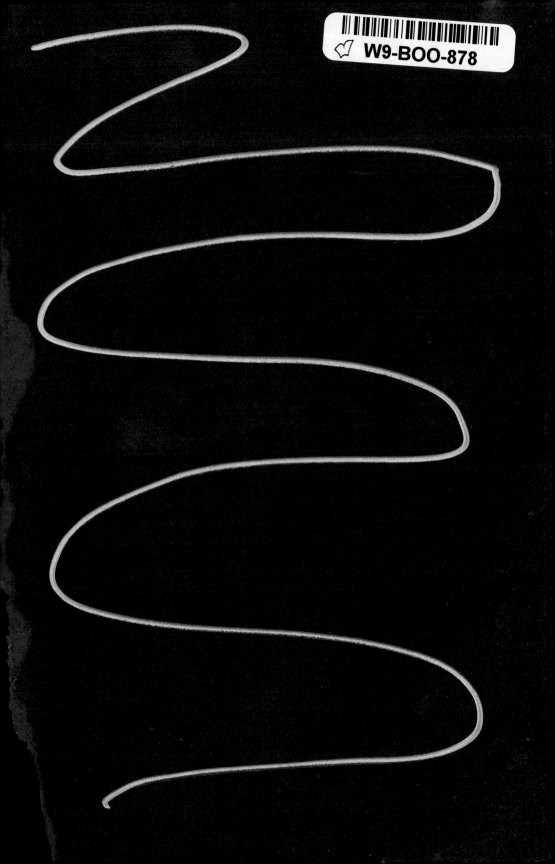

The Persian Night

The
Persian Night

Iran under the

Khomeinist Revolution

Amir Taheri

ENCOUNTER BOOKS

New York and London

First edition published in 2009 by Encounter Books, an activity of Encounter for Culture and Education, Inc., a nonprofit, tax exempt corporation.

Encounter Books website address: www.encounterbooks.com

Book design and composition by Wesley B. Tanner/Passim Editions, Ann Arbor. Manufactured in the United States and printed on acid-free paper.

♾ The paper used in this publication meets the minimum requirements of ANSI/NISO Z39.48-1992 (R 1997) (Permanence of Paper).

FIRST EDITION

Library of Congress Cataloging-in-Publication Data
Taheri, Amir.
        The Persian night : Iran under the Khomeinist revolution / Amir Taheri.
               p. cm.
        Includes bibliographical references and index.
        ISBN-13: 978-1-59403-240-0 (hardcover : alk. paper)
        ISBN-10: 1-59403-240-8 (hardcover : alk. paper) 1. Iran—Politics and govern-
ment—1979–1997. 2. Iran—Politics and government—1997– I. Title.
        DS318.825.T34 2008
        955.05'4—dc22
                                                                                    2008035220

Look at our times: A handful of impostor-clerics,

Having learned a couple of suras for deceit,

Having no notion of reason and science;

Unaware of what man is about;

Desperate like asses in search of fodder.

All they care about is eating and fornicating.

They fear not God, have no shame of men,

They have cast aside notions of honor.

They seek nothing but loot and plunder,

Alien they are to the rules of faith.

O, Unique Prophet of God!

For the sake of your ummah,

for the sake of Allah,

Rise from your garden tomb in Medina,

Behold who is ruling your followers.

O, Muslims! The time has come,

To send the Koran back to Heaven.

For, although its name is still with us,

Its content has come to naught.

Sanai Ghaznavi

Contents

Preface

In Persian mythology, the fall of Jamshid, the shah of the Pishdadi dynasty, heralded the longest night in the history of the world. During that fateful night, a priest-king of Arab origin named Azidhak (Zahhak) ruled Iran on behalf of Angarmainu, the symbol of the devil for ancient Persians. Many Iranians see the Khomeinist revolution of 1979 and the regime it produced as a real-time recurrence of the legend, but hope that this new "longest night" will prove shorter.

This essay will examine the inner history of the Khomeinist movement and trace its ideological and cultural roots. Is it a natural offshoot of Islam—which itself was an alien faith imposed on Iranians by the sword fourteen centuries ago—or a strange beast in Islamic dress?

In recent years, especially since the election of Mahmoud Ahmadinejad as president, the Islamic Republic has positioned itself as the leader of a global jihad against the so-called "infidel" camp led by the United States. The low-intensity war that Khomeinism launched against the United States in 1979 has been propelled into a new phase that could lead to full-scale military confrontation. This essay shows how Khomeinism is genetically programmed for war, but also considers how it can best be resisted and ultimately defeated, so that Iran may close the chapter of revolution and return to the global mainstream as a nation-state.

The Persian Night

1

The World's Number-One Power

Shaking his clenched fist defiantly, President Mahmoud Ahmadinejad of the Islamic Republic in Iran looked as if he had a historic message to deliver during one of his trademark provincial tours in April 2008. "Today," he said, "everyone knows that the Islamic Republic is the number-one power in the world. We are standing up to the American Great Satan and we are not alone." His audience of grim-faced men with ferocious beards and women covered in forbidding hijabs roared in approval.

A few weeks earlier, in February, Ahmadinejad had inaugurated an international conference titled "The World Without America!," attended by dozens of anti-American radicals from all over the world. Two months later, in an address marking the nineteenth anniversary of the death of Ayatollah Ruhallah Khomeini, the founder of the Islamic Republic, Ahmadinejad blamed the United States for "the ills of mankind," notably the creation of Israel, and predicted the imminent demise of both. "You should know that the criminal and terrorist Zionist regime which has sixty years of plundering, aggression and crimes in its file, has reached the end of its work and will soon disappear off the geographical scene," he said. "As for the satanic power [the United States], the countdown to the destruction of its empire of power and wealth has begun."

Ahmadinejad and his foreign minister, Manuchehr Mottaki, routinely define their policy as one intended to create "a world without America." The aim of the Khomeinist regime is to dictate the policies of the United States and of all other nations. As the many versions of anti-Americanism go, this is certainly an innovative one.

To be sure, Ahmadinejad did not invent the militant anti-Americanism that he adopted as the key theme of his presidency. Nor was the claim that the United States was at war against Islam something new to Ahmadinejad's audiences; he was harping on a theme they had known for almost three decades. The Islamic Republic had been at war against the "Great Satan" since November 4, 1979, when a group of "students" stormed the U.S. embassy in Tehran and held fifty-two of its diplomats hostage for 444 days. President Jimmy Carter's national security advisor, Zbigniew Brzezinski, called it "an act of war." The Carter administration, however, did not adopt that analysis, but tried, in a strange fit of denial, to portray the event as merely a diplomatic incident.

Carter saw Khomeini as a religious man rather than the founding father of Islamist terrorism. In a letter to Khomeini, he wrote as "one man of God to another." Carter's advisors mostly shared his illusions. His ambassador to the United Nations, Andrew Young, hailed Khomeini as a "twentieth-century saint." The U.S. ambassador to Iran, William Sullivan, saw Khomeini as a "Gandhi-like figure." They were deaf to the cries of "Death to America!" that reverberated in Tehran, and they ignored daily calls by Khomeini to wage war against the United States. With a few honorable exceptions, American policymakers have perpetuated that denial to this day.

Now in its third decade, this is a strange war. It has no easily recognizable fronts, nor is it fought with regular armies in set battles that military experts could analyze. It is not a cold war either, for the two sides on occasion have heated things up. In 1982 and 1983, suicide-commandos recruited, trained, and armed by Tehran had attacked the U.S. embassy and a U.S. Marines' dormitory in Beirut, killing almost 300 people, including 241 American soldiers. In April 1987, a U.S. naval task force in the Persian Gulf engaged the Islamic Republic's navy and sank its principal ships in a twelve-hour battle. Tehran has pursued a low-intensity war against the United States and its allies in more than a dozen countries, from Argentina to Pakistan, killing or kidnapping scores of Americans and citizens of countries allied to the United States.

In 2006, American authorities started to point the finger at Tehran as the source of funding and arms for a wide range of insurgent groups fighting the U.S.-led coalition forces in Iraq. In 2007, the United States formally held Tehran responsible for the death of at least 157 American soldiers in Iraq. In 2008, General David Petraeus, the U.S. central commander in Iraq, left no doubt that the Islamic Republic was now at war against the United States in the Iraqi theater; it had become clear in March and April that Iran's special units, known as the Quds (Jerusalem) Force, were involved in attempts by Shiite militias to control several Iraqi cities, notably Basra.[1] The U.S. media presented General Qassem Suleymani, commander of the Quds Force, as "the most powerful man in Iraq today." He was the man orchestrating the Islamic Republic's efforts to prepare for seizing control of Iraq if and when, under a new president, the United States decided to cut and run. In a report to the Congress, the Central Intelligence Agency (CIA) stated that Tehran had contacts with al-Qaeda and that helping the Taliban in Afghanistan was "the official policy" of the Islamic Republic.

* * *

The phrase "We are at war with the United States" had been established as a mantra of the Islamic Republic even before the mullahs led by Ayatollah Ruhallah Khomeini took power in Tehran in February 1979, and every president of the Islamic Republic has repeated it as a principle of the Khomeinist revolution. Khomeini saw the United States and the Soviet Union as modern versions of the Byzantine and Persian empires of the seventh century A.D., when Prophet Muhammad launched his message of Islam.

Muhammad wrote to Emperor Heraclius of Byzantium; to Negus, the monarch of Abyssinia; and to Persia's King of Kings, Khosrow Parviz, inviting them to submit to Islam. The Prophet's offer was simple: Convert to Islam and secure a place in paradise—or cling to your beliefs and face the sword of Islam. The Persian king ordered his security services to find the "insolent letter writer" and bring him to the court in Ctesiphon, capital of the Persian Empire at the time. According to Islamic folklore, Muhammad escaped capture only because Khosrow Parviz was murdered by his son and designated heir Qobad, a sure sign that Allah was angered by the impudence of the Persian monarch. Within a decade the Persian Empire had disintegrated, with most of its territory falling to the armies of Islam. The Byzantine emperor and the Abyssinian monarch, on the other hand, replied to Muhammad in brief but polite terms. According to Islamic folklore, this is why Byzantium managed to prolong its life by several centuries, while Abyssinia escaped Muslim conquest altogether.

The tradition of writing letters calling on non-Muslims to convert expanded under Ali Ibn Abi-Talib, the Prophet's cousin and son-in-law and the fourth caliph. Muhammad Ibn Hassan, the last of the twelve imams of Shiism, known as the "Hidden Imam" (whose return Ahmadinejad regards as imminent), also used letters to communicate with the outside world, though he addressed most of his epistles to Muslims in general and his partisans in particular. But as tradition demanded, he was unwilling to settle for anything less than the full and unconditional conversion of all humanity to his version of the faith.

Khomeini saw himself as a second Muhammad, given the mission by Allah to revive a moribund Islam. Some of his devotees granted him an even more exalted status. The poet Mehrdad Avesta praised Khomeini as a "celestial being" representing all the prophets that God has ever sent to mankind, including Abraham, Moses, Jesus, and Muhammad. According to the poet, angels, having observed Khomeini's ability to shed blood, bowed and prayed to him. Inspired by the "Example of the Prophet" (*Sirat al-Nabi*), Khomeini invited the "emperors" of the United States and the Soviet Union to submit or face the rage of "the only true faith." In 1987, he actually wrote a letter to Mikhail Gorbachev inviting him to convert to Islam. The Soviet leader politely declined.

Two decades later, Ahmadinejad wrote to the U.S. president, George W Bush, and to the German chancellor, Angela Merkel, reprising the invitation to submit to Islam. His letter contained a crucial message: The regime in Iran is the enemy of the international system and is determined to weaken and destroy it. Western commentators had dismissed Khomeini's letter to Gorbachev as another sign of the ayatollah's senility. They also mocked Ahmadinejad's epistolary exercise as the product of a fifty-year-old teenager's *folie de grandeur.* That, however, was a misreading of an Islamist's mind. Ahmadinejad believes that the Hidden Imam is about to return and that the Islamic Republic is obliged to provoke a "clash of civilizations" in order to hasten that event. He also believes, as he asserts in his letter, that the liberal-democratic model of market-based capitalist societies has failed and is being rejected even in its Western homeland.

When the Soviet empire collapsed in 1991, two years after Khomeini's death, his successors viewed this as a sign that Allah was delivering on his promise of making Muslims the masters of the world. Exaggerating the importance of the Soviet defeat in Afghanistan, where U.S.-backed Islamic warriors (mujahedin) seemed on the verge of winning against the Communist regime in Kabul, the mullahs saw these events as a victory by Islam over the infidels. "The next target," promised Ayatollah Sadeq Khalkhali, one of Khomeini's closest associates, "is the American Great Satan."

The Iranian mullahs, in fact, had played no role in hastening the fall of the USSR. The Islamic Republic had maintained full diplomatic relations with the Soviet-backed regime in Kabul and prevented the Afghan mujahedin from using Iranian territory as an operational base or safe haven. The Sunni Muslim groups that had actually fought the Soviets in Afghanistan—with support from Pakistan, Saudi Arabia, Kuwait, the United Arab Emirates, and the United States—mocked Shiite Iran's victory claim and saw the fall of the Soviet Union as a triumph for their own brand of Islam. They, too, regarded the United States as the next target for destruction, as they spelled out at the Popular Arab Islamic Conference held in Khartoum in 1993.[2]

The gathering at the Sudanese capital, presided over by Hassan al-Turabi—the "sheikh" of Sunni radicalism to his friends and the "Pope of Islamist terror" to his enemies—marked a major point in the history of Islam's ambitions for global conquest. For the first time it brought together Sunni and Shiite leaders in a common strategy to take on, humble, and ultimately defeat the leading "empire of the infidel," the United States of America. The unity shown in Khartoum was a contrast with the disunity that Muslim powers had shown throughout the Crusades, when rival Sunni and Shiite rulers had at times allied themselves with the Crusaders against other Muslim rulers. With the fall of the Soviet Union, Islamists of all persuasions saw their brand of Islam as the alternative to the global democratic-capitalist system represented and defended by the United States.

While Islamists believed they were at war with the Great Satan, the United States under both Republican and Democratic administrations pretended not to notice. In the French proverb, the animal defends itself when attacked.[3] The United States, however, often preferred to turn the other cheek or run for cover. After the murder of 241 Marines in their sleep in 1982, for instance, President Ronald Reagan withdrew the U.S. task force from Lebanon, despite the fact that it had been sent under a United Nations Security Council mandate and at the invitation of the Lebanese government to protect the Palestinians.[4] Even when a small group of Sunni *ghazis* (raiders in religious wars) attacked the Twin Towers of the World Trade Center in New York in 1993, killing seven people and injuring almost a thousand others, Washington refused to recognize the event for what it was: an act of war. In 1996, it was Shiite *ghazis* who attacked a U.S. target in Al Khobar, Saudi Arabia, killing nineteen American servicemen. Again the U.S. administration chose to sweep the incident under the carpet and even tried to appease Tehran with the offer of a "grand bargain" a few months later.[5]

In Khartoum, Turabi had emphasized the importance for jihadi Islam of winning control over at least one major oil-exporting Muslim nation. The war to bring the Great Satan to its knees was bound to be long and would require the resources of the state. After all, Islam's early conquests had been made possible by Muhammad's success in controlling the only viable state in Arabia at the time, Mecca—the hub of international trade between the Indian subcontinent, Persia, and Byzantium. Osama bin Laden, a native of Saudi Arabia, the world's biggest exporter of crude oil, was assigned the task of capturing control of the kingdom for jihad. The jihadists from Tehran did not face such a problem. They already controlled the resources of a major, indeed potentially the most powerful, Muslim nation. And they were determined to use the resources of Iran in the service of a global campaign against the "enemies of Islam," especially the United States.

2

The Haven of Jihad

Since the 9/11 tragedy, much has been written about "neo-terrorism," described as transnational and supposedly having no need of support from the classical structures of a state. Nevertheless, terrorists are not ethereal beings operating beyond the confines of physical reality. They need populations from which to recruit, bases of operation, and safe havens. More importantly, they also need a point of reference, a source of inspiration, an ideological home.

The Vatican may be the world's tiniest state, but it is the beacon of light for hundreds of millions of Catholics. Constantinople, though reduced to the position of an infidel outpost on the edge of the Muslim Ottoman Empire, was nevertheless the "Second Rome" for vast numbers of Christians in Europe and the Middle East for centuries, until its fall in 1453. While the Soviet Union was not in direct contact with all Marxist-Leninist groups throughout the world (some of which hated it and fought against it), to hard-left groups everywhere it was living proof that socialism works, even if imperfectly. The ramshackle administration created by the Taliban in Afghanistan was not much of a state by any standards, yet it was enough to satisfy the needs of many jihadi groups between 1997 and 2001. As a state, Iraq under Saddam Hussein likewise provided most of the services that some Islamist terror groups required, minus ideological inspiration.

With the fall of the Taliban and Saddam Hussein, Islamist radicals lost two of the states they relied upon in their jihad. In a sense, they have also lost Sudan, the original host of the jihadi congress. The generals who dominate the regime in Khartoum have scripted out Hassan al-Turabi, who led the gathering in 1993, and replaced his policy

of "permanent revolution" with that of "Islamism in one country"—
a choice encouraged by Canadian and Chinese companies that have
discovered substantial reserves of oil in Sudan. General Omar Hassan
al-Bashir, Sudan's "strongman," sees Saudi Arabia as a model Islamist
state, oil-rich and posing no challenge to the United States or its allies.
Syria, also on the U.S. government's list of "state sponsors of international terrorism," could provide all the support that jihadi groups
require, and it does so to some extent with respect to Iraq, Lebanon,
and the Palestinian territories. It falls short on one crucial point, however: because the regime is secular and the country is dominated by
a heterodox sect that most Muslims regard as heretical, Syria cannot
supply the vital element of ideological inspiration. Moreover, it supports terrorist groups only when their activities serve its own interests
as a state with limited regional ambitions. The Syrian regime does not,
indeed cannot, permit itself the luxury of dreaming of world conquest.
Syria is too small, too poor, and too unsure of itself to seek a fight in
the premier league. All this leaves a gap that only the Islamic Republic
in Iran could pretend to fill, at least in part.

At the level of individuals and groups acting on their own, terrorism
could be treated as a type of criminal activity. When sponsored by a state
and used as a weapon in a low-intensity conflict and asymmetric war
against other states, terrorism must be seen as a form of war and treated
accordingly.

One factor sets the Islamic Republic as a sponsor of international
terrorism apart from other regimes on the State Department's blacklist, such as Syria, Cuba, and North Korea. Those three regimes view
politics through the classical concept of choosing between friend and
enemy. They regard the United States as a hostile power to be resisted
and fought, at least for the time being, but do not seek to destroy it or
force its citizens to adopt their own values and way of life down to the
last detail. By contrast, the Islamic Republic in Iran is a messianic power
dedicated to spreading the "the only true faith" to every corner of the
globe. It regards the United States not as a mere enemy, a political term,

but as a *foe*, a word with religious overtones. With an enemy, one could negotiate a ceasefire, even a limited peace. With a foe, there can be neither peace nor ceasefire.[1] The ultimate goal cannot be limited to exacting concessions—though this could be a tactical objective—or even defeating it in battle; the foe must be forced to transform itself into a friend, or else be extinguished. In Cuba, Venezuela, Syria, and other places where anti-Americanism is encouraged by the state, the slogan is "Down with America" or "Yankee Go Home." In the Islamic Republic in Iran, the slogan is "*Death* to America!" Invented by Khomeini in 1979, the phrase has accumulated a religious charge beyond its original political purpose.[2] Three decades later, the Islamic Republic has once again put that old slogan at the center of its global strategy.

The present leadership in Tehran, a mixture of mullahs and soldiers, is persuaded that it has inherited the mantle of the Soviet Union as the principal challenger to a global system created by the West, portrayed as corrupt, hedonistic, cowardly, and vulgar. Muhammad Khatami, a mid-ranking mullah who acted as president of the Islamic Republic between 1997 and 2005, has described the Enlightenment as a tragedy in human history and the progenitor of colonial and imperial wars that have caused much grief to mankind. The regime's aim, therefore, is to defeat the ideology of the Enlightenment by leading humanity back to a medieval way of life in which religion—in this case exclusively Islam in its Khomeinist version—provides the organizing principle of society. The Khomeinists believe it is their historic mission not only to "revive" Islam, which they claim expired soon after Muhammad's death, but also to resume its campaign of global conquest.[3]

At first glance, any suggestion that the Islamic Republic in Iran is in a position to challenge the world's sole superpower might sound outlandish. After all, the United States' defense budget is almost twice the entire Iranian gross domestic product. There are four times as many Americans as there are Iranians. Moreover, the United States has many powerful allies, whereas the Islamic Republic has none. But the outcome of low-intensity war such as the Islamic Republic has been waging against the

United States is not determined by the same factors that apply in conventional warfare. To train a single U.S. Marine for action costs around $500,000, while the Islamic Republic invested less than $50,000 to kill 241 U.S. Marines in Beirut. The Iranian-made projectiles that killed Americans and Iraqis in Iraq in 2008 cost less than five dollars to manufacture. Members of the Mahdi Army, a Shiite militia financed by Iran in Iraq, received ten dollars a month in wages, compared with $250 that the average soldier in the new Iraqi army receives from the U.S.-backed government in Baghdad. The entire operations of Hezballah in Lebanon and Hamas in Gaza cost Tehran under $1 billion a year, compared with some $200 billion that the United States spends annually in Iraq.

For the Khomeinist regime, terrorism is something of a cottage industry fed by small but judicious investment in groups and operations that can do maximum harm at minimum cost. In West Africa, using Shiite communities of Lebanese and Syrian origin that have been resident there for generations, the Islamic Republic has created a network of influence such as the United States has failed to build despite pouring in billions of dollars in aid. The Khomeinist project is to transform the "Islamic" aspect of the West African tribes and nations into hostility towards the West, especially the United States. Tehran has also built a network of influence in many Muslim countries with the shrewd expenditure of relatively small sums, backed by a passionate anti-American rhetoric. In Afghanistan, Pakistan, Central Asia, and even the Indian Muslim community, the Khomeinist revolution is marketed as the only force capable of challenging Western domination of the world.

Another reason why traditional measurements of power are inadequate in assessing this situation is the domestic difficulties that any U.S. administration faces in using American power against an active adversary, as well as a misunderstanding of asymmetric warfare on the part of some American politicians. For example, in May 2008 the Democratic presidential candidate, Barack Obama, mocked those who he said were "obsessed with Ahmadinejad," noting that the U.S. defense budget was a hundred times larger than that of the Islamic Republic. True, the United

States could obliterate Iran in a total war; the crucial question is whether the American political system would allow any president to do so. Senator Obama forgot that a good part of the U.S. budget was spent on sophisticated and costly materiel that is irrelevant in a low-intensity asymmetric war. The Khomeinist strategy is based on the assumption that the United States, hampered by domestic political squabbles, would never be able to deploy a significant portion of its immense power against a foe like the Islamic Republic in a conventional war. Thus, Tehran perceives all those expensive fighter-bombers, aircraft carriers, laser-guided weapons, and other sophisticated gadgets—not to mention the immense nuclear arsenal—as little more than impressive figures in strategic charts. What matters is not the possession of power but the will to use it.

In that regard, Iran's leaders believe they have the edge over their American enemies. Ideologues in Tehran assume that Afghanistan and Iraq were the last wars that an American president could start, and that most U.S. opinion-makers would prefer a return to the pre-9/11 situation in which Americans were killed in small but steady numbers over a long period. These assumptions are based on a belief that the very concept of war, once glorified by Aristotle as the noblest of human pursuits, has been redefined as a tragic necessity at best, or a collective crime. For some segments of American opinion—indeed, of Western opinion in general—war is now in the same category as other best-forgotten secrets of the human family such as cannibalism, slavery, and incest. But in the Islamic Republic, war is presented, in the words of Khomeini, as "a blessing from Allah."

3

The Focus of the Universe

As an Islamic Republic over the past three decades, Iran has often behaved as a typical ideological power. Nevertheless, Khomeinist behavior both at home and abroad cannot be divorced from the physical realities of Iran's existence as a nation.

History, geography, demography, and natural resources are key factors in determining what Iran does. In its present shape, Iran is one of the world's twenty largest countries and the fifteenth most populous, with over 75 million inhabitants. Yet it ranks 44th in economic terms, reflecting a relative decline over the past three decades. Iranians like to assert that their country is located in one of the world's most strategically complex regions, making it "the Focus of the Universe." The Iranian landmass is separated from Europe, Africa, Central Asia, and the Indian subcontinent by just a single country in each case. Iran is the country with the third-largest number of neighbors, after Russia and China.[1] Of the world's eight acknowledged nuclear powers, two are immediate neighbors of Iran and three others are located in the vicinity.[2]

Another factor that contributes to Iran's geopolitical importance is energy. According to official estimates, Iran owns almost 12 percent of global reserves of crude oil and the second-largest reserves of natural gas. Since the early 1900s, when Iranian oil started to flow into world markets, Iran has consistently been one of the five biggest exporters of crude. It also has the longest coastline on the Persian Gulf, where its Arab neighbors account for a further 48 percent of the world's known oil reserves. Add to that Iran's presence on the Caspian Sea, home to 10 percent of global oil reserves as well as vast amounts of natural gas, and Iran's position as the major hub in global energy production becomes more apparent.

As a regional power, Iran has been involved in all the conflicts that have shaped regional politics since the disintegration of the Ottoman Empire after the First World War and the collapse of the Soviet Empire eight decades later. In a sense, none of the region's problems—from instability in Afghanistan and Iraq to the power struggle in Lebanon and the century-old Arab-Israeli conflict—could be resolved without input by Iran. In most cases, the Islamic Republic has pursued policies that have contributed to the sharpening of conflict in such places as Iraq, Lebanon, and Israel-Palestine.

Iran also has important ethnic, cultural, and historic ties to all its neighbors. In its present shape, Iran is the remnant of three successive empires of ancient history: the Achaemenid, the Arsacid, and the Sassanid, which included virtually all of present-day Iran's neighboring lands. The historical, cultural, and linguistic sediments of these empires continue to affect the region's politics. Iranic languages—including Persian, the national language of Iran—are spoken in one form or another throughout the Iranian periphery.[3] In Tajikistan and Afghanistan, local forms of Persian (known respectively as Tajik and Dari) serve as official languages. Other Iranic languages are spoken in parts of Russia, Pakistan, the Persian Gulf states, Iraq, and Turkey.[4] In addition to Persian, a number of other languages of the Iranic family are used in various parts of the country. Four versions of Kurdish are spoken by some 4.5 million people in three provinces and Kurdish enclaves in Khorassan in the northeast. Baluchi is the native tongue of some 1.8 million people in the southeast. Gilaki, spoken by some 1.5 million people in the Caspian littoral, and Taleshi, the language of almost a million people, again on the Caspian, also belong to the Iranic family. Non-Iranic languages used in Iran include Azari, a form of Turkish with a heavy admixture of Persian vocabulary, the native tongue of some 12 million Iranians; and two versions of the Turkmen language, spoken by 1.8 million Turkmen Iranians, mostly living in the northeast.[5] Finally, there are some two million Iranians whose mother tongue is Arabic, another non-Iranic language.[6] Despite this linguistic diversity, almost all Iranians apart from the Arab and Turkmen minorities, about 4 percent of the population, are from the same historic Iranian ethnic stock as shaped by thousands of years of interbreeding.

At first glance, Islam too might seem a unifying factor; after all, some 98 percent of Iranians are born Muslims. But a majority of Iran's non-Muslim minorities have at least as much of a claim to a historic link with the land as their Muslim compatriots. Iran's Chaldeans and Assyrians, just over 150,000 souls, lived in northwestern Iran long before the first Iranian tribes appeared more than five thousand years ago. The Armenian minority, about 300,000, also has a history of thousands of years in the Iranian plateau. The same is true of Iranian Jews, now numbering under 50,000. In fact, Iran has been home to the oldest Jewish community with an uninterrupted presence anywhere in the world. Unlike most other countries, where religious minorities are often urban professionals with no link to the land, Iran's minorities cover the entire social and economic spectrum. Iran is perhaps the only country outside Israel that has Jewish peasants, and the only one outside Armenia where Armenians still work the land.

Two other religious minorities, the Zoroastrians and the Baha'is, stand out because they represent two surviving made-in-Iran religions—the oldest and the newest. Zoroastrianism emerged as the principal religion of most Iranian peoples almost a thousand years before Christ. It offered the earliest version of monotheism as an organized religious doctrine and remained Iran's national faith until the Arab invasion in the seventh century A.D. Today there are no more than 45,000 Zoroastrians in Iran, but the world's estimated two million Zoroastrians continue to regard Iran as "holy land." More importantly, perhaps, Zoroastrianism continues to provide the template of existence for most Iranians, despite their formal attachment to Islam. There is some truth in the claim—made in 1996 by the late Sheikh Abdul-Aziz Bin Baz, the Grand Mufti of Saudi Arabia, among others—that Iranians never quite succeeded in abandoning Zoroaster for Muhammad.[7] The Baha'i faith, based on the teachings of two Shiite clerics from Shiraz, is the newest Iranian religion, assuming its definitive form towards the end of the nineteenth century. Persecuted in Iran, especially since the establishment of the Khomeinist regime, it has re-emerged as a faith with a universal message and has attracted millions of adepts elsewhere, including the United States.

The Khomeinist ideology has tried hard to deny or ignore the central fact of Iran's existence as a nation, its unity in diversity. The regime's propaganda has attempted to reduce Iran's rich and complex identity to a single component: Islam. Even then, the regime ignores the diversity of Islam as practiced in Iran. To start with, Muslim Iranians are divided between Shiites and Sunnis, the former accounting for 86 percent of the population and the latter 12 percent. The word "Shiite," moreover, is an umbrella term that covers a range of heterodox beliefs and practices. These include the Ismailis, the Ahl e Haqq, the Ali-Allahis, the Yazidis, and the Heydaris.[8] Even mainstream Shiites, known as the Jaafaris, are divided into dozens of schools, Sufi fraternities, and religious traditions.

As long as Iran was known simply as Iran—that is to say, until the mullahs seized power in 1979—this diversity was accepted as a fact and celebrated as a "divine gift."[9] The use of the adjective "Islamic" to describe the regime created by Khomeini posed the question of which Iranians were Muslims and which were not, and, perhaps more importantly, what was meant by Islam. Thus Islam, rather than serving as a unifying element, became a divisive force, especially in the ever shifting and constricting definitions presented by the regime to suit its political interests. As Khomeini once observed, being a Muslim was not enough to give an Iranian the right to seek a place in the leadership; one had to be "committed to the system."

4

The Triple Oxymoron

The system that Khomeini created and his successors perfected is officially called the Islamic Republic *of* Iran. These words amount to a triple lie, for the system is neither Islamic nor republican, and it certainly is not Iranian.

The adjective "Islamic" in this context is based on the assumption that Islam offers a model of government, but that is far from the truth. The Koran, Islam's fundamental text, presents no thoughts on how to organize a government; there is not a single mention of such terms as "government" or "politics." Muhammad acted as a ruler, general, and spiritual guide for over a decade, but refused to create a system that could be defined without himself at its center. The absence of any clear rules, let alone model of government, was at the root of the civil wars triggered by the Prophet's death.

Islamists present Muhammad's decade-long reign and the three decades in which the Muslim community (*ummah*) was ruled by his four immediate successors, the "Well-Guided Caliphs," as a "Golden Age." That would be true if gold had the color of blood. Muhammad's rule was marked by eleven wars, countless raids against trade caravans, and the massacre of tribes that refused to convert or pay tribute. Of the four Well-Guided Caliphs, three were assassinated, two of them in dynastic and sectarian conspiracies.[1] Their reign was dominated by uninterrupted war—first inside Arabia, where tribes who had reverted to their original faiths after Muhammad's death were massacred by the armies of the first caliph, Abu-Bakr, and his successor Omar, and then across the borders against the Persian and Byzantine empires. Under Osman a new layer of violence was added in the form of dynastic feuds, which led to full-scale civil wars during Ali's caliphate. The Golden Age also failed to produce a system of law beyond the pre-Islamic tribal codes that Muhammad had adopted with some modifications. Islamists claim that there could be no Islam without the Shariah, a compendium of pre-Islamic Arab tribal rules with an admixture of Jewish, Byzantine, and Persian practices; but there was no Shariah during the Golden Age. It was not until five decades later under the Umayyid caliphs, by then based in Damascus, that Byzantine and Persian judges and theologians developed the Shariah as a body of common law.

Because there has never been an Islamic model of government, the term "Islamic" could be used to describe virtually *any* political system, and it has been during the past fourteen centuries. The Umayyids and the Abbasids claimed that their rule was Islamic, just as did the Turks and the Mongols, new converts to Islam who conquered the Middle East and Central Asia. Some scholars have argued that because Islam makes a distinction between what is religious duty (*shar'e*) and what concerns the nonreligious aspects of life (*urf*), all governments in Islam have been and must be secular in the sense of a separation between mosque and state. In those terms, the only nonsecular Muslim state was the Fatimid Caliphate in Egypt, in which the caliph held both sacred and temporal authority. Other scholars insist that an Islamic government should be modeled on that of Muhammad in Medina, where he acted as both temporal and religious ruler. Still others solve the problem by attaching the term "Islamic" to almost any system of government. Today, Pakistan, Afghanistan, and Mauritania each describes itself as an "Islamic Republic," something that Iranian mullahs dismiss as a "sordid claim."[2]

To a majority of Muslims, however, it is Khomeini and the regime he created that could be accused of making sordid claims. To start with, Khomeini was a Shiite and as such belonged to a community that accounts for just 12 percent of the world's estimated 1.3 billion Muslims. Furthermore, Khomeini's views belonged to a small minority within the Jaafari "Twelver" Shiite community.[3] Other Shiite groups such as the Ismailis, Nizaris, and Zaydis—not to mention more heterodox groups such as Alevis, Nusairis, and Druze—would shudder at the thought of living in an "Islamic" republic like the one Khomeini created. Of the grand ayatollahs of the 1970s and 1980s, when the "Islamic Republic" took shape, none but Khomeini himself endorsed the system.[4] Some Shiite theologians, along with almost all their Sunni counterparts, regarded Khomeini as an "innovator," a term of abuse in Islamic polemics, and the system he created as a "satanic novelty" (*bid'ah shaytaniah*).

A majority of Muslims, divided into four schools (*mazahib*) of Sunni theology, have always been ambivalent at best on whether Shiites should be regarded as Muslims. On the surface, the difference between Shiism and Sunnism seems to be over the matter of Muhammad's successors. Sunnis respect the succession as it happened, while Shiites believe that Muhammad had meant his cousin and son-in-law Ali to succeed him, but the plan was derailed because of conspiracies by Muhammad's closest companions and immediate successors, Abu-Bakr, Omar, and Osman, with the help of Ayesha, the favorite among the Prophet's twenty-five wives. As to why Ali didn't protest the usurpation of his right, but instead served under the three caliphs that preceded him, Shiites claim that he was merely practicing *taqiyyah* or dissimulation to save his life and bide his time. To confuse his enemies further, Ali even offered one of his daughters, Hafsa, as a teenage bride to Omar, his archrival, and volunteered to serve in the usurper's armies for conquest beyond Arabia. The question of succession, however, only scratches the surface of a deeper doctrinal schism. One could argue that Shiism, although an offshoot of Islam, has developed into a distinct religion in which the Koran and the Prophet—and, as some scholars have argued, even Allah—are assigned cameo roles, while the imams take center stage.[5]

Shiism's divergence from Islam starts with major doctrinal innovations. Islam, as presented in the Koran and through sayings (*hadith*) attributed to Muhammad and his companions, is a radically monotheistic creed. Contrary to claims by Muslim scholars, it was not Muhammad who discovered or invented Allah as Supreme Being. Allah was the name that the Hanifs, a pre-Islamic sect of Arabs influenced by Judaism, gave to a god whom they regarded as superior to other gods. Muhammad's own father was called Abdallah (Slave of Allah) long before the future Prophet received his celestial message. Abdallah and its variations, such as Abdul-Mutallib (the name of Muhammad's uncle) and Abdul-Malik, were popular names among Arabs prior to Islam. What distinguished Muhammad's faith from that of the Hanif was its uncompromising monotheism: Allah was no longer presented as the Greatest of Gods but the *only* God.

The earliest war cry of Islam, *Allah Akbar!* (still in use as part of the Azan, or call to prayer), means "Allah is the Greatest" and reflects the Hanif influence. Soon a new slogan superseded it: *La ilah il-Allah,* which means: "There is no God but Allah." During the twenty-three years of Muhammad's prophetic mission, anyone who bore testimony to the uniqueness of Allah was considered a Muslim. After his death, his two immediate successors added a second article of faith: an acknowledgement of Muhammad's position as a messenger of Allah. Thus, to become a Muslim one had to repeat a new formula: "There is no God but Allah, and Muhammad is his Messenger."[6]

Some early Muslims were uneasy about the elevation of Muhammad's prophecy to the same level of importance granted to the oneness of Allah. The first two caliphs, however, needed the change as part of a propaganda effort against several "false prophets" who claimed to be Muhammad's heirs as Allah's messengers. The most successful among them, one Musaylamah—branded by Muslims as *al-Kazzab,* "the False One"—managed briefly to win over a majority of the Arab tribes. To prevent the emergence of more false prophets, thus removing the prospect of endless tribal wars in the name of rival "messengers of Allah," the caliphs agreed to a further dilution of the strict monotheistic creed. Reinterpreting some verses from the Koran, they declared that Muhammad was not only *a* messenger of God, but his *very last* one. The term used to describe Muhammad was *Khatam al-Anbia,* "the Seal of the Prophets." The fact that the Koran uses the term in a poetic rather than a literal sense and applies it to other prophets as well (notably Joseph) was ignored. Muhammad *had to become* the last prophet, even if that meant a theoretical restriction of Allah's boundless powers, including the power to change his mind and dispatch other messengers.

Still later, as Islam slowly began to develop a theology and organize itself as a religion, a third article of faith was added: the belief in resurrection (*Ma'ad*), the idea that on a given day all who had existed and died would return to life for a final judgment by Allah. The fact that an official text of the Koran had not been established until a quarter of a century after the death of the Prophet, and then in a manner that has raised many questions, facilitated the evolution of doctrine to suit the political needs of the day.

At the time of Muhammad's death in 632 A.D., it was sufficient to believe in the oneness of Allah to be accepted as a Muslim. By 635, one also had to believe that Muhammad had been Allah's very last prophet and that Islam was the final divine message to mankind. A decade later, even that was no longer sufficient: one was also required to believe in resurrection.

This doctrinal triptych remained unchallenged until the emergence of Shiism as an organized faith during the lifetime of Imam Jaafar Ibn Muhammad (702–765).[7] Since Jaafar has not left any writings, it is difficult to know what role he actually played in developing Shiism. One thing appears certain: he was a student of philosophy who devoted his life to learning and speculation. Some of his disciples developed the initial form of the Shiite doctrine from sayings attributed to him, though it is not certain that Jaafar regarded himself as Shiite in the sense the term was used after his death. Among his pupils were Abu-Hanifah, the founder of the Hanafi Mazhab, the largest of the four schools of Sunni Islam, and Malik Ibn Anas, who was to found the Maliki Mazhab, another school of Sunni Islam. More interestingly, perhaps, another pupil of Jaafar was Wasil Ibn 'Ata, the man who founded the Mutazelite school of rationalism, later destroyed by the Abassid caliphs as a heresy.

One of Shiism's basic claims is that Muhammad's three immediate successors as caliph were usurpers who had come to Islam with hidden agendas to destroy it from within. Yet Jaafar named two of his sons after the two first caliphs, Abu-Bakr and Omar. More importantly, Jaafar does not appear to have subscribed to the idea of guilt by association, alien to Islam in its original Koranic form but a key doctrinal point in Shiism. While Jaafar may well have upheld his family's claim to special treatment in the realm of Islam, it is not at all certain that he wished to introduce a fundamental reinterpretation of the faith.

Nevertheless, remarks attributed to Jaafar were used as the basis for adding two new principles to the three doctrinal principles of Islam as established before the eighth century. The first was *Adalah* (justice), meaning that men should strive to fulfill God's will in this world rather than wait for divine justice in the hereafter. This was a revolutionary departure from the original message of Islam based on the concept of an all-powerful, all-knowing Creator whom man could never properly understand. By making efforts to understand and carry out the will of God an article of faith, Shiism claimed an active role for man in deciding and shaping worldly events—something that original Islam would have seen as *lèse majesté*.

The second new article of faith was the concept of *Imamah* (imamate). This theory is based on the assertion that the world—indeed, the universe as a whole—in order to be sustained, needs the presence of an infallible guide who represents divine power. The problem is that God has created no more than fourteen infallible human beings and will never add to their number. The first of these is Muhammad. Next comes his cousin and son-in-law, Ali, followed by eleven of Ali's male offspring from his marriage to Fatima, the Prophet's daughter. Fatima herself completes the list, though as a woman—the only one among the fourteen infallibles—she is excluded from the "chain of imamate" set up by Allah to "complete the prophetic chain." Equal in status to Muhammad, the imams are superior to all the other 124,000 prophets that Allah has sent since Adam, including Abraham, Moses, and Jesus. Muhammad Baqer, the fifth imam, is quoted as saying: "If the imam is taken away from the world even for an hour, the earth and all that is on it will shake like waves that rise from the ocean." Jaafar Sadeq is quoted as saying: "If the earth is left without an imam even for one second, it will sink."[8] The imams are the *hujjat* or "proof" of God's existence, and those who don't believe in them cannot be regarded as Muslims. By that definition, some 88 percent of Muslims would be regarded as "unbelievers" because, being Sunnis, they do not share the cult of the imams.

The concept of imamate modifies one of the fundamental aspects of Islamic doctrine: the direct relationship between man and the Creator. Islam excludes all possibility of intercession, as man will face divine judgment alone. According to Islamic tradition, Muhammad tried to intercede with Allah on behalf of his own parents. The Prophet argued that since his parents had died while he was still a boy, and thus long before Allah transmitted his message of Islam, it was unfair to treat them as unbelievers consigned to hell for eternity. Allah rejected the argument, because there could be no intercession in Islam. The Shiite system, however, is based on intercession. The imams could save you from the fires of hell, and so could mullahs who know the formulas to persuade Allah to change his mind. Under the Khomeinist regime, the intercessory claims of Shiism have generated an expanding industry of indulgences, employing tens of thousands.

In its extreme versions, Shiism even casts doubt on Muhammad's own version of his prophetic mission. According to Shiite theology, Allah had initially intended to choose Muhammad's cousin, Ali, as Prophet. Archangel Gabriel was dispatched to Arabia to find Ali and deliver the divine message to him. Arriving in Mecca, Gabriel saw two Arabs sleeping side by side on a mat, half dazed by the intense heat. The two were Muhammad and Ali. Gabriel could not tell them apart, as both were roughly the same size and wore similar flowing robes (*deshdash*). Taking Muhammad to be Ali, the archangel delivered the message to the wrong man. By the time Allah realized that a mistake had been made, it was too late to reshoot the scene, so to speak. Thus Muhammad became the Prophet, with the understanding that the younger man would succeed him as leader of the Islamic *ummah*. The overwhelming majority of Muslims find such beliefs heretical and painful.

Khomeini went so far as to castigate God himself for having allowed Abu-Bakr, Omar, and Osman—branded "evil men"—to become caliph in usurpation of Ali's divine right. In his book *Kashf al-Asrar* ("Revelation of Secrets"), Khomeini writes: "We worship a God and believe in Him whose every act is in accord with wisdom, and not a God who builds a majestic edifice of justice, rectitude and divine magnificence, and then Himself demolishes it by giving the reins of government to tyrants and scoundrels such as Yazid, Muawyyah, and Osman."[9] Khomeini further asserts that the three caliphs who preceded Ali conspired to delete references to his right of succession from the Koran.

This claim defies the Muslim belief that the Koran—unlike Jewish and Christian scriptures that have been "tampered with"—has come down in its original, authentic form as dictated by Allah to Muhammad. The Koran as known to Muslims today was compiled, edited, and authorized under Osman, regarded by Shiites as one of the three "evil men" who succeeded Muhammad. Shiites believe that the only true and complete text of the Koran was held in secret by Ali and will be revealed only at the end of time when the Hidden Imam returns to cleanse the world of Sunnis and infidels. The Mahdi will also bring with him two books "superior to the Koran." In the Islamic Republic, the belief that the Sunnis have tampered with the Koran is so strong that editions of the text published outside Iran are banned and treated as contraband by customs agents. (The Sunni nations repay the compliment by banning Korans printed in Iran.)

Shiite texts make scant reference to the Koran itself, almost always preferring to quote the imams or treatises compiled by the clergy; they attach greater importance to the sayings of the imams than those attributed to the Prophet. Shiites justify this emphasis by claiming that those who related the Prophet's sayings, as Sunnis, could not be regarded as true believers, and thus their reports are unreliable or downright mendacious. The first task of the Hidden Imam on his return is to "kill all Sunnis everywhere" before proceeding to massacre the non-Muslim infidels.

In the official calendar of the Islamic Republic, the imams are celebrated or mourned for 64 days each year, including a 40-day mourning period for Hussein bin Ali, the third imam, who was martyred in 680 in a struggle for power against the Umayyid Caliph Yazid. The Prophet Muhammad, by contrast, is remembered on just one day. Even his birthday is not a public holiday, while the birthday of the Hidden Imam is the most important feast in the Shiite calendar.

Shiite theological tradition rejects virtually all positions taken by Sunni scholars. Until a school of divinity was opened at Tehran University in the 1930s, no Sunni theologians were studied at Shiite seminaries in Iran. Shiites also refuse to pray alongside Sunnis. Although the text of the prayer itself is only slightly different, the divergence in style is instantly noticeable. Shiites complete the mandatory Islamic prayer with special incantations peculiar to themselves, known as *du'a*, addressed to the imams rather than God. More significantly, Shiites have modified the original text of the Azan (call to prayer) by adding two verses that fundamentally reorient its message.[10]

Because non-Shiite Muslims are not regarded as true believers, the Islamic Republic does not allow Sunnis to build and maintain mosques or other places of worship in any part of Iran where they do not constitute a majority of the population. In Tehran there are some three million Sunni Muslims, but not a single Sunni mosque. One of the last acts of the shah's regime in 1979 had been to grant a license for a Sunni mosque in the Tehran suburb of Yussuf-Abad, along with 5,000 square meters of land and a sum equivalent to $300,000 for building the mosque. A few weeks later, the mullahs seized power, and the mosque was never built. In 1992, the only Sunni mosque in the Shiite "holy" city of Mash'had was burned down. Efforts to rebuild it have been vetoed by the authorities.

The Khomeinist regime also refuses to allow Iranians who do not share its narrow religious creed to hold positions of authority in the public sector. Christians, Jews, and Zoroastrians are excluded as a matter of course, but Sunni Muslims fare no better. No Sunni could become the "Supreme Guide" or the president of the Islamic Republic;

nor does one find any Sunni cabinet minister, provincial governor, or senior diplomat in Iran. Over the three decades of the Khomeinist domination of Iran, scores of Sunni scholars and clerics have been murdered or executed on trumped-up charges. The latest wave of executions came in the spring of 2008 when three Sunni prayer leaders in southeast Iran were hanged in public.[11]

The Islamic Republic has imposed a ban on names that most Muslims regard as quintessentially Islamic. Iranian parents are not allowed to name their children after Abu-Bakr, Omar, or Osman, collectively branded as the "Dirty Three" (*Thulatha al-Mulawwatha*). The name of Ayesha, Muhammad's only virgin bride and favorite among his twenty-five wives, is also banned, as are a host of other names associated with the first three caliphs. Mullah Muhammad Baqir Majlisi (1616–1698), the foremost authority on Shiite doctrine, claims that Ayesha poisoned Muhammad because she wanted her father, Abu-Bakr to become caliph instead of Ali. Among Shiites, Ayesha is vilified as a scheming, witchlike figure of loose morals and evil designs. To say a woman is "like Ayesha" means she is both dangerous and seductive in a *femme fatale* style. Ayesha joins Abu-Bakr, Omar, Osman, and Muawyyah, the founder of the Umayyid dynasty, to form the "Evil Five" (*Khamseh Khabitheh*).

Shiites have designated the ninth day of the month of *Rabi al-Awwal* on the Arab lunar calendar as the "Sweetest Day" because it marks Omar's murder by an Iranian war prisoner. Known as *Omar Koshan* (the Killing of Omar), it is a day of festivities when crowds of believers stream to the mausoleum of Firuz, the man who killed the second caliph, near the central Iranian city of Kashan. People gather in village and city squares to burn effigies of Omar, cursing the man who sent his invading armies to Iran. The caliph's name is used as an adjective denoting extreme ugliness and the height of evil. Saying that something or someone is *Omari* (Omar-like) indicates utmost revulsion.

Many Sunni Muslims wonder how anyone could pretend to be a Muslim while equating three of the four Well-Guided Caliphs and the Prophet's favorite wife with absolute evil. Because they regard the Khomeinist system as doctrinally suspect, many Muslim spiritual leaders, both Sunni and Shiite, will not even travel to Iran; some now regard it as part of the infidel realm. Despite offers of large bribes and other enticements by the Islamic Republic, no major Sunni theological figure has agreed to visit Iran since the mullahs seized power in 1979. A grand conference organized in Tehran in the spring of 2008 to work for a "convergence of Islamic schools" attracted only junior Sunni theologians from a few countries. Worse still for the Khomeinist regime, the Sunni theological establishment, represented by the Al-Azhar Academy in Cairo, has all but reneged on an agreement signed with the Iranian clergy on a mutual recognition of Sunni and Shiite schools as legitimate expressions of Islam. The concordat had been negotiated throughout the 1940s with support from the Iranian and Egyptian states when they were linked at the top through the marriage of the shah of Iran to Fawziah, a sister of King Farouq of Egypt. It was ratified in 1949 by Grand Ayatollah Muhammad Hussein Borujerdi, then the *primus inter pares* of the Shiite clergy in Qom. Most Sunni-majority nations today persecute their Shiite minorities. For example, Shiites are not allowed to build a mosque in Cairo or to organize mourning processions in Saudi Arabia.

Pursuing a tradition known as *tabarra* (exoneration), Shiites are asked to do whatever they can to distinguish themselves not only from the infidels but also from Sunnis. The mullahs make sure that none of the important Islamic days on the Shiite calendar coincide with those on the calendars of Sunni Muslims. Thus, the fasting month of Ramadan, common to all Muslims, always starts and ends a day earlier or later in Iran than in other Muslim countries. Where they are in a minority, and thus likely to be in danger, Shiites are advised to practice *taqiyyah* (dissimulation) to hide their faith. On such occasions, they may even present themselves as ardent Sunnis. Where Shiites are a majority and face no risks, however, they ought to do whatever possible not to look and behave like Sunnis. They must sport distinctive beards, wear special styles of clothing, and, in the case of women, adopt their own form of hijab. The necessity for Shiites to mark themselves out from Sunnis is explained by one of the younger apologists of Khomeinism thus:

> Our prophet is different from the prophet of the Sunnis, the reason being that our historical profile of the prophet is fundamentally different from that held by Sunnis. . . . Our image of the imams and even of the Koran is different from that current among Sunnis. There are many Shiite traditions about the imams that our ulema [i.e. clerics] regard as a significant commentary on specific Koranic verses.[12]

Shiite efforts to mark themselves out from other Muslims could also be witnessed in the architecture of Iranian mosques and other edifices related to the cult. Mosques throughout the Muslim world where Sunnis are a majority have only one minaret, a symbol of Allah's uniqueness. In Iran, mosques have two minarets: one symbolizing Allah, the other the principle of imamate. The tile work in Sunni mosques depicts abstract shapes or the name of Allah in stylized calligraphy. In Shiite mosques, however, the tile work presents stylized names of the "Five Immaculate Ones": Muhammad, his daughter Fatima, his cousin and son-in-law Ali, and the prophet's two favorite grandsons, Hassan and Hussein. Often, the slogan *Ya Ali* ("O Ali!") takes precedence over the more broadly Islamic one of *Ya Allah!* All this represents a substantial dilution of Islam's militant and uncompromising monotheistic message.

While it is clear that the overwhelming majority of Muslims do not consider the system created by Khomeini to be Islamic, it is not at all certain that Shiites would regard it as a true reflection of their faith either. Khomeini started playing fast and loose with Shiite doctrine almost immediately after his supporters, backed by armed Communist and Islamic-Marxist gangs, had seized power in 1979. He orchestrated a campaign to call himself "the imam" rather than a mere ayatollah as he was according to the Shiite clerical hierarchy. Thus Twelver Shiites suddenly found themselves with thirteen imams rather than twelve, a development that created confusion about the role that the twelfth imam, the Awaited Mahdi (of whom more later), was supposed to play.

* * *

If it is neither Islamic in the eyes of most Muslims nor even properly Shiite in the eyes of other Shiites, could we at least consider the Khomeinist system a theocracy, as some commentators have suggested? If theocracy means a system of government based on the claim that all power emanates from a divine source, the answer is yes. Khomeini and his successor as Supreme Guide, Ali Khamenehi—a mid-ranking mullah elevated to the position of ayatollah by his supporters—have claimed to represent divine power on earth. Both have also claimed the supreme leadership of all Muslims, Sunni as well as Shiite, throughout the world, a claim enshrined in the Constitution of the Islamic Republic.

If, on the other hand, theocracy means a system of rule by the clergy, the Khomeinist "republic" would not qualify. One reason is that Shiism, like Islam in general, has never had an organized "church" with an easily recognizable clerical hierarchy. Almost anybody could grow a beard, don a turban and flowing robes, and claim to be a mullah. A survey by the Iranian Endowments Office in 1977 revealed that over 250,000 men claimed to be mullahs at the time.[13] An astonishing 20 percent were categorized by the survey as "illiterate" or "semiliterate." Moreover, men could switch from a clerical career to other pursuits and back again at any time. Ali-Akbar Bahremani, better known as Hashemi Rafsanjani, was a small building contractor and pistachio grower in southeastern Iran in the 1970s. Then in 1978 he donned a turban, shed his European-style suit for an Arab-style robe and mantle, or *aba,* and asked his friends to call him Hojat al-Islam (Proof of Islam), a clerical title for mid-ranking mullahs. Just over a decade later, he was president of the Islamic Republic and reputed to be the richest man in Iran. Another example: Muhammad Khatami-Yazdi also started adult life as a civilian, including a spell as director of a travel agency in Tehran. With the gathering of the revolutionary storm in the late 1970s, he grew a beard, donned a turban, and exchanged his suit for a mullah's gear, claiming the title of Hojat al-Islam. A quarter of a century later, he was president of the Islamic Republic, and subsequently a frequent guest at interfaith conferences around the globe.

Rafsanjani and Khatami were not the first to become mullahs for the occasion. In the sixteenth century, as the Safavid shahs imposed Shiism on Iran by the sword, thousands of opportunists cast themselves as mullahs to profit from the new regime. Because there were no Shiite clerics in Iran at the time, the Safavids had to import mullahs from Lebanon. But these Lebanese imports did not speak Persian and could not communicate with newly Shiified Iranians. Eloquent Persians filled the gap in the market, becoming mullahs with the blessing of the Lebanese newcomers and splitting the profits with them.

There has been a reverse traffic also, with mullahs leaving the cloth for a range of reasons, not always opportunistic. When Reza Shah, the founder of the Pahlavi dynasty and the first architect of modernization in Iran, launched his anticlerical campaign in the 1930s, many mullahs shaved their beards and cast off their turbans to join his administration. Some former mullahs—including Ali Dashti, Muhammad Sajjadi, and Allameh Vahidi—became chief theoreticians of Pahlavi's secularist vision for Iran.

After the Khomeinist revolution, some mullahs were so disgusted with the cult of personality built by the ayatollah that they decided to abandon the cloth and, in some cases, go into exile. Yahya Nassiri, a mullah who had played a key role in the early days of the revolution, suddenly disappeared from the scene in what his relatives jokingly described as his "Grand Occultation." Among those who went into exile were such prominent mullahs as Abbas Mohajerani and Ali Tehrani.[14] Some leading Iranian mullahs who happened to be abroad during the revolution refused to return home even for brief visits because they regarded the Khomeinist system as heretical. Among them were Grand Ayatollah Abol-Qassem Mussavi-Khoei, Grand Ayatollah Ali-Muhammad Husseini Sistani, and Ayatollah Mahmoud Hojat Qomi.

Inside Iran, a majority of grand ayatollahs opposed the doctrinal bases of the proposed Khomeinist system from the start. Ayatollah Mahdi Rouhani declared the Khomeinist system to be "neither Islamic nor Shiite, but despotic." Hojat al-Islam Kamaleddin Ganjeh'i went further. To him, the Khomeinist system was a creation of Taghut (the Rebel), an Islamic designation for Satan.

With the liberation of Iraq by a U.S.-led coalition in 2003, the main Shiite "holy" cities of Najaf and Karbala, which had been isolated from the outside world by Saddam Hussein for three decades, became accessible to Iranians once again. This enabled thousands of Iranian mullahs to leave Qom, Mash'had, and Tehran for Baghdad, Najaf, and Karbala. In most cases, they explained their move by saying that the system Khomeini had imposed on Iran was "un-Islamic." Khomeini's own grandson, Hussein Mussavi Khomeini, a mid-ranking mullah who in 2003 moved to Najaf, the city of his childhood and early youth, told a press conference in Baghdad that the system created by the late ayatollah "had no right to be described as Islamic."

More recently, a younger generation of mullahs has opposed the Khomeinist system on both doctrinal and political grounds. They include Hassan Yussefi Eshkevari, Hadi Qabel, and Mohsen Kadivar. Even some of Khomeini's most prominent early associates have become opponents of a system they regard as un-Islamic if not anti-Islamic. The best known among them is Grand Ayatollah Hussein-Ali Montazeri, who had been Khomeini's heir-designate as Supreme Guide until their doctrinal quarrel and separation in 1986.

In fact, the opposition of the Shiite clergy to Khomeini's Islamic Republic has been consistent and widespread. While individuals dressed as mullahs occupy many of the highest positions in the system, including that of Supreme Guide, clerics also account for a large number of the regime's opponents. Over the past three decades, mullahs and students of theology have been jailed by the regime in higher proportions than people from any other social stratum. At times, the clash between Khomeinism and the Shiite clergy has become so intense that the regime has ordered the execution of some mullahs—something that no previous Iranian government dared do. Among the mullahs executed are Hojat al-Islam Muhammad Daneshi, a member of parliament; Hojat al-Islam Fakhreddin Hejazi, a popular preacher and televangelist; and Hojat al-Islam Mahdi Hashemi, an aide to Grand Ayatollah Montazeri.

Perhaps the most important clash between the clergy and the Khomeinist establishment came in 1982 when the regime arrested Grand Ayatollah Muhammad Kazem Shariatmadari, one of the six major "sources of emulation" for Shiites. In an unprecedented act of interference by the state in clerical affairs, the Khomeinist government announced that Shariatmadari had been "defrocked," a Christian term that had no parallel in either Shiism or Islam. The grand ayatollah, who had millions of "emulants" or religious followers, was kept under house arrest until his death four years later. Another grand ayatollah kept under house arrest until his death, in 2006, was Hassan Tabatabai-Qomi of Mash'had. Ironically, Shariatmadari and Qomi had saved Khomeini's life in 1963 by interceding with the shah on his behalf. Shariatmadari had gone even further and issued a fatwa (religious edict) promoting Khomeini from Hojat al-Islam to Ayatollah.[15]

The Shiite clergy includes some of the bitterest critics of the Khomeinist system. Ayatollah Hassan Sane'i has repeatedly ruled that the regime calling itself Islamic Republic is "as removed from Islam as the moon from earth." Ayatollah Kazemeini Borujerdi has labeled the Islamic Republic "a conspiracy against God and believers."[16] Ayatollah Mahmoud Tabatabai-Qomi has charged the Khomeinist leadership with "total and systematic betrayal of Islam." In an interview he asserted: "No one should call this regime Islamic. Trying to understand what these people [leaders of the regime] are doing by referring to Islam would only cause confusion."[17] Ayatollah Jalaleddin Taheri Khorramabadi, once an ardent Khomeinist and head of the notorious Imam Committee in Isfahan, turned against the regime in 1998, branding it "the rule of the corrupt, by the corrupt, for the corrupt."

The Khomeinist regime was never accepted as an "Islamic republic" even by Shiite organizations that had long fought for greater influence in shaping Iranian politics. The most important of these in terms of membership and financial resources was the so-called Mahdavieh Charitable Society, founded and for almost fifty years led by Ayatollah Ali-Akbar Halabi.[18] The society included a secret organization known as Hojatieh, devoted to fighting the Baha'i faith. By 1980, however, it had become clear that Halabi would not support the strange "Islamic" soup that Khomeini was cooking with ingredients borrowed from Marxism-Leninism and fascism. Halabi objected to Khomeini's "innovative" tendencies and specifically to his claim of imamate. Others took issue with Khomeini's militant anti-Sunni posture. One such critic was Ayatollah Nematallah Salehi Najafabadi, who wrote a book calling on Shiites to tone down their extremist views as a step towards pan-Islamic reconciliation. Written in the 1970s, the book was published and then immediately banned in 1985, six years after its author's assassination by killers allegedly linked to Khomeini.[19]

* * *

Before the Khomeinist revolution, Iran was already a Muslim nation and had been so for almost fourteen centuries. It had a constitution under which no legislation that contravened Islamic principles could be enacted. Non-Muslims could not attain high positions in the civil or armed services. Every year, Iran sent the single biggest contingent of pilgrims to Mecca, and more than ten million pilgrims went to the "holy" city of Mash'had. All children at secondary school had to take religious education and study classical Arabic in order to read the Koran. The state-owned radio and television networks allocated countless hours to religious programs. There were more than eighty high-level theological seminaries, plus full faculties of divinity offering courses up to and including the Ph.D. level. Iran also ranked high in the number of books published on Islam and produced some of the most beautiful Korans. In short, no one could deny Iran's existential reality as a Muslim nation.

Of course, there is no universal model for a Muslim nation. In Iran's case, the pre-Islamic past remains present, partly through certain aspects of the Twelver faith. Iran also has a history of more than four centuries of contact—often conflict-ridden but at times friendly and fruitful—with Western nations, from which it has borrowed heavily. Its first constitution, promulgated in 1906, was modeled on that of Belgium, with alterations to take the principles of Islam into account. Until the Khomeinist takeover, Iran had a parliament that, though manipulated by the executive, had a secure position in the national conscience as an important institution. Since 1911, there had been regular general elections, first every two years, then every four. Liberals, democrats, social-democrats, nationalists, and nihilists had all made their contribution to the collective consciousness at different times. In the 1950s, the Iranian Communist Party, called the Tudeh (Masses), became one of the largest Communist organizations outside the Soviet bloc. Iran had a privately owned press with a history of over 150 years, as well as Western-style academies, some linked with leading American universities.

Even so, whether Iran was a Muslim country was never the issue. None of the shah's opponents, not even Khomeini, ever claimed that Iran had abandoned Islam; they couched their criticism of the regime in nationalist, *tiersmondiste*, and populist terms. In 1978–79, the shah faced three parallel currents of opposition. One consisted of various leftist groups, some of them armed, who set aside their internecine feuds, dreaming of a "proletarian revolution." Another current emerged out of the Westernized middle class, which had secured material prosperity and now sought political power against an authoritarian regime. The third current belonged to what can only be described as the forces of fascism in Iranian society, which used an "Islamic" terminology.

The leftist camp knew that it could never mobilize enough muscle in the streets to neutralize the shah's army and police. The middle-class opposition also lacked muscle power and, more importantly, feared "the street." In the final analysis, the street could be mobilized only in the name of religion. This was how Iran's communists, socialists, social-democrats, democrats, liberals, etc., all rallied to the banner of Khomeini while claiming—and some of them believing—that they were fighting for greater individual and public liberties. To challenge an authoritarian regime, they brought to power dark forces led by a small group of mullahs and their nonclerical associates. It was a sight to see: at once comical and tragic. Socialists, liberals, and secularist democrats began growing beards, buying carnelian rosaries, and even conjuring a patch of piety on their foreheads. They started peppering their discourse with Koranic quotations, often with amusing effects because there are Arabic letters that Persian speakers cannot pronounce, and made a point of showing up at the mosque at least on Fridays. High-society women who used to fly to Paris to renew their wardrobes adopted the newfangled revolutionary headgear, invented by Imam Musa Sadr in the 1970s and inspired by the headgear of Christian nuns in Lebanon, and launched the fashion of organizing "holy table" parties where guests communicated with the Hidden Imam with the help of a mullah. The entire country became a vast theater stage on which tens of thousands of men and women were amateur actors playing "Islamic" roles. All this, however, could not hide the truth that the Khomeinist revolution and the regime it created were basically secular inventions and that the label "Islamic" was a lie.

For three decades, official Islam in Iran has been whatever the ruling mullahs and their praetorian guards want it to be at any given time. Khomeini had forbidden music in accordance with his understanding of Islam, but in 1980 he decided that Islam should allow music, as long as it supported the revolution and, not so incidentally, also contributed to his own personality cult. Even the ban on singing was lifted in the case of men, provided that they sang revolutionary songs in praise of the Supreme Guide. Khomeini had ruled that anyone who caught the caviar-bearing fish or ate the eggs would go straight to hell; but when he learned that Caspian fisheries generated $200 million for his treasury each year, he lifted the ban. Catching the fish and taking out the eggs were declared licit, though marketing them required special dispensation. This was an excellent device to make some mullahs rich by providing the required "religious cap" (*kolah e shar'ee*) for the business.

The ayatollah had promised to shut down all banks as "places of usury," in accordance with Islamic rules. By the end of 1979, however, the state had taken over all Iranian banks, providing endless sources of wealth for mullahs and their associates. Insurance companies had a similar experience: Islam regards insurance as sinful because it is an effort to pre-empt the will of God. If Allah intends to burn your house or wreck your car in an accident, who are you to try to obstruct his will through insurance? Worse still, how could a true believer try to provide for his family after his death? Was he not arrogating to himself the power of Allah as Sole Provider? In 1979, insurance was unknown in most Muslim countries, but it was big business in Iran. The mullahs seized all the insurance companies, and they were not prepared to kill the goose that laid so many golden eggs. Once again, Khomeini accommodated Islam with the interests of his associates by decreeing insurance to be licit only in his own Islamic Republic, thus closing the Iranian market to foreign insurance firms.

The traditional Islamic penal code does not provide for imprisonment. Those charged with any crime are to be tried before the first sunset after their arrest, and resulting penalties are either corporal punishment (including capital punishment), or fines in cash or kind, or in many cases only a cautionary sermon. Recidivist thieves may have one finger or a whole arm chopped off in public, but in most cases they go free after a caning and a fine. Even in murder cases, the guilty could walk free if the family of the victim offers pardon and receives the "blood tithe" (diy'ah), fixed by Islamic jurisprudence. Khomeini's Islamic Republic takes a different approach. The regime has executed over 100,000 people, mostly on charges that would never stand in a traditional Islamic court. It has hanged gay men from cranes in public, although the Koran only demands that homosexuals be cautioned and "allowed to go." Scores of women accused of adultery have been stoned to death in city squares, again in direct contravention of explicit Koranic rules. Under the shah, the maximum number of political prisoners in Iran was 3,000; in the early 1980s, the number climbed to over 150,000. Since then, more than five million Iranians have been sent to prison for lengths of time varying from a few hours to decades, often on spurious charges.

Khomeini boasted that he alone had authority to decide what is Islam at any given time, and even to suspend the basic principles of Islam. His successor Ali Khamenehi, being a junior mullah, has not had the effrontery to make such claims; but his propagandists compensate by asserting that whatever he decides has "divine sanction" as the authorized version of Islam. The Khomeinist revolution and the system it produced, although based on a peculiar reading of Islam, could hardly be called Islamic as understood by the overwhelming majority of Muslims and scholars of Islam. Thus the first word in the Khomeinist regime's name, the Islamic Republic of Iran, is a manifest lie.

5

Democracy as Enemy

The second identifier of the Khomeinist regime, the term "Republic," also amounts to a lie. An English dictionary defines the word as: a state or a nation in which supreme power rests with the citizens entitled to vote, and is exercised by representatives elected directly or indirectly by them and responsible to them.[1]

To understand a civilization, it is important to understand its vocabulary; if it was not on their tongues, it was not likely to have been on their minds either. None of the principal Muslim languages—Persian, Arabic, and Turkish—had a term for "republic" until the end of the nineteenth century. The word chosen as an equivalent is *jumhur,* which the leading Persian dictionary defines first as "grape juice distilled until half its volume evaporates, leaving half that is mildly intoxicating" and thus allowed under the rule of Islam forbidding the consumption of alcoholic drinks.[2] Thus *jumhur* and its variations *jumhuri* and *cumhuriyet* are used as equivalents of "republic," a word of Latin origin, only incidentally. Even in the political sense, most Arabic, Persian, and Turkish dictionaries offer a narrower definition than their counterparts for Western languages. Here is the leading Persian dictionary's definition: "A form of government in which the head (the president) is elected by the people of the country for a limited period."[3] For most Islamic leaders, the concept of a republic is little more than a rhetorical prop, as illustrated by the Libyan dictator Muammar Kaddhafi's invention of the word *jamahiria* to describe his particular form of despotism. Etymologically, the word designates an occasion on which a great deal of *jumhur* (mildly intoxicating grape juice) is imbibed, a kind of Islamic bacchanalia with reduced risks of hangover.

As for Khomeini, there is no evidence that he even knew the words "republic" or *jumhur* until he seized power in 1979. The term is never mentioned in any of his books written and published between the 1940s and the 1970s or any of his sermons before 1979. The term he always used was *hokumat Islami*, which means "Islamic rule"—specific enough to appeal to those who dreamed of religious government but vague enough not to alert the monarch's secret service, SAVAK (State Intelligence and Security Organization). During the revolutionary season of 1978–79, the term "Islamic rule" formed part of the triptych chanted by crowds in the streets of Tehran.[4] Khomeini's most directly political book, *Hokumat Islami* ("Islamic Government"), describes a system as far from republican as can be: all power belongs to Allah and is exercised by the Infallible Imams, and in their absence by a theologian acting in *walayat e faqih*, an obscure term open to multiple interpretations. Prior to Khomeini, the most widely accepted meaning was "custodianship by the theologian," referring to the tutelage of orphans, widows, and mentally handicapped individuals by mullahs. Khomeini's position, an "innovation" in the eyes of most Shiite theologians, abolished the customary distinction between the concepts of *walayat* (religious custodianship of the faithful) and *ze'amat* (leadership of society in secular matters).

Ayatollah Muhammad Hussein Tabatabai, possibly the most original of Shiite theoreticians of the twentieth century, had tried to develop common ground between Shiism and the Iranian people's thirst for democratic rule, demonstrated by over a century of struggle against absolutism culminating in the Constitutional Revolution of 1906 and the first elected parliament in a Muslim country. Arguing that Islam was in harmony with natural law, Tabatabai claimed that natural law required every society to have a "superintendent" (*sarparast*). In Shiism, he argued, that function was represented by the *walayat*. The question was who should exercise the function of *walayat*—the people as a whole, the clergy as a whole, a committee of mullahs, or a single theologian?

Tabatabai provided no answer, leaving the theoretical possibility of a system in which the people as a whole would be regarded as the vicar of Allah on earth. No doubt, Tabatabai had an eye on the 1906 Constitution, under which monarchy was "a gift bestowed by God" on the people of Iran. In other words, the nation as a whole was its own monarch; it was only the exercise of the power of monarchy that was bestowed on an individual. On this basis, a constituent assembly formed in 1912 dethroned the reigning Mohammad Ali Shah Qajar, who had taken up arms against the new democratic system. In 1925, another constituent assembly took the monarchy away from the Qajar dynasty and handed it over in trust to the Pahlavis. In both cases the message was clear: power belonged to the people, who could delegate or withdraw it as they wished.

Khomeini, by insisting that *walayat* be performed by a single mullah or in some ill-defined circumstances by a committee of mullahs, violated the principle of national sovereignty. It is not clear why Khomeini agreed to abandon the term "Islamic Rule" for "Islamic Republic." One plausible explanation, offered by some of the ayatollah's associates in the early days of the revolution, is that he was persuaded to adopt the term "republic" to reassure Communist and liberal allies.

Because most Iranians had never heard of Khomeini, let alone his weird ideas, until 1978, it was not clear how much support he actually enjoyed within the revolutionary movement. Much of the violence that pushed the shah's back to the wall was organized by leftist or Islamist-Marxist groups, some of whose leaders had trained in Cuba, China, North Korea, Communist South Yemen, and in Palestine Liberation Organization camps in Lebanon. They killed police officers and gendarmes, robbed banks, set public buildings and means of transport on fire, and terrorized the citizenry by setting up roadblocks on major roads. As for strikes, especially in strategic industries like energy and transport, the organizing was done by the well-trained cadres of the Tudeh (Masses) Party, a Communist outfit created by the Soviet Union during its occupation of northern Iran in 1941–46. Many of those who joined the revolutionary revolt, perhaps even a majority, believed they were fighting for an end to personal rule by the shah and certainly did not imagine they would end up under an even harsher personal rule by a mullah.

To allay their suspicions, Khomeini made full use of the Shiite arsenal of deception. He practiced *kitman* (concealment) by keeping his true intentions hidden. He practiced *taqiyyah* (dissimulation) by pretending to be a fighter for democracy. By the spring of 1979, weeks after the fall of the shah's regime, the broad coalition that had swept Khomeini to power was beginning to fragment. The leftist and Islamist-Marxist parties, still armed and capable of threatening the mullahs, began to campaign for a "people's republic" or a "people's democratic republic." The word "republic," designating a system in opposition to monarchy, was the only term on which everyone within the revolutionary coalition agreed. Khomeini had no choice but to adopt it, albeit with the inevitable adjective "Islamic."

Most of the men invited by Khomeini to write the constitution of the Islamic Republic believed they were required to build a more or less democratic system. The text that provided the basis of their work was a translation of the Constitution of the French Fifth Republic.[5] They also referred to Iran's Constitution of 1906, itself a translation of the Belgian Constitution. According to Grand Ayatollah Hussein-Ali Montazeri, who chaired the earliest meetings of the so-called Assembly of Experts set up to write the new constitution, the participants believed that they were expected to establish a "people-based" government. "Khomeini made many promises that we also repeated on his authority," Montazeri says. "The masses came forward in response to those promises and made many sacrifices. In reality, however, those promises were never realized."[6]

In the final days of the assembly's work, Khomeini instructed it to write the new constitution around the concept of *walayat e faqih*, ending all democratic illusions among the members. The new constitution gave the *wali e faqih* unlimited powers, including the authority to suspend the rules of Islam if necessary. The *wali e faqih* had to be an Iranian born of Iranian parents and a Twelver Shiite, but was declared to be the leader of the Muslim *ummah* throughout the world. At the same time, however, the text provided for the election of a president of the republic and a unicameral Islamic Consultative Assembly based on direct universal adult suffrage. Nevertheless, the *wali e faqih* was given the power to dismiss both the elected president and the parliament.[7] That Khomeini's system could not be a republic was made clear by Ayatollah Muhammad Beheshti, regarded by some as the regime's strongman until his assassination in 1981. Having created his political faction and named it the Islamic Republican Party (IRP), Beheshti told the central council of his movement that the term "republic in its Islamic interpretation" meant only "a rejection of hereditary monarchy" and not a Western-style system in which power belongs to the people.[8]

In fact, the term Islamic Republic is an oxymoron, because no republican system could be based on Islam. In a republic, power belongs to the people, even if in practice that might mean *some* of the people only, and the power may be exercised through elected representatives. The rule of the people, the *demos*, is democracy—a concept that is alien to Islam. There was no word for democracy in any of the Muslim languages until the 1890s, when the Greek term entered Muslim languages with little change: *democrasi* in Persian, *dimokraytiyah* in Arabic, *demokratio* in Turkish. There is not even a term for "politics" in the Muslim languages. The word *siassah*, now used as a synonym for "politics," initially meant whipping stray camels into line. The idea is to goad people onto the right path as the ruler sees it; the closest translation may be "regimentation." In a broader context, the verb form of *siassah* means meting out punishment or even assassination. Rather than the concept of *polis*, evoking citizenship with rights and duties, there is the *ummah*, the community of believers. It is no accident that early Muslims translated numerous ancient Greek texts but never those related to political matters. While the great Avicenna (Ibn Sina) wrote a commentary on Aristotle's *Poetics*, there was no translation of Aristotle's *Politics* in Persian until 1963.

There were some Greek concepts that Muslim scholars simply did not understand. Averroës (Ibn Rushd) was caught in an endless muddle because he could not imagine what tragedy and comedy meant. Another such concept was equality, the basis for democracy. *Isos*, the Greek word for "equal," is used in more than two hundred compound nouns, including *isoteos* (equality), *isologia* (equal or free speech), and *isonomia* (equal treatment). Again, we find no equivalents in any of the Muslim languages—aside from words such as *barabari* in Persian and *sawiyah* in Arabic, which mean juxtaposition or leveling.

The idea of equality is unacceptable to Islam, for the nonbeliever cannot be the equal of the believer. Even among believers, only those who subscribe to the three so-called Abrahamic religions—Judaism, Christianity, and Islam—known as the People of the Book (*Ahl el-Kitab*), are regarded as fully human. (Under Iranian influence, some Muslim scholars also include Zoroastrians among the People of the Book.) Here is the hierarchy of human worth in Islam: At the summit are free male Muslims. Next come Muslim male slaves. Then come free Muslim women, followed by Muslim slave women, then free Jewish and/or Christian men, then slave Jewish and/or Christian men, then slave Jewish and/or Christian women. (There is even a hierarchy for animals and plants. Seven animals and seven plants will assuredly go to heaven, while seven others of each will end up in hell.)[9]

Each category has specific rights to be respected, but not *equal* rights with others. For example, non-Muslims have the right to produce and consume alcoholic drinks, something forbidden to believers. Non-Muslim men also have the privilege of deciding whether or not to grow a beard, a freedom denied to their Muslim counterparts. However, non-Muslim men are not allowed to have more than one wife, and certainly no concubines and/or temporary wives, a privilege granted to their Muslim counterparts. The People of the Book have always been protected and relatively well treated by Muslim rulers, but often under a form of apartheid known as *dhimmitude,* in which non-Muslims pay a poll tax called the *jeziyah.* The status of the rest of humanity, those whose faiths are not recognized by Islam or who have no faith, has never been spelled out, although wherever Muslim rulers faced such communities they often treated them with a measure of tolerance and respect (as in the case of Hindus under most Muslim dynasties of India). In the early 1990s, a heated debate took place in the seminaries of Qom, the "holy" city south of Tehran, on whether the Japanese, not being among the People of the Book, had a soul. The majority opinion seemed to suggest they did not.

In Islam, there cannot be democracy, rule of the people, because power belongs only to God: *al-hukm l'illah.* The man who exercises that power on earth is known as *Khalifat al-Allah,* the regent of Allah. The *Khalifah* or caliph, however, cannot act as legislator, since the law has already been spelled out and fixed forever by Allah; it only remains to be interpreted and applied. Islam divides human activities into five categories from the permitted to the sinful, leaving little room for ethical innovations.[10] There is some space in which different styles of rule could develop, but no Islamic government can be democratic in the sense of allowing common people equal shares in legislation as citizens.

To say that Islam is incompatible with democracy should not be seen as a disparagement of Islam; in fact, some Muslims would see it as a compliment because they sincerely believe that their idea of rule by God is superior to rule by men. Islam has its own vision of the world and man's place in it. Islamic tradition holds that Allah has always intervened in the affairs of men, notably by dispatching 124,000 prophets or emissaries to inform the mortals of his wishes and warnings. The great Persian poet Farid ud-Din Attar says:

> I have learned of Divine Rule in Yathrib [Medinah].
> What need do I have of the wisdom of the Greeks?

A later poet, Nasser Bokharai, insists that Islam can never be compatible with "Greek Reason":

> All science of Greece was pushed to one side
> When [Muhammad] presented his absolute theory of existence.

Hafez, another medieval Persian poet, blames man's *hobut* or Fall on the use of his own judgment against that of God:

> I was an angel and my abode was eternal paradise
> Adam [i.e. man] brought me to this place of desolation.

The eminent Persian poet Rumi mocks those who claim that men can rule themselves:

> You do not reign even over your own beard,

Which grows without your permission.

Therefore, how could you pretend,

To rule on right and wrong?

In Muslim literature, the worst that can happen to man is being forsaken by God. Thus Rumi pleads:

Oh, God, do not leave our affairs to us—For if you do, woe is us.

The expression "abandoned by God" sends shivers down Muslim spines, for it spells the doom not only of individuals but also of entire civilizations. The Koran tells stories of tribes and nations that perished when God left them to their own devices.

Just as Islam brands philosophy as *Yunani* (Greek), thus alien and dangerous, some Muslims couple the word "democracy" with the adjective *gharbi* (Western), a foreign import if not an imposition. Most Islamist thinkers regard democracy with horror. Khomeini called it "a form of prostitution" because he who gets the most votes wins the power that properly belongs to Allah. Ali Shariati, a popular Islamist pamphleteer, called democracy "a veil of chastity worn by a whore." Sayyed Qutb, the Egyptian who became the ideological mentor of al-Qaeda, spent a year in the United States in the 1950s. There he found "a nation that has forgotten God and been forsaken by Him; an arrogant nation that wants to rule itself." In 2003, Yussuf al-Ayyeri, one of the leading theoreticians of today's Islamist movement, published a book in which he warned that the real danger to Islam did not come from American tanks and helicopter gunships in Iraq but from the idea of democracy and rule by the people.

The Pakistani preacher Abul-Ala Maudoodi, another of the Islamist theoreticians now fashionable, dreamed of a political system in which human beings would act as automatons in accordance with rules set by Allah. He said that Allah has arranged man's biological functions in such a way that their operation is beyond human control. For our non-biological functions, notably our politics, Allah has also set rules that we have to discover and apply once and for all so that our societies can be on autopilot, so to speak. Sheikh Muhammad bin Ibrahim al-Jubair, a Saudi theologian, claimed that the root cause of all contemporary ills was the spread of democracy. "Only one ambition is worthy of Islam," he liked to say, "the ambition to save the world from the curse of democracy and to teach men that they cannot rule themselves by manmade laws. Mankind has strayed from the path of God; we must return to that path or face certain annihilation." The Indian Sunni leader Enayatallah Mashreqi, influenced by Leninism in the 1930s, created the *Khaksar* (Down to Earth) movement to seize political power and save the subcontinent from "contamination" by the "Western disease of democracy" in which Hindus and Muslims would be treated as citizens with equal rights. He could not understand a system in which "a cow-worshipping Hindu" would have the same rights as "a proper Musulman."

Those who claim that Islam *is* compatible with democracy should know that they are not flattering Muslims; many would feel insulted by such an assertion. How, they would ask, could a manmade form of government, invented by the heathen Greeks, be compared to Islam, God's final word to man, the only true faith?

Islam rejects the idea of granting "the common folk" a decisive say in the affairs of the *ummah*. On at least twenty occasions, the Koran describes the majority of people as "ignorant and uninformed" (*akthar-hum layaalamun*). On almost as many occasions, it describes them as "unwise," "lacking the power of discernment," "ungrateful," "corrupt," "misguided," and "deniers of the Truth." In at least seven suras of the Koran, Allah advises his Prophet not to take the views of the majority into account: "For if you follow the majority, they shall lead you away from the path of Allah."

In the past fourteen centuries, Muslims on occasion have created successful societies *without* democracy. Conversely, there is no guarantee that democracy will not produce disastrous results. (Hitler was democratically elected.) Democracy has always had numerous critics and enemies, even among its own citizens.

In ancient Athens, the birthplace of democracy, Plato viewed the concept of rule by the people with skepticism. The *Protagoras* has Socrates ridiculing the title character's claim that democracy is the best form of government. Socrates points out that men always call on experts to deal with specific tasks, but when it comes to the more important matters concerning the city, they allow every citizen an equal say.

In response, Protagoras relates the founding myth of democracy: When man was created, he lived a solitary existence and was unable to protect himself and his kin against more powerful beasts. Consequently, men came together to secure their lives by establishing cities; but the cities were torn by strife. Zeus realized that things were going badly because men did not have the art of managing a city (*politike techne*). Without this art, man was heading for destruction. So Zeus called in his messenger, Hermes, and asked him to deliver two gifts to mankind: *aidos* and *dike*. *Aidos* is a sense of shame and a concern for the good opinion of others. *Dike* is respect for the rights of others and implies a sense of justice that seeks civil peace through adjudication. Before setting off, Hermes asked a decisive question: Should I deliver this new art to a select few, as was the case with all other arts, or give it to everyone? Zeus replied with no hesitation: To everyone. Let all have their share! "Hence it comes about, Socrates," concludes Protagoras, "that people in the cities, and especially in Athens, listen only to experts in matters of expertise, but when they meet for consultation on the political art, i.e. on the general question of government, everybody participates."

Traditional Islamic political thought is closer to Socrates than to Protagoras. The common folk, *al-awam*, are regarded as "animals" (*al-awam kal anaam*), so the interpretation of the divine law is reserved only for experts. In the Islamic Republic of Iran, there is even a body called the Assembly of Experts (Majlis Khobreghan). Political power, like many other domains, is reserved for the Select, or *khawas*, who in some Sufi traditions are even exempt from the ritual rules of the faith. The "common folk" must do as they are told either by the text and tradition or by fatwas issued by religious experts. Khomeini referred to the common folk as *mustazafeen* (the feeble ones), thus putting a majority of Iranians in the same category as orphans, vulnerable widows, and the mentally handicapped.

In the Greek tradition, once Zeus has taught men the art of politics, he does not attempt to rule them. They are largely on their own. Zeus and other gods do intervene in earthly matters, but always episodically and mostly in pursuit of pleasures and childish pranks. Polytheism by its nature is pluralistic and tolerant, open to new gods and to new views of old gods. One could mock Zeus as a promiscuous old rake henpecked and cuckolded by Juno, or worship him as justice deified—in the same city and at the same time. This would not be possible in monotheism, especially Islam, the most militantly monotheistic of the three Abrahamic faiths. The God of monotheism does not discuss matters or negotiate with mortals. He decrees—the Ten Commandments on stone tablets, or the Koran that was already composed and completed before Allah sent his Hermes, Archangel Gabriel, to dictate it to Muhammad. The Koran starts with a command: Read! In the name of Thy God the Most High!

Islam is about certainty, while democracy is about doubt. In democracy there is changing minds and sides, but there is no changing of one's mind in faith. To use a more technical terminology: democracy creates a series, faith builds a nexus. Democracy is like people waiting for a bus. They are of different backgrounds and have different interests. We do not care what their religion is or how they vote. All they have in common is their desire to get on that bus. And they get off at whatever stop they wish. Faith, however, is internalized, turned into a nexus. It controls man's every thought and move, even in his deepest privacy. Democracy is serial and polytheistic. People are free to believe whatever they like and engage in whatever religious rituals they wish, provided they do not infringe on others' freedoms in the public domain. Islam cannot allow people to do as they think best, even in the privacy of their bedrooms, because God is always present, everywhere, all-hearing and all-seeing (*Sam'ee wa Baseer*).

Khomeini's magnum opus, *Hal al-Masa'el* ("Solution to Problems"), suggests "the right way of doing things" for every imaginable human activity, from cutting one's nails to copulating, belching and farting, and going to war. The ayatollah tells us that when entering a lavatory, we have to put our left foot first. And when caught in a "swarm of locusts," we must not try to eat the locust that has once managed to escape from our hand. If we have had sex with our donkey, we have to take the beast to another village and sell it to an individual we do not know. If a man is sleeping in a room above his aunt's room, he must be careful that if there is an earthquake and he falls through the ceiling on top of his aunt, he does not copulate with her in the confusion; and if he nevertheless does copulate with her and a female child ensues, he does not take her as a concubine. The ayatollah's advice is: do nothing on your own; when faced with any problem, ask the experts. Allah has provided answers for all questions ever asked or to be asked until the end of time.

There is consultation in Islam, as the Koran stipulates: *Wa shawerhum fil amr.* (And consult them in matters.) But the consultation thus recommended is about specifics only, never about the overall design of society. At the same time, Islamic consultation cannot be institutionalized. The individual believer asks questions from the "expert" and receives answers, but then it is up to him whether or not to do as the "expert" suggests. The ruler consults anyone he likes, but in the end, the decision is his and his alone.

In democracy, there is a constitution that could be changed or amended. In Islam there is the Koran, the immutable word of God, beyond change or amendment. Islam means surrendering oneself to the will of Allah in exchange for the safety and security he offers. The typical Muslim dreams of *'afiyah,* which, roughly translated, means "exemption from divine punishment." To achieve *'afiyah* you have to do exactly as told, at every moment of your life. That means constant awareness of God throughout one's waking hours. The Persian poet Rashid Vatvat (twelfth century) put it this way: "Remember God, so that He forgets you!"

In the Koran, the word for belief is *iman* (security) and for the believer *mu'min* (one who is secure). The ultimate promise of Islam is to lead men back to the security of the unborn fetus in its mother's womb. The fetus has no cares; it is cared for by forces it does not know or understand. It is no accident that the two adjectives used most to describe Allah, al-*Rahman* (Master of the Wombs) and al-*Rahim* (the Wombster), both come from the same stem, *raham* (the womb). Only by implication have these terms, invoked at the start of all but one of the Koran's 114 suras, come to mean also "the merciful and the compassionate." (The name of Abraham, common grandfather of monotheism, means "Father of the Wombs" in Hebrew and Arabic.)

Mehdi Bazargan, the man who became prime minister in the first government set up by Khomeini, described the system created by the ayatollah in these terms:

> His Holiness the Imam [Khomeini] has described Islamic gov-
> ernment as one in which the Supreme Guide acts as the immov-
> able guardian of immature people. The source of this guardian-
> ship is the same Divine Mandate that has come to him from the
> Twelve Pure Imams. Therefore, just as an immature child has
> no right to dismiss his guardian, people, too, have no right to
> raise questions about the decisions of the Supreme Guide.[11]

To his credit, Khomeini had never tried to hide his contempt for "the common folk." In his book *Walayat Faqih* ("Custodianship of the Theologian") he wrote: "People are ignorant, incomplete, imperfect and in need of perfection. . . . There is no difference between the Custodian of the community and the guardian of children."[12] Khomeinist theoreticians have always dismissed elections as a trick invented by the West to give people the illusion of sharing power. Ali Shariati devoted a good part of his voluminous output to denouncing the idea of democracy as anti-Islamic. "What is the value of the votes of people who sell it for a ride or a bellyful of soup? And that is without mentioning the votes of the enslaved sheep, the votes of the donkeys and cows," he wrote in his book *Umma and Imamate.* "Leadership cannot be born from the votes of the common folk, a common choice that emerges from the misguided masses. The imam chooses his goals based on the Truth. Which Truth? The Truth revealed by Islamic ideology."[13]

The idea of separating right and morality is alien to religious thought.

It started making inroads in the West from the seventeenth century onwards, first thanks to Hobbes, and later, to Spinoza, Thomasius, and Goethe (in his *Sayings and Truth*). In Islam, however, that separation has not taken place; and because of Islam's nature as an all-encompassing doctrine, it may never take place.

6

Iran and Anti-Iran

The regime that Khomeini invented is called the Islamic Republic *of* Iran. It would be more accurate, however, to say the Islamic Republic *in* Iran. Khomeini and his associates regarded Iran as just a part of the broader Islamic *ummah*. They had no particular feeling for Iran as a land and a civilization, let alone an ideal. The late writer Reza Mazluman, murdered in France by hit men from Tehran, quipped that the Islamic Republic of Iran was not an official political designation but "the name of the disease that has afflicted our nation."

On February 1, 1979, Khomeini boarded an Air France chartered jet to return to Iran after sixteen years of exile in Turkey, Iraq, and France. Over two hundred associates, aides, and journalists accompanied him. Moments before the aircraft was to land in Tehran, a French journalist, Paul Balta, asked Khomeini what he felt on "returning home, after so many years." Khomeini's answer was simple: "Nothing!"[1] To the ayatollah, Iran was nothing but "a piece of land," a base for his global ambitions in the name of his version of Shiite Islam. As he stepped out of the plane, the many thousands who had gathered to greet him at Mehrabad Airport expected him to kneel, kiss the soil of Iran, and offer a prayer for its people. None of that happened. The ayatollah even refused to bless the Iranian flag that someone had offered him. Months later, as master of Iran, he was to replace the national flag with one of his own, symbolizing his fascist rule.

Khomeini and his associates never tried to disguise their hatred of the very idea of Iran as a nation with a distinct history, culture, and identity. In the early days of the revolution, one of Khomeini's closest aides, Sadeq Khalkhali—nicknamed "Judge Blood" for his role in sentencing thousands of people to death in mock Islamic tribunals—even suggested changing the name of Iran to Islamistan (Land of Islam). Three decades later, the foreign minister Manuchehr Mottaki suggested changing the name of the Persian Gulf to the "Gulf of Friendship" so as to please Iran's Sunni Arab neighbors.[2] Even before returning to Iran, Khomeini had worked hard to prevent the revolutionary movement from assuming patriotic colors. He had spoken of "Islamic rule" (*hokumat Islami*) in opposition to "national government" (*hokumat melli*). The various councils and committees he had created to run the revolution were all described as "Islamic." The word "Iranian" appeared nowhere. When someone suggested that he issue a special message on the occasion of Now-Ruz (New Day), Iran's ancestral New Year, predating Islam by some fifteen centuries, Khomeini lost his temper. "That is for the Magus [Magians], not for Muslims!" he shouted.[3]

Receiving a group of Iranian students in France in October 1978, Khomeini warned against "nationalist feelings," saying: "Nationalists are feeding on the leftover of the *Gabr*," a pejorative term for Zoroastrians. "They are opposed to the very foundations of religion. They want to return to the same aggressive and people-killing *Gabrs* [*sic*] and speak of pan-Iranism and the principles of being Iranian."[4] Addressing another group of Iranian visitors three months later, Khomeini again spoke of Islam's incompatibility with nationalism. "Up to now, we had problems with the nationalist ambitions of Muhammad Reza [the shah]," he said. "Now we have to cope with the problem of nationalism and democracy and similar things. You should not believe any such things."[5] Khomeini made countless other attacks on the very idea of Iran as a nation-state and insisted that loyalty to Iran, or indeed to any other nation-state, is a form of *sherk*, a Koranic term that means associating other gods with Allah. The idea is that loyalty to Allah should be exclusive. The homeland of a Muslim is his faith.

To show that he could never accept the Iranian solar calendar in which days and months bear pre-Islamic Persian names, the ayatollah always used the Islamic lunar calendar in which the months bear Arabic names. The committee set up to write the new constitution in 1979 recommended the creation of a parliament and suggested that it retain the name of the old one set up after the Constitutional Revolution of 1906: the National Consultative Assembly. Khomeini was furious. To him, the adjective "national" was anathema. The Khomeinist parliament was called the Islamic Consultative Assembly (Majlis Shuray e Islami). In February 1983, marking the anniversary of his revolution, Khomeini received the president of the Islamic Republic along with a number of foreign Islamist militants. He told them that the Islamic Republic was "the home of every true Muslim," and added: "Basically, we do not recognize a country named Iran. We have an Islamic Republic located in Iran but it belongs to Muslims everywhere."[6]

One of the first moves of the new regime was to change the Iranian national emblem of a lion wielding a sword, with a sun rising behind it. This was replaced by the word "Allah" in stylized calligraphy, in the original Arabic rather than the Persian equivalent, "Khoda." More interestingly, the calligraphy did not follow any of the Persian styles established over the previous fourteen centuries. The idea was to make a clean break with the past, in accordance with Khomeini's claim that pre-Islamic Iran had been a land of "darkness and barbarity" and that Islamic Iran, too, had lost its soul until his seizure of power in 1979. "This child of the Muslim nation is being born again," Khalkhali said, referring to Iran. What Khomeini either did not realize or chose to ignore was that the image of lion and sun was a symbol of Iranian Islam, more specifically in its Shiite form. For centuries, Ali, the first imam of Shiism, has been known as *Assad-Allah* (the Lion of Allah). The Safavid dynasty, which imposed Shiism on Iran in the sixteenth century, had adopted the image in honor of Ali. The pre-Islamic Iranian symbol had been the hawk (*shahbaz*), regarded as the Shah of the Birds. Later, the image of the rising sun was added to recall Iran's pre-Islamic past, but it was not meant to minimize the role of Islam. The idea was to show that Iran, an ancient nation, claimed a leading position in Islam thanks to Ali and his sword, known as *Dhul-Fiqar* (Double-Edged).

The ayatollah also replaced the Red Lion and Sun that had served for six decades as the Iranian equivalent of the Red Cross. Instead, he adopted the Red Crescent, in line with Arab and other Muslim countries. In doing so, he ignored the fact that the crescent for centuries had been the symbol of Iran's Ottoman enemies in countless wars, while the lion had symbolized the Iranian side.

Some of the ayatollah's associates even wanted to change the name of the Iranian currency, the rial, a modified version of the Spanish word *réal*, meaning "royal." To them, the word was associated with Iran's 2,500-year monarchic tradition and thus had no place in an Islamic system. The ayatollah, however, was persuaded not to make the change by a number of scholars who argued that the rial had been the currency of Muslim Spain and was now Saudi Arabia's currency, and thus the name was acceptable as an Islamic term.

To tone down Iran's Iranian-ness, *Iraniyat* in Persian, the ayatollah suppressed several national festivals dating back to pre-Islamic days. The national calendar was reorganized to reduce the number of days designed to celebrate *Iraniyat* and replace them with special occasions to promote the ayatollah and his revolution. Khomeinists also tried to destroy the remains of some of Iran's best-known archaeological and historic sites, such as Persepolis, the first capital of the Achaemenid Empire, which had been burned and destroyed by Alexander of Macedon. It was thanks to strong popular protests against such moves that the ayatollah had to back down. In May 2008, Khamenehi paid a publicized visit to the southern province of Fars, the heartland of Iran's ancient culture and birthplace of the first Persian Empire. Local authorities, expecting the Supreme Guide to respect a well-established tradition, had included a visit to Persepolis. Registered as part of the cultural heritage of mankind by UNESCO, the site is the most popular destination for Iranian and foreign tourists alike; it attracted more than ten million visitors in 2007. Some regard the ruins as a kind of shrine to Iranianism. But Khamenehi had no time for Persepolis. "Those ruins are leftovers of tyrants," he told the local authorities, according to the official Islamic Republic News Agency. "Iran achieved glory only after the arrival of Islam."

Iranians, however, have always thought otherwise. Persian poetry and prose over the past 1,100 years is a hymn to what Iranians believe was one of the greatest civilizations, built long before Islam appeared in Arabia. Some leading Persian poets and writers were clearly not Muslims, although they took care to hide behind fake Islamic identities to protect their lives. Others adopted Islam as part of their broader Iranian identity. For them, Islam was *part* of Iran, and they could take from it what they found worthy. The typical *diwan* (collected verse) of a Persian poet starts with a sonnet or an ode in praise of God, followed by homage to Muhammad. But once these obligations are out of the way, the poet feels free to use a palette of religious, philosophical, mythological, and cultural references far greater than anything Islam could offer. This is how the poet Rumi put it: *From the Koran, we took the kernel, To donkeys, we threw the skin.*

* * *

Khomeini did not consider himself Iranian by blood, but claimed to be a *sayyed* (master), that is to say a descendant of the Prophet through Mussa bin Jaafar, known as al-Kazim (the Self-Restrained One), the seventh imam of Shiism, and thus of Arab stock—a claim reflected in Khomeini's family name, Mussavi. Some writers have questioned the claim to be a *sayyed*, pointing out that the ayatollah's grandfather, Ahmad, never mentioned it. The tombstone of Khomeini's grandfather does not call him a *sayyed*, an unlikely omission if he had believed himself to be one. It seems that the family decided to claim sayyedship during the final years of the ayatollah's father, Mostafa.

Until the twentieth century, Iranians did not have family names. It was only in the 1930s that national identity cards were issued and Iranians were asked to choose family names. The ayatollah's family adopted the name "Hindi" ("Indian"), presumably to distinguish itself from thousands of other families who also claimed to be Mussavis, that is to say descendants of the same imam Mussa al-Kazim, reputed to have had dozens of concubines who produced scores of children.[7] The choice of Hindi was not because the family were of Indian origin, as their enemies later suggested, but because one of their ancestors had spent time in Kashmir propagating Shiism in the eighteenth century. Some of Khomeini's relatives, including his nephews, still bear the name Hindi, which Khomeini himself used as a *nom de plume* in his poems.[8] The name Khomeini refers to the central Iranian village of Khomein, where the ayatollah was born; it was added to his name because the registrar of patronyms would not let him be designated with the name Mussavi alone. (There were too many Mussavis all over the place and the state wanted to distinguish them from one another.)

The ayatollah's father used the word *sayyed* to underline his Arab origins. In Shiism, being a *sayyed* carries honorific as well as material advantages. When a *sayyed* enters a room, others must stand up and offer him the place of honor. Looking at the face of a *sayyed* first thing in the morning heralds a good day. Believers should reserve a portion of their income as an offering to *sayyeds*, in cash or kind. This is known as *sahm e sayyed* (the *sayyeds'* share) and is considered a means of "cleansing" ill-gotten wealth.[9] Inventing a role for themselves as "intercessors" (*shafi'e*), a function that did not exist in Islam, the *sayyeds*, genuine or not, claim they can negotiate deals with Allah on behalf of individuals, to obtain lesser punishments or even divine forgiveness. "Pay a *sayyed* and buy peace in the hereafter," says one favorite dictum of the mullahs. *Sayyeds* also perform miracles, such as helping barren women to conceive, the chronically sick to recover, failing businesses to improve their bottom line, and impotent men to regain the vigor of youth. According to extremist Shiites, Allah created the whole universe solely to please the family of Muhammad. Thus, serving Muhammad's descendants, the *sayyeds*, is the highest of religious duties for any Muslim.

But how does a person become a *sayyed*? One may base a claim of sayyedship on a genealogical tree (*shajareh nameh*) obtained from a professional forger, at a hefty price. Or one may rely on a declaration by another *sayyed* of good reputation. It works like this: The prominent *sayyed* convenes the local notables and reports that he has just had a dream in which the Prophet—or if one is more ambitious, one of the twelve imams—appeared, usually riding a white horse. The holy rider called on the dreamer to wake up and inform everyone that so-and-so is a *sayyed*, without knowing it. "Go and tell everyone that they are blessed with the presence of a *sayyed*, a man of pure Arab blood in their midst, a child of my very flesh," the rider said. Another way of "discovering" a *sayyed* is by examining an individual's face, especially the part between the eyebrows. If the inspection reveals a vein that is likely to swell in anger, the individual in question is pronounced a *sayyed*. The protruding vein is supposed to be peculiar to Hashemites, a clan of the Arab Quraish tribe of which Muhammad was a member. (It is known as *rag-e-Hashemi*, the "Hashemite vein.") Countless families of *sayyeds* have started with an individual discovering such a vein between his eyebrows.

There have been claims of sayyedship on even more spurious grounds. Historians have been perplexed by the extraordinarily high number of *sayyeds* in the frontier areas of Khorassan, Iran's province bordering on Central Asia. The Russian scholar Ilya Pavlovitch Petroshevsky provided a clue in his seminal work *Eslam Dar Iran* ("Islam in Iran"), where he showed that the newly Islamicized Turkic and Turkmen tribes frequently raided the region to capture Persians as slaves for sale in the markets of present-day Turkmenistan and the Chinese province of Xinjiang. The local Persians discovered that claiming to be a descendant of the Prophet protected them against capture and enslavement. Thus in the seventeenth century the number of *sayyeds* in the region soared. But then something unexpected happened: a change of taste in the slave markets made ownership of *sayyeds* fashionable. As the price of *sayyed* slaves rose, numerous families suddenly discovered that they had no relation to Muhammad after all.

The idea of tracing one's ancestry to Muhammad through his cousin and son-in-law Ali was first made popular by the Safavids, a clan of Kurdish adventurers who converted Iran to Shiism by force, starting in the sixteenth century. Although they certainly had no Arab blood, the

Safavids needed the claim of sayyedship to back their ideological war against the Sunni Ottomans. They also helped foment the legend that Hussein, Ali's second son and the third imam of Shiism, had married Princess Shahrbanu, a daughter of Yazdegerd III, the last Sassanid emperor. This was a clever propaganda trick because it persuaded Iranians that the new Safavid version of Islam was based on an ancient blood connection with Iran. After all, if Shahrbanu had really married Hussein, all nine subsequent imams, including the most important one, the twelfth and last, were half Iranian by blood. The fact that the story was a hoax did not matter to the mullahs. They well knew that Hussein, age twelve at the time the marriage is supposed to have taken place, was thousands of miles away from Iran in Medina. Nor were they bothered by the fact that Yazdegerd had had no daughter named Shahrbanu. Their aim was to make Shiism more acceptable to Iranians.

In the eighteenth century when Agha Muhammad Khan, the eunuch founder of the Qajar dynasty, turned Tehran into his capital, he asked the mullahs to find some "holy place" that would lift the nondescript city out of its obscurity. The mullahs duly obliged by announcing that the Hidden Imam had visited them in dreams to point them to a spot where, unbeknownst to all for over 1,200 years, his grandmother Bibi (Lady) Shahrbanu was buried. The spot was transformed into a shrine and became a place of pilgrimage with a host of *sayyeds* on hand to perform all sorts of miracles. After Khomeini's seizure of power in Tehran, the number of Iranians describing themselves as *sayyeds* exploded. At one point in 1982 even the secretary general of the Soviet-sponsored Tudeh (Masses) Party claimed to be the grandson of an ayatollah and a *sayyed*.[10] Tens of thousands of people added the title *sayyed* to their names as a means of enhancing their social status and/or securing access to rare goods and services. Individuals who had pure Persian—that is to say non-Islamic—names replaced these with Arabic names, some describing them as the "slaves" or even "dogs" of this or that imam.[11]

It is difficult to estimate the number of those who claim to be *sayyeds*. Judging by names in the Tehran telephone directory, they could account for around 2 percent of the population. The overwhelming majority, however, have little or nothing to do with the family of the Prophet or any other Arab clan, for the Arabs who settled in Iran as conquerors numbered no more than a few hundred thousand and were absorbed into the native population within two or three generations. Over thousands of years of existence in one political form or another, Iran has absorbed ethnic elements from many different origins: Elamite, Anshanite, Sumero-Akkadian, Arab, Turkic, Mongol, and Tatar, to name but a few. To be sure, not all who claim to be *sayyeds* put their Arabo-Islamic identity above their love for and loyalty to Iran. History is full of *sayyeds* who fought and died for Iran, at times against the very Arabs with whom they claimed kinship. Khomeini and his associates, however, have used the title as a device in their anti-Iran campaign. Four of the six men who have become president of the Islamic Republic since 1979 have claimed to be *sayyeds*.[12] One of the remainder, Ahmadinejad, claims to be half *sayyed* since his mother is supposed to be a descendant of Muhammad. It was to reap the benefits of this connection that Ahmadinejad's father in 1950 changed his family name from Saberian to Ahmadinejad, meaning "from the stock of Muhammad." Among high officials of the Khomeinist regime at any given time, a large number claim descent from the Prophet through the imams.

* * *

According to Khomeini, Muslims cannot speak of national identity since Islam does not divide the believers into nations. "All this talk about being Iranians and what we should do for Iran is not correct," the ayatollah told visitors to his home in September 1979. "The claim that we must pay attention to national identity and patriotism is completely baseless."[13] In another meeting, he claimed that nationalism was a Western invention used to sow dissension among believers. "How many slaps in the face we have had because of this idea of a nation," he said. "Nationalism is a conspiracy by colonialists. We say: those who talk of the nation should go get lost!"[14] Patriotism is a form of corruption, Khomeini said in another speech.

We have to be very attentive so that some Satans [*sic*] do not use the names of Iran and the land of Iran as a means of diverting us from our beloved Islam. Whatever corruption we have suffered from has come from this idea of nationality and patriotism. Beware that bringing up such ideas is designed to cause divisions. One of the issues that the architects of colonialism raise is patriotism.[15]

Khomeinist theoreticians claimed that the very idea of Iran as a nation is a Western imperialist invention meant to undermine Islam. This is how Sayyed Mir-Hussein Mussavi Khamenehi, Khomeini's prime minister from 1981 until the post was abolished in 1989, put the ayatollah's position on the subject:

The colonialists wanted to separate our nation from its Islamic identity. This conspiracy started in an organized way in our country and left destructive consequences. There were calculated moves to promote nationalism, the revival of dead bones to claim that the Iranian system was eternal. In architecture, for example, we had to seek inspiration in [pre-Islamic] Achaemenid architecture. The idea of reliance on a pre-Islamic Iranian system of values, and recalling the history of the Achaemenids, the Sassanids, and other Iranian dynasties before Islam, was exported to our country from the West as part of efforts to de-Islamicize it. The emphasis was put on nationalist values and concepts such as blood and soil that we encounter in nationalism. The marking of the millennium of Ferdowsi's birth in 1934 and the purging of the Persian language of Arabic words were Western conspiracies to destroy Islam. At the same time, they were bringing the ruins of Persepolis out of the earth in which they had been buried for thousands of years to fabricate a history and force our nation to feel proud about it. But that history was alien to Islam; it was a history that had died thousands of years ago.[16]

The new regime coined code words to designate its ideological enemies, including terms for democrat, liberal, secular, and leftist (*chapi*), but the worst insult was reserved for those labeled "patriotic" (*melli*). The Khomeinists regretted that the Arab invaders who brought Islam to Iran had failed to destroy the national consciousness of Iranians, as had been the case with other nations conquered by the armies of Muhammad. "To emphasize our Iranian-ness is a deviation," declared Ayatollah Sayyed Muhammad Mussavi Khoiniha, deputy speaker of the Islamic Majlis, one of the rising stars of Khomeinism at the time. "When they [the West] want to deceive people, they bring up the issue of national identity. The very concept of a nation is alien to Islam. What does national mean? As a Muslim I feel no obligation to fight for a homeland minus Islam."[17]

Proud of their claimed Arab ancestry, the Khomeinists launched a campaign to Arabize the Persian language by injecting it with hundreds of Arabic loan words. An Indo-European language, Persian has never felt comfortable in the alphabet borrowed from Arabic after the Arab conquerors succeeded in destroying the Persian characters that had previously been used. Nader Naderpour, who was one of Iran's most popular contemporary poets, described Persian language as "an Aryan soul in a Semitic body."

The story of how Persian survived the Arab invasion would read like a narrative in the style of magical realism, since the Arabs did everything they could to destroy it. They burned all the Persian books they could find and demolished more than seven hundred libraries, including one at Ctesiphon, the capital of the Sassanids, that contained over forty thousand volumes, an impressive figure for the seventh century. Omar, the second caliph, explained the rationale for the *auto da fe* organized by the Arabs: "If the books of others are in conformity with Our Book [the Koran], they are superfluous and a waste of space. If they are in contradiction with it, they must be burned." The Arabs feared that Iranians would continue to read their own books, including Zoroastrian texts, and eventually revolt against alien Islamic rule. At the time of the Arab invasion, the most popular Persian religious text was the book known as *Zand va Pazand* ("Truth and Counter-truth"), which explained the basic tenets of Zoroastrianism and the principal arguments of its critics. Omar made the reading of this book a capital crime, and he invented an Arabic word for it: *zandaqa,* a term used even today to describe anyone who deviates from Islam. The person guilty of the capital crime is called *zandiq,* "he who reads books other than the Koran," and if he refuses to stop doing so after three warnings, he should be put to death. Later, the Iranian poet Mahyar Daylami, who had learned Arabic in order to "insult the Arabs in their own language," wondered how "a people with just one book could teach others with whole libraries?"

It took the Arabs almost eighty years to conquer most parts of Iran, forcing those who wished to read "other books" to flee to still-free areas of Iranian-ness such as the Caspian Sea littoral and parts of Central Asia. For nearly two centuries, no text of enduring value was produced in Persian. (If any were, none survived.) Iranians know that period as the "two centuries of silence" in which their existence as a nation seemed threatened.[18] In those two centuries, Iranians lost their alphabet and had to adopt the Arabic one with some modifications.[19] At the same time, thousands of Arabic words crept into the most widely spoken form of Persian at the time, known as Pahlavi. (The reverse traffic also existed, although on a smaller scale, with hundreds of Persian loan words entering the Arabic vocabulary.)[20]

The two centuries of silence ended with a poem written by one Abu-Hofs Soghdi, a farmer from Central Asia who appears to have remained a Zoroastrian while assuming a Muslim appearance. Only the first line of his sonnet has survived, but every Iranian knows it as the first cry of a nation reborn. As the poet Massoud Farzad put it in the 1960s, "The baby cried, and everyone knew that he was still alive—alive after two centuries of being strangulated by a vicious invader." The first line of Soghdi's sonnet is: *How does the wild doe roam in the plain? She has no friends— friendless, how does she abide?*

For the next 1,200 years, generation after generation of Iranians believed that Soghdi's doe symbolized Iran—wounded, friendless, and turned to the wild in an epic struggle for survival. By the tenth century, however, it had become clear that Iranians would never share the fate of Egyptians, Syrians, and North African Berbers, among other nations conquered by Islam that lost their identities and became Arabs. The text that made sure Iran would remain Iran was Ferdowsi's *Shahnameh* ("Book of Kings"), which narrates the nation's mythological past, plus a few episodes of its history under the Sassanids, in almost pure Persian.[21] Ferdowsi (935–1020) reminded Iranians that they had been a proud nation, builders of empires and civilizations. He castigated the Arabs for their "violence, ignorance, and fanaticism"; they were "imbibers of camel milk and devourers of lizards." Fortune and fate had helped them destroy the Iranian civilization; but that was not the end of the story. Iran was eternal, and would return as a great nation and builder of civilizations.

When Ferdowsi wrote his epic, the Arabs had already vanished from the Iranian scene. The faith they brought had survived, albeit in a form that might have surprised Muhammad himself.

Centuries later, the Khomeinist regime launched a new campaign against the Persian language. But this provoked a reaction among Iranian writers and poets who tried to resist the regime-sponsored trend by purging their work of Arabic loan words. In the 1930s, the Iranian Academy set up by Reza Shah had already opened the way by replacing some five thousand Arabic loan words with Persian equivalents, often made from ancient Pahlavi stems. Iranian nationalists made a point of writing what they called *Parsi Sareh* (Purified Persian). One of their leaders, Zabih Behrouz, argued that since man thought with words, it was important to establish what words were used to form those thoughts. "An Iranian who thinks with Arabic words risks ending up thinking like an Arab," he wrote. "If we wish to become Iranians again we have to start thinking with our own words."

The fear that Iranians might further distance themselves from the Arabs, and thus from the religion of the Arabs, persuaded Khomeini to reduce the number of hours devoted to the study of Persian at schools to provide more time for the teaching of Arabic. Government propaganda presented Arabic as "the language of Allah" or even "the sacred language" (*zaban moqaddas*), although in the Koran nothing but Allah is described as "sacred." At a meeting with university deans in November 1982, Khomeini lashed out at one of the academics who had suggested that teaching Arabic at schools was a waste of time, as Arabs produced no scientific or literary work that could justify the effort. "Do not say that the Arabic language is not ours!" the ayatollah shouted. "The Arabic language belongs to Islam and Islam belongs to all. Our writers must not fall into the trap of Persianization. Our textbooks must be purged. The Persian names of our streets must change so that we become independent."

Khomeini's plea on behalf of Arabic was echoed by one of his lieutenants, Ali-Akbar Bahremani, better known as Hashemi Rafsanjani. In June 1985, delivering a sermon at the campus of Tehran University, he called on students to "love, cherish, and praise" the language of the Koran. "For us the Arabic language is the most noble of languages in the world and a divine gift to mankind as a whole," he said. "We are greatly attached to this language." While the teaching of Arabic proved a failure because the overwhelming majority of Iranian children were not interested, changing the names of streets proceeded briskly. By the end of 1983, the names of almost all Iranian mythological figures, kings, heroes, poets, scholars, and generals had disappeared from public places. Instead, Iranians found the names of obscure Arab historic figures, mullahs with an Arab background, and even the names of Arab terrorists, such as the man who murdered Egypt's President Anwar Sadat in 1981.[22]

Ironically, neither Khomeini nor Rafsanjani, nor indeed a majority of the mullahs, ever learned enough Arabic to conduct a conversation or write in that language. In 1979, an attempt by Khomeini to speak Arabic in an interview with Algerian television in Tehran turned into farce when the ayatollah came out with a mongrel version of the language that the visiting media men could not understand. They decided to switch to French, using an interpreter for Khomeini, who spoke Persian. Only one of the six individuals who have acted as president of the Islamic Republic has spoken Arabic.[23]

7

Unwelcome Faith

Khomeini and his associates have tried to persuade the Iranians, and the world outside, that Iran welcomed Islam with open arms. Some Islamist apologists, such as Ali Shariati, have echoed the claim and tried to prove that Iranians gladly accepted Islam because they were tired of the "unjust social system" under the Sassanids. Judging by historical records, however, the opposite was the case. By most accounts, a majority of Iranians refused to convert to Islam until some three centuries after the fall of the Sassanid Empire.

At the time of the Arab conquest, no one quite knew what Islam actually was. The Koran was not written down until a generation later. Even then, few Iranians knew enough Arabic to read it in the original, and no Persian translations appeared until four centuries later. In any case, the religious authorities regarded the translation of the Koran as a questionable if not reprehensible act and discouraged believers from consulting vernacular texts. Islamic law, or Shariah, was not codified until over a century after the conquest, mostly thanks to Iranian and Greek converts in the Levant. The Arabic language itself was little more than an oral tradition with no fixed grammatical rules and certainly no written lexicon. The grammar and lexicon were established by a number of Iranians, among them Sibuyeh and Ruzbeh (better known as Ibn Muqaffah), who pretended to be Muslim converts but continued to practice their ancestral Zoroastrian faith in secret.

The Koran orders Muslims to battle against those "who do not believe in Allah and those who follow their own faith, even those who have (their own) books until they convert to Islam or agree to pay a poll tax."[1] This was the message that Muslim emissaries from Caliph Omar brought

to the Sassanid King of Kings, Yazdegerd III: Accept Islam or submit to
Arab rule! Yazdegerd wrote back to reject the blackmail. He described
Omar's religion as "a cult of terror and plunder." Various versions of the
two letters have remained in circulation ever since as part of the never-
ending dialogue/conflict between Iranian nationalism and Islam.

The Iranian monarch's refusal triggered wars that lasted more than
fifteen years and decimated the population of the country. According to
historians, over 100,000 Iranians died in the battle of Jalula alone.[2] Iranians fought the invaders in Nahavand, Hamadan, Shushtar, Ahvaz,
and Ctesiphon. In Estakhr, the people resisted for six months and, once
they had surrendered, refused to convert or pay the poll tax. The Arabs
ordered a general massacre in which nearly the whole of the population,
some 150,000 souls, perished. There were similar massacres in Rey, near
present-day Tehran; in Sistan, a province on what is now the Afghan
frontier; in Qom, south of Tehran; in Shapour, in the province of Fars;
and in Gorgan, close to the Caspian Sea. In Yazd, central Iran, a small
army led by Mehrbanu, one of Yazdegerd's daughters, fought the Arabs
for almost twenty years. Another small army of resistance fighters under
Piruz, a son of Yazdegerd, fought the invaders in Central Asia before
eventually seeking refuge in China.[3]

Iranian chroniclers have recorded the utter amazement caused by the
Arab "passion for loot, plunder, and destruction." It was as if the Arabs,
being children of the desert, wished to reduce everything to the level of
the sand dunes they had grown up with. They were comfortable only
with things horizontal. To these tent dwellers, any building was something both to marvel at and to fear. They cut down trees, laid waste to the
artful walled gardens known as *paradais* (the origin of the English word
"paradise"), and pulled down any building that was taller than a camel
standing up. Abu-Ubaida bin al-Jarrah, one of the Arab generals, was
outraged to see that the Iranian capital had countless buildings that were
grander than Allah's Precinct at Mecca, where the black stone known
as the Ka'aba (the cube) was located. Non-Muslims were not allowed to
have buildings taller than those in which Muslims lived.[4] Whole cities

were destroyed, their inhabitants forced to flee or taken into slavery.

Some of those sent into slavery ended up as mercenaries in future Islamic conquests thousands of miles away. Nearly half the army that conquered southern Spain for Islam consisted of slaves and mercenaries from Isfahan, in central Iran. Iranian mercenaries and slaves also participated in the capture of Sicily and Corsica by Muslim armies.

For generations, the atrocities committed by the Arab invaders were not forgotten; some are remembered in Iranian folk songs and stories to this day. The history of the "two centuries of silence" is also filled with accounts of Iranian revolts against Arab oppressors. According to most historians, not a year passed without some part of the occupied territories being shaken by rebellion. Iranians created secret societies that in later centuries transformed themselves into Sufi fraternities. Rebels gathered in the charred remains of old Iranian cities laid waste by the Arabs. The urban wastelands, known as *kharabat* (the ruins), became havens of peace where Iranians could recite their new Persian poetry, drink forbidden wine, recall ancestral liturgies, and nurse their national chagrin. They also kept alive the memory of Iranian resistance against the invaders. Those urban wastelands, which still dot the Iranian landscape, provided refuge for anti-Arab rebels such as the Khorram-Dinan (Followers of the Felicitous Faith, i.e. Zoroastrians)—people who had rallied to the standard of Babak Khorramdin, who fought the forces of the caliph for over a decade before being betrayed, captured, and crucified.

Under Muawyyah, the founder of the first Muslim monarchy, the Arabs decided to create permanent settlements in various parts of the occupied territories to discourage further revolts. Between 662 and 682 A.D., an estimated 50,000 Arab soldiers and their families, some 300,000 people, were settled in Khorassan, the Iranian province bordering on Central Asia. The settlers mixed with the local population, starting a process that was to continue until the end of Arab domination some 150 years later. Rather than Arabizing Iranians, however, Muawyyah's scheme led to the Iranization of the settlers. By the start of the ninth century, outside the lowlands of Khuzestan where Arabic speakers had lived under Iranian rule, not a single Arabic-speaking village or neighborhood existed anywhere on the vast Iranian plateau.

The belief that Arabs and Persians were worlds apart permeates the works of many great Iranian poets. The Arabs are depicted as a people who love fighting, plunder, and the visible rituals of their faith. Iranians, on the other hand, are presented as a people of great spirituality who love beauty and dislike showing off their religiosity. The Arabs are concerned with appearances, the outside of things; the Iranians with the "inner truth" of existence. In a famous poem, Attar tells the story of a wealthy Arab who "falls among a bunch of Persians" and loses his worldly wealth, but he is extremely happy nevertheless. When his Arab friends wonder how this can be, he says that he "lost the superficial to gain the essential."

Some Iranians even considered the Arabs incapable of understanding the message of Islam. Here is the Persian poet Sanai Ghaznavi (twelfth century):

> If the Arab were the protector of the faith,
> The man who fires the furnace would be master of the sun and the moon.
> It is the Persian who could build [civilization].
> The Arab is good for marauding and raiding.
> Bulahab was from the very soil of Yathrib.*
> However, he couldn't value the call to prayer.
> Salman, on the other hand, was a Persian
> Who strived hard for the faith.
> Who could forget his love of Persian
> Or take the crown of honour from Salman's head?

Soon after the Arab invasion, some Iranians tried to build up Salman, known to Islamic history as Salman Farsi (the Persian Salman), into a co-founder of Islam. A soldier in the King of Kings' army and a mysterious figure, Salman seems to have traveled to Arabia after quarreling with his superiors. There he met Muhammad and decided to help promote the

---

* Bulahab was a wealthy Arab cursed by the Prophet for rejecting Islam. Yathrib was the ancient name for Medina, Muhammad's adopted hometown.

new prophet's message. Although claims that he might have been the author of the Koran must be discounted, there is no doubt that he was close to Muhammad and acted as his chief military strategist in a number of key battles that helped Islam defeat its early enemies. The Prophet's attachment to Salman was clear when he decided to build seven mosques for his closest companions in Medina: he devoted the largest mosque (still standing) to Salman.

* * *

Among the many innovations that the invaders introduced into Iran was slavery. Persian society had been hierarchized in accordance with a loose system of castes, at the apex of which stood the warrior class, including the royal family and the aristocracy, with the farmers constituting the base of the pyramid. The intellectual elite, known as *dabiran* or bureaucrats, stood in the middle along with artisans. There were no slaves. The Arabs, on the other hand, had no caste system but always had slaves. The capture of new territories provided them with fresh opportunities for a flourishing slave trade that, having started in Mesopotamia, soon expanded into Central Asia in the east and North Africa through the Levant, and continued until the twentieth century.

Religious intolerance was another of the innovations that the invaders brought to Iran. Although Iran had experienced the consequences of bigotry on occasions, including the massacre of Mazdakites under the Sassanid King Khosrow Anushiravan in the seventh century, the overall attitude of Iranians towards followers of other faiths was one of tolerance. The many Christian sects that faced persecution because of schisms in the Roman Empire always found a home in the Sassanid Empire. Many followers of Arianus fled to Iran after being chased out of North Africa and the Levant by Roman emperors. They founded the Persian Church of Christ, which the Romans attacked as "the Persian Party." No doubt, part of the welcome accorded to Roman schismatic fugitives was due to political calculations: the Sassanids missed no opportunity to foment discord within the Roman Empire and its successor, the Byzantine Empire. Iranians were also used to seeing people of other faiths in high places. They had seen their monarchs take Jewish and Christian wives while many non-Zoroastrians reached the highest echelons of public service. Muslims, however, had no tradition of tolerance at the time. Non-Muslims were given the choice either to convert to Islam or to pay a poll tax that most of them, impoverished by the collapse of the economy, could not afford. As a result, many of Iran's religious minorities immigrated to lands still free of Arab domination. They left behind names of villages and whole areas that recall a Christian or Jewish past. In addition to Jews and Christians, hundreds of thousands of Zoroastrian Iranians immigrated to India, taking with them as many of the sacred texts as they could save from Arab rage.

The invaders tried to break the will of the Iranians just as they had done with Syrians, Phoenicians, Greeks, Egyptians, Libyans, Vandals, and Berbers that fell under their rule. This is how Muawyiah spelled out his policy in a letter to one of his provincial governors:

> If you wish to tame the Iranians, remember that they cannot
> be kept in rein except with the method of Omar bin Khattab [i.e.
> the second caliph, whose armies began the conquest of the Sas-
> sanid Empire]. These people, you ought to humiliate. You ought
> to hit their heads so hard that they cannot raise them. Reduce
> their income to a minimum, and give them as little sustenance
> as possible. They are best kept in check when hungry. Because,
> once they are well fed the first thing they think of is revolt.
> On the war front, dispatch them to the front-line so that they
> become the first targets of the enemy. Make sure that they are
> inflicted with whatever hardship and punishment possible. I
> repeat: humiliate and crush them, and see how they bow their
> heads to your rule.[5]

Although a majority of Iranians started to convert to Islam from the middle of the ninth century, they did not tone down their hatred of the Arabs as invaders and destroyers of their ancestral culture. According to one study, the Arab invasion, the active part of which lasted fifteen years, cost Iran the equivalent of half a century of its gross domestic product in modern terms. In a sense, Iran never recovered from the damage done to its economic infrastructure. Many of the underground water channels, known as *kariz* and *qanat*, an Iranian invention, were never repaired, leaving vast tracts of once cultivated land exposed to desertification. As for the windmill, another original Iranian invention, it all but disappeared from the plateau. The invaders also destroyed hundreds of dams that had enabled Iranians to develop a sophisticated irrigation system in a land that depended on seasonal rain. The result was the loss of agricultural production on a vast scale, especially in Khorassan and Central Asia. The systematic chopping down of trees by the invaders, especially on the central plateau, led to a rapid extension of Iran's two inner deserts, *Dasht e Kavir* and *Kavir e Lut*, enabling Arab desert-dwellers to feel more at home. Some contemporary Iranian writers have argued that Iran never recovered from the physical and spiritual damage done to it by invading Arabs. To them, repairing that damage remains the central task of the current generation of Iranians.

Some of the Zoroastrian fire temples destroyed by the invaders were later revived as Islamic holy shrines, often claimed as the burial ground of someone related to the imams. But some major ruins were left to oblivion, covered by the fog of fantasy and myth. The ruins of Persepolis, the capital of the first Iranian Empire, came to be known as *Takht-e-Jamshid*, or the Throne of Jamshid, a mythical monarch. The Mausoleum of Cyrus the Great at Pasargad, in the southern province of Fars, was taken to be the tomb of King Solomon's mother. Azargoshasp, the largest of all fire temples, located in Azerbaijan, was renamed *Takht Suleiman* (Solomon's Throne). It was not until the nineteenth century that many of these ruins were properly studied, regaining their original names and identities. As the mist of centuries lifted, Iranians began to rediscover their pre-Islamic past; and the more they discovered, the greater the pride they took in their ancient culture and civilization.

It is this pride that the leaders of the Islamic Republic, from Khomeini to Ahmadinejad, have identified as the greatest threat to their anti-Iranian regime. As Ayatollah Muhammad-Taqi Mesbah-Yazdi, Ahmadinejad's theological master, put it:

> We have had all this talk of Iran and Iranian-ness from the beginning of our revolution. Even Bazargan [Khomeini's first prime minister] spoke of Iran. But Bazargan was an honest man; he wanted Iran for Islam, not the other way round. Today, we face people who want Islam for Iran. Even worse, there are those who are prepared to sacrifice Islam for Iran. We, however, do not care about Iran. What we care about is Islam.[6]

A quarter of a century earlier, the first president of the Islamic Republic spoke of how Khomeini kept launching new ideas to trigger new crises. "His Islam cannot function without crises. He doesn't care what happens to Iran."[7]

Iranians have adopted Islam, but in the process have subjected it to substantial changes. But, unlike many other nations that became Muslim, they could never quite forget their pre-Islamic past. Anyone familiar with Persian literature—which in its modern form spans a period of over a thousand years—would know that it regards Islam as no more than one part of a much broader Iranian identity. Persian literature's humanism, love of beauty, praise for wine and other "celestial gifts," and celebration of diversity stand in sharp contrast to the bigotry projected by people like Khomeini in the name of Islam. In Persian literature, steeped in nostalgia about ancient and eternal Iran, most heroes are pre-Islamic. This is one of the roots of the national schizophrenia from which Iran has suffered ever since, a subject that we will examine more closely later.

8

A Strange Beast

The so-called Islamic Republic of Iran is a triple lie on a grand scale. It is neither a republic nor Islamic in the sense acceptable to most Muslims. And, although located in Iran, it certainly is not Iranian. What kind of beast, then, is the regime invented by Khomeini? To start with, it is an ideological regime in a post-ideological age. It has mixed up elements of Islam with half-understood ideas from Western radicalism, both left and right, and added a bit of *tiersmondiste* rage, real and fake, ending up with a deadly cocktail known as Khomeinism. Iran today is a rentier state, heavily dependent on income from oil, which is used to purchase domestic support and finance terrorism abroad. It is a terrorist regime towards Iran's own population as well as other nations.

The first person to describe the Khomeinist regime as "fascist" was Maxime Rodinson, a French scholar of Islam. At a discussion in 1981, having just returned from a visit to what he jokingly described as "Khomeini's kingdom" (*le royaume du Khomeiny*), Rodinson explained that he had at first regarded the anti-shah revolution as an Islamic version of "liberation theology," a form of left-wing Christianity then fashionable in Latin America. "Now, however," he said, "I see that what Khomeinism has taken from the left resembles what the fascists took from socialism. Fascism is entering Iran, perhaps the Muslim world, in the guise of Islamic revival."[1]

Not all of Rodinson's compatriots agreed with his analysis. Michel Foucault saw something different when he visited Tehran in the autumn of 1978, as the Khomeinist revolution was gathering pace. He saw "an explosion of spiritual energy in the streets . . . a sudden intrusion of religion in the affairs of the city." Foucault, of course, later changed his tune, especially when the mullahs who had seized power thanks to that "spiritual energy" started hanging his homosexual friends, alongside everyone else, in the streets of Tehran.

The active phase of the revolution lasted no more than four months, during which the self-styled "soldiers of Allah" robbed numerous banks, cut the throats of lowly officials including traffic wardens, disfigured women by throwing acid at their unveiled faces, and set fire to hundreds of cinemas, bookshops, concert halls, girls' schools, restaurants, and other "places of sin." In a single incident in August 1978, over four hundred people were burned alive at Cinema Rex in Abadan, set on fire by one of the commandos that Foucault had admired. The commando had blocked the emergency exits from the outside and destroyed firefighting equipment to make sure that a maximum number of people would die. The Supreme Guide of the revolution, Khomeini, dismissed the incident as "a sign of the rage of our youth."

Foucault was not alone among Western leftists to be seduced by Khomeinism. Some of the historic figures of the May 1968 student revolts in Europe visited Iran during these troubled days to see their fantasy revolution take shape in a Third World country. Like impotent voyeurs, they watched the tragedy imposed on Iran by a revolution they could only dream of in their own countries. In 1967, a group of radical West German students, working with their Iranian counterparts in Frankfurt and Hamburg, had tried to kill the shah during a state visit by blowing up his cortege with a booby-trapped Volkswagen. Now that the shah was being blown up by an explosion of popular anger on the streets of his own cities, no Western revolutionary worth his salt would want to miss the show. For Western return-ticket revolutionaries, watching the Iranian tragedy was—and for some, still is—a way of obtaining vicarious pleasure without a price in pain. Just as quite a few Western pedophiles travel to Third World nations to gratify the bestial tastes they cannot easily indulge at home, aging European and American revolutionaries flocked to Iran to see a revolution such as they no longer hoped to see in their own countries, and they tried hard to describe it as a "people's revolution."

Originally, the Khomeinist leadership itself had hesitated to use the "Islamic" label, speaking instead of a "popular uprising" (*qiyam mardomi*) so as to attract leftist groups and reassure the middle classes that feared religious rule. Soon, however, they realized that they needed Islam to mobilize the muscle required to neutralize the shah's armed forces. The poor and downtrodden would not fight for any leftist ideology; only the claim that Islam was in danger could persuade them to join the revolt. The "Islamic" appellation did not please the Western intellectuals, but their Iranian counterparts in various Communist outfits—from Moscow-backing to Mao-adulating to Fidel-adoring to Trotsky-nostalgic and Titophile—willingly adopted it. A "people's revolution," after all, was *their* business, not that of the mullahs who were clearly leading the Iranian revolt at the time. To those leftist ideologues, the "Islamic revolution" was an Oriental version of the bourgeois-democratic revolutions dreamed of in the West; it represented the resolution of contradictions between the nation and imperialism, paving the way for a later "proletarian revolution."

But the "Islamic" label has impeded a proper understanding of what has happened in Iran over the past thirty years. It has also prevented a correct analysis of similar developments in other Muslim countries. Those who later became conscious of the inadequacy, not to say outright impropriety, of the term "Islamic" to describe the Khomeinist revolt and the government that it produced have tried to further complicate matters by injecting the term "fundamentalism," or *intégrisme* in French. Instead, the revolution of 1978–79 and the system it created should be regarded as the product of a large-scale mimetic enterprise. It is a violent intrusion into Iranian reality of Western dystopic ideas and methods, which, as Rodinson and others have observed, could be properly explained with reference to ur-fascism or generic fascism.

Latin Americans divide dictatorships into *dictadura* and *dictablanda*, a word play that distinguishes "hard" from "soft" regimes. One could also speak of "hard" and "soft" fascism. A system need not fulfill all the conditions set by, say, Adolf Hitler or Benito Mussolini or even Juan Perón to be described as fascist. Two cousins may look and behave differently yet bear a family resemblance—*un air de famille,* as the French say.

What are the main characteristics of generic fascism and how do they apply to Khomeinism?

First, all fascist movements and systems are totalitarian inasmuch as they seek to control all aspects of individual and community life. They are one-party systems. In Iran the slogan is "Only one party: the Hezballah!" Fascists reject diversity and scorn alternative lifestyles. The state and the dominant party must dictate every movement of all citizens at all times. Khomeini's book *Hal al-Masa'el* ("Solution to Problems") includes more than six thousand fatwas regulating every issue, from Weltanschauung to rules for urinating. The totalitarian state wants to control the past as well as the present and the future, stopping history at points it deems suitable to its own designs.

The second characteristic of generic fascism is that it is deeply anti-religious, even when it pretends to be religious. In Iran, the mosques have been turned into supermarkets and centers for distributing consumer durables. A Tehran joke puts it well: Before the mullahs, we used to pray in private and drink in public; now we drink in private and pray in public! Numerous mosques are used as offices of the Imam Committees (*Komiteh* in Persian), the parallel police created by Khomeini in the early days of the regime. On occasion, mosques are used as temporary prisons for criminals and for political opponents of the regime. Hardly any new mosques have been built in Tehran since Khomeini came to power. Instead, the regime has financed the building of *takeyh* and *husseinieh,* meaning Shiite centers for political rallies disguised as religious ceremonies. The Khomeinist regime has made a mockery of Shiite rules for choosing the *marja taqlid* or "source of imitation"—rules that go back more than three centuries.[2] More than three hundred mullahs and students of theology have been executed and thousands are in prison, while many others have fled into exile. Koranic and religious studies have been cut from six hours a week to four; the remaining two hours are used for a study of "the political thoughts and acts of Imam Khomeini." More than a hundred religious seminaries have been closed, and all of Iran's grand ayatollahs have been put under house arrest on different occasions. People going to Mecca for the Hajj pilgrimage are chosen in accordance with quotas fixed by revolutionary organizations. Tens of thousands of Muslims in Iran have been executed or killed in clashes with government forces.

The third characteristic of generic fascism is a cult of tradition, which in practice often means reviving old superstitions. All that man needs to learn is assumed to be already present in some cryptic message of either religious or pagan provenance. The idea is to return to the source, which could be ancient Hellas, the Rome of the Caesars, or the imagined Medina of the seventh century. The past is idealized, the present vilified, the future painted as fantasy. In Iran, regime-backed mullahs try to justify their oppression of women, religious minorities, and dissidents on the grounds of *sonnat*, "tradition."

Under Khomeinism, all sorts of superstitions long dead in Iran have been revived and used as the centerpiece of a growing industry under the banner of tradition. Iranian newspapers are full of advertisements for what is presented as "faith services," where one learns how to contact those who claim to ensure success at university entrance examinations, in finding well-paid jobs or wealthy spouses, and in overcoming illness. All sorts of fortunetellers, charm-makers, soothsayers, magicians, and astrologers are on the market. Some pretend to predict the future by opening the Koran at random and interpreting the verses. Others have a little bird pick from among a number of small envelopes the one that contains the answer to your question. Still others read the future by slowly pouring a handful of sand on the ground. In almost every town and village there is at least one individual who claims to be in contact with the Hidden Imam. Each year, several men are arrested on the charge of pretending to *be* the Hidden Imam.

This industry of the absurd assumes giant proportions in the village of Jamkaran, some eighty miles southeast of Tehran. According to legend—taken as fact by the faithful—the Hidden Imam, who disappeared in 941 A.D., visited a pious local man in a dream and asked him to build a mosque in the village. The imam's implicit promise was that once the mosque was built, he would visit it to lead the prayer that would mark his Grand Return. A modest mosque was built and the legend was propagated that the village well was connected to a well in Samarra, Iraq, some seven hundred miles to the west, where the twelfth imam had started his Grand Occultation. Because Samarra was no longer a Shiite city, the assumption was that the imam would reappear in Jamkaran to be among "his own people."

In 1972, the government of Prime Minister Amir Abbas Hoveyda financed the building of a road to make Jamkaran accessible from Qom. At that time, Iraq's Shiite shrines were closed to Iranians because of bad relations between Baghdad and Tehran, and Hoveyda intended for Jamkaran to become an alternative to Iraqi shrines. Qom, about a hundred miles south of Tehran, has for decades made a fortune from the mausoleum of Massoumah, a sister of Imam Reza, the eighth imam of Shiism. The "holy" sister, whose very existence is questioned by historians, is supposed to have died there of dysentery at the age of nine. The village of Qom grew into a town in the eighteenth century as the Shiite "holy" cities in Iraq fell under Ottoman rule and were closed to Iranians. With a population of 1.2 million, Qom today hosts more than three hundred Shiite seminaries and research centers, which constitute a veritable industry employing an estimated 150,000 people. On Hoveyda's orders, a modest inn was also constructed in Jamkaran to host a few dozen pilgrims. It was not until the 1990s, however, that a group of young entrepreneurs discovered Jamkaran's commercial potential. By 2000, many of the estimated 12 million pilgrims who visited Qom also spent a few hours in Jamkaran.

Ahmadinejad is supposed to have visited Jamkaran in 2005 to ask whether the Hidden Imam would support his presidential candidacy. The Hidden Imam is supposed to have endorsed the mayor of Tehran, even though public opinion polls at the time gave him support rates of under 1 percent. Since then, Ahmadinejad has promoted Jamkaran as the most

important site for Muslim pilgrims, and its mosque has been reclassi-
fied as *Masjed Muqaddas* (Holy Mosque), a title that even the mosques of
Mecca and Medina do not bear. In 2008, the president allocated $17 mil-
lion to expanding the mosque and providing additional facilities for pilgrims. He has held several meetings of his cabinet in the mosque, where
secretaries of state and other senior officials have received rosaries made
of the mud extracted from Jamkaran's soil. The government has commissioned the composition of special Jamkaran prayers and set up research
groups to produce books on miracles attributed to the Hidden Imam and
Jamkaran.

It is not only esoteric products with an Islamic accent that have
become fashionable in the Khomeinist republic. A huge market has also
developed for all kinds of esoteric oeuvres imported from the lands of the
infidels: Nostradamus, Joseph de Maistre, *Protocols of the Elders of Zion,*
biographies of Pythagoras and Cagliostro, books on alchemy, and the
like. There is even Khomeini's own assessment of ancient Greek philosophy, where he presents Socrates as the first "monotheist Muslim" and as
the victim of "a Jewish conspiracy." The idea is to reject rationalism and
to inject into Iranian society a syncretism in which rulers run a super-
market of superstitions.

The fourth characteristic of generic fascism is its rejection of modernity. While mullahs can be seen flying in helicopters and wearing glisten-
ing Colts under their mantles, the modern world to them is essentially
the product of a "Judeo-Christian conspiracy." Malaysia's former prime
minister Mahathir Mohamad went further in October 2003 when he told
a summit of the Organization of the Islamic Conference that the modern world was a "Jewish creation." He also claimed that the Jews had
"invented" such modern ideas as democracy, human rights, and communism. Because rejecting modernism means rejecting the achievements of humanism since the Enlightenment, de Maistre's critique of
the French Revolution is appreciated by the ruling mullahs in Tehran.
Khatami, the mullah who acted as president of the Islamic Republic
between 1997 and 2005, frequently quotes de Maistre in his criticism of

"Western" rationality. Modern ideas such as the intrinsic worth of the individual, freedom of conscience, and the rule of law are spurned as "Western" or "colonial" values to be resisted at all levels. In an address at the University of Florence in 1998, Khatami branded the Renaissance as the starting point of "human decline into barbarity," a time that "led to imperialism and the burning of weak countries by the strong." Khatami's fellow mullah Ayatollah Muhammadi Gilani likes to describe modernity as "the cult of unbridled sex, wife-swapping, and sodomy." In his weekly live television series in the 1980s, the ayatollah portrayed the West as a modern version of Sodom and Gomhorra. (The authorities decided to end the series when they realized that it actually made the West more popular by presenting it as a kind of Shangri-la where carnal pleasures denied to frustrated young Iranians were readily available.)

The fifth characteristic of generic fascism is the cult of the chief. There are, of course, many nonfascist systems that also practice such a cult, but in those cases one only has to obey the chief; one does not necessarily have to love him or acknowledge him as a guide in all aspects of life. In Iran, on the other hand, the cult of Khomeini has developed into a secular religion. He is called imam, thus turning Twelver Shiism into a cult of the Thirteen. His iconic image is carved into giant rocks and shaped in cedar forests on mountain slopes. Prayers start and finish with his name. His *fatwas* remain valid forever, annulling a well-established Shiite principle under which an ayatollah's rulings die with him and cannot be followed unless endorsed by a living authority. The Supreme Guide of the day has the constitutional right to suspend the basic principles of Islam, but cannot cancel the *fatwas* of the dead chief. The slogans *Khoda, Koran, Khomeini* ("God, Koran, Khomeini") and *Allah Akbar, Khomeini Rahbar* ("God is One, Khomeini is the Leader") remain the war cries of Hezballah in Iran and other Muslim countries where the party has branches. (In Arabic the slogan is: *Allah Wahed, Khomeini Qa'ed!*) Men, women, and children march in front of ten-foot portraits of the "Imam" in Tehran and Beirut, giving the salute. The titles *Pihsva* and *Rahbar,* used to describe the leader, are Persian equivalents of the German *Fuehrer*. The imam belongs to the same tradition of political iconography as the Fuehrer, Il Duce, the Caudillo, the Zaim, and the Rais.[3]

This is how one of the earliest theoreticians of "Red Shiism," Ali Shariati, described the role of the leader in the ideal Shiite system:

> The imam does not [stand] alongside the executive; he is not connected with the state, and has no coordination with the policies in place. He has direct and exclusive responsibility for the community's politics. The direct leadership of the economy, the armed forces, culture, foreign policy, and the administration of all other internal affairs are also his. This means that the imam is both the head of state and the head of government. Shiism counsels obedience to the imam on the basis of the [Koranic] verse that says: Obey Allah, obey the Prophet, and obey those in charge of your affairs. The phrase "those in charge of your affairs" means the imam. God has put obedience to imam on the same level as obedience to Himself and to His Prophet. In Shiism, this obedience extends to the vicars of the imam.[4]

Khomeini himself demanded blind obedience to the Leader: "If [the imam] orders you to capture such-and-such a place, set such-and-such a house on fire, wipe out such-and-such a group that is harmful to Islam, you have to obey. For [the imam] orders only what is just. Obeying him is incumbent on all. Anyone refusing will be a rebel against God."[5] His disciples have taken this position further: "In this country, people today see their national identity, culture and history reflected in the presence of the imam," the *Islamic Review* editorialized in 1983. Khomeini's tomb, in a mausoleum south of Tehran, is officially designated a *haram* (shrine) and described with the adjective *muqaddas* (holy). In Islam, no one and nothing but Allah could be described as "holy." Mecca is honored with the title "the Generous"(*Al-Mukarramah*) and Medina is known as "the Luminous" (*Al-Munawwarah*). The Khomeinist regime took the cult of the chief to new boundaries in 1990 by starting an industry for manufacturing hadiths (sayings or anecdotes) related to the ayatollah, thus equating him with Muhammad and the twelve imams.

In 2008, a similar operation was launched for Khamenehi, the junior mullah who had succeeded Khomeini as Supreme Guide in 1989. Since then, every one of his sayings and doings has been recorded, interpreted, and used as authoritative sources along with the Koran and the prophetic hadiths. State-owned media are full of panegyrics for Khamenehi, showering him with the kind of adulation that would have made any shah blush. In April 2008, the Islamic Republic News Agency reported in deadpan language that the famous flowers of Shiraz were "smelling twice as sweet" because of Khamenehi's visit to the city. (Only a week earlier, Shiraz had witnessed an explosion that claimed scores of lives.) One of the titles often used for Khamenehi is *Tali'eh Khorshid Tashayyu'e,* which means, in literal translation, "the advance ray of the Shiite sun."

The sixth characteristic of generic fascism is its exploitation of social and economic grievances. It recruits from among the lower middle classes, poor peasants driven into cities, and pseudo-intellectuals who look for certainty and fear doubt. Hatred, envy, jealousy, and suspicion are major themes in the discourse of generic fascism. The "dispossessed" (*mustadhafeen*) are told that while they are suffering, others live fantastic lives of luxury.

Well-to-do Iranian "protest intellectuals" used to buy secondhand clothes in the bazaar to present themselves as being among the *mustadhafeen.* This led to a whole new style of clothing known as *khaksari* (down-to-earth), in which expensive material is treated to look rough. By wearing his notorious five-dollar shirts, Ahmadinejad presents himself as a *khaksari* model. The *khaksari* style rejects Western clothes and condemns the wearing of neckties or bowties as a sign of "submission to the Crusaders." One of the charges brought against Muzaffar Baqai, an early ally of Khomeini who soon turned against him, was that he wore bowties to underline "the submission of Islam to the infidels." Ironically, the necktie, mentioned in the *One Thousand and One Nights* and Islamic histories, was invented in Baghdad in the ninth century by Jaafar Bar-maki, the Iranian grand vizier of the Caliph Haroun al-Rashid, as a way of hiding his long neck. It was with one of his neckties that Barmaki was eventually strangled on the caliph's orders. Today, however, Islamist fascists regard the wearing of a necktie as a sign of ill-gained wealth.

A true Muslim may cheat and steal and embezzle, amassing vast for-tunes, as is the case with many Islamist fascists in Iran and elsewhere. What he may not do is flaunt his wealth. In the early days of the revolu-tion, much was made of Khomeini's supposedly austere lifestyle; only later did people learn that he and his family possessed vast tracts of land in and around Qom and were proud owners of a cement factory and a number of smaller businesses. Ahmadinejad, too, has made much of the fact that he lived in a modest bungalow and drove a battered old car. Much is also made of Osama bin Laden's decision to abandon his life of luxury and live in caves in Afghanistan. Looking poor is honored, while such words as "rich" and "wealth" are used as terms of abuse.

The wealthy at home are to be detested, and foreign powers hostile to the regime are branded as "the rich powers" or "the wealthy empires." This terminology implies that the regime will keep the masses stuck in poverty. Fascism does not and cannot promise a good life of comfort and ease, because once such a living standard is attained, people might begin to demand pluralism and freedom.

The seventh characteristic of generic fascism is xenophobia. To Hit-ler, of course, the Jews were the "other" to be most feared and hated. Mussolini warned the Italians that they might become "Africanized" and turned "subhuman." The "other" may be defined not only by race or eth-nicity, but also by religious or political beliefs or by ideological "devia-tions," real or suspected. In this "us versus them" worldview, anyone could cease being one of "us" and become one of "them." To remain one of "us" requires total obedience and complete acceptance of the politi-cal line of the day. In this Manichean duality, the "other" is blamed for all the shortcomings and failures on "our" side. Even when we massacre revolutionary comrades and brothers, the fault lies with the "other" who deceived them and made them abandon the right path. Some apologists of the Khomeinist regime have even blamed the "other" of the moment for what Bazargan called "the ultimate failure of our revolution."

In Iran, the "us versus others" culture has developed into an intricate system of relations within the establishment. Those who belong to the "us" camp are known as *khodi* (literally, "of our own"). All others are branded as *ghayr* (literally, "other") or *biganeh* ("foreign"). Often the *khodi* are allowed to say and do things that could lead to imprisonment or death if said and done by the *ghayr*. In 1979, Sadeq Qotbzadeh was one of Khomeini's closest aides, and thus a *khodi* par excellence. He was forgiven everything, including his dalliances with questionable ladies in Paris when he visited the city as foreign minister of the Islamic Republic. Two years later, having become *ghayr*, he was hanged as a "traitor to Imam and Islam" because he had been imprudent enough to criticize the ayatollah.

Many other labels are used against the "other," including *gharbzadeh* (literally, "West-smitten") and *elteqati* (literally, "mixer," meaning someone who tries to mix Islam with modern ideas). The term *munafiq* (hypocrite) is used for Islamist-Marxists who, having first allied themselves with the mullahs, broke with them and took up armed struggle. Over the past three decades, the Khomeinist regime has targeted different groups and nations as the "other" to be hated, among them Baha'is, ethnic Kurds, Afghan immigrants, and gays and lesbians. But the status of "other" has remained unchanged in three cases: women, the United States of America, and Jews.

The eighth characteristic of generic fascism is its cult of death. From the Phalangists' *"Viva la muerte"* and the Nazis' love for the scalp symbol to the Islamist fascists' passion for martyrdom, we see love of death, often linked to hero worship. The martyr instantly goes to paradise. The poor, illiterate Iranian teenagers sent into Iraqi minefields during the 1980–88 war were given plastic keys to hang from their necks; they were called "keys to paradise" (*mafatih al-jinan*). The regime employed professional actors to play the role of the Hidden Imam, appearing at decisive moments to urge the child soldiers to flood the minefields or jump under enemy tanks to stop them. Dressed all in white, the actor playing the Hidden Imam would appear on an elevation near the encampment of the child soldiers and call on them through a megaphone to start the final phase of their journey to paradise.[6] On arrival there, the hero-martyr would immediately have access to seventy-two perpetual virgins.

Khomeini's most favored dictum was "To kill and be killed are the supreme duties of Muslims." Islamist fascists often wear shrouds during street demonstrations to symbolize their readiness to die at any moment. One of the "holy" places of the Khomeinist regime is the graveyard known as Behesht Zahra (Paradise of Flowers) in a Tehran suburb. Originally built to meet the needs of the capital until 2020, the graveyard was filled within the first decade of Islamist fascist rule. At the center of the vast sprawl stands the notorious "Fountain of Blood," a concoction of iron and concrete spouting a red, viscous fluid. Most of those buried in the Behesht Zahra are teenage boys or young men killed in the Iran-Iraq war or in the ethnic revolts that have shaken the regime since its inception. They are the martyrs whose blood "irrigates the tree of Islam," as Khomeini liked to say. The religious fascist never names a street or a public edifice after a living person: only those who died for the movement are honored. For example, the street on which the Egyptian embassy in Tehran stands is named after Khalid Showqi al-Islambouli, the assassin of President Anwar Sadat. By contrast, the Egyptian Nobel laureate Neguib Mahfouz is never named except to be insulted.

The Islamic Republic has adopted black, the color of death and mourning in Iranian culture, as its favorite hue. Visitors to Iran experience a visual shock by the sea of black they see everywhere in the cities. One has to travel to rural areas to see the eternal Iran of bright colors. (The irony is that the color of Muhammad's Bani Hashem clan was green, while black was the color of Bani Abbas, the clan that persecuted Shiites for centuries.) Dozens of official ceremonies in the Islamic Republic center on themes of death and mourning. The months of Muharram and Safar on the Arabic lunar calendar are reserved for mourning Hassan and Hussein, the second and third imams. In all Muslim countries, the fasting month of Ramadan is an occasion for evening feasts and light-heartedness, because the first verses of the Koran are supposed to have been dictated to Muhammad during that month. In the Islamic Republic, by contrast, Ramadan is a grim season of wearing black and mourning Ali, the first imam. The Khomeinists expect Iranians to wear black on no fewer than sixty days each year, marking the "martyrdom" of various imams and other real or imagined heroes of Shiism. One of Iran's most popular novelists, Fereidun Tonkaboni, describes the culture promoted by the Khomeinist regime as "an inhuman culture, a culture of sadness and mourning, a culture of death and nihilism. This is a culture that forbids happiness and joy. . . . The only thing not forbidden in the Islamic Republic is death and shedding tears at funerals for the dead."

The Khomeinist version of fascism has turned death into its proper territory. Khomeinists love the dead better than the living. They regard themselves as a superior race not only because they are prepared to kill in cold blood, but also, and especially, because they are ready to die. They have nothing but contempt for those who wish to live. In his pseudo-Nietzschean moments, Khomeini saw the desire to live as a fundamental weakness of human character. His ideal man was prepared to die for the cause because he was prepared to do everything else for it, including lie, cheat and kill. Khomeinism is above morality, a discourse that has no audience in death's territory. It was in this spirit that Khomeini in 1981 issued his notorious fatwa ordering children to spy on their parents and report their anti-Islamic activities, while parents were told that their religious duty required them to denounce their offspring if they engaged in anti-regime schemes. A Tehrani witticism put it thus: "The shah had tried to teach Iranians how to live, and failed. Khomeini taught them how to die, and succeeded." According to Khamenehi, it is "by dying for his faith that a Muslim becomes truly alive."[7]

The ninth characteristic of generic fascism is its fear and hatred of freedom. It speaks of "the people," but this is a chimera to prevent citizens from taking initiative. There is no system of delegating power, and thus no accountability. Nor can the "just" government be replaced through free elections. Khomeini admitted that his chief motive in fighting the shah's regime was that it might have evolved into a Western-style democracy, which he called "a form of prostitution." Khamenehi is equally straightforward: "In the Koran and the sayings of the Prophet, there is no talk of liberty or freedom of speech and belief."[8] Freedom, he often insists, is acceptable only if its aim is to strengthen the Islamic system.

This view is based on the works of an earlier advocate of Islamist fascism, Hussein Tabatabai, who wrote:

> Some exegetes have tried hard to prove that there is freedom of conscience in Islam. They have referred to the verse: "There is no constraint in faith." What I can say here is that monotheism is the foundation stone of all Islamic principles. Thus, how could Islam decree any freedom of conscience? In all its legislation, Islam has relied on nothing but monotheism, prophecy, and resurrection. If there is freedom, it is within that circle. If we accept freedom outside that circle we have undermined the foundations of our faith.[9]

The mullah Morteza Motahari claims that freedom is only a pretext for sexual license. "In Western societies," he writes, "freedom is summed up in the freedom of lusts and desires. Western freedoms, in the name of equality for women, promote sexual license and corrupt the souls of maidens and young ladies."[10] If Allah granted man any freedoms, according to Khomeinism, it was not on an individual basis. The human individual has no meaning outside the *ummah*, which is a theatrical device—like "the people" or *"Das Volk."* This is perhaps why Khomeini and his successors have spoken of "the *umma* that is always present on the stage to play the role required of it."

The generic fascist hates parliaments, political parties, and institutional politics in general. He feels at home in mass rallies, street marches, and flag-waving shows. In Iran, people appear at such rallies in theatrical costumes: volunteers for martyrdom wear shrouds and crimson headbands, while women are hidden under a mass of black drapery. It is reminiscent of the Nazis' passion for choreographed mass gatherings. Key government decisions are announced not at the parliament but at gatherings of militants on Fridays at the campus of Tehran University. The principal yardstick for choosing government officials is not expertise but loyalty. Khomeini used to say: "Don't talk to me about economists. Economics is for donkeys." Khamenehi likewise has attacked those who dare suggest that the nation might need specialists to rebuild its shattered economy. "We need devoted people," he said. "We need people who believe in our system. A specialist who doubts is worse than any enemy."[11]

The tenth characteristic of fascism is its love of uniforms, and Khomeinism uses uniforms in a variety of ways. Mullahs wear special gear marking them out from the common folk. The most prominent item of a mullah's clothing is the turban. The larger the turban, the higher is the wearer's claim to status within the clerical hierarchy; the most imposing turbans, requiring up to six meters of cloth, are reserved for grand ayatollahs. A black turban identifies the wearer as a *sayyed*, a descendant of the Prophet and thus doubly deserving of deference. White turbans are for clerics who do not claim Arab blood; they are known as *a'am* (common). Another feature of the mullahs' attire is the long, Arab-style robe. Unlike the Greeks in ancient times and the Arabs up to the present day, Iranian men never wore robes or skirts. Iranians invented trousers for men more than 2,500 years ago and have always associated the wearing of skirts with femininity.

Mullahs are not alone in marking themselves out by their clothing. The regime employs several corps of professional supporters, the largest of which is the Ansar Hezballah (Friends of the Party of Allah). These are street fighters who dress in battle fatigues and wear the Palestinian checkered *kufiyah* around their necks, in the same way that leftist students do in the West. Acting as an Iranian version of Mao Zedong's Red Guards, these violent thugs are used by the regime to terrorize opponents on university campuses, in factories, and on city streets.

The regime's most widely used tools of uniformization are the hijab for women and the beard for men—both props in a campaign of visual terrorism, designed to frighten opponents and enforce conformity. In 1982 the regime passed a law imposing the hijab and what was called "modest dressing" on women. In April 2006, the Islamic Majlis (parliament) passed a broader law mandating "Islamic dress" for both men and women. We shall discuss the hijab later when we examine the regime's obsession with controlling women. As far as beards are concerned, wearing or not wearing them has become one of the perennial issues of Iranian politics.

One of the first measures of the Khomeinists in 1978 was an effort to force Iranian men to grow beards. The slogan "Death to Those Who Shave" appeared on the walls; and several youths were disfigured by acid thrown at their clean-shaven faces. Those who wished to assume a revolutionary identity stopped shaving. Later, growing beards became sometimes a necessity and sometimes a device for self-ingratiation with the authorities. At government offices, clean-shaven men are either ignored or humiliated, while those sporting the revolutionary beard are received attentively.

In most cultures, facial hair has been associated with historic or religious missions. The classical image of Zeus in Hellenic culture or God in Semitic culture is a man with a long white beard. Old Testament prophets are represented with beards, as are most Christian saints. More recently, beards have made an appearance in secular creeds, on Marx and Engels and their Russian disciples from Plekhanov and Martov to Lenin and Trotsky—although the last two wore only goatees (also known as Vandykes). Fidel Castro and Ernesto "Che" Guevara, the Argentine T-shirt revolutionary, also had beards. Mao Zedong and Kim Il Sung did not grow beards, apparently because they were genetically incapable of doing so.

Although Ayatollah Fazl-Allah Mahallati once claimed that no man could become a true Muslim without growing a proper beard, there is no evidence that early Muslims, those of the so-called Golden Age, detected any sacred qualities in facial hair. According to his biographers, including Ibn Kathir, Muhammad himself sported a goatee. The Persian poet

Farid ud-Din Attar lampooned the mullahs for growing big beards. In one verse, Attar depicted the fate of "an idiot with a huge beard" who is choked and killed by it when his boat capsizes. Another poem relates the story of a pious man who, despite his prayers, never feels well. He asks Moses to ask God why this is so. God answers:

> *He has forgotten all about us,*
>
> *So preoccupied with his beard he is.*
>
> *Tell him to first forget about his beard,*
>
> *So that he may reap some rewards.*

The poet Sanai also mocked those who grew beards:

> *How could any follower of Mostafa**
>
> *Grow the beard and moustache of the ignorant?*

The Sufi poet Rumi poked fun at the mullahs who wore beards to back their claim of discernment:

> *You cannot rule your own beard*
>
> *Which grows, and goes white—*
>
> *regardless of your wishes.*
>
> *How then could you claim*
>
> *To rule over Good and Evil?*

More recently, Iraj Mirza, the great Persian satirist of the early twentieth century, wrote poems mocking beards. Iraj Mirza himself wore a moustache and expressed understanding of clerics growing Vandykes in imitation of Muhammad. Anything beyond that, however, he considered a prop for charlatanry and tartuffery. In one poem, he complains about the fact that he has to shave every day even while he is losing the hair on top of his head, and he wonders: couldn't Allah reverse the process?

The Persian word for beard is *rish,* which also means "wound" or "injury"; another meaning is "corruption" or "going to waste." The popular expression "its beard has grown" refers to something that has gone bad or been exposed as untrue. According to the medieval satirist Suzani Samarkandi, *rish-jonbani* (literally: "shaking a beard") is a worse breach of etiquette than belching or letting off wind in public.

* "The Chosen," one of Prophet Muhammad's titles.

By contrast, the Arabs use the euphemism *mahasin* (benedictions) to describe beards. It is in imitation of Muhammad that Saudi officials and theologians grow Vandykes plus a moustache. The more radical Sunnis, known as Salafis (meaning predecessors or ancestors), distinguish themselves from Saudi Wahhabis by growing a more fulsome beard but no moustache. The Khomeinists also go for longer and denser beards.

Over the years, deciding who is who by style of beard has become a popular sport with Iranians. Called "beard spotting" (*rish shenasi*), the technique enables the observer to place a man by the beard he grows. The mullahs with the greatest pretensions to learning and piety grow the longest beards. Many dye their beards jet black or various shades of red with the help of henna. Those who wish to give an impression of detachment from the transient do not dye their beards. Most others opt for a salt-and-pepper look to make them appear old enough to impress the populace but young enough to avail themselves of teenage "temporary wives," or *sigheh.* Nonclerics who wish to emphasize their piety without being mistaken for mullahs grow bushy round beards that are carefully trimmed and dyed, and often perfumed with rosewater. Mullahs who wish to portray themselves as "moderate" or open to a "dialogue of civilizations" choose beards that do not dominate their faces. A goatee is kept in deference to the Prophet, but it is extended by long sideburns to distinguish the wearer from the Saudis. A trim moustache is also added to show that one does not sympathize with Salafis like bin Laden. Those who wish to hedge their bets—that is to say, advertise their Islamism while appearing "modern"—have opted for what is known in the West as designer stubble, achieved with an electric shaver that does not cut the facial hair from the root. This "modern" type of beard was authorized by Ayatollah Mahmoud Taleqani, one of the "useful idiots" that Marxists and fellow travelers promoted as a religious facade in the early days of the revolution. He ruled that Islam banned the use of razors that cut facial hair completely, but an electric shaver was acceptable because it allowed some of the hair to remain. The Stalinists who collaborated with the fascist mullahs in the first phases of the revolution distinguished themselves by maintaining two-day stubble dominated by a thick bushy moustache in memory of the Soviet despot. The Mujahedin Khalq (People's Holy Warriors), Marxist-Islamists who helped Khomeini come to power but later broke with him, mark themselves out by shaving off their beards and growing signature moustaches in imitation of their Supreme Guide, Massoud Rajavi.

Khomeini, ignorant of history and most other things, did not realize that—except for clerics who sported Vandykes—the growing of beards had not been a Shiite tradition until the seventeenth century, when it was imposed by the Safavid Shah Tahmasp with a royal edict. Tahmasp had a dream in which the Hidden Imam apparently demanded that "men of True Faith" not discard what Allah had made to grow on their faces as a sign of his blessing. After Tahmasp's reign, however, most men reverted to the custom of shaving their beards but growing ferocious moustaches.

Because the regime attaches such importance to facial hair, its opponents use shaving as a sign of protest. Television news footage and photos of public gatherings published by newspapers are censored to make sure they do not show too many clean-shaven men. To further emphasize their individuality, young men grow their hair long or spiked, and wear T-shirts with Western inscriptions. A Western visitor would be surprised how many young Iranians wear T-shirts and caps that advertise various American baseball teams.

The eleventh characteristic of generic fascism is the cult of war, both foreign and civil. It conceives of existence as a Manichean struggle between Good and Evil. While other messianic movements may also instigate wars, Islamist fascism uses war as a highly desirable tool in creating the new man and the ideal society. Khomeini described war as a divine blessing. Where open warfare is not feasible—perhaps because one is not sure of winning—it is necessary to maintain the "war spirit" by provoking conflicts. It is also essential to pick adversaries who will show one up as a hero. Thus, the Iran-Iraq war was not presented as a conflict with Saddam Hussein, described by Khomeini as a "nincompoop who had better commit suicide." No, Iraq and Saddam Hussein were too small for a great heroic revolution! The Khomeinists said they were at war against the United States, and better, against "World Arrogance"; they were fighting to defeat the Americans, liberate Palestine, and wipe Israel off the map! Conveniently ignored was the fact that the United States and Israel, at a crucial stage, helped Iran get the weapons it needed to continue the war and avoid defeat by Iraq.

Over the past thirty years, the Khomeinist regime has led Iran into an eight-year war with Iraq, a two-year border war with Afghanistan (1998–2000), and a proxy war against Israel, waged through the Lebanese branch of Hezballah, since 1983. It has also been engaged in low-intensity warfare against the United States. The various wars provoked by the Khomeinist regime at home and abroad have claimed the lives of over a million people—the vast majority of them Iranians. This is a regime with war written in its political DNA.

More importantly, perhaps, the Khomeinist regime has been at war against the Iranian people almost continuously for the past three decades. It has crushed revolts by ethnic minorities with savage brutality. In 1979, a unit of the Islamic Revolutionary Guard Corps, the regime's praetorian guard, organized a massacre in the Kurdish village of Naqada, in the province of West Azerbaijan, killing more than nine hundred people, mostly women and children. Almost thirty years later, Turkmen were massacred in the province of Golestan, on the Caspian Sea, by another unit of the IRGC. The regime's repressive forces have been engaged in low-intensity wars against Baluch and Kurdish rebels, in southeastern and western provinces respectively, for the past two decades.

Linked to the fascist cult of war is a readiness to use terrorism, both before and after attaining power. Franquist death squads remained in operation three decades after the victory of the Phalange. SS death squads were always on hand to eliminate real or imagined opponents long after Hitler had sat down at the window that opened on the Unter Den Linden. Khomeini issued his first death fatwa in 1946, against a leading intellectual (Ahmad Kasravi). The Khomeinist regime today has several death squads known as Thar Allah (Blood of Allah) and Avengers of the Imam. Numerous prominent politicians and mullahs who had initially cooperated with the new regime have been assassinated in the past thirty years. In the late 1990s under the presidency of Khatami, hundreds of intellectuals, along with spiritual leaders of Sunni Muslims, Christians, Jews, and Baha'is, were murdered by official death squads, their corpses thrown by the roadside. Mrs. Shirin Ebadi, Iran's Nobel Peace laureate, puts the number of those murdered at "over four hundred" and claims to have full documentation about at least half the cases. The man who orchestrated the murders was the mullah Qorban-Ali Dorri Najafabadi, who worked as Khatami's minister for intelligence and security. (Under Ahmadinejad, he works as chairman of the High Administrative Tribunal.) A series of books and articles by the dissident journalist Akbar Ganji has revealed the extent of high-level official involvement in the killings. (The books cost Ganji five years in prison and eventually exile.) Abroad, death squads from Tehran have killed 127 dissidents, most of them intellectuals, in sixteen countries including the United States and several European nations.

That the Islamic Republic practices terrorism as official policy was established at a trial in Berlin on April 10, 1997. The Berlin Criminal Court was dealing with a case concerning the murder of two Iranian Kurdish dissident leaders and their two interpreters in a restaurant in the German capital in 1992. After years of investigation and cross-examination, the court reached a unanimous verdict: the murders were ordered and planned at the highest level of the Islamic Republic's leadership. Four officials were named as participants in the crime: the Supreme Guide, Ali Khamenehi; the president of the Islamic Republic, Hashemi Rafsanjani; the minister for intelligence and security, Ali Fallahian; and the minister for foreign affairs, Ali-Akbar Velayati. Of the four "murdering Alis," as the quartet is known in Iran, all but the last were mullahs. In 2007, a court in Buenos Aires found the government of the Islamic Republic responsible for a terrorist operation in July 1994. A unit of Hezballah, acting on orders from Tehran, blew up the headquarters of the Israel-Argentine Mutual Jewish Association in Buenos Aires, killing 86 people and injuring 250. The Argentine court demanded that "red alert" international arrest warrants be issued against a number of Khomeinist officials, including the four "murdering Alis."

Eventually, however, the Executive Committee of Interpol issued "red alert" notices against only one of the four Alis, Fallahian, along with four other Islamic Republic officials. The four are General Mohsen Rezai; a former IRGC commander; General Muhammad-Reza Asgari, the deputy defense minister; General Ahmad Vahidi, military advisor to the Supreme Guide; and Mohsen Rabbani-Amlashi, a mullah attached to Khamenehi's office. Also in the 1990s, the French antiterror judge Jean-Louis Bruguière sought arrest warrants for a number of other Islamic Republic officials in connection with a series of assassinations of Iranian dissidents in France. The officials included Muhammad Gharazi and Hussein Sheikh Attar, both former members of the Islamic Republic's Council of Ministers, as well as Muhammad Hejazi, a senior official of the IRGC. No other regime in recent history has seen so many of its highest officials implicated in political murders at trials taking place in countries where the rule of law is respected.

In an extended interview published by the pan-Arab daily newspaper *Asharq Alawsat* on May 14, 2008, a senior Iranian ayatollah spoke of how he had helped create both the Lebanese branch of Hezballah and the armed wings of the Palestinian movement Hamas. A former ambassador of the Islamic Republic to Damascus, Ayatollah Muhammad Hassan Akhtari, spelled out the crucial role played by the Islamic Revolutionary Guard Corps in "recruiting, training, arming, and deploying" groups that the State Department in Washington, along with governments in more than two dozen other countries, officially designates as "terrorist." "Hezballah, Islamic Jihad for the Liberation of Palestine, and Hamas are legitimate offspring of our Iranian revolution," Akhtari boasted. The leader of the Lebanese branch of Hezballah has always boasted that his movement "owes everything" to the Islamic Republic.

Not all terrorist movements are fascist, but all fascist movements and states include a strong element of terrorism. Generic fascism leads to the creation of a kakistocracy, rule by the worst elements of society—elements that resort to terrorism when their masters deem it necessary. Since 1989, Tehran has hosted an international gathering of terrorist organizations every February. Known as the Ten Days of Dawn, the event attracts scores of terror groups from more than seventy countries across the globe.

Some Western analysts believe that Sunnis and Shiites, divided as they are by deep theological differences, could not come together to fight the United States and its allies. The truth is that Sunni and Shiite extremists have always been united in their hatred of the United States and their desire to "bring it to destruction," in the words of Taliban leader Mullah Muhammad Omar. To understand the problem with Islamist fascists, it is important to set aside the Sunni-Shiite divide and focus on common hatreds. Theology is useless here; what we are dealing with is politics. For Khomeini and his successors, the slogan "Death to America" is as important as "Allah is the Greatest"—hence the ayatollah's insistence that it be chanted at all public meetings and repeated after each session of the daily prayers. To that end, Khomeinists have worked with anyone, not only Sunnis but even Marxist atheists.

For more than a quarter century, Tehran has been host to the offices of more than three dozen terrorist organizations, from the Colombian FARC to the Palestinian Hamas, and including half a dozen Trotskyite and Leninist outfits. The regime also finances anti-American groups and parties of both the extreme right and the extreme left in Europe and the Americas. Ahmadinejad has bestowed the Muslim title of "brother" on Cuba's Fidel Castro, Venezuela's Hugo Chávez, Bolivia's Evo Morales, and Nicaragua's Daniel Ortega. Communist North Korea is the *only country* with which the Islamic Republic maintains close military-industrial ties and holds joint annual staff sessions. For years, until a recent change of policy, Tehran financed and offered shelter to the Kurdistan Workers' Party (PKK), a Marxist movement fighting to overthrow the Turkish Republic. This support reflected Tehran's displeasure with Turkish membership of NATO and ties with the United States.

The suicide attacks that claimed the lives of over 300 Americans, including 241 Marines, in Lebanon in 1983 were joint operations of the Khomeinist Hezballah and the Marxist Arab Socialist Party, linked to Syrian intelligence services. For almost three decades, the Syrian regime has been the closest ally of the Khomeinist regime, despite the fact that Shiite clerics regard the Alawite minority that rules in Damascus as heretics. George Ibrahim Abdallah, the Lebanese maverick who led a campaign of terror in Paris in the 1980s on behalf of Tehran, was a Christian. So was Anis Naqqache, who led several death squads sent to kill exiled Iranian leaders. Tehran's surrogate in Lebanon, Hezballah, formed an alliance in 2006 with a Maronite Christian faction led by the ex-general Michel Aoun to oppose the democratic majority bloc that favors close ties with the West. In May 2008, Hezballah armed gangs attacked the Sunni Muslim districts of Beirut in a massive show of force. To terrorize the populace, they burned social clubs and libraries, ransacked offices of the independent media, looted luxury shops, and killed over sixty people. While Hezballah was terrorizing Sunni Muslims, Aoun's supporters were moving into Christian districts to intimidate their coreligionists.

The Islamic Republic has financed and armed the radical Afghan Sunni Hizb Islami (Islamic Party) since the 1990s. It also financed the Front for Islamic Salvation (FIS), a Sunni political-terrorist outfit in Algeria between 1992 and 2005. In 1993, a senior Iranian delegation led by Ayatollah Mehdi Karrubi, the speaker of the Islamic Parliament, attended the Popular Arab Islamic Conference organized by Hassan al-Turabi, nicknamed "the Pope of Islamist Terror," in Khartoum. At the end of this anti-American jamboree, a nine-man Coordinating Committee (known as the Majlis al-Shuyukh or Assembly of Elders) was announced, and Karrubi was a member. The fact that Karrubi was a Shiite mullah did not prevent him from sitting alongside Sunni sheikhs.

In 1996, a suicide attack claimed the lives of nineteen American servicemen in Al Khobar, eastern Saudi Arabia. The operation was carried out by Hezballah in Hejaz, an Iranian-financed outfit, with the help of the Sunni militant group called "Sword of the Peninsula." In 2000,

Sunni groups linked to al-Qaeda killed seventeen U.S. servicemen in a suicide attack on the USS *Cole* off the coast of Yemen. This time, a Shiite militant group led by Sheikh al-Houti, Tehran's man in Yemen, played second fiddle in the operation. In Tajikistan and Uzbekistan, Tehran has for years supported two Sunni movements, the Rastakhiz Islami (Islamic Awakening) and Hizb Tahrir Islami (Islamic Liberation Party). In Azerbaijan, Tehran supports the Sunni Taleshi groups *against* the Azeri Shiite majority—because the Taleshi Sunnis are pro-Russian and anti-American, while Shiite Azeris are pro-American and anti-Russian.

There are no Palestinian Shiites, yet Tehran has become the principal source of funding for radical Palestinian Sunni groups, notably Hamas and Islamic Jihad, along with half a dozen leftist-atheist mini groups. Tehran is the only place on earth where all Palestinian terror groups maintain offices. The Hamas leader Ismail Haniyeh refuses to pray alongside his Iranian hosts during his visits to Tehran, but when it comes to joining Khomeinist crowds in shouting "Death to America" he is in the forefront. With Arab oil kingdoms no longer as generous as before, Iran has emerged as the chief source of funding for Hamas. The national budget that came into effect on March 21, 2008, allocated over $2 billion to the promotion of "revolutionary causes." Much of this money was earmarked for Hamas and the Lebanese branch of Hezballah.

In Pakistan, the Iran-financed Shiite Tehrik Jaafari (Jaafari Movement) joined a coalition of Sunni parties to govern the Northwest Frontier Province, until they all suffered a crushing defeat in the 2008 parliamentary elections. The fact that Sunnis and Shiites in other provinces of Pakistan continued to kill each other did not prevent them from developing a joint anti-U.S. strategy that included the revival of the Afghan Taliban and protection for the remnants of al-Qaeda. Almost all self-styled "holy warriors" who go to Iraq on a mission of murder and mayhem are Sunnis, yet most pass through Syria, a country dominated by a sect with a militant anti-Sunni religious doctrine. The 9/11 Commission report states that Tehran was in contact with al-Qaeda at various levels before the 2001 attacks. Tehran has acknowledged the presence of al-Qaeda figures in

Iran on a number of occasions and has arranged for the repatriation of at least thirteen Saudi members in the past five years. The bin Laden family admit that at least two of Osama's sons, Sa'ad and Seyf al-Islam, have lived in Iran since 2002. It was in Tehran that Osama bin Laden met the Tajik Islamist leader Abdallah Nouri in the 1990s. Since 2002, eyewitness reports suggest that scores of Taliban leaders and several al-Qaeda figures spend part of the year in a housing estate near the village of Doust Muhammad on the Iranian frontier with Afghanistan. These reports are hard to verify because Tehran has declared large segments of eastern Iran a "no-go" area, even for its own state-owned media.

The regime uses Khomeini's writings and speeches to justify support for "Jihad against the enemies of Islam"—what others would regard as terrorism. Here is how Khomeini justifies terror and war:

> Those who say that Islam should not kill, don't understand [it]. Killing is a great [divine] gift that appears [to man]. A religion that does not include [provisions for] killing and massacre is incomplete. Those who claim that Jesus was averse to killing and war, harm his prophetic mission. The prophet has a sword to fight with. Why do you insist on reading the Koran's merciful verses and not verses that urge killing? Killing is the same as mercy. Our imams were all military [men] and killed people.[12]

Finally, the twelfth characteristic of generic fascism is its rejection of the normal language of society. All brands of fascism invent their own vocabularies and literary styles. Mussolini's affected Latinism was at times hilarious, while Ezra Pound's "pure Aryan lingo" was intriguing. The German used by Hitler and Goebbels was closer to the argot of Munich beerhouses than to the language of Kleist or Goethe. Jean-Marie Le Pen is careful about his *imparfait du subjonctif.* The backbone of the Khomeinist newspeak version of Persian is a list of over three hundred words and terms, most of them new coinages. The total vocabulary of this newspeak is around two thousand words, quite sufficient for a fascist type of system. Anything more might lead people into the temptation of thinking. In Khomeinism, as in all forms of fascism, what matters is *zikr,* the incantation of authorized texts, rather than *fikr,* or critical thought. Fascism destroys the normal syntax in an unconscious bid to pre-empt the development of rational thought and critical analysis.

Islamist writers had always tried to subvert the Persian language by bringing it closer to Arabic. The late Jalal al-Ahmad, a Stalinist who converted to Islamism in the 1960s, often wrote Persian with a pseudo-Arabic syntax. (In Persian, the order of words is subject, object, verb; in Arabic it is verb, subject, object.) Khomeini went further than al-Ahmad by doing away with *all* order. His speeches and writings reflect his inability to think clearly beyond repeating his anti-American leitmotiv in a jumbled style. The effect is often so hilarious that many Iranians read Khomeini's writings for entertainment at informal gatherings. It is only in the United States that the ayatollah's work is presented as "philosophy" and taught to unsuspecting university students.[13]

Besides imposing its own vocabulary, generic fascism also employs censorship. Khomeini censored his own collection of poems, which appeared in a limited edition only after his death, and his *Hal al-Masa'el* ("Solution to Problems") was "purged of unsuitable ideas" before being published. The censorship list in Tehran reads like a who's who of Persian and world literature and thought: every imaginable writer or poet of importance in any language is either totally banned or heavily censored in the Islamic Republic. Even classics of Persian literature are "edited" to remove ideas that might undermine the regime. The largest department in the Ministry of Islamic Guidance and Culture is the one in charge of censorship. (There, a blind man heads a special unit to censor movies: he listens to descriptions of cinematic scenes and decides which to cut!) Newsreels and photos are edited or airbrushed to eliminate those who have broken with the regime and give those in the ascendancy higher profiles. Successive editions of Khomeini's works are edited and partly rewritten to remove embarrassing passages and add new ones to justify the current policies.

* * *

What happened in Iran in 1978–79, and the system subsequently created, has a mainly if not exclusively political relationship with Islam and Shiism. The Khomeinist system is a *beda'a* (innovation) ultimately opposed to Islamic as well as Persian philosophy, theology, and political thought and practice. Its roots can be found in generic fascism, a largely Western product that has invaded Iran in a dramatic instance of mimetic madness. This mimesis is Westernizing Iran more than the nation's previous 150 years' experience with the gradual assimilation of some aspects of Western life. One of Khomeini's closest associates in the early phases of the regime, Mehdi Bazargan, argues that even the use of the term "revolution" to discuss the ayatollah's seizure of power was a sign of Westernization. "Revolution is in essence an import from the West," he writes, "something alien to the culture of Iranians and Muslims."[14] The argument is based on the fact that none of the main languages of Muslims contained a word for "revolution" as used in a political sense in European languages. The Arabic word *enqelaab*, which means "counterfeiting," was originally used in Persian to mean "sudden change of weather." (Arabs still use it in that sense.) It was only after the 1930s that some writers started to use *enqelaab* in the sense of a political revolution. Initially, Khomeini and his advisors had thought of presenting their movement not as a revolution but as a *nehzat*, an Arabic word meaning "awakening." It was under the influence of his Stalinist allies that the ayatollah decided to sanction the term *enqelaab* (revolution).

One of Iran's best-known philosophers has written a book arguing that by ideologizing Islam, the Khomeinist movement is, perhaps unwittingly, introducing the West into all aspects of Iran on a scale never known before.[15] The problem is that the West is coming to Iran in its totalitarian version, just as it had come to other developing nations in its socialist or communist versions. Bazargan recognized this when he portrayed the Khomeinist revolt in these terms: "Those clenched fists, dour faces, and cries calling for death and violence were more reminiscent of a Communist class revolution than an image of Allah's mercy."[16] He rejected the claim that street demonstrations against the shah gave legitimacy to the

Khomeinist regime: "The fact that some people gathered and marched in the streets of Tehran or on the campus of the university, even if their number is estimated at around one million, in a city that had seven or eight million inhabitants, does not imply majority support for the rulers' legitimacy."[17]

A mixture of political immaturity, opportunism, and outright irresponsibility led Iranian liberals, democrats, socialists, and social-democrats to transfer power to the fascist movement led by Khomeini. Many Iranian intellectuals failed to recognize the wolf disguised as the grandmother. The beards, the turbans, the *mishlahs* (a kind of shawl worn by men), the *miswaks* (toothbrushes made of sandalwood), the piety patches on foreheads, the *qamis* (a men's long shirt), the beards—pogonophilia gone mad—do not demonstrate that Khomeinism is a *religious* movement. These props of terror are as representative of Islam as the uniforms of Mao's Red Guards were of China's Confucian tradition. Those who thought they could ally themselves with fascism to win power against a regime they did not like were not familiar with the proverb about falling from the frying pan into the fire. Almost all the intellectuals that the shah had detained for brief periods were shot, imprisoned, or driven into exile by Khomeini even though they had signed the "devil's pact" with him—or maybe *because* they had done so. They fought a regime they disliked, rightly or wrongly, by supporting a movement that disliked them.

The Iranian people are the primary victims of Khomeinism just as the Germans were the first victims of Hitlerism and the Russians of Leninism. The main lesson that Muslim intellectuals must learn from the Iranian tragedy is that they should not abandon their core political beliefs. Today, most regimes in the Muslim world are corrupt and despotic, and must be fought as enemies of their people; but this must be done from positions that are more humane, more progressive, and more democratic than those of the regime in place.

9

The Feeble Ones

The Islamic Republic of Iran has three phobias: women, Jews, and America. Of these three, perhaps the strongest is the regime's fear and hatred of women, often referred to as *zaeefeh* (the feeble ones).

In fact, the first issue that turned Khomeini from a quietist mullah into a political activist was the shah's decision to enfranchise women as part of a package of social and political reforms in 1962. In a cable to the monarch, Khomeini, still using deferential terms, warned that giving women the right to vote and seek election amounted to an attack on Islam.[1] The shah ignored the cable, and women were enfranchised. Later, the shah went further by asking parliament to pass a landmark law that removed most of the inequalities women had suffered since the advent of Islam. Women were granted the right to sue for divorce, as well as protection against "repudiation," an Islamic practice under which a man could divorce any or all of his four wives without even informing them. The new law, known as the Family Protection Act, made Iran the first Muslim nation to acknowledge women as citizens with equal rights.

Khomeini and other reactionary mullahs never forgave the shah for it. When they eventually seized power in 1979, they realized that the enfranchisement of women was perhaps the most difficult of the shah's reforms to undo. This particular genie would not return to the bottle. Iranian women were strongly attached to their newly won right and would not give it up without a fight. While the shah's reforms did not remove all discrimination against Iranian women, they did open the way for a massive influx of women into the labor market. In 1977, the last year for which data are available before the mullahs took power, over 160,000 women worked in public service, nearly half of them in education. Women were present in all sections of the administration as well as the army and the police. There were 317 woman judges and advocates, the first in the Muslim world; 107 woman diplomats up to ambassadorial level; several woman mayors of cities; and woman members of parliament and senators. One of the nine justices of the Supreme Court was a woman.[2] And every government since 1968 had included at least one woman cabinet minister.[3]

The first demonstration against the Khomeinist regime was held in Tehran on March 8, 1979, less than a month after the ayatollah had seized power. Marking the International Women's Day, the demonstration attracted over half a million people, both men and women, who wished to warn the new regime that canceling the shah's reforms would be resisted. The Khomeinists tried to crush the demonstration by sending Hezballah shock troops, armed with chains, knives, and baseball bats, to hit the protestors and if necessary kill them. The attackers, however, were beaten back by groups of young men who had come to protect the women. Then the Khomeinists decided to postpone efforts to undo the reforms. In the new constitution drafted for the Islamic Republic, the right of women to vote and seek election to the unicameral parliament was maintained, although women were implicitly barred from seeking the highest positions of state, including that of Supreme Guide and president of the republic.[4] Women were also purged from some professions.

Having failed to cancel the rights won by women over decades of struggle, the new regime tried to contain what it saw as a strategic threat to its vision of a "pure Muhammadan Islam" (*Islam naab Muhammadi*). School textbooks were revised to propagate the theme of women's subservience to men. Primary school textbooks under the shah featured illustrations of two children, one girl and one boy, in a series of events designed to help teach important lessons. Both children had pure Persian, non-Islamic names, Dara and Azar, and they were depicted wearing the kind of clothes that Iranian children typically wore at the time, sometimes in jeans with matching T-shirts. The new Islamic textbooks changed the children's names to Ali and Fatima, after the Prophet's son-in-law and daughter. The new illustrations show Fatima wearing the mandatory hijab, and never in short dresses or trousers. She is scripted out of activities, including sports, that are supposed to be "un-Islamic" for the female of the species. Whereas Dara and Azar were neighbors attending the same mixed school, the regime of gender apartheid required that a boy and a girl not be seen together under any circumstances unless they were recast as brother and sister. Fatima appears always deferential towards her brother, while the text urges sisters to adopt her example. There is no mention of duties that Ali might have towards his sister.

Ayatollah Abdul-Karim Mussavi Ardebili, who acted as the Khomeinist regime's chief justice for years, put the new regime's view of the whole issue in his usual stark terms: "A woman's basic duty is to be a slave to her husband." Iranian women, however, never bowed to the agenda of gender apartheid. In 1980, less than a year after the establishment of fascist rule, women held a series of seminars and conferences—often in universities that had been shut down on Khomeini's orders—to campaign for women's rights. These conferences provoked violent reactions, not only from Hezballah militants who beat up the women and disfigured some by throwing acid at them, but also from some female members of the new establishment. One such woman said: "Opening a debate over women's rights is a Western phenomenon and sign of antimonotheist views, which sadly have permeated our society as well. This phenomenon is the effect of the illness of the antimonotheist culture."[5] The dean of the Alzahra University, an institution for women, went further, saying: "Women should avoid thinking about matters [related to] the rights of women and men. This is the task of the clergy and religious scholars, not of women."[6]

Under Khomeinism, tens of thousands of women were fired from their posts in the public sector on a variety of pretexts. All women judges were expelled on the ground that Islam forbids a woman to sit in judgment over cases that involve men. The purge of women from the public sector did particular damage to the nation's educational system. Under the shah, women had accounted for more than 40 percent of teachers in primary schools. Now, however, women were not allowed to teach boys on the pretext that they would "feminize" the future warriors of Islam, who needed manly qualities to face the infidels in battle. Having closed down mixed schools and many girls' schools, the new regime had no need of so many woman teachers. Women were also thrown out of the army and the police. In a regime claiming that any physical contact between a man and a woman not related by blood or marriage would be an attack on Islam, there was no place for policewomen or female soldiers.[7]

In the end, however, it was the hijab that represented the new regime's most potent instrument for enforcing its view of women's place in society. Like women in most societies, Muslim women over the centuries had worn a variety of head coverings, with such names as *chador, rusari, ruband, chaqchur, maqne'a, burqah,* and *picheh,* These had tribal, ethnic, and generally folkloric origins, and were never associated with religion. In Senegal, Muslim women wore colorful headgear but went topless.

The Khomeinists encouraged the wearing of a special form of hijab from 1977 onwards as their revolutionary movement gained momentum. Styled like a hood, it covers the woman's ears so that she does not hear things properly, and it prevents the woman from having full vision of her surroundings. This form of hijab was invented in the early 1970s by Musa Sadr, an Iranian mullah who won the leadership of the Shiite community in Lebanon. Being totally new to Iranians, this hood-like hijab served to identify the wearer with Khomeinist Islam. Initially, a few hundred militant women wore the neo-hijab of Islamist fascism; but by 1979, when the mullahs seized power, the number wearing it had multiplied by the thousands.

Persian literature over the centuries is full of anti-hijab sentiments. The twelfth-century poet Suzani believed that Caliph Omar invented the tradition of covering women because he had several ugly daughters he hoped to marry off without letting potential husbands see them in advance:

> *Blessed is Omar, the great Caliph*
> *Who ordained that the ugly be covered;*

Saving us, lovers of beauty,

from eye-sores in city bazaars.

Similarly, the novelist Javad Fazel writes that Atossa, a dowager queen in the pre-Islamic Persian Empire and known as a nymphomaniac, invented the hijab. Realizing with horror that she was growing a beard while going bald, Atossa launched the fashion of wearing the veil.

One of medieval Persia's greatest poets, Saadi, claimed that only ugly women wished to cover up:

Beauty cannot bear to be covered,

Shut the door on her,

she sticks her head out of the window!

Saadi also claimed that a woman's concealment could drive a man to distraction:

Do not cover yourself, oh housebound moon,

[Your cove] could lead me to madness.

I dream of melting in you,

Others I hold with horror and alienation.

The modern poet Iraj Mirza (d. 1926) offers a verse tableau in which a man pursues and propositions a fully covered female believing she is a prostitute, only to discover that she is his own sister.

Radical Islam's obsession with covering women's hair is a new phenomenon. In 1981, Abol-Hassan Banisadr, the first president of the Islamic Republic, announced that scientific research had shown that women's hair emits rays that drive men insane with lust. To protect the public, the new regime passed legislation in 1982 making the new form of hijab mandatory for all females above six years of age, regardless of religious faith. Violating the hijab code is punishable by one hundred lashes of the cane and six months imprisonment. By the mid-1980s, a form of hijab never seen in Islam before the 1970s had become standard headgear for millions of Muslim women all over the world, including Europe and North America. Many younger Muslim women, especially Western converts, were duped into believing that the neo-hijab is an essential part of the Islamic faith.

The 1982 dress code also imposed dark colors as the only ones authorized for the hijab. This produced a semiotic scheme in which the color of a woman's hijab indicated her political leanings. Hard-line Khomeinists chose black or dark blue. Islamist-Marxists, who broke with Khomeini in 1981, preferred brown or light blue. Those who hated Khomeinism manifested their hatred by wearing white, yellow, or green, thus technically breaking the law. Shirin Ebadi tried to distance herself from the Khomeinists by wearing a red hijab soon after being awarded the Nobel Peace Prize.

Muslim women anywhere in the world could easily see the fraudulent nature of the neo-Islamist hijab by going through their family albums: they will not find a single picture of a female ancestor who wore the cursed headgear now imposed upon them as an absolute "must" of Islam. This fake Islamic hijab is thus nothing but a political prop, a weapon of visual terrorism; it is a symbol of a totalitarian ideology inspired more by Nazism and Communism than by Islam, and is designed to promote gender apartheid. And yet this prop of visual terror was presented by Khomeinist ideologues as a fundamental value—as "a pillar of Islamic existence," in the words of Khatami, and as "our most effective weapon against the enemies of Islam," according to Rafsanjani. One well-known female Khomeinist wrote, "The superpowers know that hijab is the foundation of Islamic government and that to conquer the Persian Gulf and plunder its oil resources, they must first eliminate hijab."[8]

To counter the Islamist claim that the hijab blocks the dangerous, lust-provoking rays emanating from a woman's hair, some women have proposed other forms of hijab. One Iranian designer came out with a wig made of horsehair, thus ensuring that a woman's own hair remains hidden while she still "looks like a normal human being." Some Iranian actresses suggested they be allowed to appear in plays and films wearing wigs made of animal hair. The French cosmetics firm L'Oreal tried to market a transparent hijab that would show a woman's hair but keep its "dangerous rays" locked in. The Khomeinists would have none of it; they wanted women to be seen in public in a state of submission.

To the new style of Islamic headgear for women was added another mandatory item: a thick, all-covering overcoat in dark colors that women are forced to wear in every kind of weather. That this was a complete invention having nothing to do with Islam is indicated by the fact that the mullahs didn't even find a Persian or Arabic word for it, so they called it a *manto*, from the French word *manteau*. In 2004, President Khatami authorized an experiment under which twelve girls' colleges with all-female staff in Tehran were to allow their pupils to take off their *manto* within the school premises. To make sure that the girls and their teachers were not exposed to "stolen gazes" from men, six-foot-high plastic extensions were added to the walls around the buildings. "With the new walls, the school looks like a prison," commented Ms. Shamloo, the headmistress of one school participating in the experiment. "But inside it we feel free!" Khatami had approved the experiment after a nationwide study showed that the imposition of hijab on girls from the age of six caused "serious depression and, in some cases, suicide." Three months later, the experiment was abandoned after coming under attack by more hard-line Khomeinists. The newspaper *Jumhuri Islami* (Islamic Republic), owned by Khamenehi, lashed out against "this slippery slope towards scandal." "Casting off the hijab encourages the culture of nudity and weakens the sacred values of Islam," the paper warned.[9] Rafsanjani went further, telling a Friday prayer gathering in Tehran that "a strand of woman's hair emerging from under the hijab is a dagger drawn towards the heart of Islam."

The harm that Islamism is doing to Muslim women is not limited to the evil headgear. Under the Khomeinist regime, as in every other Muslim country, the number of women out of work is at least twice that of men. Women's wages are less than a quarter of men's. In Iran under Khomeinism, as in most Muslim countries, women cannot travel without the written permission of a male guardian. And yet Tehran has been the venue for numerous seminars and conferences on women and Islam, designed to prove that Western women have become "objects" to be used as props in commerce and pornography. One constant tune of these seminars is that girls need to be educated, but the fact is that Muslim girls have already kept their end of the bargain as far as education is concerned. They have all the degrees they need, but are not allowed to leave home without a chaperon or wear the clothes they like. They cannot get the jobs they merit or choose whom to marry. The Tehran seminars are a far cry from the first congress of Muslim women held in Kazan, then part of the Russian Empire, in 1875, at which over eight hundred women delegates unanimously voted for "full equality of sexes, and the abolition of all discrimination."

* * *

Khomeini and his followers base their anti-woman position on the Koran and the hadiths. In the ninth century, a Persian scholar named Abdallah al-Bokhari decided to collect and edit the sayings of Muhammad, so he traveled all over the Muslim world and interviewed 1,080 people, mostly in Hejaz on the Red Sea, gathering 600,000 hadiths—a fantastic number. (The Prophet should have lived at least three hundred years to have had time to feature in so many anecdotes.) Mercifully, Bokhari knew the limits of the ridiculous. He decided to keep only 7,275 hadiths, which he published in his magnum opus: *Sahih* ("The Correct") or *Tariq al-Mostaqeem* ("The Right Path"). For the Shiites there were 2.5 million hadiths because they had twelve imams who also had anecdotes related to them. The hadiths have led to the creation of an industry employing tens of thousands of people: the *muffasserin* (exegetes), the *fuqaha* (theologians), the experts in Shariah. In many cases, the most enduring impact of the hadiths has been an occultation of the Koran itself, as issues are often discussed in terms of the hadiths rather than through a meticulous reading of the Koran. One cannot calculate all the damage that has been done to Muslims over many centuries as a result of judgments based on apocryphal anecdotes, not to say downright inventions. Every aspect of life has been affected, including the status of women.

Some writers admit that women are discriminated against in Muslim societies but also claim that Islam brought an improvement over the situation of women during the preceding *Jahilyah* period—the period of darkness, as Muhammad called it. We are told that before Islam, especially in the Arabian Peninsula, women were treated as subhuman and never allowed to attain positions of responsibility. We are also told that the Arabs had a habit of burying newborn baby girls. Islam, we are told, changed all that.

This simplistic view is used to justify discrimination and injustice today, although it lacks a factual foundation. The Arabian Peninsula before Islam had known quite a few woman rulers. Queen Zenobia is still remembered. So is Belqees, the famed Queen of Sheba who charmed the Prophet Solomon. There was also Semiramis, the Mesopotamian temptress, a beautiful but brutal character who would have her lovers put to death once she tired of them. Even at the time of the Prophet Muhammad himself, some women were prominent and powerful figures in Arabia. The notorious Hind—who is said to have devoured the innards of the Prophet's uncle Hamzah after the battle of Ohud—played a leading political role in Mecca. Muhammad's first wife, Khadijah, was a successful businesswoman engaged in export-import on a fairly large scale. She gave Muhammad his first and only job, until Allah chose him for the prophetic mission. Some women, for example the mother of the future Caliph Muawyyah, were among the richest individuals in Arabia. Women in Persia and Byzantium, although never given equal status with men, were nevertheless able to play their part in society. The Sassanid Empire, which was overthrown by the Arab invasion, counted two reigning queens among its monarchs.

In Arabia, there certainly was a barbarous custom of burying newborn baby girls, but it could not have been widespread or the population would not have increased as dramatically as it did in the decades that preceded the coming of Islam. By the same token, the live burial of girls did not stop with Islam; there are fully documented cases of the practice continuing long after the Prophet's death. In one instance the Caliph Muawyyah buried a girl alive and rode his horse on the burial spot. (Even today in China there are reports of newborn girls being put to death by couples who prefer a boy under the government's one-child-only policy.)

Pre-Islamic society in Arabia was not as anti-female as it is portrayed by those who try to blacken it so that Islam will appear more brilliant in comparison. Pre-Islamic Arab poetry is full of passion for women. Such folk tales of love and passion as *Antar and Ablah, Leyla and Majnun,* and *Wameq and Azra* clearly show that women were something more than breeding machines or de facto slaves of men. The fact that most idols in pre-Islamic Arabia were goddesses is also significant. Mecca's three principal idols at the time of the Prophet were female: Lat, Manat, and al-Ozza. Even the sun, considered male in Persian mythology, was taken to be female in Arabia and worshipped as a goddess. It is therefore not true that pre-Islamic Arabia was no more than a living hell for women. What Islam did was codify the rules applied to women and define their rights and responsibilities. In some areas, such as marriage and inheritance, the existing tribal customs were adopted with little or no modification.

On the other side of the issue, some writers blame Islam for having burdened women with restrictions and humiliations that supposedly did not exist in pre-Islamic society. This view is also incorrect. In fact, one could argue that Islam on balance improved the status of women, though without giving them the full legal equality that the modern world demands. What is certain is that Muhammad was no misogynist. He is quoted as having said: "Three things I enjoy above all: Women, perfumes, and daily prayers!" Whether or not this quotation is authentic, we know that Muhammad enjoyed the company of women; he married twenty-nine of them, and according to his biographers he always treated them with kindness and respect.

The Koran does not offer any emphatic, unchangeable rules regarding the status of women. To be sure, it assumes that society will retain a patriarchal structure in which women are deprived of many rights and allowed only a secondary role. In this respect, the Koran reports on things as they were at the time; it does not portray an ideal state of affairs.

Virtually all of the Koran's specific positions regarding the status of women are included in the sura of al-Ahzab (the parties). Here we learn about rules of marriage and divorce.

O, believers! When you marry believing women
and then divorce them before you've touched them,
you have no period to reckon against them;
so make provision for them, and set them free
with kindness.
O Prophet! We have made lawful for you
Thy wives whom thou hast given their dowers
And what your right hand owns, spoils of war
That God has given you, and the daughters of
your uncles paternal and your aunts paternal,
Your uncles maternal and your aunts maternal who
Have emigrated with you; any woman believer,
If she gives herself to the Prophet and if the
Prophet desires to take her in marriage for you
Exclusively, apart from other believers—
We know what we have imposed on them
Concerning their wives and what their right hand owns
That there may be no fault in you:
God is All-Forgiving, All Compassionate.
You may put off whom you wish of them,
And whom you wish thou may take;
And if you seek any you have set aside
There is no fault in you. So it is likelier they
Will be comforted, and not sorrow, and everyone of them will be pleased with
　　　what you give her.
God knows what is in your heart;
God is All-Knowing, All-Clement.
Thereafter women are not lawful to you,
Neither for you to take other wives in exchange
For them, though their beauty please you, except what your right hand
　　　owns;

God is watchful over everything.

The rules spelled out in detail here are clearly addressed to the Prophet and are intended to define his rights and limits in matters regarding marriage and divorce. At no point is there the slightest hint that these are supposed to be universal rules applied till the end of time.

One of the numerous problems that exegetes of the Koran have always faced stems from a peculiarity of the Arabic language, which lacks a verb that is of crucial importance in Indo-European languages: *to be*. It is hard to convey an exact notion of time in Arabic, and one is never quite sure whether something is described as it is or as it should be. Constructing a precise system of law is difficult on so tentative a basis.

Those who argue that the status of women is defined as permanently inferior in the Koran also say that the book's version of the Creation myth presents Eve as inferior to man and guilty of being the first to taste the forbidden fruit.[10] The Koran, however, never implies any guilt on the part of Eve. As for woman's inferiority, here is what the Koranic verse says: "It is He who created you out of one being (*nafsan*) and made of him his espouse, that he might rest in her." In this verse, the word *nafs*, for the primeval being out of which God created both man and woman, is linguistically masculine; but one should not read too much into this. When we say "mankind" in English, this does not mean that we are talking only about men. In French, the word for telephone is masculine but the word for television is feminine. In Arabic, almost all noble attitudes such as honor, pride, honesty, and courage are feminine. Does it mean that men are excluded from them?

Anti-woman commentators, like Khomeini, also point out that the Koran implies that man was created before woman, and use this as an argument in favor of their claim that men are masters of women. That, however, is nothing more than a chronological precedence. After all, it is man *and* woman who together ensure the survival of the species. Creating one creature before another is not, on its own, a sign of discrimination.

In languages that ignore gender, there is no such problem with the reading of the Koranic text on Creation. In Persian, the primeval being (*nafs*) from which man and woman were created has no gender. Thus, the verse could be read like this: "It is He who created you man and woman from a single being." The absence of linguistic gender in Persian makes it difficult to use the Persian Koran to support male chauvinistic positions.

To some Iranian writers and poets, covering women was a purely Arab tribal obsession. The poet Nasser Bokharai mocked the Arabs for wanting to cover whatever is denoted by a word of the feminine gender— even the Ka'aba, the great black stone in Mecca, which is always covered in black drapes:

> *The kaaba, because it has a feminine gender,*
> *Is kept behind the purdah like graceful brides.*

Once a year, the drapes are removed for laundering or for replacement. On such occasions, the "forbidden precinct" is closed so that men cannot see the black stone without its hijab.

Centuries of anti-woman propaganda and action related to the hijab are based on the following passages from the Koran, also in the sura of al-Ahzab:

> *O believers! Do not enter the house of the Prophet*
> *without an invitation for a meal, and come on time.*
> *When you are invited, enter; and when the party is over,*
> *Leave.*
> *Do not stay on for chitchat. That is hurtful to the Prophet*
> *And he is too shy to tell you.*
> *But Allah is not shy to tell you the truth.*
> *And when you ask the Prophet's wives for any object*
> *Ask them from behind a curtain [hijab]; that is more proper*
> *For your hearts as well as theirs.*
> *It is not for you to hurt the messenger of Allah,*
> *Neither to marry his wives after him, ever. Surely,*
> *That would be a monstrous sight in the eyes of God.*

Further on we read the following:

> O Prophet! Tell your wives and daughters
>
> and other believing women to draw their veils [hijab]
>
> close to them; so that it is likelier
>
> they will be known, and not hurt. Allah is All-Forgiving,
>
> All-Compassionate.

Any unprejudiced reading of this verse would see it as a recommendation, not a stricture—a distinction that is always clear in the Koran. The point becomes more obvious when we study the background to the passages. Muslim theologians have always attached great importance to the study of the background of each sura. This is known as *asbab nozul* (reasons for revelation). What is curious, however, is that almost no effort has been made to apply the same technique to the passages regarding the issue of the hijab.

The passages in question came to the Prophet in Medina in the fifth year of the Hegira (literally: emigration), his flight from Mecca to Medina in 622 A.D. The Prophet had just married his cousin Zaynab bint Jahsh and had asked one of his aides, a man called Anas Ibn Malek, to organize a wedding party. The party was attended by almost all members of the Muslim community in Yathrib (later renamed Medinat al-Nabi or the City of the Prophet). A meal was served, at the end of which the guests wished the Prophet and his new bride well, and then left. Three guests, however, continued to "chitchat" and showed no signs of intending to leave. The Prophet wanted to be alone with his new bride but was too shy to ask the three to leave; he kept going from room to room in the hope that they would depart. It was in this time of agitation that the verses regarding the hijab descended from heaven. The Prophet pulled a curtain between himself and Anas Ibn Malek, who was present in the house, and recited the verses. Thus the original hijab referred to in the sura is the curtain that separates the Prophet from Anas Ibn Malek, not the headgear that prevents women's hair from emanating "dangerous rays that drive men crazy."

As for the second passage quoted above: The fifth year of the Hegira was a particularly difficult one for the Prophet. The defeat of his forces at the battle of Uhud and the siege of Yathrib by the Meccan armies during the Battle of the Ditch (*khandaq*) had created tension in the small Muslim community. At such low moments, quarrels within a community are to be expected; and in those days, most quarrels involved women. In any case, women captured in war were regarded as booty. It was necessary to mark out Muslim women from others; hence the recommendation about the hijab.

The word *hijab*, however, does not mean the veil. It comes from the Arabic word *hujb*, which means "capacity." Hijab could appear in three aspects, the first being visual. A dust storm could create a hijab that covers the sun. The Ka'aba wears a hijab because it is covered by a sheath of cloth. Many caliphs in Islamic history wore masks to hide their faces from their subjects. A legend popular in most Muslim countries claims that Muhammad himself always wore a mask to protect his followers from being burned to death by the brilliance of his visage. One of Muhammad's most popular nicknames is Muahhreq, literally "Fire-Raiser," because his gaze was said to ignite a fire when and if he so wished. Persian classical poetry often refers to Muhammad as "the Wearer of the Medinan Burqah and the Meccan Mask."

The second aspect of hijab is spatial, relating to physical space. Muslim houses had inner and outer parts (*andaroun* and *biroun*); the inner parts were declared *haram* (forbidden) to unauthorized people. In this context, the hijab divides these two spaces. The concept of "harem" developed from this aspect of hijab.

But the most important aspect of hijab is the ethical one: the distinction between right and wrong. This aspect should not be ignored in favor of the purely visual one.

The Koran uses the word "hijab" seven times. The first refers to the curtain behind which Mary, mother of Jesus, hides herself from her relatives when she is with child and does not want her condition to be revealed. The second instance of hijab is at the end of the Prophet's wedding party, when he draws a curtain between himself and one of the lingering guests. The third is when the Prophet's wives and daughters and other Muslim women are recommended to mark themselves out from infidel women, slaves, and women captured in war and considered as booty, so that they are not harmed. In the fourth instance, a curtain separates the believers from the damned on the Day of Reckoning. The fifth time, hijab is a curtain that protects the Prophet from being burned by the light emanating from the divine face during his encounter with Allah in his journey to the seventh heaven on the back of his horse Buraq. The sixth and seventh times the word hijab appears, it is a curtain that prevents the unbelievers, the idolaters, from seeing the One and Only God.

To reduce all these different aspects of the hijab to a piece of cloth behind which women are supposed to hide their hair (and sometimes their faces) requires a great deal of bad faith, both of which the Khomeinists have in abundance. They and other Islamist fascists do not demand that women mask their faces, but do insist on the wearing of a headscarf that covers all of a woman's head, leaving only her face exposed. The obsession with covering the hair is difficult to justify on any grounds; for if we interpret the hijab of the verses that we have cited to mean a veil behind which women could hide, then what matters is hiding the face, not the hair. But for Islamist fascists, the purpose of the hijab is not really to protect women from supposedly lustful men; the purpose is to deny women their rights and put them in a subordinate position.

Obsession with covering women dictates part of the Islamic Republic's foreign policy as well. Throughout the 1980s, the Khomeinist regime spent substantial sums to persuade Senegalese Muslim women not to appear topless in public. The going rate for covering the breasts was around two dollars a month, paid in cash by agents of the Khomeinist embassy in Dakar. In the 1990s, the Islamic Republic was paying Muslim women in war-torn Bosnia-Herzegovina an average of five dollars a month to cover their hair. In Western Europe and North America, the mission to persuade Muslim women to cover up is assigned to special "Offices of the Supreme Guide" that act as unofficial embassies, thus avoiding laws and rules applied to diplomatic legations.

* * *

Khomeinists often criticize the West for having turned women into mere objects in male-dominated societies. But it is Khomeinism itself that treats women as objects at the disposal of men for sexual gratification and procreation. In his *Tahrir al-Wassilah* ("Release of the Means"), a kind of do-it-yourself book addressed exclusively to men, the ayatollah fixes the age at which a "woman" could be taken as a temporary or permanent "wife" at nine. This is because the Prophet took his favorite wife, Ayesha, when she was only nine years old. The founder of the Islamic Republic rules that a man should not have sex with his wife, whether temporary or permanent, if she is below the age of nine, but allows other "gratifications," such as "touching with lust, embracing and foreplay, even if [the female child in question] be a nursing baby." If, however, a man ignores the rule and, in effect, rapes the baby girl, his only punishment is that if he ends up divorcing the female in question, he will not be able to marry any of her sisters. If the baby girl dies on account of the rape, her supposed husband will have to pay blood money to her relatives. Even then, the price of a woman's blood is half that of a man's.

Khomeini also sanctions prostitution, provided that it is covered by the Shiite tradition of *mut'ah*, the taking of "temporary wives." In the chapter on "copulation" (*nikah*) in the same book, he writes: "Temporary marriage with an adulteress is allowed, even though she is a notorious prostitute. [But this must be done] with displeasure. Once copulation is done with her, she should be advised to give up her profession."[11] Khomeini also claims that men who take temporary wives, for periods lasting from one hour to ninety-nine years, are performing "a high religious duty." The Islamic Republic has a policy of encouraging "temporary marriages" under which men can obtain sex in exchange for the payment of a fixed sum to women who agree to enter into such contracts. Once the contract runs out, the man has no obligations towards the woman or any child that she might bear from him. The phrase "like the child of a temporary wife" has entered the Persian language to describe a person or a business that is nobody's responsibility. Many women have been drawn by poverty into the "temporary marriage" business, especially in shrine cities such as Mash'had and Qom. In Tehran, an estimated fifty thousand women, many of them war widows, are reportedly engaged in the "temporary marriage" business.

That Khomeini and other contemporary Islamists are more reactionary than their peers centuries ago is illustrated by the fact that one of the ayatollah's first acts in power was to forbid the admission of women into theological courses at universities. The so-called "Science of Faith" (*Ilme-Din*), he said, was far too noble to be made available to mere women. In contrast, Emineh Begum, sister of Mullah Muhammad Baqir Majlisi, the true founder of Shiite theology in the seventeenth century, was allowed to study theology and achieved the position of ayatollah. She also took part in the compilation of her brother's *Bahar al-Anwar* ("Sea of Lights") in 132 volumes, which remains the largest encyclopedia of Shiite theology.

Four centuries later, Iranian women are denied the right even to study their religion. As "feeble ones," they are supposed to be incapable of handling "the weighty matters of faith." Women have also been slowly edged out of public life. There has also never been a woman in the Council of Ministers, although Massoumeh Ebtekar, one of the "students" who held American diplomats hostage in 1979–80, worked as Khatami's assistant on environmental issues.[12] Whereas the last pre-revolutionary parliament counted thirty-two women as members, the latest general election in Iran reduced the number of women in the Islamic Consultative Assembly, the Khomeinist ersatz parliament, from thirteen to just eight. In 2008, Iran was behind its Muslim neighbors in terms of women's representation in parliament. Iraq and Afghanistan had instituted special quotas for women's representation; Iraq had 44 and Afghanistan 68 women parliamentarians. The parliament in Turkey, another neighbor of Iran, included 46 women. In Pakistan, also a neighbor of Iran, women occupied 20 percent of the seats in the national parliament. During the three decades of Khomeinist domination in Iran, three major Muslim nations—Bangladesh, Pakistan, and Turkey—had women as prime ministers, while women had risen to senior ministerial positions in 27 others. Iran, which had pioneered the rise of women in politics as early as the 1960s, had fallen to the bottom of the list on that score.

The Western democracies have done little to help Muslim women in their struggle for freedom and equality. Leading Western ladies—including former Irish president Mary Robinson and Danielle Mitterrand, wife of the late French president François Mitterrand—have frequently visited Tehran and other Islamic capitals wearing the evil neo-hijab. The list of topics that the European Union has raised in its twenty-five-year "critical dialogue" with the Khomeinist regime has twenty-two items. Not one is concerned with the Islamist gender apartheid. Some European and American leftists have even praised the fascist neo-hijab in the name of "cultural diversity" or "anti-imperialism."

10

The Prophet and Women

The Khomeinists' fear and hatred of women is not limited to a misreading of certain passages of the Koran. During the past fourteen centuries, an abundant anti-woman literature has been produced by a succession of mullahs and others who make their living by juggling with Koranic precepts. This literature is based on just two hadiths, both of questionable authenticity.

The first was related by one Abu-Bakarah, a wealthy businessman of Basrah in the seventh century, and is quoted by Bokhari in his *Sahih*. The hadith is brief: "Abu-Bakarah says: I heard the Prophet say that a people who bequeath their affairs to a woman shall not prosper!" These few words have been and are still being used as an excuse for claiming that women must be excluded from politics and government.

Let us examine the background of the hadith: When did the Prophet utter these words and in what context? According to Abu-Bakarah, the source of the hadith, the Prophet expressed the opinion when he heard that Princess Azarmidokht, a daughter of the Sassanid Emperor Khosrow Parviz, had taken the crown as empress of Persia. The hadith, if true, relates nothing but a comment made by the Prophet on an event in a foreign country that was suffering from internecine feuds and political turmoil at the time. Had the Prophet wanted to exclude women from politics and public life in general, he could have said so clearly and distinctly. And had God wanted the same, his divine wish would have been expressed in the Koran itself. The Koran treats of issues such as settling disputes over the ownership of camels, for example, but at no point does it disqualify women from holding public office.

Moreover, there is good reason for believing that Abu-Bakarah's hadith is made of whole cloth. Abu-Bakarah came up with his hadith twenty-five years after the date at which he claimed to have heard it. Do you remember what you had for lunch yesterday? Abu-Bakarah, like most people in his time, was illiterate and did not keep a diary. He had been a slave freed by the Prophet and had become extremely prosperous under Islam. But at the time he came up with this hadith, his fortune was seriously threatened in Basrah. It was after the famous Battle of the Camel between the partisans of Ali, the fourth caliph, and an army of rebels led by Ayesha, the widow of the Prophet. Ayesha's forces had suffered a serious defeat in which they lost thirteen thousand men and Basrah had been captured by Ali's forces. It was an excellent time for Abu-Bakarah, who had originally sided with Ayesha, to protect his fortune by switching to the winning side. The hadith he presented became his insurance policy. His fortune remained intact.

The same Abu-Bakarah, however, had a history of untruthfulness. Under Caliph Omar, he had been sentenced to be whipped in public for giving false testimony.

The fact that Ayesha was a woman was in no way considered a reason for disqualifying her from leadership either of the army or of a future government. Even Ali himself never used gender as part of his propaganda against the Prophet's rebellious widow. Ayesha's army included many generals who had fought under the Prophet, men like Talhah and Zubayr. They had never heard the Prophet say that women should not assume leadership. Even such a highly respected man as Abu-Mussa Ash'ari, the governor of Kufah who had been appointed by Ali himself, refused to join the caliph in the civil war.

Abu-Bakarah's hadith is clearly described as a falsehood by Tabari (838–923 A.D.), the greatest historian of Islam and a leading authority on the Muslim system. That Abu-Bakarah was a shameless fabricator can be established when one examines his subsequent inventions. After Ali's assassination and the establishment of Muawyyah as caliph, the same Abu-Bakarah came up with another timely hadith: "I heard the Prophet say that his grandson Hassan would be a man of reconciliation!" This was, of course, a device to persuade Hassan, Ali's eldest son, not to contest Muawyyah's legitimacy as caliph. The reconciliation was quickly arranged and the Umayyid dynasty consolidated its position. Abu-Bakarah was rewarded with a number of highly profitable government contracts.

The hadith invented about women in 656 (year 36 of the Hegira) has been "strengthened" by another anti-woman hadith from Abu-Hureirah, the source of thousands of hadiths. Abu-Hureirah says: "I heard the Prophet say that if three things appear between a man who prays and the *qiblah* [the direction of Mecca], the prayers will be null: women, donkeys, and dogs."

This insulting little piece of male chauvinism would not have merited any attention had it not formed the foundation for hundreds of supposedly learned treatises against women. Imam Muhammad Ghazzali, Ibn Jowzi, and many others have used this hadith of Abu-Hureirah as the basis for their anti-woman teachings. On that basis, they have pronounced women to be unclean, less than human, and even the incarnation of satanic energy on earth. The literature of Islam is full of lengthy papers on whether or not women have souls!

Once again, however, we are faced with a despicable fabrication by a disreputable character. A Yemeni slave called Abd al-Shams (meaning "slave of the sun") was freed by the Prophet and given the nickname Abu-Hureirah ("father of Hureirah") because he often had with him a kitten named Hureirah ("Little Silken One"). He disliked the name and often asked the Prophet to give him a new one. Although Abu-Hureirah was in the Prophet's service as domestic help for less than three years, he later became the source of no fewer than 53,000 hadiths concerning Muhammad—an average of 49 each day! Could anyone take such a man seriously? Unfortunately, many Islamist scholars have done so for centuries and still do so today. Many of Khomeini's positions on a range of social, economic, and ethical issues are based on hadiths made up by Abu-Hureirah. One Arab Islamist, Abdul-Mun'em Saleh al-Ala'i, has written a whole book in defense of Abu-Hureirah. In this book, published in 1983, al-Ala'i claims that "imperialists and Zionists" try to cast doubt on Abu-Hureirah's veracity in order to weaken Islam! How could Muhammad equate women with donkeys and dogs?

In rebutting the basic anti-woman arguments of the fundamentalists, we do not intend to portray Islam as a religion that is especially generous towards women, or to claim that the inferior status of women in Islam is the result of misinterpretation. Islam certainly treats women as inferior, but not in ways that Islamists want us to believe. Those who refuse to acknowledge that one root of women's inequality in Islamic societies could be traced to the Koran itself render no service to Muslims. On the other hand, those who blame Islam exclusively for the existing inequalities are also wrong. Women suffer from inequality in virtually all cultures and all religions of the world. Even the Western democracies with their undoubted achievements in the legal domain still treat women as less than equal. But we must oppose the misuse of Islam as a means of perpetuating and even deepening the injustice done to women.

Some Muslim writers have tried to exculpate Islam by blaming foreign influences for the deterioration in the status of women. Muhammad-Jamal Jayhun blames the Persians, arguing that Muslim women were treated as full equals until the Abbasid Caliphate was Persianized and adopted old Persian traditions. Another writer, Mrs. Aqlal Khalifah, blames the Ottomans, even claiming that Ottoman Turks introduced polygamy to Arab countries they conquered! She forgets explicit Koranic rules about taking up to four wives and a virtually limitless number of concubines. Yet another writer, Mrs. Ghada al-Kharsah, detects a Zoroastrian conspiracy and blames the Barmakid family for having destroyed the equal position of women in Islam.[1]

The truth, however, is that Islam, like other monotheistic faiths, does not treat women as fully equal to men. But it is also true that most modern Islamists, including the Khomeinists, are even more anti-woman than Islam as initially presented by Muhammad and his immediate successors. For example, the rule of stoning women to death on a charge of adultery does not exist in the Koran or the sayings of the Prophet. It is one of the many pre-Islamic Arab rules that Muhammad cast aside. Under Muhammad's rules, adultery is virtually impossible to prove.[2] Even if proven, it is punishable only by the public caning of both partners. Modern-day Islamists, Khomeini among them, have revived the pre-Islamic Arab rule and claimed it as an integral part of Islam's "divine immutable code." The same is true of many other so-called "divine laws" of the Islamic Shariah that could be traced back to pre-Islamic times and were revived and canonized for reasons of expediency many centuries later. Over the past three decades, at least 120 women have been stoned to death in the Islamic Republic on a charge of adultery, often on the basis of hearsay. In other cases, women who have suffered rape have been sentenced to death or sent to prison for supposedly provoking men to manifest their basest instincts.

Wherever possible, the Khomeinist regime has driven women out of the public sphere. Women are no longer allowed to work as judges or serve in senior diplomatic and political positions. A generation ago, female music stars filled the Iranian artistic sky, with such divas as Delkash, Marzieh, Gugush, Mahasti, and Haideh achieving cult status. Today, not a single female singer is allowed to perform outside private homes. Film scripts are written, or censored, to minimize the role of women. Even foreign films are edited to exclude women as far as possible. Women's sports have been ghettoized in a few facilities reserved for the "feeble ones" on the fringes of the cities, complete with high walls to make sure that women are neither seen nor heard.

It is not surprising, therefore, that women have been in the vanguard of the struggle for freedom and democracy in Iran. Tens of thousands of women have been sent to prison over the past three decades and at least 120 have been executed on a charge of "waging war on Allah."

11

The Eternal Conspirator

If women have been vilified because of their gender, Jews have been the object of Islamist hatred and violence because of their faith. This hatred dates back to the days of Muhammad's rule in Yathrib, the cosmopolitan city to which Muhammad fled when he was informed of a plot to kill him in Mecca. The date of that flight, the Hegira, marks the start of the Islamic lunar calendar. Muhammad's choice to settle in Yathrib was not a spontaneous decision; it had been carefully prepared and negotiated over several months. One inducement was the prospect of protection by two friendly tribes who lived around the city. Another was the certainty that the Jews who formed the city's largest community at the time would not resent the addition of a new religious community to their multi-faith hometown. Since Jews did not wish to convert others, they represented no threat to new converts to Islam.

Muhammad's initial friendly ties to the Jews of Yathrib helped his enemies in Mecca spread rumors that portrayed him as a Judeophile who wished to build up his adopted hometown as a commercial rival to his native city, thus realizing one of the oldest dreams of Arabia's Jews. Muhammad had made himself interesting to Jews by linking his religion to Abraham and not pretending that it was a new faith. The fact that almost 90 percent of the Koran is built around Jewish tales, with Jewish prophets in leading roles, must have further reassured the Jews of Yathrib. In the Koran, Moses is mentioned by name over ninety times, while Muhammad is named only once. Joseph is called the "Seal of the Prophets" (*Khatam al-Anbia*), a title that was later reserved for Muhammad himself. Muhammad's initial admiration for the Jews is reflected in one of the most famous hadiths attributed to him: "Hearken what the People of Israel say, and do not question it!"

In time, however, relations between Muhammad and the Jews of Yathrib deteriorated as the new Prophet demanded that non-Muslims convert to his faith or pay a poll tax. Muhammad now asserted that Islam had superseded Judaism and Christianity, the older messages from Allah. Several Jewish tribes reached an accommodation with their former guest and new ruler, and managed to preserve their existence, albeit in reduced circumstances, for several more decades under Islam. Three tribes, however—the Banu-Nuzair, the Banu-Qaynaq, and the Banu-Qurayzah—refused Muhammad's offer and were put to the sword, their women taken as slaves and their property seized as war booty. In the case of the Banu-Nazir, the quarrel seems to have started over money. The Prophet had come to ask for a loan to finance his next operation against the Meccans. Although they had provided similar loans in the past, this time the Jews refused. It seems that Muhammad somehow believed that the Jews wished to assassinate him, and he decided to strike first. Since then, Islamic culture has been steeped in anti-Jewish prejudice, although most Muslim rulers never allowed this to lead to the kind of atrocities that Jews experienced in Christian Europe. In the mind of the average Muslim, whether Sunni or Shiite, the Jew is the quintessential conspirator who, prompted by unspecified dark motives, tries to destroy the existing moral and political order.

Some Western writers believe that hostility towards Jews among Muslims is a byproduct of the conflict over Palestine. But even a cursory look at Islamic literature—in Arabic, Persian, and Turkish—would reveal the Jew as the menacing "other" to be watched and contained, and, when perceived to be dangerous, killed.

Sunni Muslims claim that a Jew named Abdallah Ibn Saba created the cult of Ali and thus the entire Shiite school soon after the death of the Prophet as part of a Jewish conspiracy to divide Muslims and prevent Islam from conquering the world. He is supposed to have asserted that since all prophets had a designated successor, it was not natural for Muhammad to die without naming his heir, and that Ali had been named as Muhammad's successor (*wassi*) not only in the Koran but also in the Old Testament.[1] At the time Ibn Saba is supposed to have conducted his mission, there was no official text of the Koran as yet. At any rate, the Sunni claim that Shiism was a conspiracy plotted by a Jew continues to this day.

Shiites repay the compliment by claiming that Ali was denied his right of immediate succession to Muhammad as a result of a Jewish conspiracy. According to this theory, the Jews approached Abu-Bakr, the man who was to succeed Muhammad as the first caliph, and persuaded him to infiltrate the entourage of the new prophet as their agent with a view to preventing Ali's succession, thus "corrupting" Islam from the start. Here is one Shiite account of the supposed conspiracy: "Before he went into hiding, the twelfth imam said: On the advice of a Jew, he [Abu-Bakr] agreed to verbally recite the confessional formula of Islam, hoping that the Prophet (Peace Be Upon Him) would leave rulership and authority to him. But he [Abu-Bakr] had remained an infidel at heart."[2]

Sunni and Shiite scholars do not say how it was that a single Jew, although cursed by Allah and destined for the deepest recesses of hell, succeeded in splitting the Muslims and dramatically changing the course of Islamic history.

Despite all this, anti-Semitism had never struck root in Iran. Although Jews on occasion were subjected to enforced conversion to Islam, they never suffered the pogroms that their counterparts experienced in Europe. The 1906 democratic constitution had recognized Jews as an Iranian community and reserved one seat for them in the National Consultative Assembly (parliament). There were no Jewish ghettos in Iranian cities, and despite deep-rooted Islamic prejudices, Jews were allowed to live a more or less normal existence. Occasional attempts at inciting anti-Jewish revolts seldom attracted popular support.

Initially, Iranians regarded the creation of Israel as a Jewish state with some ambivalence. They had no love for the Arabs, and they were glad that the British were driven out of another corner of the Middle East. Thus the Iranian government's decision to extend de facto recognition to Israel and allow it to open a special office acting as an embassy in Tehran in 1949 sparked little opposition even from the mullahs. At the time, Iran's leftist parties, including the Communist Tudeh (Masses) and the social-democratic Zahmatkeshan (Laborers), welcomed the creation of Israel as a victory for the global anticolonial movement. Leftist Iranians pointed to the fact that Israel had a socialist government and expressed admiration for the kibbutzim movement as a model for destroying the feudal landlords in Iran itself. Over the years, many figures of the Iranian left, including a few who later joined the Khomeinist revolution, visited the Jewish state at the invitation of the Israeli trade union movement, the Histadruth, and came back with glowing accounts of a new nation using religious faith in the service of socialism.[3] Although some prominent mullahs did express displeasure at the creation of the Jewish state, the Iranian clergy did not adopt a systematically anti-Israeli position. Khomeini himself never made an anti-Israeli remark until the early 1960s. In the early 1950s, he had established close ties with the Fedayeen Islam (Self-Sacrificers for Islam), a Shiite terrorist group modeled on the Egyptian Muslim Brotherhood (Ikhwan al-Moslemeen). The group did make occasional noises about fighting "the Jews in Palestine" but never took any action in that direction.

In the early 1960s, hatred of Israel was injected into Iranian politics as part of the Cold War. In the 1950s, Iran had joined the Baghdad Pact, later to become the Central Treaty Organization (CENTO), thus emerging as part of the *cordon sanitaire* that the Western powers, led by the United States, were building around a hostile USSR. Although the United States was not a full member of the alliance—which initially grouped together Britain, Turkey, Iraq, Iran, and Pakistan—it was clear that the pact was part of Washington's strategy to contain Moscow. (Iraq withdrew from the alliance after the 1958 coup d'état that destroyed the pro-West monarchy in Baghdad.) By 1960, three key Arab states, Egypt, Syria and Iraq, had switched to the Soviet side and embarked on an aggressive campaign of propaganda and sabotage against pro-West regimes in Turkey, Iran, and Saudi Arabia. Having gained momentum thanks to a military coup that ended the pro-British imamate in Yemen, the new Arab radical regimes used the slogan "liberating Palestine" as a war cry to rally Arab and other Muslim masses to their side.

In 1960, the Egyptian dictator Gamal Abdel Nasser, architect of pan-Arab nationalism, created a special unit for a massive propaganda war against the shah's regime in Iran. The state-owned radio Sowt al-Arab (Voice of the Arabs), broadcasting from Cairo, launched a special Persian-language program to attack Iran and alert its people to the "crimes committed by Jews in Palestine." Egyptian secret services established contact with Iranian opposition figures both inside and outside Iran with offers of financial and political support. Emissaries visited Qom to sound out the mullahs, some of whom had never forgiven the shah's father, Reza Shah Pahlavi, for having banned the hijab and the turban and curtailed the influence of the clergy in the 1930s. At least one emissary also contacted Muhammad Mossadeq, a veteran politician who had served as prime minister under the shah on two occasions but ended up as a symbol of opposition to the Pahlavis. (Mossadeq angrily turned down Nasser's offer of money and support.)

Meanwhile, the Soviet Union, too, had altered its initially friendly policy towards Israel and increasingly identified the Jewish state as an active member of the "enemy camp" led by the United States. As a result, the Iranian left, which had been ambivalent towards Israel, also adopted a hostile position. By the time Israel had defeated its Arab enemies in the Six Day War of 1967, it had become a prime target of attack by both Islamist and leftist anti-shah groups in Iran. As far as the small number of radical anti-shah mullahs was concerned, Israel provided a convenient excuse for presenting their deep-rooted anti-Jewish sentiments as nothing but political opposition to a Jewish state that had usurped the rights of the Palestinians.

The anti-Israel position of Iranian opposition groups, both Islamist and leftist, hardened over the years. Hundreds of young Iranian radicals enrolled in special courses in guerrilla warfare and urban sabotage run by various Palestinian groups, including Yasser Arafat's Al-Fatah

(Victory). The more leftist opponents of the shah received training in camps run by George Habash's Marxist People's Front for the Liberation of Palestine (PFLP) in Lebanon. (The program ended in 1975, when the PFLP was put on the shah's payroll on the advice of Saudi Arabia's King Faisal Ibn Abdul-Aziz.)

When Khomeini launched his first revolt against the shah's social and political reforms in 1962, he used hatred of Israel as a major theme in his campaign. He claimed that the shah was working for the Jews and Baha'is and against Islam. Forced into exile, first in Turkey and later in Iraq, Khomeini had greater opportunities to meet Arab, especially Palestinian, emissaries who offered him support. From 1970 onwards, Colonel Muammar Kaddhafi's regime in Libya emerged as a major source of support for Iranian opposition groups, including the Khomeinists. In 1971, the Soviet-sponsored Tudeh (Masses) Party concluded a tactical alliance with Khomeini, then in exile in Iraq. The Tudeh emissary, Reza Radmanesh, underlined "joint opposition to the existence of Israel" as a key factor in the unity of Marxist and Islamist opponents of the shah. The informal alliance was later expanded to include an even more surprising partner, the cashiered general Teymur Bakhtiar, a former head of the shah's secret service who, motivated by personal ambition, had turned against his former patron. A refugee in Lebanon but a frequent visitor to Iraq, Bakhtiar had to adopt an anti-Israeli profile to please his Arab protectors.[4]

Faced with the combined opposition of the Soviet bloc and its radical Arab allies in the context of the Cold War, the shah and his advisors soon identified Israel as a strategic ally. Like Iran at the time, Israel did not want a Middle East dominated by pan-Arabism, from which Iranians, Turks, Kurds, Christians, and Jews would be excluded. The pan-Arab regimes called for the destruction not only of Israel but also of Iran as a nation-state. Nasser invented the term "Arabian Gulf" to replace "Persian Gulf," the historic and universally recognized name for the body of water that separates Iran from the oil-rich Arab monarchies. He and his counterparts in Syria and Iraq also called for the secession of Iran's oil-rich province of Khuzestan, which they dubbed Arabistan (Land of the Arabs). By 1965, Iranian intelligence services had ample evidence that radical Arab regimes were financing and training members of several Iranian opposition groups. In 1968, Arab radicals also launched the so-called People's Front for the Liberation of Occupied Arabian Gulf (PFLOAG), a Marxist guerrilla outfit whose members were trained in Cuba, North Korea, East Germany, and South Yemen, with the aim of toppling the Sultan of Oman and seizing control of the strategic Strait of Hormuz, the chokepoint of Iran's oil-based economy. Seen from Tehran, it was obvious that Iran and Israel shared the same enemies.

Because Israel was perceived as a friend of the shah, his opponents had no difficulty in regarding the Jewish state as an enemy. While the left tried to present its opposition to Israel in secular terms, Khomeini, emerging as the principal spokesman for radical mullahs, seized every opportunity to foment hatred of Jews as a whole. In a sermon in Qom on April 13, 1963, he told his supporters: "I know that you do not want Iran to lie under the boots of the Jews." Later he called the shah "a Jew in disguise," accusing him of taking orders from Israel. He claimed that the central political theme of contemporary life was an elaborate and highly complex conspiracy by the Jews—"who controlled everything"— to "emasculate Islam" and dominate the world thanks to the natural wealth of the Muslim nations. In 1963, he told a crowd of theological students that their fight was not just against the shah but also against the Jewish state. "Israel does not want the Koran to survive in this country," Khomeini said. "It is destroying us. It is destroying you and the nation. It wants to take possession of the economy. It wants to demolish our trade and agriculture. It wants to grab the wealth of the country." Always careful to trace his current hatred of Israel to Islam's deep-rooted suspicion of the Jews, Khomeini accused them of having tried to falsify the Koran "just as they had falsified the Torah." He also accused them of leading a global campaign against Islam. Later, in his first openly political work, *Islamic Government*, the ayatollah claimed that Jews wished to dominate the world, adding that since "they are a cunning and resourceful group of people, I fear that . . . they may one day achieve their goal." Then in September 1977, he declared, "The Jews have grasped the world with both hands and are devouring it with an insatiable appetite; they are devouring America and have now turned their attention to Iran and still they are not satisfied." In August 1978, as the Khomeinist revolution gathered momentum, a Persian translation of the *Protocols of the Elders of Zion*, the notorious anti-Semitic tract forged by the Russian tsar's secret services in the nineteenth century, was printed and widely circulated in Iran. The man who financed it was a certain Haji Mahdi Araqi, a close associate of Khomeini.[5]

In 1980, soon after the start of the Iran-Iraq war, official propaganda began to portray Khomeini as the leader who would realize the Arab dream of wiping Israel off the map of the Middle East. For some fourteen centuries, Iranians had known Jerusalem as Beit al-Muqaddas (House of the Holy). The Khomeinist regime abandoned that name in favor of Quds (Holy), the Arab name for Jerusalem.[6] It also launched the slogan "Through Karbala to Jerusalem," to underline its claim that the war was really aimed at liberating Palestine and destroying Israel.

To back this claim, the traditional machines for fabricating hadiths were set in motion. Here is one hadith as narrated by Ayatollah Mahdi Rezvani, deputy chairman of the Islamic Majlis's Defense Committee, in July 1982:

> His Holiness Imam Jaafar Sadeq spoke thus: Before the rise of His Holiness the Mahdi (May Allah hasten his return), a man from the noble progeny of the Prophet will rise in Iran. His soldiers will fight for eight or eighteen months, weapons in hand, heading for Beit al-Muqaddas [Jerusalem]. There is also a saying from the pulpit by the Commander of the Faithful [the first Imam, Ali] that at some point Jews coming from the West will conquer Palestine and set up an Israelite state there. On such a day, Muslims are bound by the chains of colonialism. Again, His Holiness Imam Jaafar Sadeq said: When Israel spreads

corruption on earth, God the Most High will dispatch His most ardent special believers who are inflexible and war-seeking from Qom to Iraq. These will first conquer Iraq and then ally with Arabs to liberate Palestine. When they enter Palestine, they will go house to house and bunker to bunker in search of Zionist Jews to pull them out and cut their heads like buffaloes until not a single Jew is left alive in Palestine. The Holy Prophet Himself said: I see a people who start a war in the context of a revolution, earning divine victories from beginning to the end. The leader of this revolution is Iranian and sends his forces to Jerusalem.[7]

Rezvani's forecast that the war would last eight to eighteen months proved wrong. The Iran-Iraq war, provoked by Khomeini but started by Saddam Hussein, lasted eight years, claiming a million lives and ending in a draw. The ayatollah's "Volunteers for Martyrdom" got nowhere near the Iraqi city of Karbala, let alone liberating Jerusalem.

The "cursed Jew," however, came to Iran's support whenever he found an opportunity. In 1981, Israeli bombers destroyed Iraq's French-built nuclear center at Osirak, south of Baghdad, preventing Saddam Hussein from making the bomb that he had always said he needed to make up for his country's geographic and demographic disadvantages against Iran. (That Saddam Hussein would not have hesitated to hit Iran with nuclear weapons was later illustrated by his decision to use banned chemical weapons that killed over 50,000 Iranians and maimed more than 100,000 others.) In 1985 and 1986, Israel also helped persuade the Reagan administration in Washington to ease a U.S. ban on the sale of arms to Iran. In an operation designed by Israel, a large quantity of U.S.-made antitank missiles were shipped to Iran, helping the Iranians neutralize Saddam Hussein's superior armored divisions and taking the war into Iraqi territory. Israel had to stop its military aid, however, when a Tehran faction led by Ayatollah Montazeri leaked details of the secret deals, also involving the Reagan administration, to discredit the faction led by Khomeini who had approved the scheme. (This led to the so-called Irangate scandal.) Ahmadinejad, then serving in the Islamic Revolutionary Guard Corps (IRGC), was among the first Iranian troops to enter Iraqi territory, partly thanks to weapons shipped from Israel.

Nevertheless, as Israel celebrated its sixtieth birthday on May 8, 2008, Ahmadinejad described the Jewish state as "a dead rat." Addressing members of the Islamic Majlis, he said: "The Zionist regime, having been slapped by the nation of Lebanon, is like a dead rat that has reached the end of the road." Mocking Israel's birthday celebrations, he added: "Today, the very philosophy of the Zionist regime's existence is being questioned. This usurper and fake regime is destined for decline and fall." Referring to President Bush's decision to attend Israel's birthday party, Ahmadinejad said: "Those who think they revive this stinking corpse with birthday festivities are badly mistaken. And those who take part in such festivities should know that their names will be registered in the list of criminals. They should know that regional nations hate this fake and criminal regime, and if the smallest and briefest chance is given to regional nations, they will destroy [it]." In the same speech, he linked the "elimination of Israel" with his own "mission" to prepare the world for the return of the Hidden Imam. He said: "Our mission in the arena of foreign affairs is to present the idea of Pure Islam as the only path for the salvation of mankind to all nations. We have to smash the existing models in the world."[8]

Indeed, soon after his election as president, Ahmadinejad had grabbed world headlines by describing Israel as "a cancerous tumor" that had to be wiped off the map. Addressing a conference called "The World Without Zionism" held October 2005 in Tehran, he described the creation of Israel as "a move by the Oppressor of the World [the United States] against the Muslim world." He said, "The clashes in the occupied land are part of a war of destiny. The outcome of hundreds of years of war will be defined in Palestinian land." He then recalled that Khomeini had said: "The usurper regime that occupies Jerusalem must be wiped off the slate of time."

Ahmadinejad predicted that "the annihilation of the Zionist regime will come" with events that he did not specify. "The Muslim *ummah* will not allow its historic enemy to live in its heartland," he said, claiming that the Israel-Palestine conflict was part of a bigger war between Islam and the United States. He warned Palestinian and other Arab leaders that making peace with Israel could expose them to "the seething wrath of Muslim masses." "Anyone who signs a treaty that recognizes the entity of Israel has signed the surrender of the Muslim world," he shouted.

Reviving Khomeini's bellicose rhetoric, Ahmadinejad promised "full and total victory" in what he called a "historic war" over who would set the agenda for mankind: Islam or the oppressor infidels led by the United States as manipulated by the Jews. This war, he said, "dates back hundreds of years. Sometimes Islam has advanced. Sometimes nobody was winning. Unfortunately, over the past three hundred years, the world of Islam has been in retreat," he lamented. "One hundred years ago the last trench of Islam fell, when the oppressors went towards the creation of the Zionist regime. They are now using it as an advance base to spread their aims in the heart of the Islamic world." At the same time, he assured his audience, "There is no doubt that the new wave [of attacks] in Palestine will soon wipe off this spot of dishonor [Israel] from the face of the Islamic world."[9]

Ahmadinejad's comments stirred up a storm of protest all over the world, including within Iran itself. In an attempt to cool things down, the Supreme Guide Ali Khamenehi came out with a statement apparently distancing the regime from the president. Speaking in November 2005, Khamenehi implicitly ruled out any Iranian attack on Israel:

> We hold a fair and logical stance on the issue of Palestine.
> Several decades ago, the Egyptian statesman Gamal Abdel
> Nasser, who was the most popular Arab personality, stated in
> his slogans that the Egyptians would throw the Jewish usurpers
> of Palestine into the sea. Some years later, Saddam Hussein, the
> most hated Arab figure, said that he would set half the Palestin-

ian land on fire. But we would not approve of either of these two remarks. We believe, according to our Islamic principles, that neither throwing the Jews into the sea nor setting the Palestinian land on fire is logical and reasonable. Our position is that the Palestinian people should regain their rights. Palestine belongs to Palestinians, and the fate of Palestine should also be determined by the Palestinian people. . . . We have suggested that all native Palestinians, whether they are Muslims, Christians, or Jews, should be allowed to take part in a general referendum before the eyes of the world and decide on a Palestinian government. Any government that is the result of this referendum will be a legitimate government.[10]

It was not hard to see that Khamanehi's "fair and logical" solution to the Israel-Palestine problem, if implemented, would achieve the same goal as set by Khomeini and Ahmadinejad: the destruction of the Jewish state. Palestinians from all over the world as well as those in Israel, the West Bank, and Gaza would be allowed to decide whether or not the Jewish state should live. Non-Israeli Jews, however, would be excluded from the proposed referendum. Khamenehi's formula was not original. It was first proposed in 1989 by the Libyan dictator Muammar Kaddhafi, who called it "the democratic way to end the life of the Zionist enemy."

In any case, Khamenehi's statement may have been little more than a tactical move to ease international pressure on the Islamic Republic. Soon after the Supreme Guide had spoken, his senior representative, Muhammad-Hassan Rahimian, told an audience of Khomeinist mullahs in Tehran that a war with Israel was inevitable. "The Jew remains the most obstinate enemy of the pious," he said. "And the main war shall determine the destiny of mankind. . . . The reappearance of the twelfth imam will lead to a war between Israel and the Shiites."[11]

More importantly, Ahmadinejad himself did not seem to take much notice of Khamenehi's pirouette. In several interviews with the world media, including American television networks, he refused to deny that he desired Israel's destruction. To underline his determination to put the fight against Israel at the heart of his presidency, Ahmadinejad devoted most of his speech at an Islamic summit conference hosted by King Abdullah Ibn Abdul-Aziz of Saudi Arabia in Mecca in December 2005 to what he called "the Zionist threat to Islam." He claimed that most Israelis were European Jews who had no place in "the heart of Islam." He then dismissed the Holocaust as a myth invented by the West:

> Why have they come to the very heart of the Islamic world
> and are committing crimes against the dear Palestine using
> their bombs, rockets, missiles, and sanctions? . . . The European
> countries have imposed the illegally established Zionist regime
> on the oppressed nation of Palestine. If you have committed the
> crimes, then give them a piece of your land somewhere in Eu-
> rope or America and Canada or Alaska to set up their own state
> there. They have invented a myth that Jews were massacred
> and place this above God, religions and the prophets. The West
> has given more significan ce to the myth of the genocide of
> the Jews, even more significance than to God, religion, and the
> prophets; [it] deals very severely with those who deny this myth
> but does not do anything to those who deny God, religion, and
> the prophets. If you have burned the Jews, why don't you give a
> piece of Europe, the United States, Canada, or Alaska to Israel?
> Our question is, if you have committed this huge crime, why
> should the innocent nation of Palestine pay for this crime?[12]

Ahmadinejad's "Holocaust denial" speech raised another and bigger storm. Once again, some Islamic Republic officials, including the foreign minister, Manuchehr Mottaki, with some Western "useful idiots" in tow, tried to claim that the president had not really meant what he said. Mottaki claimed that Ahmadinejad had tried to draw attention to how the West was trying to "impose its narrative of events." Most of the "useful idiots" played semantic games with the president's phraseology and ended up blaming the West and Zionists for distorting his views. They claimed that truth was relative and that each culture was entitled to its own version of it. Ahmadinejad, however, would not let himself be redefined by Westernized bureaucrats like Mottaki, or by "useful idiots" from American universities. While self-appointed exegetes were telling the world that he neither wanted Israel wiped off the map nor doubted the Holocaust had happened, one of Ahmadinejad's senior advisors was preparing the first Holocaust denial conference ever organized by a member state of the United Nations. The man in charge was one Muhammad-Ali Ramin, a German-educated militant of the Iranian branch of Hezballah with close connections to neo-Nazi groups in Germany. For years, Ramin was advisor on psychological warfare to Ali Larijani during the latter's tenure as director of the state-owned Islamic Radio and Television in Tehran.[13]

Ramin's hatred of the Jews, as reflected in the standard speech he has been delivering at Hezballah seminars and "courses for cadres," is structured around traditional European anti-Semitic themes rather than the more superficial dislike and distrust of Jews current in the Muslim countries of the Middle East. For him, the Jew is the quintessential "other" not only in religion but also in ethnic and racial terms. For years, Ramin had proposed holding a Holocaust denial conference, but both of Ahmadinejad's immediate predecessors, presidents Rafsanjani and Khatami, had rejected the idea. Ahmadinejad had a more favorable view, and on December 12, 2006, he addressed the final session of the conference that Ramin had dreamed of and organized with government money.

The list of participants at the Tehran conference reads like a who's who not only of those who oppose Israel on political grounds but also of individuals who make no secret of their racial and religious hatred for Jews. Many of Ramin's neo-Nazi friends from Germany, Belgium, and France were in attendance, thanks to all-expenses-paid invitations from the president of the Islamic Republic. Present also were a crowd of self-styled historians who make a living out of their claim that the Holocaust either did not happen or, if it did, was not as terrible as the Jews said. One such "esteemed scholar," as described by the conference brochure, the American Veronica Clark, claimed that the Jews had made money in Auschwitz. Another, the Frenchman Robert Faurisson, compared the Holocaust to one of Lafontaine's fables and other fairy tales. The former Ku Klux Klan leader David Duke informed the audience of how the Jews influenced American policies, and Frederick Toben, the Australian president of the Holocaust Denial Institute, spoke of how Jews used "the myth of genocide" as a "murder weapon" against others, notably the Palestinians. A Belgian convert to Islam, Leonardo Clerici, electrified the audience with his prediction that Jews were destined for ultimate destruction. Also present were members of the anti-Israel Orthodox Jewish sect Neturei Karta, in their traditional gear. They told anyone who wished to listen, including reporters from the Islamic media, that although they did not deny the Holocaust, they prayed for the destruction of Israel.

The organizers of the conference also offered an exhibition of photos, books, and "documents" supposedly proving that the Holocaust never happened. These were meant to support the real theme of the conference: that Israel could claim no legitimacy based on a crime that had never taken place. Ramin made no secret of his belief that "the issue of Holocaust could be solved with the destruction of Israel."

In his speech, Ahmadinejad praised the conference for shaking "the very raison d'être" of the Jewish state.[14] He added: "The life-curve of the Zionist regime has started its descent, and it is now on a downward slope towards its fall. . . . The Zionist regime will be wiped out, and humanity will be liberated."[15] Ahmadinejad's belief that the fate of Israel would be determined in the broader war that Islam was supposed to wage against the infidels was reflected in his first substantial speech on his policies as president in October 2005: "We are engaged in the process of a historic war," he said. "This war has been going on for hundreds of years. We must measure the depth of the disgrace that the enemy [has inflicted on us] so that our sacred rage rises like a wave and strikes our enemy."[16]

One of Ahmadinejad's predecessors as president of the Islamic

Republic, Hashemi Rafsanjani, had evoked the prospect of a thermonuclear exchange that would end up with Israel's annihilation. Speaking in December 2001, Rafsanjani asserted that "the use of even one nuclear bomb inside Israel would destroy everything" while the Muslim world, if attacked in retaliation, could easily afford to lose millions of "martyrs." He concluded: "It is not illogical to contemplate such an eventuality." And Rafsanjani is often regarded in the West as a moderate.

12

Esther and the King

The idea of the Jew as the quintessential enemy of the natural order is a key theme in the Islamic Republic's propaganda. The Ministry of Islamic Guidance and Culture has financed the publication of hundreds of books accusing the Jews of having "betrayed God" by rebelling against his commandments. Jews are blamed for the death of Jesus, although the Koran, and Islam in general, never made such a charge—if only because they believe the Son of Mary did not die on the cross at all. Khomeinist literature accuses Jews of having "altered" the sacred scriptures brought by Moses and Jesus and having attempted to falsify the Koran as well. Khomeinists also claim that Jews planned the Crusades in order to divide the Muslim world. Conveniently ignored are the fact that Iran was not involved in most of the Crusades, and that in some of them it sided with Christian powers against rival Sunni Muslim caliphates and emirates. Because they import a good part of their anti-Semitism from the West, Khomeinists pay no attention to the fact that no Muslim historian ever claimed that the Jews played any role in the Crusades except that of helping the Muslims whenever and wherever they could.

Jews are credited or blamed for many major events in the past three thousand years. Khalkhali claimed that the Jews sent "the beautiful spy Esther" to seduce Cyrus, a Persian princeling of no consequence, to encourage him to create an empire, liberate the Jews from Babylonian captivity, and help them rebuild their temple in Jerusalem. "Cyrus was young and full of lust," the ayatollah writes, "and his blood boiled with passion for the Jewess." Esther was so effective that not only did she succeed in persuading Cyrus to give up his homosexuality and become heterosexual, but also helped him build his empire and release the Jews from bondage.[1]

Khomeinist literature blames the Jews for the French Revolution of 1789 and the Bolshevik Revolution of 1917. It claims that Jews invented Communism through Marx, who divided mankind according to class rather than religious belief, as in the Islamic system. Khomeini himself claimed that the Universal Declaration of Human Rights, and the idea that all human beings are equal, was a Jewish invention designed to enable Jews to achieve high positions in societies where their minority status limited their progress. He said that a cabal of Jewish conspirators prompted the British-Indian novelist Salman Rushdie to write *The Satanic Verses*, for which Khomeini issued a death fatwa against him. The 9/11 attacks on New York and Washington were launched by Jews to persuade the United States to start a war of conquest against Muslim nations. Jews paid Danish artists to come up with cartoons of the Prophet Muhammad. Jews have been buying land in Iraq under American occupation in the hope of expanding Israel to the River Tigris. The destruction of the Mosque of the Two Imams, a Shiite shrine in Samarrah, Iraq, was also the work of Jews. According to Ahmadinejad, "The Zionists have placed themselves in control of a substantial part of the financial, cultural, and media sectors." Having blackmailed Western democracies for sixty years, they are now trying to become rulers of the whole world.

Despite the presentation of the Jew by the Khomeinist regime as the ultimate "other" and object of hatred, anti-Semitism has failed to find a wide audience in Iran. Leaving aside what one might call "vulgar anti-Semitism," there is no evidence that hatred of the Jews has any echoes in contemporary Persian literature and art. Part of this is because the overwhelming majority of Iranian writers, poets, and other "producers of culture" reject Khomeinism as a form of anti-Iranian fascism. The main reason, however, is that the average Iranian, though he may sympathize with the widely and constantly reported sufferings of the Palestinians, cannot identify with the Arabs, whom he regards as an ancestral foe. The fact that the only major war that Iran has fought in the past three hundred years was started by an Arab nation—Iraq under Saddam Hussein—makes it hard for most Iranians to contemplate an Irano-Arab front against Israel.

So, why has the Khomeinist regime tried to present itself as an advocate of the most radical anti-Israeli, not to say anti-Jewish, strategy? The answer lies in the regional and even global ambitions of a regime in search of hegemony and empire. If Iran were to use Iranian culture and the Persian language as vehicles for projecting those ambitions, the regime would have to tone down its Islamic pretensions, thus losing its principal claim to legitimacy.

Iranian nationalists have often dreamed of recreating the Persian Empire, albeit in its most modest version, and they also seek recognition by the West as a member of the broader Indo-European family of peoples. The author and journalist Rahmat Mostafavi remarked that the word "Iran" came from the same root as the word "Eire," the name adopted by the Irish Republic. Both meant "Land of the Noble," and signaled the "common ancestry of Iranians and Europeans from the Caspian Sea to the Atlantic Ocean." Mostafavi also claimed that Iran was separated from its "kith and kin" in Europe by "alien races such as Turks and Arabs." The poet Lotfali Suratgar demanded that European nations recognize Iran's "heroic resistance on their behalf" against invaders from the depth of Asia:

> For a thousand years, as the world slept,_
> Iran guarded the gates of Europe
> Against the invading Tatars.

There was, however, no prospect of the Western European powers accepting Iran as an equal ally and partner. French presidents from Charles De Gaulle to Valéry Giscard d'Estaing visited Tehran to shower the shah with praise and laud Iran's "great contributions to culture and civilization." All German chancellors from Ludwig Erhard to Helmut Schmidt also visited Iran, as did the queen of England and senior British political leaders. The European Common Market acknowledged Iran's importance by offering it the status of an associate partner. That was not good enough for the Iranians, who realized that no matter what they did, they would never become more than a small fish in the big European pond. Today, with Iran stuck in one of the darkest nights of its long history, it is even less likely that Europe, now a club of twenty-seven nations and the most powerful economic bloc in the world, would offer anything more enticing.

For obvious reasons, the Khomeinist regime cannot play the cards of Iranian culture and the Persian language. And even if it did so, this might generate some enthusiasm for Iranian leadership only in a few places, notably Afghanistan and Tajikistan.

What about Shiism as a vehicle for Iran's ambitions? Here, too, the limitations are evident. An Iran that claims leadership only in the name of Shiism might, at most, attract the support of some 15 percent of the world's estimated 1.3 billion Muslims. Even then, it is not at all certain that Arab Shiites, who form a majority of the population only in Iraq and Bahrain, would wish to be led by a non-Arab power. Thus, Iran cannot claim regional leadership in the name of either Iranianism or Shiism.

One theme that Iranian nationalists share with their Khomeinist enemies is that of "being alone." Most nations are part of a larger family that could provide them with adequate space to ensure their security and help them achieve their full potential. Most nations of Europe, sharing historical, cultural, and religious roots, have come together in the European Union. More broadly, the Western nations, led by the United States, form a common family under the banner of the Atlantic Alliance or the Organization for Security and Cooperation in Europe (OSCE). The Arabs have their League of Arab Nations. In the New World, there is the Organization of American States (OAS), plus a number of regional groupings. African nations nurture their common roots through the African Union. Turkey is part of a family of Turkic nations stretching from Europe to Central Asia. China and India, though too big to need anyone, are nevertheless projecting power and influence through their respective "kith and kin" communities around the world. Iran, being Persian and Shiite, is all alone.

The only way that Iran could claim leadership was by casting itself as an Islamic power seeking a new world order as shaped by Islam rather than the "Judeo-Christian conspiracy." Iran's claim of leadership in the

Muslim world is not fanciful. For centuries, Iran in its various incarnations was one of only three nations—along with the Ottoman Empire and, from the nineteenth century onwards, Egypt—that set the agenda for the Muslim world. The Ottoman Empire no longer exists. Its successor, the Turkish Republic, advertising its secularism, has been out of the Islamic orbit for too long to seek a leadership role among Muslim nations. Having dropped its Arabic alphabet in favor of the Latin, Turkey has also rewritten its history to de-emphasize the role of Islam. Even under a conservative pro-Islam government, Turkey's ambition to become a member of the European Union remains unchanged. Egypt, too, has dropped out of the competition for the leadership of Islam. More than half a century of autocratic rule, from Nasser to Hosni Mubarak, has turned Egypt into an Islamic no-man's land.

None of the other Muslim nations is in a position to claim the leadership of Islam. Saudi Arabia has a great deal of money but a small population. It is also hamstrung by its Wahhabism, which a majority of Muslims regard with suspicion if not outright hostility. Moreover, its Wahhabi religious establishment has failed to produce anything resembling a current of creative theological thought.[2] The four most populous Muslim countries are Indonesia, Bangladesh, Pakistan, and Nigeria, while India has three times as many Muslims as does Iran. However, none of these countries ever played a leading role in Islam or has the intellectual wherewithal to claim it today. Iran's leadership claim could be based on a number of facts. Even today, Iran has one of the two or three largest economies in the Muslim world. It is the fifth largest Muslim nation in terms of population. Of the fifty-seven Muslim nations of the world, twelve are Iran's neighbors. Iran is the only Muslim nation to have direct geographical links with all major components of the Muslim *ummah*: Arabs, Turks and Turkic peoples, and Central and South Asian nations.

While Khomeini believed that only "permanent revolution" could ensure the survival of the Islamist rule in Iran, his succesors Banisadr, Rafsanjani, and Khatami tilted towards the idea of "revolution in one country." They argued that the Khomeinist system still had to crush its enemies at home, especially Iranian nationalists and the middle classes seduced by Western ideas. Ahmadinejad, on the other hand, follows the example of Rajai, the second president of the Islamic Republic, who believed that the Khomeinist revolution in Iran could achieve its "divine mission" only by spreading to other Muslim countries. Boasting that he is "the second Rajai," Ahmadinejad regards "exporting revolution" as necessary for the regime's survival in Iran itself.

The idea of promoting Iran as the leader of the Muslim world had even tempted the shah, albeit only briefly. In 1968, the shah led the move that culminated in the first Islamic Summit, held in Rabat, the capital of Morocco, in April 1969. He also became one of the founders of the Organization of the Islamic Conference (OIC). By the early 1970s, however, he had decided that playing the Islamic card could lead to a clash with his Western allies, thus leaving Iran exposed in the face of the permanent Soviet threat, while emboldening his domestic enemies among the mullahs. Nevertheless, encouraged by Iran's rising economic and military power, the shah developed hegemonic dreams of his own. In 1975 he came up with a proposal for the creation of a "Common Market of the Indian Ocean," to encompass some fifty African, Middle Eastern, and Asian nations, including India and Australia.[3]

The shah realized that the historic decline of Islam as a force on the international stage had ended in the mid-twentieth century and could be followed by a period of rapid ascent, provided that Muslim nations modernized their economies. It was in this context that the shah thought of promoting Iran as the leader of an Islam in the ascendant. At the start of the twentieth century, there were only two independent Muslim nations: Iran and the Ottoman Empire.[4] By the end of the century, that number had risen to fifty-seven. In the same period, the number of Muslims rose from some 8 percent of the world's population to almost 25 percent. (Iran's own population rose from six million to almost seventy million.) Significant Muslim minorities began to take shape in over a hundred non-Muslim countries around the globe. The rising importance of oil—of which some 60 percent of all known reserves happen to be in Muslim lands—added a new dimension to the "return of Islam" as a force to reckon with on the international stage. Despite all this, however, the shah could never have sold the idea of Iranian leadership in the name of Islam. His own ambiguous attitude towards Islam represented an insurmountable hurdle, as did Iran's majority Shiite faith, and the nationalistic narrative of his regime.

Promoting Iran under a Khomeinist regime as the leader of Islam is no easy task either. Few Muslims, even among Shiites, would endorse the claim made in the Khomeinist constitution that the Iranian Supreme Guide is the spiritual and temporal leader of the *ummah* throughout the world. Iran's majority Shiite faith remains as much of a hurdle as it was under the shah. This is why some Khomeinist reformists, like Abdul-Karim Sorush, suggest that the regime modify aspects of its Shiite discourse to reassure the Sunnis. That, however, could threaten one of the main pillars of the regime's claim of legitimacy. What the Khomeinist regime needs is a temporal, that is to say political, message with which to sell the idea of Iran's leadership to other Muslim nations. Ahmadinejad knows that Muslims, though divided, all yearn after some vague political unity that might revive the real or imagined Golden Age and make Islam the master of the world. In other words, while there could never be a unified religion named Islam, a united political movement under the label of Islam is quite possible.

Ahmadinejad is not the first to make such an analysis. Go to any mosque anywhere in the world, including those in European and American cities, and what you hear is a political, not religious, discourse. You would hear of the sufferings of the Palestinians and, occasionally, Kashmiris and Chechens, and how the infidel West is trying to undermine Islam with "Islamophobia." Translations of articles and books by well-known anti-Americans, some from the United States itself, are read aloud and commented upon to shed more light on the "constant conspiracies of the American Great Satan" to destroy Islam and devour the world. Because Islamic theology died over a century ago, you are unlikely to hear much that resembles a proper religious discourse. To be sure, God often makes a cameo appearance, mostly to promise to burn Israel and bring down the United States. Of what the Persian poet Nasser Khosrow called "the "Science of Faith," however, you would find no sign.[5] What you would see is Islamism, a political movement that dreams of revenge and reconquest. The modern Islamist dismisses all talk of spirituality as "a plot hatched by the infidels" to demobilize the Muslim masses and frustrate their efforts to destroy Israel, reconquer Spain, liberate Kashmir, and eventually rule mankind under the banner of Muhammad. Khomeini's dream and that of Ahmadinejad is to gain control of the global Islamist movement in the name of common *political* goals. The starting point of this quest for leadership must be Iran's geopolitical habitat in western Asia, a region where Arabic-speaking peoples are a majority.

Now, what is the message that might galvanize those Arabs? Moderate politicians and movements might suggest such themes as democracy, human rights, economic development, and the rule of law. These, however, are not themes that a regime such as the one Khomeini imposed on Iran could adopt without provoking derision. Such a regime must appeal to religious bigotry, xenophobia, class hatred, and whatever other base instincts are most easily provoked.

In the late 1950s and early 1960s, a generation of Islamists had cut its ideological teeth by adopting the cause of Algerian independence against France. Some—like Banisadr, Qotbzadeh, and Yazdi—adored Franz Fanon before they discovered Khomeini. Even then, few Iranians sympathized with the Algerian National Liberation Front and its use of terror as an instrument of politics. The Islamists were enraged in 1962 when Hassan Arsanjani, the shah's minister for agriculture, unveiled a plan to invite forty thousand of the French living in Algeria, known as *pieds-noirs*, to come and settle in Iran, where they would be given farmland and credit to build a new life. Today, however, there is no Muslim people engaged in an anticolonial war of liberation; or if there is, as with the Chechens in Russia and the Uighur in China, they have no kith-and-kin who could be mobilized for a global war against the infidels.[6]

The only theme that the Khomeinist regime might use to find an audience among the Arabs is one that has resonated with at least some of them since the 1950s: hatred of Israel. Israel has all the qualifications to become the ideal scapegoat for the Arab audience that Ahmadinejad seeks. To start with, Israel is Jewish and thus presumed heir to "the Jews who made Muhammad suffer in Medina." Israel is also the "outsider" because millions of its citizens, though perhaps no longer a majority, have Western backgrounds. Being a democracy also makes Israel the opposite of the despotic Khomeinist system. Having adopted a capitalist market economy, Israel is perceived as a challenge to the Islamo-fascistic populism that Khomeinists present as their political ideology. In any case, Israel must be doomed because it has already had a woman as prime minister, and, as Muhammad is supposed to have said, a nation ruled by a woman is bound to perish.

Because of all these factors, the Khomeinists see Israel as something more than a mere political enemy or rival. Israel is a *foe,*[7] which cannot be placated or accommodated, let alone turned into a friend. Muhammad had urged peace and reconciliation with the factions of the Qureysh tribal confederation that he regarded as mere enemies. In dealing with such enemies, one could persuade them to convert to Islam, or sign a truce renewable every ten years by mutual consent. With a foe, however, there could be neither peace nor truce.

The Khomeinist regime hopes to achieve a number of objectives by adopting the destruction of Israel as its cause. It will attract the attention of the Arab intelligentsia, a good part of which has built its vision of the world around deep hatred of Israel. Hatred of Israel also provides a bond between the Islamic Republic and the broader Arab masses who are suspicious of Iran's Shiism. The same is true of the remnants of the left in the Middle East, to whom an anti-Israel stance is part of a broader anti-imperialist strategy that Khomeinism, too, claims to espouse.

Using the "destroy Israel" slogan as the only theme that could unite Muslims, Tehran hosted a conference called "The End of Israel" on May 26, 2008. Organized by the so-called Justice-Seeking University Students

Movement, the conference drew participants from the United States, Venezuela, Argentina, Chile, Paraguay, Nicaragua, Cuba, and France, plus Pakistan and eleven Arab countries. According to the official Islamic Republic News Agency, the participants were "distinguished academics" who would "examine, analyze and debate President Ahmadinejad's assertion that the Zionist enemy state will soon come to an end."

Ahmadinejad's message to the Arabs is simple: Forget that Iran is Shiite, and remember that today it is the only power capable of realizing your most cherished dream, the destruction of Israel. The Sunni Muslim Brotherhood promised you it would throw the Jews into the sea in 1948, but failed. Pan-Arab nationalists, led by Nasser, ushered you into one of your biggest defeats in history, enabling Israel to capture Jerusalem. The Baathists under Saddam Hussein promised to "burn Israel," but ended up bringing the American infidels to Baghdad. Yasser Arafat and the Palestinian "patriots" promised to crush the Jewish state, but turned into collaborators on its payroll. Osama bin Laden and al-Qaeda never gave two hoots about Palestine, focusing only on spectacular operations in the West to win publicity for themselves. Sheikh Ahmad Yassin and Hamas did all they could to destroy Israel but lacked the power, like flies attacking an elephant. The only force now willing and able to help realize your dream of a burned Israel and drowning Jews is the Islamic Republic as created by Khomeini.

Although the preceding is presented as a verbal caricature, it exposes exactly how many Arabs have received Ahmadinejad's message. A visitor to Arab capitals could easily ascertain this for himself by dropping in to any teahouse or mosque or bazaar and talking to the locals at random. (Arabs and many other Muslims in Europe and the United States are likely to express similar views in support of the Islamic Republic's anti-Israel posture.) This does not mean that the Arabs are naïve enough to buy the bundle offered by Ahmadinejad. Most know that the Islamic Republic has neither the intention nor the power to take on Israel in open warfare. What they hope for is that the Islamic Republic will devote part of its resources to making life increasingly unbearable for the Israelis, through low-intensity war waged by the Lebanese branch of Hezballah as well as Hamas and half a dozen other Palestinian groups financed by Tehran. In any case, what do the Arabs have to lose? If Ahmadinejad succeeds in wiping Israel off the map, so much the better; if he fails, the Arabs would not be any worse off. One Saudi personality, speaking perhaps only half in jest, claims that the prospect of endless war between Iran and Israel should delight the Arabs. "Shiites and Jews killing one another?" he quips. "Allah himself couldn't promise anything better!"[8] After all, Sunni Arabs regard both Iranians and Jews as eternal foes of Arabism and Islam. The Iraqi Sunni politician Taha Yassin Jizrawi, who was Saddam Hussein's vice president, wrote a book titled *Jews, Persians, and Flies: Three Things That Allah Should Not Have Created.*

Ahmadinejad might want to ponder whether he is making a good long-term investment by propelling the Khomeinist regime towards war with Israel. He might also recall the proverb: Beware of what you wish for! Suppose that Ahmadinejad, helped by the Hidden Imam and Jesus Christ, whom the mullahs describe as "the Mahdi's special assistant," succeeded in destroying the state of Israel. But would he be allowed to enter Jerusalem in triumph? Not likely. The Palestinians, both Arab nationalists and Sunni Islamists, would consider him as much of an outsider as Israeli Jews. Even supposing he were welcomed in Jerusalem, he would still face a major problem from another direction: as a Shiite, he could not pray in Sunni mosques; and, as he surely knows, there is not a single Shiite mosque in the whole of Palestine. What would Ahmadinejad do? Would he pray in the Mosque of Omar, named after the second caliph, who is the most hated man of all history in the eyes of Shiites? As a child, Ahmadinejad's Shiite parents must have taught him that he should wash his mouth three times after pronouncing the name of Omar even to curse him. Would the Khomeinist president go to the Dome of the Rock, built by the very Umayyid caliphs who "martyred" Hussein bin Ali, the third imam of Shiism and Iran's most revered saint, by severing his head, and then mutilated his corpse? What would the Hidden Imam say of such behavior? Would Ahmadinejad just go around in Jerusalem as if his newly liberated friends were not the same Sunni *Nassibis* that the Hidden Imam will put to the sword?

While politics in the shape of hating the "other" unites Muslims today, religion has always divided and will continue to divide them. Today, Israel is the quintessential "other." If it were gone, Muslims would be forced to think about and talk of religion among themselves. Then they would find out how dangerous and deadly a politicized religion can be. Ahmadinejad must have an inkling of this already. He has seen how Hamas leaders behave on their visits to Tehran. They come to pick up millions of dollars, often crisp greenbacks in leather cases, but refuse to pay homage to Khomeini at his so-called shrine, something no Sunni Muslim worth his salt would ever do. Hamas leaders also refuse to pray alongside their Iranian Shiite hosts. Sunni Arabs are not alone in regarding Iran as a political ally but a religious enemy. Shiite Arabs, too, have difficulty accepting Iranian hegemony, especially under a Khomeinist regime.

Since 1982, the Islamic Republic has spent some $30 billion helping Lebanon's Shiite community. It has created a branch of Hezballah in Lebanon, training and arming its militia to the point that in 2008 it was regarded as the strongest military force in the country. And yet, with the exception of Hezballah's secretary general Sayyed Hassan Nasrallah and a few of his associates, all of them creatures of the Iranian secret services, few Lebanese Shiites accept religious leadership from Iran. Despite generous cash handouts, the number of Lebanese Shiites who regarded Iran's Supreme Guide, Ali Khamenehi, as *marja taqlid* ("source of imitation" in religious matters) did not exceed a few thousand in 2008. The overwhelming majority of Lebanese Shiites were followers of Grand Ayatollah Sistani in Iraq or the Lebanese Ayatollah Sayyed Hussein Fadlallah in Beirut. Almost two decades of Iranian largesse has produced no more than a few thousand religious followers for Khamenehi among Shiites anywhere, including in Iran itself. Sheikh Na'im Qassem, number two in the Lebanese Hezballah leadership and thus one of Tehran's point men in Beirut, puts it this way: "We look to Ayatollah Khamenehi as a political leader!" Qassem has missed the point: Khamenehi claims political leadership on the ground that he is a *religious* leader.

Ahmadinejad might find out that helping Arabs destroy Israel was not such a good idea after all. For six decades, most of the negative energies of the Arabs have been directed against the Jewish state, but with Israel gone, those energies might seek a new target. One possibility is Turkey, because of its supposed oppression of the Arabs during the Ottoman Empire and its refusal to hand over the province of Iskanderun, where ethnic Arabs form a majority, to Arab rule. But inciting Arabs to hatred of Turkey, a predominantly Sunni Muslim nation, would not be easy. The designer target for those negative energies is Iran, which is Persian and Shiite, and now it is aggressively expansionist.

Today, the United Arab Emirates claims ownership of three Iranian islands, a claim endorsed by every single session of Arab foreign ministers or heads of state since 1995. Most Arab states have already rebaptized the Persian Gulf as the "Arabian Gulf." Many Arabs, both nationalists and Islamists, regard Iran's oil-rich province of Khuzestan as an "Arab land" that must be either attached to Iraq or allowed to become an independent state. According to an Iraqi foreign minister, speaking only half in jest, the claim is based on one key fact: Khuzestan has palm groves, and wherever dates grow is part of the Arab world![9] For a decade, the song "From the Atlantic Ocean to the Persian Gulf," by the Egyptian pop star Abdul-Halim Hafiz, promised Arabs a new empire built partly on the ruins of Iran.[10]

Once Israel is out of the equation, Ahmadinejad's Arab allies might well thank him and quickly move on to other issues. Might they not demand to know why Iran's twelve million or so Sunni Muslims suffer religious restrictions of the kind that even Israel never inflicted on its Sunni Muslim citizens? Khalid Mash'al, the leader of Hamas and a member of the Sunni Muslim Brotherhood movement, might entreat "Brother Mahmoud" to allow Iranian Sunnis to build their own mosques and present their version of Islam to their Iranian Shiite brethren. Arabs might also ask how it is that the children of Iran's Arab minority are not allowed to study in their own language, the language of Allah himself, which Khomeini called "far superior to all other languages of mankind." Even Israel allowed its Arab citizens to study in their native tongue, publish Arabic-language newspapers and books, and stage plays and make films in Arabic. Could the Islamic Republic of Iran, the "liberator" of Jerusalem, be more repressive towards Arab Muslims than Israel, that "stain of shame on the map of the Middle East"? Ahmadinejad might want to contemplate another question: is it wise to speak of wiping nations off the map? Would it not set a precedent that Arab radicals could one day use against Iran, as did Saddam Hussein and his gang in the 1980s when they spoke of "wiping the Persians off the map"?

In any case, Ahmadinejad should not assume that Arabs were born yesterday. Over the past six decades, Arabs have seen how hatred of Israel has been abused to justify policies and ambitions the cost of which they had to bear. The Arab feudal regimes spoke of "liberating Palestine" as a priority that overrode all other issues—such as individual liberties, the rule of law, and social reform. The military regimes asked the Arabs to be patient with despotic rule until after Israel is wiped out. Nasser tried to annex Syria in the name of "liberating Palestine." He sent his army to Yemen as a "prelude to liberating Palestine." Today, Arabs watch as Iran extends its dominion over Syria and Lebanon, again in the name of "liberating Palestine." For the first time since the seventh century A.D., Iranian troops have reached the Mediterranean through Syria and Lebanon, treating both as part of an Iranian glacis in the heart of the Middle East.

Ahmadinejad's militant rhetoric against Israel, signaling a return to Khomeini's most extreme positions, has failed to resonate with most Iranians—something that the maverick president may end up accepting as fact. His predecessor, the mullah Muhammad Khatami, also toyed with anti-Israel themes in the early stages of his presidency. On October 24, 2000, he told an Iranian television audience, "In the Koran, God commands [us] to kill the wicked and those who do not respect the rights of the oppressed. . . . If we abide by human laws, we should mobilize the whole Islamic world for a sharp confrontation with the

Zionist regime. . . . If we abide by the Koran, all of us should mobilize to kill." Soon, however, Khatami realized that while presenting the Jews as the enemy might appeal to hardcore Khomeinists such as himself, the message would not sell with Iranians at large.

It is not easy to present Israel as a threat to Iran, let alone a Muslim world of 1.3 billion people. There is no history of enmity between Iranians and Jews. On the contrary, most historical narratives on both sides radiate with genuine warmth and mutual affection. Ancient Persians helped save the Jews from extermination in Babylon. Jews always remained loyal to Iran, fighting and dying for it whenever given an opportunity. Even when Israel was reborn as a state, few Iranian Jews were prepared to choose it over Iran. Iran and Israel do not face any of the problems that set one nation-state against another. There is no border dispute between them. They are not competing over access to rare natural resources or markets. They do not suffer from a collective memory of hatred and war. Any Western visitor to Iran would quickly realize that Iranians do not hate Jews and would not be prepared to sacrifice them for the Arabs. This lack of a popular base for a policy of hatred and war may well prove to be the ultimate check on Ahmadinejad's messianic illusions.

Before Ahmadinejad wiped Israel off the map, moreover, he would have to deal with the third "other" in the Khomeinist demonology: the American Great Satan, which, although weakened by its internal squabbles and surrounded by squeamish allies, remains the world's sole superpower. Between Ahmadinejad and the light of day stands the shadow of a heavily armed foe that has all but encircled the Islamic Republic and, its tergiversations notwithstanding, remains capable of doing quite a bit of mischief.

13

The Great Satan

In April 2008, Tehran hosted a conference designed to bring the many different Islamic sects closer together in the name of *taqrib* (religious convergence). Over one hundred individuals from all over the world addressed the gathering, among them Ahmadinejad and Rafsanjani. None of these speakers, however, addressed the officially declared purpose of the exercise—the quest for theological common ground among Islam's many different sects, especially Sunnis and Shiites. The only issue on which all speakers were in harmony was the depiction of the United States as the "arch-enemy of Islam."

This was not surprising, as anti-Americanism had been a key theme of Khomeinism since the seizure of the U.S. embassy in Tehran in November 1979. At that time, the ayatollah had circulated his notorious dictum "America Cannot Do a Damn Thing!" This meant that the United States, while still powerful, would not be able to stand against the rising tide of the global Islamic revolution. In other words, there was a draw between Islam and America. The spring conference in Tehran introduced a new analysis, encapsulated in the slogan inscribed on the lectern from which speakers addressed the congregants: "America Is Going to Fall!"[1]

Khomeini had always regarded the United States as the latest incarnation of "impiety and perfidy." He dubbed it "the Great Satan," claiming that it embodied an ancient force for evil throughout history. In an audience he granted to the leaders of the "students" who had taken the American diplomats hostage in Tehran, the ayatollah spoke of "the very long history that we have with these people," meaning the Americans. "This matter does not belong to today or yesterday," he said. "It is two thousand years that the United States has colonized us."[2]

Some of Khomeini's confidants, including his son Ahmad, have suggested that the ayatollah developed his rabid anti-Americanism after the success of the revolution, when elements from the left along with the Soviet embassy in Tehran started to spread rumors that the United States was planning to stage a coup against the new revolutionary regime. The Soviet-controlled Tudeh (Masses) Party hammered on the theme that the core issue of the revolution was "the contradiction between the people and imperialism led by America."

Some of Khomeini's closest associates had also converted to chic French-style anti-Americanism and blamed the United States for all the ills not only of Iran but of the Third World as a whole. Mehdi Bahar, a critic of the shah, had set the tone in the early 1970s by publishing a book under the title *Heir to Colonialism*, blaming the United States for the continuation, in "substantial parts of the world today, of the misery and despotism caused by the European imperial powers." For his part, Banisadr claimed that the United States, as "the principal force of imperialism," was trying to weaken Muslims' religious beliefs in the name of national cultures. "The very notion of culture is an Imperialist notion designed to loosen the people's [bonds] with faith," he wrote. "It was colonialism that propagated the idea of art and culture as domains separate from faith. . . . Any activity, whether economic or cultural, if not motivated by and wholly in the service of faith is satanic activity."[3] Years later, Khomeini himself expressed a similar fear—that the United States was trying to persuade Muslim nations to adopt its own model of the separation of church and state. He wrote: "A religion that places the material and spiritual resources of Islamic and non-Islamic countries at the disposal of superpowers; that exhorts the people to believe that religion is separate from politics—that religion is the opiate of the masses. However, such a religion is no longer the true religion, but it is a religion which our people call American Islam."[4]

But in 1979, there seemed to be no reason for Khomeini to fear the United States. President Carter had helped the revolution by exerting pressure on the shah to appoint a caretaker government and go into exile.

Being a born-again Christian, Carter regarded Khomeini as a man of faith and thus, despite differences in religion, a kindred soul. Documents seized at the U.S. embassy in Tehran show that the administration was in contact with key figures of the revolution inside Iran and did nothing to temper their growing radicalism. William Sullivan, Carter's ambassador to Tehran, believed that the shah was meeting his "comeuppance" and fully deserved it.[5] Zbigniew Brzezinski, Carter's national security advisor, dreamed of turning Iran into the principal link of a chain of Islamic nations around the USSR.

On the whole, the American intelligentsia was also sympathetic to the revolution. Few Americans would shed tears over a monarchy, especially one vilified by their media for more than a decade. Also, the word "revolution" resonates well with many Americans who associate it with their own war of independence. At times, American sympathy for Khomeinism was expressed in almost lyrical tones. An article in the *New York Times* said: "Many consider this revolution as the most beautiful moment in Islamic history." It went on to predict that Khomeinism would become "a model for humane government," something that "we, too, need." Khomeinism was neither fanatical nor anti-American, the writer declared. On the contrary, all indications were that "it would transform Iran into a law-based and fully democratic society."[6] All this at a time that Khomeinist militants were throwing acid in the faces of women who refused to cover themselves, while self-appointed Islamic judges did overtime work in revolutionary tribunals issuing death fatwas and putting their enemies in front of firing squads.

In 1979, soon after the mullahs seized power, Carter sent Khomeini a warm congratulatory letter. His man at the UN, a certain Andrew Young, praised Khomeini as "a twentieth-century saint." Carter also tapped his closest legal advisor, Lloyd Cutler, as ambassador to the Khomeinist regime. A more dramatic show of U.S. support for the mullahs came when Brzezinski flew to Algiers to meet Khomeini's prime minister, Mehdi Bazargan. It was love at first sight—to the point that Carter approved the resumption of military supplies to Iran, even

as the mullahs were executing Iranians by the thousands, includ-
ing many whose only "crime" was friendship with the United States.
The Carter administration's behavior convinced the mullahs that the
United States was a "paper tiger" and that it was time for the Islamic
Revolution to highlight its hatred of America. "The Carter administra-
tion's weakness was a direct encouragement to [anti-American] hard-
liners," wrote Ibrahim Asgharzadeh, one of the hostage-takers at the
U.S. embassy, years later.[7]

Khomeini was not the first ruler of Iran to face the problem of dealing
with the Americans. The United States had appeared as a major player
on the Iranian scene during the Second World War when it organized a
massive transfer of food and weapons to the Soviet Union through Iran.
The Americans had arrived in Iran after Soviet and British troops had
invaded the country, chased away its monarch, and forced it to abandon its neutrality and join the Allies against the Axis. At the end of the
war, the British withdrew their troops in accordance with an agreement
signed with the Iranian government in 1941. The Soviets, however, refused
to withdraw and used the Red Army to set up two breakaway "republics"
in the Iranian provinces of Kurdistan and Azerbaijan. This was not the
first time that the Soviet Union tried to annex a chunk of Iranian territory. Between 1917 and 1921, it had helped its local allies create a secessionist regime in the Iranian coastal province of Gilan on the Caspian
Sea under the name of Azadistan (Land of the Free). At the time, the
Iranian Cossack Brigade—led by Reza Khan, who was to become shah in
1925—had succeeded in defeating the secessionists while the Red Army,
too busy with the Russian civil war, had been unable to come to the rescue. But in 1945 it was obvious that the much-weakened Iranian army
was in no position to drive the Red Army, then at the peak of its glory
after crushing Hitler, out of the occupied territories.

Iran's traditional mistrust of the British, and the evident weakness of
the British Empire at the end of World War II, meant that the Iranians
could not count on Britain to help end Soviet occupation. In any case,
most Iranians were convinced that Britain was only interested in Iran's

oil and might seize the opportunity to revive old treaties with the tsars under which they had tried to divide Iran into British and Russian zones, effectively ending the country's existence as a sovereign nation. For centuries, Iranian policymakers had used a symbolic color scheme to label the various threats they thought Iran faced because of its peculiar geopolitical position. Green was the color of the Arab threat that had dominated the scene from the third decade of the seventh century A.D. to the middle of the ninth century. It had been replaced by yellow, the color of the Turkic-Mongol-Tatar threat from Central Asia that lasted for almost a thousand years and on several occasions brought Iran to the verge of extinction as a nation-state. In the nineteenth century a new threat had appeared, the threat of European imperialism, with Britain and Russia as its most powerful representatives. It was designated by the color blue. The two European empires used a mixture of war and chicanery to deprive Iran of large parts of its national territory. Russia ended up annexing the whole of Iran's possessions in the Caucasus and Central Asia. The British annexed more than half of Baluchistan to their Indian Empire and solidified Afghanistan's secession from Iran through the Treaty of Paris in 1856. They also seized a number of Iranian islands in the Persian Gulf. After the Bolshevik Revolution of 1917, a new threat was added: the threat of Communism, designated by the color red.[8]

For six decades after that, the "red threat" remained the principal source of concern for Iranian policymakers. Since the time of Peter the Great, most Russian tsars had dreamed of expanding their empire to the south to reach the warm waters of the Persian Gulf and the Indian Ocean. The Bolsheviks had revived that ambition in the name of global revolution; the Communist International leader Zinoviev spoke of "setting the East ablaze," starting with the moribund Persian state. With the victory of the Bolsheviks in Russia, Iran's traditional enemy joined the expansionist appetite inherited from the tsars with an ideological agenda that seduced a good part of the Iranian intelligentsia. The tragedy for Iran was that its reformist, pro-West intellectual elite was divided for the first time between left and right. Before Bolshevism, almost all Iranian reformers agreed on a democratic model of society inspired by Western Europe. They had achieved their first success by leading the Constitutional Revolution of 1906, which created the first constitutional monarchy, with an elected parliament, in a Muslim country. After 1917, however, the Iranian reformist elite was never able to reunite and was thus forced to ally itself either with the autocratic ruling cliques or with reactionary clerics. In the Islamic Revolution of 1979, the entire Iranian left put itself under Khomeini's command, while the reformist right that had allied itself to the shah was neutralized once he left the country. With the fall of the Soviet Empire in 1991, the "red threat" disappeared and Iran's modernizing elites were able to unite once again. But it was too late, as the Islamic fascists already controlled the country.

In 1945, with the "red threat" very much alive, Iranian leaders faced the prospect of another truncation of their country. While Stalin was busy annexing the northwestern portion of Iran, the British were reviving old schemes for setting up Khuzestan, the southwest province where 90 percent of Iran's oil is located, as a separate emirate. They were also arming their usual tribal clients, especially the Bakhtiaris close to the oil region, to prevent the central government from sending troops there.

The only power capable of helping Iran stand up to the old Russian enemy in 1945 was the United States of America. The trouble was that the Americans were not interested in Iran. With the war over, they had withdrawn their forces and cut down their diplomatic presence to a minimum. They were not even prepared to name an ambassador to Tehran. The Cold War had not yet warmed up as a central theme of American foreign policy, and President Harry S. Truman still trusted Uncle Joe. Two factors helped secure American support for Iran. The first was strong Iranian lobbying in Washington, combined with an imaginative and resolute campaign at the United Nations in New York. The high culture and dexterity of Iranian diplomats impressed the Americans. More importantly, Stalin's expansionist ambitions were exposed through his campaign to seize control of Greece through the local branch of the Communist International. The Truman administration realized that it had to draw a line in the sand. At the time, it was in a strong position to do so partly because the United States still enjoyed a monopoly of nuclear weapons. Also helpful was the fact that the Iranian leadership elite, habitually divided into rival factions aligned to rival foreign powers, for once were united in preserving the nation's territorial integrity. By November 1946, more than eighteen months after the end of World War II, Stalin's forces were finally out of Iranian territory, allowing the two "People's Republics" they had created in Tabriz and Mahabad to collapse without much of a fight. Iran was saved from yet another dismemberment that might have led to its balkanization. The experience persuaded the Iranian elite that only a strategic alliance with the United States could help Iran preserve its independence and territorial integrity against its expansionist Soviet neighbor. Some Iranian politicians and intellectuals even began to dream of playing the American card against the British, who continued to exploit Iran's oil wealth in the most glaringly unfair manner possible. In November 1947, the newspaper *Iran Ma* ("Our Iran") called for a thorough revision of the nation's foreign policy in a direction that would lead to "an abiding alliance with the democratic world under the leadership of its savior, the United States of America."

Despite their success in helping Iran push Stalin out, the Americans remained uninterested in an "abiding alliance" with a poor and underdeveloped Islamic country thousands of miles away. They were prepared to offer aid, and did so through Truman's Point Four program. They helped Iran eradicate malaria and a host of other endemic diseases, cutting down infant mortality by half in less than a decade. They organized the first Iranian units to fight locusts, whose annual attacks through the neighboring Arabian deserts claimed a quarter of the crops. By the early 1950s, the Point Four aid package was almost as large as the Iranian government's annual budget. The program included the building of roads, clinics, schools, and grain silos. Food was distributed through CARE, helping alleviate the sufferings of Iranians in areas still facing near-famine because of dislocations caused by the war. Point Four employed hundreds of Iranians, many of whom went through special courses in economics, administration, and management. From the late 1950s, Point Four alumni provided a good part of the Iranian management elite, both private and public, and helped strengthen the belief that the United States, a disinterested and generous ally, was a vital factor in helping Iran define its space between the Soviet Union and Britain. The Americans, however, would not be wooed. They were particularly reluctant to forge a military link with Iran, refusing persistent demands from Tehran to train some Iranian army officers in the United States.

Two key players in Tehran's politics at the time were especially keen to involve the United States in Iranian affairs: Ahmad Qavam and Muhammad Mossadeq. They were cousins who belonged to the Qajar clan, whose chiefs had ruled Iran as shahs from the end of the eighteenth century until 1925. Qavam had served in senior positions on a number of occasions since the 1930s. He had been prime minister in the 1945–46 crisis over Soviet attempts to annex northwestern Iran, and by all accounts his imaginative leadership, including a set of tough negotiations with Stalin, had helped Iran regain its lost territories. Mossadeq, on the other hand, had promoted himself as a perpetual parliamentary critic of whatever policy happened to be in place. He had opposed the building of the trans-Iranian railway and the package of reforms introduced by Reza Shah in the 1920s. Because he liked to call himself "Doctor" on the strength of a law degree he had obtained in Switzerland, his detractors called him "Dr. No." Though divided by politics and personal ambitions, the cousins were united in the belief that only the United States could offer Iran effective protection against its old imperialist enemies. To attract the attention of the Truman administration, Qavam created a group called the Democratic Party of Iran, borrowing heavily from the program of its American model.

For his part, Mossadeq decided to focus on a single issue: the nationalization of Iranian oil. He had seen Mexico nationalize its oil with the tacit understanding of the Truman administration. The major U.S. oil companies had also concluded an agreement with the Saudis that gave the Arab kingdom a far better deal than was offered to Iran by the Anglo-

Iranian Oil Company, later to be renamed British Petroleum, a company owned by the British government. Mossadeq knew that the United States was the only major industrial power not to have a government-owned oil company. Thus, he concluded, what mattered to the U.S. government was not ownership and control of the oilfields, but making sure that oil continued to flow to world markets. One other factor persuaded Mossadeq that the time had come for Iran to gain control of its principal source of natural wealth: The British Labour government, having just launched a comprehensive program of nationalization at home, could not oppose a similar move by Iran.

There is ample evidence that the Truman administration encouraged the idea of nationalizing Iran's oil, albeit indirectly, while taking precautions not to antagonize Washington's British allies. As the oil nationalization movement gathered momentum, the United States upgraded its diplomatic representation in Tehran, eventually naming one of its most senior diplomats, Loi Henderson, a former head of the Middle East desk at the State Department, as ambassador.[9] By the end of 1950, the idea of nationalizing the oilfields had secured massive support both within the ruling elite and in the nation at large.

The Majlis, Iran's unicameral parliament, had no difficulty recommending the appointment of Mossadeq as prime minister, a move that the shah immediately endorsed. In 1951, when Mossadeq presented his first cabinet to the shah, the Soviets saw this as a sign of growing American influence in Iran. *Pravda*, the daily organ of the Central Committee of the Communist Party of the Soviet Union, went even further by claiming that Mossadeq's premiership represented a victory by the American "new imperialists" against "the old British imperialists." Soon, the theme of Mossadeq as an "agent of American imperialism" became a favorite of the pro-Soviet newspapers in Tehran. This is how the most popular daily newspaper of the Soviet-sponsored Tudeh (Masses) Party saw the new government:

> The government of Dr. Mossadeq has taken the path of killing

the nation, lying, and obeying the colonial policy of America. Dr. Mossadeq, having miserably surrendered to American colonialism, has deemed it necessary to shower our nation with bullets and shed the blood of the most noble and independence-loving children of the nation to please the ambassador of U.S. imperialism. The path of Dr. Mossadeq's government is the path of massacring people, use of fascist methods, spreading lies, and making deals with American and English [*sic*] imperialism, and sacrificing the interests of the Iranian nation. [10]

A sign that Mossadeq wished to nurture a relationship with the United States was that he appointed his son, Ghulam-Hussein, a doctor of medicine, as his personal contact with the American ambassador in Tehran. During Mossadeq's premiership, U.S. aid to Iran rose from under $5 million a year to more than $23 million. When the British sent two gunboats to anchor opposite the Iranian oil refinery at Abadan in order to intimidate Mossadeq, President Truman informed Prime Minister Clement Attlee that the United States would not endorse military action against Iran. [11] Truman demonstrated his high regard for Mossadeq by receiving him as a head of state during a visit to the United States. At the United Nations and other international organs, the United States consistently supported Iran's right to nationalize its oil. The Truman administration also tried to broker an amicable settlement between Mossadeq and the British, and dispatched Averill Harriman, a former governor of New York and a senior figure of the Democratic Party, as special emissary to Tehran.

14

Five Days in August

B_y 1953, it had become clear that Mossadeq had reached a political impasse of his own making. He had rejected every offer extended to him by the British, including a generous one endorsed by Washington, but had not made any counteroffer. At the same time, he had dissolved the parliament, quarreled with the shah over who should command the military, declared martial law, printed vast sums of paper money and thus provoked unprecedented inflation, and broken with most of his supporters within the political elite.

For their part, the Soviets clearly hoped that Mossadeq would prove to be Iran's Kerensky, a liberal prime minister destroying the monarchy and paving the way for a Communist takeover. The Soviet secret service, the NKVD (the future KGB), had built an impressive network of agents in Iran. Directly or indirectly, it controlled no fewer than twelve newspapers in Tehran alone.[1] As it was revealed a couple of years later, the NKVD had also recruited over six hundred Iranian army, gendarmerie and police officers and NCOs in the name of "proletarian solidarity." Moscow's chief asset in Iran, the Tudeh (Masses) Party, boasted a card-holding membership of over fifty thousand, making it the largest Communist party outside the Soviet camp and China. An unknown number of NKVD sleeper agents, mostly Soviet citizens from the Caucasus and Central Asia who spoke Persian and could easily pass for Iranians, had created an underground network to be activated for an armed insurrection. Having been forced to withdraw his army from Iran just seven years earlier, Stalin dreamed of making a spectacular return. He had even thought of a legal façade for his planned military interventions. Two treaties signed between Tehran and Moscow, in 1921 and 1941, gave the USSR the right to land troops in Iran when and if Soviet security appeared to be threatened by armed conflict in Iranian territory.

Meanwhile, a coalition of anti-Mossadeq personalities, parties, and associations had taken shape with one of Mossadeq's former cabinet colleagues, Senator Fazlallah Zahedi, as figurehead. A retired major general and a relative of Mossadeq, Zahedi had been interior minister in Mossadeq's first cabinet in 1951. Two years later, however, Zahedi had emerged as leader of the opposition in the Iranian senate while also enjoying the support of several members of the lower house of parliament. But how to get rid of Mossadeq and allow Zahedi to become prime minister? The constitution required that the shah dismiss Mossadeq and appoint Zahedi in his place, but the shah would not hear of such a scheme. He had dismissed Mossadeq once before and experienced pro-Mossadeq street riots that claimed thirty-one lives in Tehran. No, he did not want any more bloodshed. Also, the shah did not like Zahedi, a member of his father's military entourage, who regarded the young monarch as a mere boy. Finally, the shah would not risk provoking an armed conflict that could give the Soviets the pretext to invoke the 1921 and 1941 treaties and send the Red Army back into Iranian territory it had evacuated seven years earlier. With the British out of Iran and turned into sworn enemies because of the dispute over oil nationalization, there was no major power to counter such a Soviet move should it come to pass. To all those who urged him to dismiss Mossadeq, including some Iranians with close ties to the British, the shah always had one answer: Who would protect us against the Russians?

The obvious answer was the United States, the same power that had helped Iran push the Russians out a few years earlier. The problem was that the Truman administration, still supportive of Mossadeq, would not give the shah the guarantee he demanded for dismissing the prime minister. By January 1952, however, President Truman had been replaced by Dwight D. Eisenhower, a Republican and friend of Winston Churchill, who had replaced Clement Attlee as Britain's prime minister. John Foster Dulles, the new U.S. secretary of state, was much more of a cold warrior than Dean Acheson, the man he had replaced. He was also the architect of what was to become known as the "quarantine the aggressor" strategy, a more dynamic version of the Truman administration's doctrine of containment against the USSR. Determined that Iran should not fall into the Soviet orbit, Dulles let himself be persuaded by the British to give the shah the guarantee he wanted. The guarantee eventually came in the form of a coded message relayed by Allen Dulles, director of the Central Intelligence Agency (CIA), to the shah's twin sister, Princess Ashraf, during a secret meeting in Switzerland, and passed on to the shah through his wife, Queen Soraya, in another secret meeting between the two women in Tehran.[2]

Buoyed by the American guarantee of support against a putative Soviet invasion, the shah signed two edicts, one dismissing Mossadeq and the other appointing Zahedi as prime minister. But when a colonel in the Royal Guard arrived at Mossadeq's residence to deliver the edict, the prime minister claimed that the document was a forgery and thus unacceptable. The colonel was arrested, and Mossadeq ordered a propaganda campaign around the theme of "an attempted military coup by British agents." Convinced that Mossadeq was determined to defy the constitution with support from the army, the shah decided to leave the country so as to prevent a direct clash.

At the time, Mossadeq held the post of minister of defense as well as prime minister and had appointed officers related to him by blood ties or political ideas to all key posts within the armed forces. One of his relatives, General Muhammad-Taqi Rihai, a brilliant French-educated officer, served as chief of staff. A few months earlier, Mossadeq had given himself "full powers," dissolved the parliament, declared a state of emergency (known as Point V under Iranian law), and arrested scores of his opponents, creating the impression that he wanted to impose personal rule or maybe even abolish the monarchy with support from the Communists. Later, he put a prize on Zahedi's head and dissolved the senate, forcing the senator to go into hiding.

As things heated up, the Tudeh threw its full support behind

Mossadeq, the man it had vilified as an "American agent" two years earlier. But the bulk of Mossadeq's original coalition had turned against him.[3] His foreign minister, Hussein Fatemi, a firebrand and a magnetic orator, seized the opportunity to call for the abolition of the monarchy at a series of public meetings, thus widening the gap between Mossadeq and the traditional, monarchist elements of Iranian society.

Surprisingly, however, Mossadeq appeared to be paralyzed, often spending most of the day in bed in his pajamas and refusing to see his ministers. When the interior minister, Hussein Sadiqi, arrived to ask what was to be done now that the shah had left the country and there was no parliament either, Mossadeq dismissed him with "a few incoherent banalities."[4] The old man had simply run out of ideas. He was one of those politicians who have one big idea—his had been the nationalization of oil—beyond which they cannot think. The Tudeh urged him to declare a transitional government with himself as president. But he couldn't; he had been appointed prime minister by the shah and still pretended that the royal decree dismissing him had been a forgery. It would not have been difficult for him to contact the shah and find out whether the decree was genuine. But he didn't. He wanted the shah in the system and did not want the shah; he didn't know what he wanted. Or, rather, there was one thing he wanted above everything else: to preserve his "good name." Like all populists, he was prepared to sacrifice almost anything to ensure that crowds continued to hail him. In those hot August days, however, Mossadeq's ambivalence and inertia persuaded the crowds that he was no longer capable of offering leadership in any direction. The crowds now in the streets were no longer Mossadeqist; they were pro-Tudeh mobs, brought to destroy the statues of the shah and his father, ransack the offices of anti-Communist newspapers, and call for a "people's republic."

In the meantime, plans by a network of CIA agents, working hand-in-glove with British intelligence "assets" in Tehran, to organize demonstrations against Mossadeq had collapsed. The reason was that the demonstrations were supposed to be triggered by the news of Mossadeq's dismissal by the shah and Zahedi's appointment. But when Mossadeq refused the royal decree on the grounds that it might be forged, the transfer of power to Zahedi could not take place. The CIA had established an antenna in Tehran in 1950 to watch the growing activities of its Soviet counterpart, the NKVD. The Americans had managed to bribe a few members of parliament, and made arrangements with two or three minor newspapers to publish stories planted by the agency. There is no doubt that by the time the shah had signed the decree dismissing Mossadeq, the CIA, using whatever assets the British had left behind, was engaged in a number of dirty tricks designed to incite public opinion against the prime minister by creating the impression that the Communists were about to seize power in Tehran.

In the end, the CIA played only a minor role in the dramatic events that led to the August 1953 uprising in favor of the shah. Mossadeq realized that the game was up for him, and as crowds of angry Tehranis moved towards his home, later to loot and ransack it, he climbed his wall with a ladder, still in his trademark pajamas, to seek refuge in the headquarters of the American Point Four next door. Zahedi, who had been in hiding and played no role in the actual uprising, emerged to seize control and invite the shah to return from his brief exile first in Baghdad and then in Rome.

Over the years, the events of those five days in August in Tehran were built up into a myth according to which the CIA had organized what amounted to a decisive change of course in Iranian history. It is virtually impossible to find a single anti-American text published after 1960 that does not refer to the "CIA plot" as something horrible, on par with the Holocaust. The narrative built around the "plot" theme is simple: Iran in 1953 was a democratic society with a democratically elected parliament, prime minister, and cabinet, supported by the overwhelming majority of the Iranian people. But then, sometime in August, the United States, which had supported Iran's democracy during the Truman administration, decided, under the Republican administration of President Eisenhower, to ally itself with the dictatorial shah against Iranian democracy as symbolized by Prime Minister Muhammad Mossadeq. The CIA sent an operative, a certain Kermit Roosevelt, to "put the shah back on his throne." Roosevelt almost single-handedly succeeded in overthrowing Mossadeq, reinstalling the shah, and earning the United States the eternal ire of all nations in the so-called Third World, before quickly flying to London for a well-deserved holiday. (As Brecht once observed: OK, Caesar did cross the Rhine in winter; but did he not have someone to make him soup and polish his boots?)

This story, born in 1960—a full seven years after the August 1953 events in Tehran—was quickly adopted by the Soviet Union as a major theme in its global anti-American propaganda campaign. Over the years, other opponents of the United States have also adopted it, as have some American academics who often thought the worst of their own nation. For more than fifty years, the story has been used to "prove" that the United States, its claims of loving liberty notwithstanding, has been an enemy of democracy in the developing world.

In recent years, one American journalist has published a book to "prove" that Osama bin Laden and al-Qaeda decided to attack the United States on 9/11 because of the "bitterness felt about those distant events in Iran." In 2006, the newspaper USA Today ran an article claiming that the "destruction by the United States of democracy in Iran" was "an established fact."

In March 2000, Secretary of State Madeleine Albright implicitly adopted the myth of "August in Tehran" and apologized to the Iranian people for it. Later that year, President Bill Clinton echoed her apology in a speech, expressing regret for "all the crimes that my country and my culture have committed" against the Iranian people. After leaving office, Clinton told an audience at the World Economic Forum in Davos, Switzerland, that during his presidency he had "formally apologized on behalf of the United States" for what he termed "American crimes against Iran." By his account, "It's a sad story that really began in the 1950s when the United States deposed Mr. Mossadeq, who was an elected parliamentary democrat, and brought the shah back and then he was overturned by the Ayatollah Khomeini, driving us into the arms of one Saddam Hussein. We got rid of the parliamentary democracy back in the '50s; at least, that is my belief."

Duped by a myth spread by the Blame-America coalition, Clinton appeared to have done little homework on Iran. The truth is that Iran in the 1950s was not a parliamentary democracy but a constitutional monarchy in which the shah appointed, and dismissed, the prime minister. Mossadeq was named prime minister by the shah twice, and dismissed by him twice. This did not mean that the United States "got rid of parliamentary democracy," something that did not exist in the first place. Having dissolved the parliament and stopped the subsequent general election in midcourse because he realized that his opponents would win a crushing majority, Mossadeq was ruling by decree in violation of the constitution. Though a popular populist, he could hardly be described as a democrat.

Clinton's claim that the United States changed the course of Iranian history on a whim would be seen by most Iranians, a proud people, as an insult by an arrogant politician who exaggerates the powers of his nation more than half a century ago. Moreover, in the Islamic Republic that Clinton was trying to court, Mossadeq, far from being regarded as a national hero, is an object of intense vilification. One of the first acts of the mullahs after seizing power in 1979 was to take the name of Mossadeq off a street in Tehran. They then sealed off the village where Mossadeq is buried to prevent his supporters from gathering at his tomb. History textbooks written by the mullahs present Mossadeq as "the son of a feudal family of exploiters who worked for the cursed shah, and betrayed Islam." Clinton's apology to the mullahs for a wrong supposedly done to Mossadeq was like begging Josef Stalin's pardon for a discourtesy towards Alexander Kerensky.

The so-called coup d'état that supposedly brought back the shah happened only in the imagination of anti-American ideologists. The Iranian army did not intervene in the events until after pro-shah demonstrators had seized most key government buildings, and then only to restore public order after the new government had been announced. Many hours of newsreel footage of the events are available in archives, including the National Film Archive in Washington, D.C., clearly depicting a popular pro-shah uprising. There are also hundreds of eyewitness accounts by Iranians who observed or took part in the events.

It is interesting that the CIA claims that all its documents relating to the events disappeared in a mysterious fire. We are thus left with two accounts. One is a self-serving book by Kermit Roosevelt, who presents himself as a latter-day, and vastly inflated, Scarlet Pimpernel.[5] The other is an official report commissioned by the CIA and written by Donald Wilber, the agency's operational director in Tehran at the time. While Roosevelt's account is obviously fanciful, Wilber's report is written in a sober, almost self-deprecating style. He shows that the CIA and the British MI6 did have a plan to foment trouble against Mossadeq after the shah had signed the dismissal decree, but the plan failed as the CIA's agents and "assets" behaved more like Keystone Kops than professional conspirators engaged in a major big-power clash in the context of the Cold War. Wilber reports that the CIA station sent the message to Washington that "The operation has been tried and failed." The British followed with their own message of failure: "We regret that we cannot consider going on fighting. Operations against Mossadeq should be discontinued."[6] Wilber blames the CIA's Iranian "assets" for the failure. The CIA had prepared "a Western type plan offered for execution by Orientals [*sic*]. Given the recognized incapacity of Iranians to plan or act in a thoroughly logical manner, we would never expect such a plan to be executed in the local atmosphere like a Western staff operation."[7]

Moscow, too, noticed the failure of the CIA-MI6 plot. For two days running, Moscow Radio broadcast an editorial by *Pravda*, the CPSU organ, headed "The Failure of the American Adventure in Iran." The editorial claimed that British and American agents had tried to foment street riots against Mossadeq but had failed because "progressive forces," a codeword for Communists and fellow travelers, had rallied behind the old leader.

The official CIA report also refutes the claim that the Americans had bribed a number of Iranian army officers to stage a coup against Mossadeq. Wilber states categorically: "In Iran we did not rely on bribery. . . . We did not spend a cent in the purchase of officers."[8] He also makes it clear that no army units were involved in the events, although a brigade led by Colonel Bakhtiar, a cousin of the shah's wife, Queen Soraya, arrived in Tehran from Kermanshah after the fall of Mossadeq.

Wilber observed part of the popular pro-shah uprising and offered his version in the report commissioned by the CIA:

> In the evening, violence flared in the streets of Tehran. Just what was the major motivating force is impossible to say, but it is possible to isolate the factors behind the disturbances. First the flight of the Shah brought home to the populace in a dramatic way how far Mossadeq had gone, and galvanized the people into an irate pro-Shah force. Second, it seems clear that the Tudeh Party overestimated its strength in the situation. . . . Third, the Mossadeq government was at last beginning to feel very uneasy about its alliance with the Tudeh Party. The Pan-Iranists were infuriated and the Third Force was most unhappy about the situation.[9]

Wilber's narrative continues:

> The surging crowds of men, women and children were shouting: *Shah piruz ast* (The Shah is victorious). Determined as they seemed, a gay holiday atmosphere prevailed, and, as if exterior pressure had been released so that the true sentiments of the people showed through. The crowds were not, as in earlier weeks, made up of hoodlums, but included people of all classes—many well dressed—led or encouraged by civilians. Trucks and busloads of cheering civilians streamed by. . . . As usual, word spread like lightning and in other parts of the city pictures of the Shah were eagerly displayed.[10]

Some Iranians believe that the CIA retrospectively built up its own role in the August 1953 events so as to restore its prestige, shattered after the Bay of Pigs fiasco in 1961. The agency needed at least one feather if it were to keep its expensive hat. Anti-Americans, especially the Soviets and their agents and sympathizers throughout the world, found it in their own interest to endorse the CIA's claim as an example of American "imperialism" in action against a Third World nation. The shah's enemies inside Iran also liked the story, as it absolved them of any responsibility for Mossadeq's failure. Blaming the foreigner for one's own shortcomings has always been popular in Iran.

Not all anti-shah and anti-American scholars have bought the CIA's claim. According to one British Marxist academic:

> There is no doubt that the US government, and specifically the CIA, played an active part in organising the coup of 19 August 1953 that ousted Mossadeq, and that this intervention was the fruit of the build-up of the US presence in Iran that had been under way since the war. However, it is misleading to attribute everything to this factor alone: Iranian nationalists tend to do so—and so, on occasions, does the CIA, keen to claim credit for a successful operation. The reality is not so simple, since the CIA intervention was only possible because of internal balance of forces in Iran, the existence of elements within the dominant class that were interested in acting against the Mossadeq regime and the weaknesses of Mossadeq's own position.[11]

Those five days in August 1953 were destined to remain the stuff of legend and myth, as well as accusations and counteraccusations, that have continued to this day. Iranian opponents of the shah cite these events as proof of his "original sin," for which he should never be forgiven. The shah's supporters, on the other hand, claim that even if we assume that the Americans played a decisive role in the outcome, we must remember that the change of prime ministers at the time helped save Iran from a Communist takeover. In any case, allegations of CIA plotting did not translate into anti-Americanism in Iran. Iranians continued to regard the United States as a valuable friend. In the 1960s, the United States became the number-one destination for Iranian visitors and students. By 1978, there were more than 150,000 Iranian students, most of them financed by their families, in the United States—by far the largest number for any nationality. At the same time, more than 70,000 Americans worked in Iran along with almost a million other expatriates from some fifty different countries.

Mossadeq himself never blamed the United States for his downfall. And it is quite possible that he was relieved to be pushed aside at a time that he had run out of ideas and lived on a day-to-day basis. He had built his career on opposition to the British and then to the two Pahlavi Shahs. In August 1953, the British were no longer there, the first Pahlavi had been dead for years, and the second was in exile in Rome. What could Mossadeq do now? What did he have to offer? A typical naysayer, he knew only how to oppose, having marketed his ideology as "a balance of negatives" (*movazeneh manfi*). After a show trial in which he amused himself by demonstrating his oratorical skills once again, Mossadeq was given a three-year sentence, which the shah commuted to one of "surveyed residence." This meant that the old man would have to live in his estate near Tehran under the watchful eyes of security agents.

Because the power struggle had taken place within a small elite, most of whose members were related by blood or marriage, Mossadeq's political and army allies received short prison sentences or were released without charge. Only one was executed: Hussein Fatemi, the foreign minister who had publicly called for an end to monarchy and refused to recant. Some of Mossadeq's close associates remained attached to the belief, or the illusion, that the United States, especially the Democratic Party, somehow supported them. In the years to come, some of them immigrated to the United States and acquired American citizenship—no sign of bitterness there.[12]

In 1978, as the Khomeinist revolution gathered pace, pro-Mossadeq figures looked to the United States to help them come to power.[13] After the Khomeinist revolution, Tudeh Party leaders blamed Mossadeq's "weakness and tergiversation" for his fall and boasted that the Communists could have helped him seize power by force if necessary. While it is true that Mossadeq offered no leadership in those crucial days, it is unlikely that the Tudeh could have staged a putsch in his support. As noted earlier, the Tudeh and their Soviet masters enjoyed the support of hundreds of army, police, and gendarmerie officers and NCOs, and they could have seized control of Tehran. At the time, however, Moscow was in no position to make such a major move on the Cold War chessboard. Stalin had passed away four months earlier and the CPSU leadership was engaged in a bitter power struggle between the first secretary, Nikita Khrushchev, and the prime minister, Grigori Malenkov. The Soviet embassy and the NKVD network in Tehran were paralyzed, unable to obtain clear instructions from Moscow. A combination of factors beyond any man's control helped Iran escape what looked like an inevitable takeover by the Soviets and transformation into the "People's Republic of Iranestan" under a red flag.

As for Mossadeq's project, the nationalization of oil, it did great harm to Iran. In 1951, Iran had not been ready to take over the industry, produce the oil, and sell it on world markets. There were just four Iranians at the mid-levels of the industry, none with any experience in macromanagement of a major business enterprise. In any case, the ownership of the oil reserves had never been in doubt. The Anglo-Iranian Oil Company had operated in less than 1 percent of the Iranian territory, with the right to explore for oil in another 4 percent. Even then, the company never claimed it owned Iran's oil, if only because such a claim would have been legally groundless and politically impossible to sustain. Ali Razmara, prime minister in 1950–51, just before Mossadeq, had reminded the people of all these points in speeches at the parliament. He had suggested negotiating a new contract under which Iran would get better terms while training the personnel needed for an eventual "Iranization" of the industry at all levels. Razmara, a professional soldier and graduate of the elite French school at Saint-Cyr, also reminded the Iranians that their inefficient and corrupt government—a government that was unable to pay its employees on time—was in no position to run the oil industry and recapture the markets in the teeth of British opposition.

Mossadeq, however, was not interested in economics or practical matters in general. Nationalization was a catchy slogan; it created the impression that Iranians were taking revenge against the perfidious Albion that had snatched so much of their territory and subjected them to so much humiliation for 150 years. But during his two and a half years as prime minister, Mossadeq managed to find only one customer for Iranian oil, an Italian company, and sold 23,000 barrels to it. The event was dubbed the "Miracle of Mossadeq" and celebrated as a great victory. In reality, it was a humiliating occasion for a nation that could recall numerous genuine victories in its history. Then the British seized the cargo and declared it "stolen property" when they captured the Italian tanker *Rosa Maria* before it had left the Persian Gulf. The whole of Iran cried, and Mossadeq, who had been hailed as a hero a few days earlier, was recast as the quintessential martyr—not a bad position for those addicted to martyrdom.

"We don't care if we are going to starve or return to the stone age," shouted Hussein Makki, the most popular of Mossadeqist politicians, in Abadan in 1951. "The spectacle of seeing the English [*sic*] pack up and run away is enough victory for us for generations to come." The fact is that few Iranians at the time had ever seen any foreigners at all, let alone "the English," who numbered around two thousand and were confined to seven oil centers in often wild and inhospitable spots in the southwest where average temperatures are in the 100s Fahrenheit for much of the year.

By the time Zahedi took over as prime minister in 1953, most Iranians realized that they had had a good party and that, having tasted revenge against "the English," they now needed to cope with the hangover. They looked to the United States to help them avoid famine, end the oil dispute, and return the economy to some level of normality. Although the government led by Zahedi depended heavily on American financial aid, it showed no interest in a formal alliance with the United States. Several key ministers in the new cabinet, who had also served under Mossadeq, urged Iran to draw closer to the Non-Aligned Movement. The shah, however, was convinced that only a formal alliance with the United States could insure Iran against Soviet expansionism. He believed that once he had that insurance, he would be able to mobilize Iran's not inconsiderable resources for projecting power in its "natural habitat." Iran had to become "the regional superpower"; that was its manifest destiny as a builder of empires.

The issue of an alliance created some tension between the shah and his new prime minister, and came to a head over Iran's membership in the Baghdad Pact, a military alliance led by Britain with the United States as an associate member. The shah was for; Zahedi against. It soon became clear that Zahedi had to go, and he was posted to Geneva as ambassador to the UN's European headquarters, a sinecure for a golden exile. Even then, influential voices within the decision-making elite still advocated a policy of nonalignment. It was under their pressure that Iran sent a delegation to the Bandung Conference, where the Non-Aligned Movement was announced formally in April 1955.[14]

The shah's campaign for a formal alliance with the United States included an offer he made to President Eisenhower during a state visit to Washington to put the Iranian army under American command, as European NATO members had done with their armies. Eisenhower politely declined. Instead, he offered a Treaty of Friendship and Cooperation, which the two nations duly signed in 1955. It stated that "there shall be firm and enduring peace and sincere friendship between the United States of America and Iran," but no military alliance. The treaty remained the basis of Irano-American relations until Khomeini seized power. Even then, since neither side has revoked the treaty, it legally remains in force. In fact, the Islamic Republic invoked it in a suit it brought against the United States at the International Court of Justice at The Hague in 2001. An ICJ judge, Shi Jiu-yong, ruled in Iran's favor, declaring the treaty still valid.

The price the shah paid for American friendship was high, and in later years he almost regretted having agreed to pay it. The Soviet propaganda machine, reinforced by the worldwide network of anti-Americans of all ilk, targeted him as "a lackey of imperialism." The myth was propagated that Iran had become a satellite of the United States and that the shah was pursuing the kind of militant anti-Communism that the Americans themselves had abandoned after the McCarthy era. But even the most ardent opponents of the shah have never been able to cite a single specific example of anything the shah did that was good for the United States and bad for Iran.

Having made major inroads into the Middle East in the 1960s by signing military pacts with Egypt, Syria, and Iraq, Moscow saw Iran as the main obstacle to Soviet hegemony over the Persian Gulf and its vital energy resources. It tried to pressure the shah into accepting a "Finlandization" of Iran, that is to say adopting a policy of neutrality in the Cold War.[15] The suggestion always angered the shah: Finland was "a tiny backwater of Europe" while Iran was "a great power in the heart of the most important region on earth." Even then, as the United States consistently refused to sign a military pact with Iran, the shah remolded his policy to accommodate aspects of nonalignment. For example, he would not allow U.S. military bases on Iranian territory.[16] Nor was he prepared to send Iranian troops to fight alongside the U.S.-led coalition in Vietnam.[17] Ignoring U.S. efforts to isolate Communist China, the shah decided to recognize the People's Republic in 1970 and sent his twin sister, Princess Ashraf, on a goodwill mission to Beijing. This was followed by an even more spectacular visit in 1971, by Empress Farah and Prime Minister Hoveyda, that turned China into one of the shah's strongest supporters, right to the end of his reign.[18] The shah also tried to diversify the sources of weaponry for Iran while launching a domestic military hardware industry that was to reach impressive scale in the 1980s. If the air force that he created almost from scratch was entirely dependent on American hardware, the army and the navy used French, Italian, British, Swiss, and even Soviet equipment and materiel. Trying not to depend solely on the United States for training the technical personnel his armed forces needed, the shah concluded agreements with thirteen other countries, including several in Europe as well as South Korea.

By the 1970s, the shah felt confident enough to start projecting Iranian power where he believed the United States was failing as defender of the free world against Communism. It was thus that Iranian troops arrived in the Sultanate of Oman to fight Soviet-backed Communist rebels. Iranian troops also appeared in southern Lebanon to prevent Soviet-backed Palestinian groups from attacking Israel. In Morocco, some four hundred Iranian military experts, along with massive Iranian arms supplies, helped King Hassan II beat an Algerian attempt to drive him out of the Western Sahara. Nearer home, the shah sent military experts and materiel to help Pakistan defeat a Soviet-backed insurgency in Baluchistan. On the diplomatic front, Iran helped persuade several countries to switch sides and join the anti-Communist camp. These included Sudan, Somalia, and most importantly Egypt under its new president, Muhammad Anwar Sadat. In 1973, Iran initiated a series of diplomatic, political, and economic moves to curtail Soviet influence in Afghanistan. Determined to play the "big power," Iran, having announced in 1961 that it no longer needed foreign aid, launched its own aid program for the developing world. Part of this aid was channeled to the OPEC Fund, which the shah helped set up.[19] The bulk of the Iranian aid, however, was disbursed through bilateral agreements with more than forty countries across the globe, mostly in Asia and Africa. Iran also helped some old allies, notably Great Britain, by lending them vast sums of money to ease their budgetary pressures on a number of occasions. To show the flag, the shah set up his own version of the American Peace Corps. Called the Legion of Mankind's Servants of Humanity, the paramilitary organization offered medical, agricultural, and educational aid to some twenty countries.

The shah regarded the United States as a fickle power whose policies could change in accordance with changes of mood in its domestic politics. Except for the eight years of the Nixon and Ford administrations, the shah's relations with the United States were never easy. He suspected President John F. Kennedy of wanting to topple him and install a military regime in Tehran as he had done in Saigon. These suspicious were fanned by the red-carpet reception that Kennedy and his brother Robert, the attorney general, had given to Lieutenant General Teymur Bakhtiar, head of the shah's secret service (SAVAK), during a visit to Washington. An earlier alleged plot, involving Brigadier General Valiallah Qarani, had also been traced to Washington. The shah regarded Robert Kennedy's encouragement of anti-regime Iranian student leaders abroad as a sign of hostile intent by Washington.

The shah believed that the period of American ascendancy would be short, perhaps no more than a few decades.[20] He was baffled by the American system in which "just anybody could become president, anybody like Ford or Carter," while "a great statesman like Richard Nixon" would be "utterly destroyed on trivial grounds."[21] His dream, therefore, was to make Iran powerful enough not to need U.S. support against the Soviets and their radical Arab allies. That meant establishing Iran as the regional "superpower," capable of defending the vital sea-lanes of the Persian Gulf, the Arabian Sea, and the Indian Ocean. Those ambitions ran counter to the global Soviet strategy and thus turned the shah into the bête noire of Communists and their fellow travelers and "useful idiots." Rather than offer a critique of the shah's strategy with reference to Iran's interests as a nation-state, his enemies preferred to present him as an "American puppet," thus drawing support from all those throughout the world, including the United States itself, who had succumbed to the irrational seduction of anti-Americanism.

15

A Universal Ideology

That the mullahs who succeeded the shah in 1979 should inherit his big-power ambitions is no surprise. Those ambitions reflect the reality of Iran as a potentially strong nation-state in a region of weak and at times unstable newly created states. There are, however, fundamental differences between the shah's vision of Iran as a regional power and the Khomeinist regime's vision of the Islamic Revolution as a messianic movement destined to conquer the world. Under the shah, Iran acted as a nation-state. Under the Khomeinists, it acts as a revolution. This dichotomy creates a Jekyll-and-Hyde situation with profound effects on Iranian foreign policy. The ambitions of a nation-state can always be accommodated within an international system based on interaction among nation-states. The ambitions of a revolution, especially one claiming a universal mission, are not so easily accommodated, if only because the first objective of every revolution is to change the status quo and cancel the rules of the game. In a speech on January 5, 2005, Ahmadinejad explained the difference this way: "We must believe in the fact that Islam is not confined to geographical borders, ethnic groups and nations. It's a universal ideology that leads the world to justice. We don't shy away from declaring that Islam is ready to rule the world. We must prepare ourselves to rule the world."[1]

The shah wanted to use American power to counterbalance the Soviet Union, thus enabling Iran to build itself as a regional power. Even then, the shah regarded the USSR as an adversary rather than an enemy, and thus amenable to compromise. He did not want to force the USSR to change its ideology or political model. All he wanted was to prevent the USSR from imposing its ideology and political model on Iran. Today there is no USSR, and the Islamic Republic hopes to take its place. All Islamic Republic leaders, from Khomeini to Ahmadinejad, have taken for granted that the principal obstacle to their dream of "exporting" their revolution to the whole world is American power.

Like Communists before them, Khomeinists regard the United States as "the enemy." The issue is not how to neutralize it but how to defeat it and force it to adopt the Khomeinist version of Islam. The shah's policy was aimed at avoiding war through diplomacy and trade. The Khomeinists, on the other hand, have war written in their political DNA. Here is how Rafsanjani, often regarded in the West as a moderate, puts it: "The weaker the U.S. becomes, the stronger [our regime in] Iran. We have some scores with America that must be settled one day. And that day may not be far off."[2] Referring to "American difficulties in Iraq," he said the United States had become "vulnerable" and had been "proved to be an empty drum." Recalling how China used the United States' defeat in Vietnam to build its own position as the principal power in Asia, Rafsanjani predicted that an American defeat in Iraq would enable the Islamic Republic to emerge in a leadership role in the Middle East.

Ayatollah Ahmad Janati, head of the powerful Council of the Guardians of the Constitution, has put the case even more bluntly: "When all is said and done, we are an anti-American regime. America is our enemy, and we are the enemies of America. . . . Just like [our] revolution destroyed the monarchy here, it will definitely destroy the arrogant hegemony of America, Israel, and their allies."[3] America is at once powerful and fragile, so its destruction and "disappearance" is both a realistic and a legitimate aim: "America seems so big, but in fact is like a paper tiger— even the slightest tremor could easily make it crumble and disappear."[4]

The Islamic Republic is probably the only place where a special course in "Anti-American studies" is offered at several universities and staff training academies. Works by anti-American authors abroad, including writers in the United States, are instantly translated and published. Throughout the developing world, the embassies of the Islamic Republic and the special offices of the Supreme Guide channel funds to anti-

American newspapers, magazines, and private radio stations. In 1988, a doctoral program in anti-Americanism was launched at Tehran University's Department of Political Science under Professor Homayun Elahi. Since that year, a committee headed by Khamenehi, then president of the Islamic Republic, and including a number of black American defectors, has worked on a project for creating a "black republic" in one of the southern states of the United States, with Mississippi regarded as the favorite.[5] The Islamic Republic has organized at least half a dozen international conferences with such titles as "A World Without America" and "America Is Heading for a Fall." In 2001, the Ministry of Islamic Guidance and Culture organized a competition for poets who imagined the "destruction of the Great Satan." Iranian children from the age of six are taught to shout "Death to America" as if it were part of their religious incantations. City walls throughout Iran are covered with anti-American graffiti, often showing the United States as a monster dragon being slain by an Islamic version of Saint George. The star-spangled flag is painted in front of many doorways to make sure it is constantly trampled underfoot. November 4, the anniversary of the raid on the U.S. embassy in Tehran, is called "Death to America Day" and celebrated as a major feast with official messages from the Supreme Guide, the president of the Islamic Republic, and other dignitaries.

Anti-Americanism is also the guiding principle of the Islamic Republic's foreign policy. Between 1979 and 1991, it inspired what amounted to an undeclared alliance between the Islamic Republic and the USSR. Iran was the only Muslim country to allow the Soviet-installed regime in Afghanistan to maintain an embassy in Tehran. The Iranian border with Afghanistan was sealed, preventing the Afghan mujahedin from attacking the Red Army from that direction. Although the mujahedin were fighting in the name of Islam, the Islamic Republic was more anxious to preserve its anti-American alliance with the Soviet Union. Anti-Americanism also meant that the Islamic Republic was the only Muslim country to maintain a firm alliance with Yugoslavia even while the dominant Serbs were massacring Muslims in Bosnia-Herzegovina and Kosovo.

Yugoslavia was the only European country to play host to Khamenehi as president in 1989. And the Serbian leader Slobodan Milosevic (later prosecuted as a war criminal) was the only European head of state to forge a personal friendship with the ayatollah.

That anti-Americanism, rather than Islam or even its Shiite version, is the guiding principle of the Islamic Republic's foreign policy is made clear in a number of other cases. As the USSR was crumbling in 1989, Rafsanjani, as speaker of the Islamic Majlis, the ersatz parliament, paid a state visit to the Soviet Union, where he told Soviet Muslims to remain loyal to the Communist regime, which he claimed was "a supporter of Islam on the global stage." In a speech in Baku, capital of Soviet Azerbaijan, he quoted the Prophet as saying that "love of country is part of faith" and called on Muslims not to break away from the USSR. "The world-devouring Great Satan is plotting to destroy the Soviet Union and dominate the whole of mankind," he said. "Muslims should not fall into the [American] trap. . . . What is [needed now] is solidarity among those who do not wish impiety to dominate."[6] Needless to say, the Azeris found the Iranian visitor's exhortations distasteful, to say the least, coming so soon after Gorbachev had organized an invasion of Baku by land, sea, and air, to crush a popular anti-Soviet uprising. The message was especially painful to Azeris, most of whom are Shiites, because it came from a Shiite mullah.

Two years later, as president of the Islamic Republic, the same Rafsanjani threw his weight behind Christian Armenia in a war against Shiite Azerbaijan, now an independent republic, over an enclave named High Qarabagh (Nagorno Karabakh) in Transcaucasus. Over half a million Azeri Shiites were driven out of their homes, many becoming refugees in Iran. And yet Tehran continued to back landlocked Armenia by helping it break an embargo imposed by Turkey and Azerbaijan. The reason was that while Azerbaijan had allied itself with the United States and Turkey, Armenia had retained its traditional alliance with Russia. Determined to punish Azerbaijan for "the sin of pro-Americanism," Tehran tried to incite the Sunni minority in Talesh, on the Caspian Sea, to revolt against the government in Baku. Ayaz Mutallibov, the pro-Russian leader of the Sunni Taleshis, became the darling of the mullahs against the Shiite and pro-American Abulfazl Ilchibey. In another former Soviet republic, Tajikistan in Central Asia, Tehran persuaded the Islamist opposition to make a deal with pro-Russian neo-Communists to exclude pro-West democratic forces from power. In Pakistan, Tehran has ordered its clients in the Jaafari Movement (Tehrik Jaafari), an Iranian-financed Shiite party, to forget its blood feud with the pro-Taliban Sunni parties and join them in a coalition to defeat pro-American candidates in two successive general elections in the past decade.

Sometimes, anti-Americanism is justified with the claim that the United States has prevented Muslims from liberating Jerusalem and destroying Israel. Here is how Rafsanjani puts it: "We give support to the mujahedin in Palestine. Hamas is zealous with regard to Sunni Islam, but because of their jihad and resistance, we supply them with aid."[7] In other words, although Hamas is a militant anti-Shiite group linked to the Sunni Muslim Brotherhood, it deserves support from Iran because of their mutual hostility to Israel and the United States. One need not be Muslim at all to attract support from the Islamic Republic. Communist North Korea, the most militantly antireligious regime today, is the closest ally of the Khomeinist regime in Tehran. What the two have in common is anti-Americanism. The same was true of the "strategic partnership" that the Islamic Republic had forged with Romania under Nicolae Ceausescu's Communist dictatorship. In December 1989, Ceausescu paid his very last visit abroad to Iran just days before he was executed upon his return home. In a joint communiqué issued in Tehran, the Islamic Republic and Romania vowed to "combat imperialism on all fronts."

That the Khomeinist regime perceives international relations as a form of war is made clear in Katami's words: "What could we do in order to enter the world scene? We need a force that the enemy [the United States] does not possess, a force superior to technology and to arms. What we need as a balancing force is the newly born, fully alert, and ready-to-sacrifice Islamic force. If the Islamic Republic is supported by such a force . . . then its movement will be taken seriously."[8]

In 1979, Khomeini had vowed to fight the Great Satan in every corner of the globe. Over the years, this has meant efforts by the Islamic Republic to forge alliances with all those who have pursued an anti-American agenda. In the 1980s, while the Reagan administration helped the Contras in Nicaragua, Tehran supplied the Sandinistas with oil, money, and arms. When the United States tried to isolate Cuba and, after the fall of the USSR and Castro's loss of Soviet aid, force it towards reform, the Islamic Republic retaliated by making up a good part of the lost Soviet aid to Cuba. When the United States helped successive Colombian governments fight the narco-Marxists of the FARC, the Revolutionary Armed Forces of Colombia, the Khomeinist regime responded by funneling funds to the FARC. When the United States supported moderate Arab regimes in Saudi Arabia, Kuwait, Bahrain, Jordan, Egypt, and Algeria, the Islamic Republic replied by financing and arming terrorist organizations in every one of those countries.

Latin America, described by Ahmadinejad as "the backyard of the Great Satan," has been the target of special attention by Tehran for decades. The first Latin American regime with which the Islamic Republic forged an alliance was Cuba under Fidel Castro. Over the past eighteen years, Iran has injected billions of dollars into Cuba's ailing economy, helping the Castro regime absorb the shock of the loss of Soviet patronage in 1991. Then, in 1993, Khamenehi set up an office to promote "convergence" among various Islamic sects, but the principal mission of the new organ, under Ayatollah Muhammad-Ali Taskhiri, was to establish contact with Shiite communities throughout the world, especially in West Africa and South America, where millions of ethnic Lebanese and Syrians have lived for decades. Soon, branches of Hezballah appeared in Brazil, Argentina, Uruguay, and Paraguay. Everywhere, these branches were instructed to cooperate with other anti-American forces, including the Bolivarists and Marxists, to accentuate the leftward trend of Latin American politics.

In the late 1990s, Tehran found a true Latin American ally in the person of Hugo Chavez, president of Venezuela. He has helped Iran create a radical axis within the Organization of Petroleum Exporting Countries (OPEC), with Libya and Algeria as occasional allies. With assistance from Chavez, Ahmadinejad is trying to win the leadership of the so-called Non-Aligned Movement, a grouping of over 150 Third World nations, some of them anti-American since the days of the Cold War. As Ahmadinejad sees it, the United States is trying to throw a lasso around the Islamic Republic with the help of allies in the Middle East, Transcaucasus, and Central Asia. Therefore, the Islamic Republic should throw a "counter-lasso" through alliances in South America, where Ahmadinejad is supporting a chain of anti-American regimes with the help of his "brother" Chavez.

Since the late 1980s, Hezballah has been building a base in Paraguay by recruiting within the Shiite community of Syrian-Lebanese origin, which represents an estimated 15 percent of the population. This base played a key role in ensuring the election of Fernando Lugo, a former Catholic bishop, as president of Paraguay in 2008, especially through a massive fundraising campaign supported by Iran and Venezuela. Lugo is known for his involvement in radical leftist political activities in the name of "liberation theology." In the 1990s he had visited Iran to pay homage at the tomb of Khomeini, a man he has praised as "a forerunner of the modern global revolutionary movement." Ahmadinejad was among the first foreign leaders to congratulate Lugo on his election as president, describing him as "a man of God." Clearly, Ahmadinejad hoped that Paraguay would now add another link to the "counter-lasso."

Both Ahmadinejad and Chavez have every reason to be pleased with their strategy. The United States is clearly in retreat in its own backyard. The Monroe Doctrine, designed to deny European powers a dominant role on the American continent, does not apply to Iran, which is determined to carve out its zone of influence in Latin America. At the start of the new century, Brazil already had a moderate leftist regime under President Luiz Inácio Lula da Silva. Since then, Bolivia has elected a leftist firebrand in the person of President Evo Morales. Chile, Argentina, and Uruguay have opted for moderate leftist governments, while Ecuador has taken a sharp turn to the left. Ecuador's new president, Rafael Correa, suspended talks for a free trade agreement with the United States and threatened not to renew the lease for the American air base at Manta in 2009. Joining the so-called "Progressist Front" of Latin American countries with leftist regimes, Ecuador has also returned to OPEC, increasing the influence of Iran and Venezuela. The Sandinistas, slightly less leftist but a lot older, have gained power again in Nicaragua under President Daniel Ortega, who highlighted his alliance with Ahmadinejad by making Iran the first country outside Latin America that he visited after returning to the presidency. One of the biggest Iranian missions abroad is active in Managua. Even in Peru, the return of Alan Garcia as president has revived the corpse of the anti-American left. In the summer of 2008, the only piece of the puzzle still tilting to the right was Colombia under President Alvaro Uribe.

Seen from Tehran, all this is confirmation of Ahmadinejad's working hypothesis that the global tide is turning against the United States and that the idea of clipping the wings of the American Great Satan is no longer merely a revolutionary fantasy. Under Ahmadinejad, Tehran has signed contracts with Caracas worth $40 billion, a huge sum considering the modest size of the Venezuelan economy. Contracts worth a further $30 billion have been negotiated with Bolivia, Nicaragua, and Ecuador. Iran's business relations with Cuba, Brazil, and Peru are also booming. Relations with Argentina have remained problematic largely because of arrest warrants issued by a court in Buenos Aires for a number of senior Iranian officials in connection with the bombing of a Jewish cultural center over a decade ago. But even there, the Islamic Republic is appearing with offers of lucrative contracts designed to rescue Latin American economies from their decade-long stagnation.

These contracts come in four sectors. The first and the largest is energy. Iran's aim is to replace as many of the U.S. companies as possible in the Latin American oil and gas industry. A joint Iranian-Venezuelan consortium hopes to dominate the natural gas sector in Bolivia while launching new exploration schemes for oil and gas in Nicaragua, Ecuador, and Peru. The second sector is armaments. None of the Latin American countries has a credible weapons industry, and the Islamic Republic hopes to fill that gap. Iran has already sold $4.5 billion worth of military materiel to Venezuela and is training hundreds of Venezuelan military personnel. The third sector is security. Iranian and Venezuelan security services have already set up a coordination committee and developed a system of exchanging information. Nicaragua was expected to join soon, along with Cuba, Bolivia, and Ecuador. Finally, Iran is investing in Latin American media. The first step in that direction came in April 2008 in the form of a $1 billion Iranian investment in developing a Spanish-language television network to compete with the major American satellite channels. As Ahmadinejad likes to tell his Latin American hosts: the Americans are going, the Iranians are coming! With crude oil prices at record-high levels, the Islamic Republic had piles of cash to throw around while the United States was heading for another bout of belt-tightening.

16

Sunrise Power against Sunset Power

For almost eight years during the presidency of Bill Clinton, one word summed up the policy of the United States towards Iran: "containment." Having labeled Iran a "rogue nation" in 1994, Secretary of State Warren Christopher sat back waiting for things to sort themselves out. Four years later, however, it was clear that the Islamic Republic, far from being contained, was spreading its influence throughout the Middle East, Central Asia, and sub-Saharan Africa. It had also built solid relations with the European Union, which had become Iran's number-one trading partner, while treating Russia and China as informal allies. The Iranian leadership had interpreted the Clintonian "containment" as an assurance that the United States would take no action to weaken their hold on power in Tehran. They felt they had a free hand to pursue their hegemonic designs wherever they found an opportunity. Even when an Iranian-sponsored hit squad blew up a U.S. military residence in Al Khobar, eastern Saudi Arabia, killing nineteen American servicemen, the Clinton administration decided to hush things up so as not to implicate the mullahs. The FBI presented the president with "ample evidence" of Iranian involvement. Clinton, however, ruled out any action against the Islamic Republic.[1] By the end of his presidency, Clinton had gone even further in attempting to placate the mullahs. His second secretary of state, Madeleine Albright, had lifted some of the sanctions imposed on Iran by three U.S. administrations and offered public apologies to the Islamic Republic.

Why did Clinton decide to give the Islamic Republic a free hand in pursuit of policies that were clearly designed to drive the United States out of the Middle East and use the region as the principal base of a global anti-American campaign? One reason may be that Clinton regarded the publicly stated intentions of the Khomeinist leadership as nothing but radical rhetoric. But is it not possible—incredible though it may sound— that he also sympathized with a regime that he regarded as revolutionary? The answer is yes, and it was provided by Clinton himself shortly after he had left office. Here is what Clinton said at a meeting on the margins of the World Economic Forum in Davos, Switzerland: "Iran today is, in a sense, *the only country* where progressive ideas enjoy a vast constituency. It is there that the ideas that I subscribe to are defended by a majority."[2] (Emphasis added.) A few days later, Clinton said in a television interview with Charlie Rose:

> Iran is the only country in the world that has now had six
> elections since the first election of President Khatami [in 1997].
> [It is] the only one with elections, including the United States,
> including Israel, including you name it, where the liberals, or
> the progressives, have won two-thirds to 70 percent of the vote
> in six elections: Two for president; two for the Parliament, the
> Majlis; two for the mayoralties. In every single election, *the guys
> I identify with* got two-thirds to 70 percent of the vote. There is
> no other country in the world I can say that about, certainly
> not my own.[3] [Emphasis added.]

So, while millions of Iranians, especially the young, looked to the United States as a model of progress and democracy, a former American president designated the Islamic Republic as his ideological homeland. But who were "the guys" Clinton identified with? There was, of course, President Muhammad Khatami, who a week earlier, speaking at a conference of provincial governors, had called for the whole world to convert to Islam: "Human beings understand different affairs within the global framework that they live in," he said. "But when we say that Islam belongs to all times and places, it is implied that the very essence of Islam is such that despite changes [in time and place] it is always valid."[4] There was also Khatami's brother, Muhammad-Reza, the man who in

1979 led the "students" who seized the U.S. embassy in Tehran and held its diplomats hostage for 444 days. And there was the Ayatollah Sadeq Khalkhali, known to Iranians as "Judge Blood," and Ayatollah Ali-Akbar Mohtashami-Pour, the man who created the Lebanese branch of Hezballah. Mohtashami-Pour is also the man who organized the attack on Pan Am Flight 103 over Lockerbie, Scotland, in 1988, claiming the lives of 271 people, most of them Americans. Clinton was identifying with "progressives" who had made Iran the world record-holder for executions, just behind the People's Republic of China, and had organized the murder of hundreds of intellectuals, Christian priests, and Sunni Muslim clerics.

Not surprisingly, the state-owned media in Tehran seized upon Clinton's utterances to counter President George W. Bush's claim that the Islamic Republic was a tyranny that oppresses the Iranians and threatens the stability of the region. Clinton's declaration of love for the mullahs showed how ill informed even a U.S. president could be. Hadn't anyone told Clinton when he was in the White House that elections in the Islamic Republic were as meaningless as those held in the Soviet Union? Did he not know that all candidates had to be approved by the Supreme Guide and that no opposition figures are allowed to run? Did he not know that all parties are banned in the Islamic Republic, and that the mullahs use such terms as "progressive" and "liberal" as synonyms for "apostate," a charge that could lead to a death sentence? More importantly, did he not know that while there was no democracy without elections, there could be elections without democracy? Clinton forgot that anti-Americanism and hatred of the West in general form the ideological backbone of Khomeinism. The former president endorsed another claim of the mullahs: that Saddam Hussein, the deposed Iraqi dictator, had invaded Iran on behalf of the United States. If true, this would mean that another Democratic president, Jimmy Carter, had engineered a war that claimed more than a million lives.

Bill Clinton's feeling of "guilt" towards Iran is inspired by what one might call the "imperialism of compassion." Those who suffer from this affliction believe that the so-called developing nations are nothing but objects of history, never subjects, and that history is made only by the major Western powers. If the people of the Indian subcontinent tore each other apart over religion and fought a series of wars that claimed millions of lives, it was all the fault of Britain. If the Arabs have produced despotic regimes that suffocate their societies, the blame rests with Western colonialism. If the Rwandans massacre each other, the fault lies with the West. The imperialism of compassion is as humiliating for the developing nations as classical imperialism was in its time, for it denies those nations a sense of responsibility, thus part of their humanity.

Seen from the Khomeinists' point of view, the United States appears like the proverbial giant with feet of clay. Gripped by self-doubt and a sense of guilt, its leaders are incapable of using even a fraction of their nation's power in defense of its interests. At the same time, many U.S. politicians simply cannot believe that others might not share their view of politics as the art of the possible in a realm of compromise. Most Americans admire a politician who can negotiate a compromise to avoid conflict. Making deals, fifty-fifty, is part of the American culture; thus the Civil War is viewed as a great national tragedy. The Khomeinist mindset is quite different. It regards compromise as degrading because the Only Truth—that is, Islam—can never bring itself down to the level of the "abrogated" faiths, meaning all other religions and creeds. Khomeini is admired because he refused all compromise. In 1978 he could have helped Iran avoid tragedy had he agreed to allow the formation of a transitional government and the holding of free elections. At any time between 1980 and 1988, he could have accepted any of the UN-brokered compromises to end the war with Iran, thus preventing hundreds of thousands of deaths. In 1988, he could have stopped a massacre of over four thousand political prisoners by accepting their "repentance." But in every case, anxious to keep his image as a tough leader intact, he rejected compromise. Khomeini was an exaggerated version of the typical Iranian "strongman" who must not, indeed, cannot show weakness. In the nineteenth century, the Qajar king Fath Ali Shah might have avoided a humiliating defeat and loss of territory by Iran had he apologized to Russia for the seizure of its embassy and the murder of its ambassador in Tehran.[5] In 1941, Reza Shah might have prevented the invasion of Iran and his own enforced abdication had he agreed to a compromise under which he would expel Nazi agents and join the Allies against the Axis. In 1953, Mossadeq might have saved himself and the nation a great deal of hardship had he accepted any of the generous compromise deals worked out by his American friends. In every case, however, the leader was prepared to sacrifice the best interests of the nation at the altar of his hubris. The generation that was swept to power with Ahmadinejad is even less prone to compromise, if only because it regards "martyrdom" as the noblest of goals.

By contrast, the American "enemy" loves life to the point that he is prepared to accept almost any humiliation and indignity to prolong it. Soon after his election as president, Ahmadinejad told a press conference that he knew "all about Americans" and boasted, "I know how their minds work." At the time, Ahmadinejad's principal "expert" on U.S. affairs was one Dr. Hassan Abbasi, a professor of strategy at the Islamic Revolutionary Guard Corps University and nicknamed "the Kissinger of Islam." He also lectured to informal gatherings of "Volunteers for Martyrdom." His main theme is that the United States lacks the stamina for a long conflict and that it is bound to "run away" from the Middle East, allowing the Islamic Republic to reshape it as the "core of an Islamic superpower."

To hear Dr. Abbasi tell it, the entire recent history of the United States could be narrated with the help of the image of "the last helicopter." It was this image that impressed the Bay of Pigs fiasco on the pages of history under John F. Kennedy. The same image in Saigon concluded the Vietnam War under Gerald Ford. Jimmy Carter had five helicopters fleeing from the Iranian desert, leaving behind the charred corpses of eight American soldiers. Under Ronald Reagan, the helicopters carried the bodies of 241 Marines murdered in their sleep in a Hezballah suicide attack. Under the first President George Bush, the helicopter flew from Safwan, in southern Iraq, with General Norman Schwarzkopf aboard, leaving behind Saddam Hussein's generals, who could not understand why they had been allowed to live so they could crush their domestic foes and fight America another day. Bill Clinton's helicopter was a Black Hawk, downed in Mogadishu and delivering sixteen American soldiers into the hands of a murderous crowd.

According to this theory, President George W. Bush is an "aberration," a leader out of sync with his nation's character and no more than a brief nightmare for those who oppose the creation of an "American Middle East." Abbasi and Ahmadinejad have concluded that there will be no helicopter as long as George W. Bush is in the White House. But they believe that whoever succeeds him, Democrat or Republican, will revive the helicopter image to extricate the United States from a complex situation that few Americans appear to understand.

Ahmadinejad believes that the world is heading for a clash of civilizations, with the Middle East as the main battlefield, and with Iran leading the Muslim world against the "Crusader-Zionist camp" led by America. In 2005, Ahmadinejad announced one of the most ambitious government mission statements in decades, declaring that the ultimate goal of Iran's foreign policy was nothing less than "a government for the whole world" under the leadership of the Mahdi, the Absent Imam of the Shiites—code for the export of radical Islam. The only power capable of challenging this vision, the United States, was in its "last throes." Bush may have led America into "a brief moment of triumph," but the United States is a "sunset" *(ofuli)* power, while the Islamic Republic is a "sunrise" *(tolu'ee)* power. Once Bush is gone, a future president will admit defeat and order a retreat, as all of Bush's predecessors have done since Jimmy Carter. Geopolitical dominance in the Middle East, Ahmadinejad's tract unequivocally stated, is "the incontestable right of the Iranian nation."

Tehran leaders believe that the U.S. defeat in Vietnam enabled China to establish itself as the rising power in Asia. They hope that a U.S. defeat in Iraq will give the Islamic Republic a similar opportunity to become what Rafsanjani calls "the regional superpower." The Khomeinists also believe that an American defeat in Iraq will destabilize all Arab regimes,

leaving the Islamic Republic as the only power around which a new status quo could be built in the region. "Here is our opportunity to teach the
Americans a lesson," Rafsanjani said in 2004. But what would constitute
a U.S. defeat in Iraq? As far as Tehran is concerned, all that is needed is
television images of American soldiers boarding those familiar helicopters and leaving behind their Iraqi allies before they are in a position to
defend themselves.

History, however, is never written in advance. It is possible that the
9/11 attacks have changed the way Americans see the world and their
place in it. Running away from Cuba, Saigon, the Iranian desert, Beirut,
Safwan, and Mogadishu was not hard to sell to the average American,
because he was sure that the story would end there—that the enemies
left behind would not pursue their campaign within the United States
itself. But the enemies that America is now facing in the jihadist archi-
pelago are dedicated to the destruction of the United States as the world
knows it today.

17

Crazy Eddie and Martyr Hussein

In May 2008, the Democratic presidential candidate Senator Barack Hussein Obama announced his plan to seek a summit with the president of the Islamic Republic, Mahmoud Ahmadinejad, in "direct talks with no preconditions." For months, Obama rallies included small groups carrying placards saying "No War on Iran," whereas "No Nukes for Iran" would have made more sense.

The attempt to fabricate another "cause" with which to bash America was backed by the claim that the mullahs were behaving badly with their nuclear ambitions because George W. Bush refused to talk to them. By way of contrast, Obama referred to John Kennedy's "leadership" in his Vienna summit with Nikita Khrushchev and during the Cuban missile crisis, an incident that has entered American folklore as an example of "brilliant diplomacy." But few bother to examine the small print. The crisis, as you may recall, started when the Soviets installed nuclear missiles in Cuba, something they were committed not to do in a number of accords with the United States. Kennedy reacted by threatening to quarantine Cuba until the missiles were removed. The Soviets ended up "flinching" and agreed to take the missiles away. In exchange, they got two things: First, the United States pledged never to perpetrate or assist in hostile action against Castro—in effect offering life insurance to his regime. Second, the United States removed the Jupiter missiles installed in Turkey as part of NATO's defenses. Instead of being punished, Castro and his Soviet masters were doubly rewarded for undoing *what they shouldn't have done in the first place.* And Castro was free to do mischief, not only in Latin America but also in Africa, the Arabian Peninsula, and the Persian Gulf, often on behalf of Moscow, right up to the fall of the USSR

Applied to Iran, the "Kennedy model" would provide the Khomeinists, facing mounting discontent at home, with a guarantee of safety from external pressure, allowing them to suppress their domestic opponents and intensify mischief-making abroad.

The second model for engaging Iran is Jimmy Carter's policy towards the mullahs. Carter has called for a "diplomatic solution," and Zbigniew Brzezinski, his national security advisor, published an op-ed blaming the Bush administration for the crisis. He wrote: "Artificial deadlines, propounded most often by those who do not wish the U.S. to negotiate in earnest, are counterproductive. Name-calling and saber rattling, as well as a refusal to even consider the other side's security concerns, can be useful tactics only if the goal is to derail the negotiating process."

Let's forget that the "artificial deadlines" for Iran to cease its uranium enrichment have been set by the International Atomic Energy Agency and the UN Security Council, and that most of the "name-calling and saber rattling" has come from Tehran. But let us recall one fact that Brzezinski does not mention: that the Carter administration *did* "engage" with the mullahs without artificial deadlines, saber rattling, or name-calling. The results for the United States were disastrous. Brzezinski's op-ed was titled "Been There, Done That," meant as a sneering nod to events that led to the liberation of Iraq. A more apt title, however, is "Been There, Done That, Learned Nothing"—a nod to Brzezinski's failure to learn the lessons of Iran even three decades later.

The third model for engaging Iran is the Clinton model. Beating his own drum, Bill Clinton has rejected the threat of force and called for "engaging" Iran. This is how he put it in a recent speech: "Anytime somebody said in my presidency, 'If you don't do this, people will think you're weak,' I always asked the same question for eight years: 'Can we kill 'em tomorrow?' If we can kill 'em tomorrow, then we're not weak." Clinton's pseudo-Socratic method of either/or-ing issues out of existence is too well known to merit an exposé. This time, however, Clinton did not ask enough questions. For example, he might have asked: What if by refusing to kill some of them today we are forced to kill many more of them tomorrow? Also: What if, once assured that we are not going to kill them today, they regroup and come to kill us in larger numbers?

Clinton did not reveal that in 1999 he offered the mullahs "a grand bargain" under which the Islamic Republic would be recognized as the "regional power" in exchange for lip service to U.S. "interests in the Middle East." As advance payment for the "bargain," as we have already noted, Clinton apologized for "all the wrongs that my country and culture have done" to Iran, whatever that was supposed to mean. The "bargain," had it not been vetoed by the Supreme Guide in Tehran, might have secured Clinton the Nobel Peace Prize he coveted, but it would have sharpened the Khomeinists' appetite for exporting revolution.

The fourth model for engaging Iran is that of Nixon in China: a U.S. president taking the trouble of traveling to Beijing for direct and unconditional talks with adversaries. This model is based on the myth that it was Kissinger's "deft diplomacy" and *Realpolitik* that made Nixon-in-China possible. Facts, however, show a different picture. To start with, they show that the dramatic trip was made possible because China, and not the United States, had changed. It is often forgotten that the initiative that eventually led to the visit came from China, through Pakistan and Iran under the shah. By 1970, the Great Proletarian Cultural Revolution—a moment of madness that had wrecked the Chinese economy and pushed the nation to the brink of famine—had run out of steam. Its principal orchestrator, Marshall Lin Biao, had died in a mysterious plane crash. The "Gang of Four," including Mao Zedong's wife and the powerful mayor of Shanghai, Yao Wen-yuan, had been neutralized by the pragmatists led by Zhou Enlai. At the same time, China, having suffered a series of military defeats at the hands of the Soviets along the Usuri River, found itself exposed and vulnerable, caught between two superpowers acting as enemies. China needed to normalize relations with the United States to counterbalance the Soviet threat and end its isolation in Asia. It took a number of measures to show goodwill towards the United States. It all but stopped support for anti-Western rebels in several places, including the Sultanate of Oman and Angola. It also reduced support for North Vietnam and indicated readiness to help broker a deal to end the war in Indochina. Beijing also dropped its longstanding demand that the United States break all ties with Taiwan and allow it to "return to the motherland," presumably by force. In other words, China had met most of the American "preconditions" as the price of direct talks.

The Khomeinist regime, precisely because it bases its legitimacy as a revolutionary power on the teachings of Islam, something it does not fully control in doctrinal terms, cannot abandon its radical pretensions as easily as did the Maoists in Beijing, who "owned" their ideology and could alter it at will. Mao could have the last word on Maoism. But no Iranian Supreme Guide could pretend to have the last word on Islam. The most zealous of Islamists would always find someone even more zealous. And since Islam's ultimate ambition is to rule the world, the only debate within it would be about ways of achieving that goal, not about its legitimacy.

Despite later attempts at waffling, Obama not only wants the United States to drop its preconditions—including, for example, that the Islamic Republic stop arming groups that kill Americans in Iraq—but also ignores demands made by the UN Security Council and the International Atomic Energy Agency. Instead, he has promised a number of goodies to the Islamic Republic even before Tehran has agreed to play ball. This kind of diplomacy reminds one of "Crazy Eddie," a character from American television advertising a few years ago. Shouting at the top of his lungs, Crazy Eddie would start by offering something for sale, usually a gadget of doubtful utility, at a ridiculously low price. Having presumably attracted the viewers' attention, he would announce that he was also offering a "free gift" for every item purchased. Shouting "and this is not all," Crazy Eddie would then proceed to add "free gift" to "free gift" until one needed a wheelbarrow to carry all the gadgets he was giving away for the purchase of a single item.

Contrary to Obama's claim, the Bush administration had been trying to "engage" the Islamic Republic at least since May 2006 when the secretary of state, Condoleezza Rice, issued a solemn statement trying to tantalize the Khomeinists with a range of Crazy Eddie–style goodies. Ms. Rice's bag of treats included security guarantees, help to modernize Iran's energy industry, an offer of high-speed Internet technology, membership of the World Trade Organization (WTO), and upgrading Iran's derelict air transport fleet. Contrary to Obama's claim, these goodies were offered with no strings attached. Ms. Rice did not even demand that the Islamic Republic stop arming terror units that were killing American troops in Iraq. Ahmadinejad, however, refused to bite. He did not want those things, or anything in particular; he wanted *everything* and was sure he would get it.

However, it was the U.S. ambassador, Zalmay Khalilzad, who came closest to the Crazy Eddie image. "The package of incentives includes active international support to build state-of-the-art light-water power reactors and access to reliable nuclear fuel," the ambassador promised in 2008. Iran would also receive spare parts for its aging U.S.-made jetliners, credit facilities through the World Bank, membership of the WTO, and a lifting of the ban on Iranian exports to the United States. But as Crazy Eddie used to say, that was not all. Later, Khalilzad offered other free gifts in an op-ed published by the *Wall Street Journal.* "We call on Iran to engage in constructive negotiations over the future of the nuclear program," the ambassador wrote. "Such negotiations, if successful, would have profound benefits for Iran and the Iranian people. The message from the U.S. to the people of Iran is that America respects your great country. We want Iran to be a full partner in the international community." Having piled on the presents, Khalilzad threw in the clincher: "If Iran respects its international obligations, it will have no better friend than the United States of America."

The trouble with all this is that the diplomats and their political masters ignore the fact that the "Crazy Eddie" technique does not work when one is dealing with "Martyr Hussein," the central figure in the Khomeinist mythology.

The ideal Khomeinist model is Hussein bin Ali, the third imam of Shiism, who was "martyred" in Karbala, Iraq, on the tenth day of the lunar month of Muharram (known as Ashrua) in 680. Hussein broke a compromise that his elder brother had reached with the Umayyid caliph in Damascus and marched into Iraq to raise an army to capture the caliphate. Very soon, however, it became clear that he lacked popular support and the material resources required for a major campaign. He ended up with only seventy-two companions and their womenfolk and children.

Caliph Yazid tried Crazy Eddie salesmanship by seeking to persuade Martyr Hussein to accept a range of "free gifts" in exchange for a compromise. Martyr Hussein was not after free gifts, however. He did not want to be *given* anything. He preferred to *take what he wanted*, which meant *everything*, and then to kill the caliph as well. He believed that Allah himself had given him a mission to capture the caliphate, conquer the world, and hoist the banner of Islam on every rooftop. Failing that, his mission was to kill as many of the "impious" as he could before securing his own martyr status. To the Shiites, as former president Khatami has said, Hussein is "the Perfect Man, the Ideal Man," an "eternal model for all of us, in every aspect of our lives." One of the most popular slogans of the Khomeinist movement is: "Every city is Karbala! Every day is Ashura!" Khomeinists tell people that Hussein regarded death as sweeter than "giving an inch."

Western politicians who don't believe in anything cannot imagine that others might believe in something so bizarre as the cult of Hussein.

The Islamic Republic resents being treated like a naughty boy who is promised goodies in exchange for better behavior. Ahmadinejad, seeing himself as a messianic figure with a world mission from the Hidden Imam, feels insulted when Westerners try to tempt him with membership of the WTO. General Muhammad-Ali Jaafari, commander of the Islamic Revolutionary Guard Corps, has poured scorn on the West's Crazy Eddie approach. "Our revolution has not yet ended," he told fellow officers in January 2008. "Our Imam did not limit the movement of the Islamic Revolution to this country, but drew greater horizons. Our duty is to prepare the way for an Islamic world government and the rule of the Lord of the Time [the Hidden Imam]."

The current radical leadership in Tehran is determined to change the future of mankind. Only Crazy Eddie would think that Ahmadinejad and Jaafari could be bribed with spare parts for Boeings or "state of the art power stations." The concept of *khod-kafai* (autarchy or self-reliance) is a central plank of Ahmadinejad's vision. It was in the name of *khod-kafai* that he ordered the resumption of uranium enrichment three years ago.

Khalilzad's biggest "free gift" was the prospect of Iran and the United States becoming "the best of friends." But this is exactly what the mullahs, led by Khomeini, revolted against in 1979. The mullahs and their Communist allies hated the shah precisely because he had made Iran and the United States best friends. The Khomeinists raided the U.S. embassy in Tehran and took its diplomats hostage in 1979 to break ties with Washington. Over the past twenty-eight years, the Islamic Republic has occasionally flirted with the idea of "revolution in one country," most recently under Khatami, who engaged in secret talks with the Clinton administration. But the regime has always reverted to the concept of "permanent revolution."

Obama might think that in calling for talks with Ahmadinejad he has come up with a great new idea. The fact is that every U.S. administration has talked to the Islamic Republic and has gotten little for the effort. Carter negotiated with the mullahs but failed to obtain the release of the hostages in time to help his re-election. Reagan negotiated with and supplied arms to the Islamic Republic. He even invited Rafsanjani's son Mehdi to tour the White House, and he sent Khomeini an autographed Bible and a kosher cake shaped like a key. All he got in return was suicide attacks against U.S. positions in Lebanon. Perhaps the most generous offer made to the Islamic Republic came in 1989 from the first President George Bush. Two weeks before his inauguration, he offered to wipe the slate clean and deal directly with the Islamic Republic as a major regional power. The answer he got came from Khamenehi, then president of the Islamic Republic:

You have nothing to say to us! We object. We do not agree to relationship with you! We are not prepared to establish relations with powerful world-devourers such as you! The Iranian nation has no need of the United States; nor is the Iranian nation afraid of the United States. . . . It is up to us to set conditions, and reject your behavior, your oppression [of other nations] and your intervention in so many parts of the world.[1]

Most recently, Washington and Tehran held direct talks in 2002 in Bonn, Germany, and in 2006 in Baghdad. The outcome was an intensification of Khomeinist mischief-making in Iraq.

Others who talked to the Islamic Republic fared no better. Hans-Dietrich Genscher, longtime West German foreign minister, built his career around the hope of bringing the Islamic Republic into the mainstream. He invented the phrase "critical dialogue"—which in practice meant a joint Iranian-European bad-mouthing of the United States. Most recently, Jack Straw, during his tenure as the British foreign secretary, visited Tehran more frequently than Washington, but failed to obtain a single concession. Russia, Kazakhstan, Turkmenistan, and Azerbaijan have been talking to Iran to determine the status of the Caspian Sea for fifteen years, without getting anywhere. Turkey has held talks with Iran since 1989 on Turkish-Kurdish rebels and the Turkish branch of Hezballah, also to no avail. In every case, the Islamic Republic has interpreted the readiness of an adversary to talk as a sign of weakness and, as a result, has hardened its position. Kuwait has been negotiating the demarcation of its water borders with the Islamic Republic since 1980—so far with no results. The United Arab Emirates has been seeking direct talks with the Islamic Republic concerning a dispute over three tiny islands in the Persian Gulf, again with no results. Negotiation is possible and could prove productive only if those engaged in it recognize each other's equal worth, at least implicitly. The Islamic Republic cannot do that for any possible negotiating partner. The reason is that it regards itself as not only the world's number-one power but absolutely the only legitimate power on earth, because it represents the only "true version of pure Muhammadan Islam." The infidel powers' very existence is a bonus to them, until the Hidden Imam returns and puts them all to the sword. As for countries that profess Islam, most are viewed as guilty of having "modified" Islam and are open to the charge of *Iltiqat* (dilution). As for countries such as Kuwait and the UAE, they are "mere midgets"; in fact, Ahmadinejad has described the oil-rich Arab states of the Persian Gulf as "gas stations, not real countries."

As the last of the revolutionary regimes, the Islamic Republic thinks its ideals should not be sacrificed at the altar of mundane diplomatic considerations. At the same time, rivalries among the Khomeinists prevent each faction from adopting a policy of compromise whether at home or abroad. Because the overthrow of the shah came with unexpected ease, the vast majority of the new regime's personnel had no time to secure a "revolutionary biography." They have tried to acquire one after the fact by talking and behaving in the most radical way possible.

Each group within the establishment is constantly watching rivals for the slightest sign of lacking in revolutionary zeal. No Khomeinist leader would be seen making the slightest concessions to an outsider without risking political demise. The regime's history is full of officials who committed political suicide by trying to play by international rules. Khomeinist diplomacy is designed to seek total triumph for the Islamic Republic and total surrender from its negotiating partners on all issues. Anyone following the official media in Tehran would soon learn that the leadership could not conceive of a "win-win" situation: It must *always* win and its negotiating partners must *always* lose.

When Ayatollah Khomeini ordered the release of the American hostages in 1980, he said he had done so as a gesture of Islamic generosity towards their families, not because of months of talks with Washington. He released them when he no longer needed them—Carter had lost the election and had been "punished" for brokering the Camp David peace accords between Egypt and Israel. Khomeini recognized no laws outside Islam as interpreted by himself. Here is how he put it: "All international laws are the product of the syphilitic minds of a handful of idiots. And

Islam has obliterated all of them. [Islam] recognizes no law except its own laws anywhere in the world. . . . Because they are [of] Divine [origin] Islamic laws are eternally fixed and unchangeable."[2]

Since 1979, the real question with regard to Iran has been simple: Should the world kowtow to the Khomeinist regime or should the Khomeinist regime accept the global rules of the game? The Tehran leadership has repeatedly made clear that it will not, indeed cannot, play by any rules except those fixed by itself. Despite periodic claims by self-styled Iran experts that the Khomeinist revolution has entered its Thermidor and, given encouragement, would opt for normalization, there are no signs that Iran has freed itself of the hysteria caused by the upheavals of 1979. Ahmadinejad makes no secret of his ambition to drive the United States out of the Middle East, replacing America's influence with Iran's in the name of the Khomeinist revolution. He is likely to interpret the "Crazy Eddie" tactics of the West as a sign of weakness and a vindication of his claim that "punching them in the face" is more productive than shaking their hands.

The International Atomic Energy Agency referred the Islamic Republic to the UN Security Council because Tehran had violated its obligations under the Nuclear Non-Proliferation Treaty. The council found Tehran guilty as charged and yet stopped short of decreeing effective punitive measures. A mere rap on the knuckles could not persuade Ahmadinejad to abandon his self-set mission to save the world from American domination. "Free gifts" would only encourage him in his belief that the tougher he gets the more concessions he will receive.

The real issue is who will shape the future of the Middle East—the United States or the Islamic Republic, or, as some naïve souls hope, both in partnership. What the United States needs is an open, honest, and exhaustive debate on what to do with a regime that claims a mission to drive the Western democracies out of the Middle East, wipe Israel off the map, create an Islamic superpower, and conquer the world for "the Only True Faith." Calling for talks is just cheap talk. It is important to say what the proposed talks should be about. In the meantime, talk of "constructive engagement" is sure to encourage Ahmadinejad's intransigence. Why should he slow down, let alone stop, when there are no bumps on the road? Even the craftiest of diplomats cannot bring Crazy Eddie and Martyr Hussein together.

18

West Stricken, Arab Stricken

The Khomeinist upheaval of 1978–79 was the first of the great revolutions to lack a corpus of ideological works on which to rely. Most of Khomeini's own writings do not deal with political issues, focusing instead on matters of personal behavior, especially with regard to religious duties, sex, and commercial transactions. Even then, the ayatollah's confused prose, limited vocabulary and muddled thinking make his writings hard to read and even harder to understand.

Might not one consider the Koran itself as the first manifesto of the movement? The answer is no. The Koran, too, does not discuss politics, but instead addresses matters of ritual and the maintenance of a thin veneer of religious loyalty. In any case, every part of the Koran has always been so open to interpretation that it could be, and has been, used by all sorts of scoundrels—from the apologists of despotic monarchy to "reformed" Stalinists, and, of course, fascists. Ehsan Tabari, the principal ideologue of the Tudeh (Masses) Party, has published several books claiming that the Koran could be read as the first draft of *The Communist Manifesto*. By contrast, Muhammad-Ali Ramin, a key advisor to Ahmadinejad, has established "thematic accords" between the Koran and Hitler's *Mein Kampf*, especially with regard to the "ever conspiring Jews."

Sometime in the early nineteenth century, the mullahs, who had once provided the backbone of the nation's intellectual elite, stopped producing anything worthwhile even in their own domain. Unable to risk theological speculation, let alone innovation, as their predecessors had done, they resigned themselves to parrot-like repetitions of shopworn clichés. When pressed to offer views on new issues of contemporary life, they shied away from taking a position by invoking the Shiite principle of *ehtiat* (caution), which means dancing around the issue, or they hid behind the formula "Allah Knows Best." In the nineteenth century, Aqa Najafi, a key ayatollah of his time, was asked by some wits what believers should do in the North Pole to honor the five daily prayers and the dawn-to-dusk fasting of Ramadan? His answer was: no good Muslim should go there if such a place exists!

In 1978–79, Khomeinism had a great deal of muscle in the streets—muscles that burned, looted, threw acid at hijab-free women, and cut the throats of kidnapped policemen. When it came to brains, however, they had only two "philosophers." One was Abol-Hassan Banisadr, a fifty-year-old "mature student" in Paris who had self-published a pamphlet under the title "Monotheistic Economics." The other was the mullah Morteza Motahari, who had once worked as "philosophical advisor" to Empress Farah and had written a column for *Zan Ruz* ("Today's Woman"), a weekly women's magazine. When exposed to the wider public, both these "big brains of Islam" proved embarrassing. Banisadr became the first president of the Islamic Republic for some eighteen months but then fled back to Paris, thus losing his place as a theoretician of Khomeinism. Motahari was soon assassinated by a group called Forqan (Discernment) created by rival mullahs, while his gospel of "blood and martyrdom," although fashionable for a time, proved eventually to have limited appeal.

The leaders of the revolution knew they had to do better. It was then that they discovered and tried to promote two other ideological "prophets." One was Jalal al-Ahmad, a Communist turncoat who had discovered "the healing touch of Islam" towards the end of his life, shortened by decades of addiction to vodka. In the 1960s he had published a pamphlet under the title *Gharb-Zadeg* ("Being Stricken by the West," translated into English as "Westoxication"). He claimed that the root cause of Iran's poverty, backwardness, and despotic political system was the "Westoxication" of its elites and urban middle classes in general. Iranians, he argued, should "return to themselves," rediscover their traditional values (which he would not spell out), and above all, be on guard against contamination by Western ideas. Interestingly, al-Ahmad opened his pamphlet with a quotation from Ernst Jünger, a major in Hitler's army and a part-time philosopher. Having advised Iranians to steer clear of the West, al-Ahmad filled his pamphlet with quotations from Western writers, revealing his own acute Westoxication.[1]

The other writer the Khomeinists discovered was Ali Shariati, who had studied sociology in Paris and died after a long illness in Southampton, England. Shariati, too, had been a talented pamphleteer and a firm believer in the toxic nature of Western civilization. In the 1970s, the shah's secret police (the State Intelligence and Security Organization, or SAVAK) had used his writings, especially his pamphlet titled "Marxism and Islam," in an ideological campaign against Marxists. Now it was the turn of the Khomeinist regime to enlist him in support of its campaign against "the corrupt, capitalist West." For the mullahs, however, using Shariati was not as easy as using al-Ahmad, since Shariati had been an outspoken critic of mullahs as self-serving collaborators of despotic regimes for over four hundred years. The mullahs, he argued, represented the Safavid version of Shiism, named after the Safavid dynasty, and not the Shiism of Ali, the first imam. Safavid Shiism was formal, hypocritical, and ultimately empty. Ali's Shiism, on the other hand, was lively, passionate and liberating. Shariati had tried to Islamicize some of the key concepts of Marxism, which he had studied under his French teacher Gurovich. He identified the term "proletariat" with the Shiite concept of *mustazaf* (the underdog), while the "bourgeoisie" was the equivalent of *mustakbar*. Shariati's confused message also included the claim that Imam Hussein's ill-fated attempt at becoming caliph was a prototype of "revolution" as understood in Europe's secular radicalism.

At any rate, the mullahs were able to extract the message they wanted: a hatred of the West as the cause of Islam's decline, and by extension, Iran's historic defeat. The infidel West was the enemy that the revolution needed, and the United States, as the leader of the infidel West, deserved special vilification. By adopting anti-Americanism as the backbone of its ideology, Khomeinism was giving a sharper focus to anti-Western sentiments that had built up over the previous two to three decades, while claiming ownership of them.

In 1979, having shut all universities for two years, Khomeini appointed a council to reorganize higher education based on his anti-Western ideology. While proceeding with the purge of academia, the council transformed itself into a philosophical club in which mullahs and their nonclerical associates soon divided into two camps. One camp was labeled "the Heideggerites," after Martin Heidegger, the pro-Nazi German philosopher who is also claimed by existentialists as a spiritual ancestor. Ahmad Fardid, a teacher of philosophy at Tehran University, who described himself as "a companion of Heidegger," was their champion. Fardid's young sidekick Reza Davari Ardakani carried the Heideggerites' banner in media appearances. The other camp was named "the Popperites," after the British philosopher Karl Popper, who devoted his life to fighting totalitarianism. Initially, the Popperites had rallied around Motahari. When he was assassinated, the Popperites promoted a nonclerical amateur philosopher named Abdul-Karim Sorush as chief spokesman. A British-educated chemist, Sorush had been appointed secretary general of the council at the start of the academic purges of 1979.

Needless to say, neither the Heideggerites nor the Popperites merited their labels. Both accepted Khomeini's claim of the right to rule in the name of the Hidden Imam, something that neither Heidegger nor Popper would have understood. The Heideggerites were chiefly interested in presenting any form of democracy as anti-Islamic and against philosophy. Davari, for example, claimed that Socrates had been sentenced to death because of his opposition to democracy and that his disciple Plato had been an advocate of the "rule by the select," which in Iran's case meant a government of the mullahs.

The Popperites insisted that the mullahs' rule should be subjected to public endorsement in elections, but were not prepared to go as far as allowing just any citizen to stand for election. All candidates had to be loyal to the regime. Nor were they prepared to admit that the government of the mullahs was bound to lead to totalitarianism in the name of religion. In a distortion of Popper's thought, his Iranian followers tried to develop the concept of "religious democracy." The trick they used was to argue that democracy was not incompatible with Islam or any other religion. This is certainly true. What they did not say, however, was that Islam is incompatible with democracy. Islam can have its place in a democratic state, but democracy has no place in an Islamic state. The idea that a state could be both Islamic and democratic at the same time is a myth that many disillusioned Khomeinists had tried to cling to since the 1990s.

Until 1989, the Heideggerites were the dominant philosophical force within the Khomeinist establishment. The then Prime Minister Mir-Hussain Mussawi and the then Chief Justice Abdul-Karim Ardebili, a businessman-cum-mullah, were confirmed Heideggerites. The Popperites started their ascendancy in the 1990s and managed to emerge as the dominant group within the regime in 1997 when one of their supporters, Khatami, won the presidency against Ayatollah Ali-Akbar Nateq-Nuri, the candidate of the Heideggerites. In the summer of 2005, however, the Popperites suffered their worst defeat when Ahmadinejad, the candidate of the Heideggerites, won the presidency. That victory put the limelight on Ayatollah Muhammad-Taqi Mesbah-Yazdi, one of Fardid's most talented pupils and the best-known mullah among the Heideggerites. Mesbah-Yazdi is Ahmadinejad's "thought-master."

It might come as a surprise to outsiders, but for the past twenty-eight years the philosophical debate in the Islamic Republic has been over a misunderstanding of a pro-Nazi German philosopher on the one hand and an even bigger misunderstanding of a liberal British philosopher on the other.

Almost three decades of supposedly Islamic rule has not produced a single Islamic philosopher. Even Mesbah-Yazdi, acclaimed by his supporters as "the most significant Islamic philosopher of the past two centuries," has little to offer besides a rehash of Fardid's misunderstanding of Heidegger. Fardid, who knew no European languages, had gleaned some knowledge of his idol, Heidegger, through partial Persian translations as well as verbal accounts by friends who spoke French or German.[2]

The Heideggerites claim that each society must identify the elite that could provide it with the best government. In the case of Islam, that elite consists of religious scholars. Once the "just rule" is established, society should admit no dissent and should, instead, mobilize all its energies against internal and external foes. The Heideggerites have also inherited a dose of anti-Semitism, both from the German philosopher himself and from his Iranian admirers. Since Ahmadinejad's election the Heideggerites have attacked the Popperites as "naïve souls deceived by a Jewish troublemaker," a reference to the fact that Popper had been of Jewish birth. The Popperites allow for a diversity of views and even "multiple readings of the sacred texts." But they, too, reject any possibility of changing the structures of the Islamic state, let alone subjecting the faith to critical scrutiny. In 2002, Jürgen Habermas, the most fashionable German philosopher alive, visited Iran as a guest of the Ministry of Islamic Guidance and was surprised by the domination of Iranian thought by "misunderstood Western philosophies."

Khomeinist propaganda uses both "schools" in support of its anti-Western, more specifically anti-American message. It also uses them against those who oppose the regime from the standpoint of Iranian patriotism. Iranian patriots see the Khomeinist regime as "Arab-stricken" (*Arab-zadeh*) and claim that it is trying to de-Iranize Iran, thus realizing the dream of the first Arab invaders. In books that have become bestsellers in Iran, albeit in samizdat form, the writer Ali-Mirfetros argues that the Khomeinist regime is trying to destroy Iran's "national identity" and transform it into part of a nondescript Islamic *ummah*. That Khomeini had no feelings for Iran as a nation-state is revealed in this statement: "We do not worship Iran, we worship Allah. For patriotism is another name for *sherk* [associating others with Allah]. I say let this land burn; I say let this land go up in smoke, provided Islam emerges triumphant in the rest of the world."[3]

Khomeinists label their enemies "Americans." To them, America is the codeword for democracy, modernity, reform, love of country—sentiments that threaten the regime. To opponents of the regime, on the other hand, Khomeinism is an attempt to impose a twisted Arab identity on Iran, deny its people basic freedoms and human rights, and turn it into an enemy of the modern world in the name of anti-Americanism. The late writer and diplomat Fereydoun Hoveyda argued a strong case in support of his thesis that anti-Americanism, rather than Islam, should be seen as the principal ideological ingredient of Khomeinism. Hatred of the United States performs several functions for the regime. It gives its supporters a unifying theme: they can direct their negative energies towards an outsider rather than against each other. It provides the regime with potential allies who are neither Muslim nor even religious. Anti-Americanism is a popular ideology in many parts of the world, including the United States itself. What could make Ahmadinejad and Hugo Chavez "brothers," if not their shared anti-Americanism? Only anti-Americanism could persuade the mullahs to impose Noam Chomsky's books as compulsory reading at Iranian universities along with Khomeini's pamphlets. And why would Bill Clinton and Sean Penn feel "a certain kinship" with Khomeinists, unless it is because of their shared belief that the United States is guilty of "crimes against weaker nations"?

Hoveyda also believed that were the mullahs ever to abandon their anti-American ideology, they would be sealing the fate of their regime. Khomeinists of all tendencies agree on three things only: compulsory hijab, compulsory beards, and hatred of America. To abandon anti-Americanism would leave the regime with nothing but beards and hijab. No Khomeinist leader could take such a risk. This is specially so because the United States remains popular among the Iranian masses.

Over the past two decades, dozens of opinion polls have shown that while anti-Americanism is rife even in U.S. allies such as Great Britain, Iran remains one of the few remaining bastions of pro-American sentiment. Despite government-imposed bans and occasional campaigns of brutal repression, American books, films, music, and other cultural products remain as popular in Iran as ever. On several occasions, Khamenehi has condemned all this as "an unhealthy madness for America" and has tried to "cure" it with police repression. What he does not realize is that part of the reason for the average Iranian's fascination with the United States is precisely that it is vilified by an unpopular regime. Frequent visitors to the Soviet Union would be familiar with the phenomenon. There, too, the state's official enmity for the United States was translated into popular goodwill towards America and a fascination with things American. This is more so in Iran's case if only because, unlike Soviet citizens, millions of Iranians have had direct experience of the United States while millions more are in almost daily contact with aspects of it thanks to the global communications revolution. The Iranian community in the United States, believed to be 1.8 million strong, has emerged as an alternative face of Iran, offering a home for writers, poets, musicians, filmmakers, and other producers of culture to continue their creative work free from state censorship and repression. Dozens of satellite television and radio channels are beamed to Iran from southern California and Washington D.C., maintaining bonds that the regime is desperately trying to break. Almost three decades after the Khomeinist seizure of power, Iranian society is more Westoxicated than ever, in the sense that such Western ideas as democracy, human rights, the rule of law, and secularism have found an audience they did not have before.

At the other end of the spectrum, the regime's efforts to Islamicize—or as Iranian patriots claim, Arabize—Iran have produced few results. Before the revolution, most Iranians ignored the Arabs if only because they had no direct contact with them. Apart from those who went to Mecca on pilgrimage, almost no Iranians traveled to any Arab country. Teaching Arabic was part of the secondary school curriculum, but few attached any importance to it. Between 1958 and 1979, few Arabic-language films were screened in Iran and fewer Arab writers translated into Persian.[4] During the same period, virtually all major European and American writers were translated into Persian and found a growing audience. American movies almost always topped the box-office lists, often ahead of Iranian films.

Almost three decades of Khomeinist attempts at de-Iranization has awakened anti-Arab sentiments that had been dormant for centuries. Most Iranians continue to look towards the West—"the natural direction of their gaze," in the words of Mostafavi—as they have always done in their history. The anti-Western discourse of the Khomeinist regime in a nation that is overwhelmingly pro-Western is another sign of the schizophrenia that Iran has manifested since the mullahs seized power.

19

State or Revolution

The seemingly erratic manner in which Iran at times takes and applies its decisions, especially in certain areas of foreign policy, has baffled more than one observer in the past three decades. In the 1980s, one might have argued that Iran's behavior, which at times included harming its own interests, was partly due to the relative inexperience of the new decision-making elite that issued from the 1979 revolution. There was also the fact that the system evolved since the revolution was neither a monolithic regime nor a typical Third World dictatorship in which decisions are made by either one man or an easily identifiable group.

Neither fact, however, explains fully why Iran at times appears unable to take and apply decisions that are demonstrably in its own interests as a nation-state. The main reason for Iran's behavior is the conflict between state and revolution—a conflict that has continued, albeit with varying degrees of intensity, since 1979.

Initially, Khomeini, who led the revolution to victory and presided over its destiny during the first decade, had intended to destroy the state structures inherited from the Pahlavi dynasty. To him, everything associated with that state was *Taghuti* (satanic) and had to be "wiped out without a trace." Muhammad-Ali Rajai, a Khomeini bodyguard who rose to become prime minister and then president of the Islamic Republic under the ayatollah, had a simple formula to explain the new regime's approach to policy: "Whatever they [the shah's regime] did, we will do the opposite." This attitude led to the cancellation of hundreds of contracts that the shah had signed with foreign nations and corporations, often harming Iran's interests by delaying or scrapping development projects. It was in that spirit that the nation's nuclear power generation project was simply canceled, meaning a loss of $4 billion in initial investments.

Khomeini's effort to replace the Pahlavi state with one of his own creation also extended to his insistence that the Constitution of 1906—which represented a rare national consensus and had nothing to do with the Pahlavis—be replaced with one written on his own orders. The ayatollah also tried to radically transform or completely replace as many of the state organs as he could. Between 1979 and 1980, he tried to replace the ministerial cabinet with his Islamic Revolution Council, a secret body of some thirty members appointed by him and answerable only to him. To give the council a coercive arm, the ayatollah created his Islamic Revolutionary Guard Corps, generally known as Pasdaran, which was to replace the national army. At the same time, the so-called Imam Committees (Komiteh) were created to replace the urban police and the gendarmerie. Mistrustful of the bureaucracy, the ayatollah placed his own men as "imam's representatives" within each government department, giving them the right of veto over all key decisions. At the provincial level, he made state-appointed governors subservient to Prayer Leaders appointed by himself.

Over time, however, Khomeini realized that he could not treat Iran as a tabula rasa on which to depict his ideal state. Many of the Iranian state institutions proved too resilient for him. He was eventually obliged to allow the regular army to exist, albeit in a truncated version and with no say in political decision-making. The regular police and gendarmerie also survived, although the Imam Committees continued to operate as instruments for distributing favor among the supporters of the revolution. Even the pre-revolutionary secret police, known as SAVAK (State Intelligence and Security Organization), managed to continue under the new name of VEVAK (the Islamic Republic's Intelligence and Security Organization), especially insofar as counterintelligence was concerned.

Other organs as well as elements of the 1906 Constitution also survived the Khomeini onslaught, but with reduced power and influence. For example, Khomeini was obliged to accept the eminently un-Islamic principle of electing a parliament that had been established in Iran since

1906. He was intelligent enough to understand that any attempt at ruling without some form of an elected parliament could turn the middle classes against the revolution. Some organs of the state the ayatollah dared not touch, even only to change their names. Thus, the National Bank of Iran narrowly escaped being called "Islamic Bank of Iran" in 1980. An attempt to rename the National Iranian Oil Company so as to inject the term "Islamic" in 1981 also failed. Further, Khomeini abandoned his initial idea of changing the country's name from Iran (Land of the Aryans) to Islamistan (Land of Islam).

All along, however, it was clear that Khomeini at best *tolerated* those state organs and political traditions that his revolution had inherited from the *ancien régime*. In time, the ayatollah's obvious dislike of Iran's state organs and traditions was reciprocated by those who represented them. Iran has one of the world's oldest state structures, dating back to the sixteenth century, with a well-established bureaucracy and a deep-rooted tradition of public service. Even in the remotest parts of the country, one encounters families who boast more than a century of state employment and public service. The Pahlavi state had been built on the Prussian model of central control that strengthened the machinery of government at all levels. From the 1960s onwards, the massive revenues produced by oil exports had given the state further means with which to acquire popular favor and strengthen its position within society. With annual economic growth rates of 10 percent or more between 1971 and 1977, the Pahlavi state tried to base part of its legitimacy on the success of its economic development program. It was also able to draw on under-the-surface nationalistic sentiments that could, when the opportunity arose, offer a rival ideology to Khomeini's radical Islamism.

Nevertheless, the key factor that aborted Khomeini's plan to destroy the "inherited Satanic state" completely was the eight-year Iran-Iraq war unleashed by Saddam Hussein. The ayatollah quickly realized that he could not fight on two fronts at once. He knew that he needed the support of the Iranian state structures, notably the armed forces, to prevent Saddam's armies from marching through an undefended land to

Tehran. Within ten days of the invasion, the Iraqis had captured almost 3 percent of Iranian territory and were knocking on the gates of such major oil cities as Ahvaz and Abadan. Hurriedly, the ayatollah called up thousands of army and air force officers, NCOs, and men released from prison, where they had languished for their association with the *ancien régime,* and dispatched them to the war front to stop the Iraqi advance.

Over the years, the revolution, the Khomeinist purges, the war with Iraq, and the internecine feuds that splintered the revolutionary camp created a system full of internal conflicts and contradictions, reflected in the "erratic behavior" mentioned above. As long as Khomeini was alive, he was able to draw on his revolutionary prestige and position as one of the top six theologians of Iranian Shiite Islam, to impose a decision whenever necessary. With his death in 1989, however, the contradictions of the system he had helped create gradually came into the open, furnishing the central theme of what is often seen as the "power struggle" in Tehran.

Some commentators have tried to reduce these contradictions to a mere rivalry between two camps often labeled "moderate" and "radical" or "reformist" and "conservative." Iranologists, recycling the old techniques of Kremlinology, have tried to discover "doves" and "hawks" in Tehran's ruling circles, without being able to identify the two camps clearly. This is partly because rival individuals and organizations often use almost exactly the same vocabulary and pursue their goals under the same slogans of revolutionary Khomeinism. The British politician Chris Patten, who served as a European Union foreign policy commissioner in the 1990s, was puzzled by the Iranian "schizophrenia." It took him some time to realize that many of the Iranian officials with whom he negotiated were "mere actors playing official roles," while faceless individuals who never met Western officials took the real decisions.

To understand why Iran behaves the way it does on any specific issue, it is essential to identify and understand the principal bodies that contribute to decision-making. These could be divided into four categories: the revolutionary organs, the state organs, the hybrid organs of the state and the revolution, and secret societies operating in parallel with both state and revolution. There is, of course, some overlapping in all cases. One must also take into account a number of para-revolutionary and para-state organs that could emphasize this or that part of their dual identity according to issues and circumstances.

The recognized organs of the revolution began to appear in the course of the 1978–79 revolutionary period, and they had no discernible existence in Iranian politics before that. The most important of these organs is the *wali e faqih* (Theologian Custodian). Often referred to as the "Leader of the Revolution" or the "Supreme Guide," this is the central institution of the Islamic Republic. The Supreme Guide represents the element of divine power that had its epiphany in the Prophet Muhammad and the twelve imams of Shiism who followed him. Because the twelfth imam, the "Awaited Guide" (Mahdi al-Muntazar), has gone into his grand occultation, the element of divine power is represented by the best of his "deputies," that is to say the man chosen as the *wali e faqih*. The first Supreme Guide, Khomeini, was of course self-appointed and never faced an election. His successor Ali Khamenehi, however, was first elected by a hastily convened gathering of mullahs and under questionable conditions, first on a temporary basis in 1989, shortly after Khomeini's death, and then for life in 1991. Under the 1979 Constitution drafted on Khomeini's orders and approved in a referendum, the Supreme Guide, representing the will of Allah on earth, has virtually unlimited powers. He can order the suspension of the basic principles of Islam itself. He can also suspend the constitution, dismiss the elected president, and dissolve the elected parliament. He is the head of all three powers—the executive, the judiciary, and the legislature—and thus the head of state. All key officials of the state—including the elected president, cabinet ministers, provincial governors, ambassadors, military commanders, and heads of state-owned companies—must be appointed by him through special decrees. He is also commander-in-chief of all armed forces and has sole authority to declare war or make peace.

Although the Supreme Guide has unlimited executive powers and controls virtually every organ of state, his office must nevertheless be classified as a revolutionary organ for a number of reasons. The first is related to legitimacy. The Supreme Guide knows that his legitimacy stems directly from the 1979 revolution. Any decline in the power and prestige of that revolution would be translated into a corresponding diminution of the position of the Supreme Guide. It is also in the context of the revolution that the Supreme Guide can exercise unlimited power. Were he to acknowledge the supremacy of the state over revolution, he would transform himself into a functionary of the state, and thus someone who is bound by the state's earthly laws and regulations.

The Supreme Guide is often in a difficult position, having to choose between the interests of the revolution and those of the state, which could happen to be in direct contradiction. In most major cases so far, the Supreme Guide has ruled in favor of the revolution rather than the state. This has often brought the Supreme Guide into barely concealed conflict with the president on issues of both foreign and domestic policy. When Khamenehi, the present Supreme Guide, was president he occasionally found himself in conflict with the Supreme Guide at the time, Ayatollah Khomeini. To be sure, the Supreme Guide always wins—or has until now. In 1989, for example, President Khamenehi realized that the fatwa issued by Khomeini for the murder of Salman Rushdie was harming the interests of Iran as a nation-state. Thus, Khamenehi publicly suggested that the fatwa be canceled if Rushdie recanted. Khomeini's response came within hours in the form of a public castigation of Khamenehi. "He needs to return to school to learn more about Islam!" Khomeini announced. If the Supreme Guide decides that someone must die because this is good for Islam, the president has no right to reject the idea on the grounds that it is bad for the state! In a more dramatic clash between the Supreme Guide and the president in 1981, Khomeini simply dismissed President Banisadr with a nine-word decree.

Because he stands above factions, at least in theory, the Supreme Guide plays a major stabilizing role within the system. He is in a position to prevent one faction from crushing the others and imposing its monopoly on power for any length of time. The Supreme Guide has an abiding interest in promoting a dose of pluralism within the system, thus opening a space for discussion and debate with himself as the ultimate arbiter. This, in turn, provides the system with political safety valves to dissipate the negative energies of the ruling elite. Thanks to the existence of the Supreme Guide as an institution, the Islamic Republic has managed to avoid the politics of the bloodbath that is practiced by many ruling elites in the so-called "developing nations." Rival factions within the Islamic Republic's ruling elite do not murder one another because the Supreme Guide is always in a position to decide who wins and who loses and for how long. Today's losers in the Islamic Republic always know that they are the reserve squad for the Supreme Guide, who could, when the time comes, send them back into the field. In 2000, Khamenehi's intervention was decisive in discouraging attempts by the security services and professional revolutionary organs to undermine, perhaps even assassinate, President Khatami. At the same time, Khamenehi was also able to persuade Khatami to jettison his moderate discourse and lead the crackdown on a nationwide student revolt.

In much of the developing world, a group that has seized power through violence of one form or another starts by massacring real or imagined opponents and then embarks on its own internecine bloodletting. In Iran, however, the Supreme Guide has prevented rival cliques within the revolutionary minority from using violence against each other. One mechanism he uses is carefully managed elections in which he must approve all candidates and all eventual winners. By taking into account the public mood, the domestic and international realities of the moment, and, above all, his own interests, which he identifies with the interests of the revolution, the Supreme Guide decides which faction should win or lose in any particular election. Thus, Iranian elections today resemble primaries in U.S. political parties, with the difference that a single individual, the Supreme Guide, could make all the difference in the end.

To some Iranians as well as foreign observers, the institution of

Supreme Guide might seem to be no different from the absolute monarchy that Iran had known for more than 2,500 years. This is why many
Iranians jokingly refer to Khamenehi as "Ali Shah." After all, the shahs,
too, had based their claim of legitimacy on the spurious concept of
"divine mandate." Persian shahs were often called "the Shadow of Allah
on Earth." Nevertheless, leaving aside superficial resemblances, the
Khomeinist Supreme Guide is quite different from the traditional Persian
shah. Part of the reason for Iran's inability to absorb its revolutionary
crisis and move on lies in that difference.

Theoretically at least, the office of the traditional Persian shah was
a unifying factor because it blended all the contradictory realities of the
nation into a single overarching institution that cut across religious,
ethnic, and class differences. Iran was one nation with one shah. The
Khomeinist Supreme Guide, to start with, claims to be the chief Shiite
priest. At the same time, as his most popular designation in official propaganda indicates, he is the "Leader of the Revolution." Thus, he cannot
claim to represent non-Shiite Iranians or counterrevolutionaries. The
traditional shahs regarded anyone who was Iranian by birth or natural-
ization as their subjects. The Supreme Guide cannot do so, if only because
he poses conditions that not all Iranians could fulfill. Revolt against a
traditional shah was never regarded as anything more than a secular
act or a crime under the penal code. Revolt against the Supreme Guide is
presented as a sin in religious terms. More than 90 percent of those executed by the Khomeinists because of their opposition to the system were
charged with "waging war against Allah" by defying the Supreme Guide.
The traditional Persian shah did not see the state as a potential rival or
enemy; the Iranian state was *his* state. For the Khomeinist Supreme Guide,
the Iranian state is no more than an instrument in his broader mission as
"Leader of the Muslim *Ummah* Throughout the World." Worse still, the
Iranian state can never be trusted to support the revolution, or, indeed,
Islam itself, on all issues and occasions. This is because the interests of
Iran as a nation-state do not always coincide with either the Khomeinist
revolution or Islam itself.

The belief that the Supreme Guide must not, indeed cannot, depend exclusively on the Iranian state structures is reflected in the parallel organs that have sprung up around the office of the *wali e faqih*. Commonly known as the "Office of the Leader" (*Daftar Rahbar*), the organization controlled by and responsible to Khamenehi is a state within the state in all but name. Never included in the official organigram of the Islamic Republic, it is not open to scrutiny by the country's legislative or judicial institutions. It is also the only organization using public money that is not subjected to state accountability. The "office" is reported to have an annual budget of around $2.5 billion, of which only part is provided by the state. It is also reported to employ around three thousand people in its various branches in Tehran alone. These figures, however, do not reflect the full size of an octopus at the heart of the Iranian reality today. The Supreme Guide controls thousands of businesses through so-called "foundations" whose chief executives and managerial boards he appoints. According to some studies, these "foundations" account for more than a quarter of the private sector of the Iranian economy, representing an annual turnover of $30 billion. Because they never open their books to public scrutiny, no one knows how much money these foundations make or what part of their profits are funneled through the Supreme Guide.

Treating the Iranian state as a potential enemy, the Supreme Guide has infiltrated its key organs thanks to a network of functionaries directly answerable to him. Every government office includes a section called "Office of the Leader's Representatives," usually headed by a mullah acting as the ideological commissars of the Communist Party did in Russia under the Bolsheviks. A "representative of the leader" shadows every state functionary above a certain rank both at home and abroad. In most capitals, especially in Muslim countries, the Supreme Guide maintains unofficial embassies—offices charged with exporting the revolution, spying on Iranian exiles, and coordinating operations with Muslim and non-Muslim radicals and anti-American groups. All these functionaries are paid by the state, but they work only for the Supreme Guide. When it

comes to "sensitive areas" such as the military, security, and media organizations, the Supreme Guide controls both the official command structures and the informal advisory groups appointed by him.

Ultimately, however, the role that the Supreme Guide plays depends
on the personality of the man who occupies the position. The first man
in that position, Khomeini, had little knowledge of Iran and even less
interest in things Iranian. Although he had composed some poetry,
mostly doggerel, Khomeini knew next to nothing about Persian literature and cared even less for it. His poems were so embarrassingly bad
that a volume published after the revolution was quickly banned when
advisors convinced him that it would harm his image. Khomeini was a
limited man, living a narrow life centered on his deep misunderstanding of Islam, his visceral hatred of the shah, and his pathological fear
of modernization and democratization. At age seventy-seven, he was an
old man when he won power, and thus very much in a hurry. He had no
time to waste trying to persuade counterrevolutionaries that they were
wrong; better to kill them by the thousands, and move on. Having lived a
confined life—first in Qom, a backwater at the best of times, and then in
exile in Turkey and Iraq—Khomeini had never developed a physical feel
for Iran and its seductive natural beauty.

Khamenehi is somewhat different. To start with, when he became
Supreme Guide, he was twenty-six years younger than Khomeini, and
thus had a different idea of the role that time plays in politics. Khomeini
had spent at least a quarter of a century dreaming of becoming ruler
of Iran and the leader of Islam in global conquest. Khamenehi had
never harbored such illusions. Circumstances, including several bouts
in prison on political charges and years of banishment to remote regions
of Iran where Shiites were in a minority, had prevented him from com-
pleting his theological studies. In 1978, he was better known as an anti-
shah militant than a theologian of any rank. He had made his name as a
revolutionary street fighter by organizing gangs of youths who attacked
cinemas, restaurants, and other "places of sin," and terrorized the urban
middle classes into joining the revolutionary movement. Indicating his

ambition to build a political rather than a theological career, Khamenehi had played a key role in the creation of new revolutionary organs, most notably the Islamic Revolutionary Guard Corps. In 1980, he had managed to get himself appointed deputy secretary of defense.

Unlike Khomeini, who never felt at home in Iran, Khamenehi regarded Iran as home and, quite possibly, even loved it as a land as well as a civilization in its own right. Khamenehi had traveled to many parts of Iran and, again unlike Khomeini, had directly experienced and shared the average life of Iranians. Having never spent time in exile, Khamenehi did not share Khomeini's feeling of being an outsider in Iran. Khomeini was unable to speak in Persian for five minutes without making at least a dozen grammatical errors—errors that gave his performance an air of standup comedy.[1] Many Iranians regarded Khomeini's "peasant accent" and inability to speak an idiomatic Persian as a sign that he had never received a proper education in that language. The fact that Khomeini never quoted any Persian poets, writers, or philosophers, and appeared to have no knowledge of the incredibly rich treasury of Persian proverbs, reinforced that belief.

In contrast, Khamenehi is a fluent Persian speaker with a standard accent understood by all Iranians. Also, he is well read in Persian poetry, philosophy, and history. Khamenehi's family hail from a village of that name in East Azerbaijan, one of the four provinces in northwest Iran where people of Iranian stock speak a form of Turkic known as Azari. However, Khamenehi spent much of his life in Khorassan, northeast Iran, the birthplace and cradle of modern Persian.

A magnetic orator, Khamenehi shines where Khomeini embarrassed himself with his whining voice, limited vocabulary and narrow vision of existence. Although he spent fifteen years in an Arabic-speaking country, Khomeini never mastered the Arab language. Khamenehi, who has never lived among the Arabs, however, is a fluent speaker of Arabic and, according to some reports, also composes occasional verse in that language. Unlike Khomeini, who hated music, Khamenehi loves "the celestial sounds" and is himself a passable player of the sitar, a traditional

Persian stringed instrument. On private occasions in the company of handpicked friends, Khamenehi is known to demonstrate his talents in singing classical Persian songs—again, something that Khomeini would have regarded with horror. There are also reports, impossible to confirm, that Khamenehi is an occasional smoker of opium, a typically Iranian middle-class affliction since the nineteenth century—something else that would have scandalized the puritanical Khomeini.

Like Khomeini before him, Khamenehi is the object of a massive cult of personality. Official flatterers describe him as a "Divine Gift to Mankind" or the "Shining Sun of Imamate." In official discourse, he is quoted more often than Prophet Muhammad or the Koran itself. Objects he has touched during provincial visits are collected and sold as icons supposed to cure disease, ensure personal success, and ward off the "evil eye." In 2008, some officials started to refer to Khamenehi as "Aqa" (Sir), an affectionate term, or as "Sayydena" (Our Master), a title usually reserved for Prophet Muhammad.

The Islamic Republic protocol requires that all senior foreign visitors, including heads of state, call on Khamenehi to pay their respect. An audience with him is presented as a "special gift." The Islamic Republic's clients throughout the world know that paying tribute to Khamenehi is part of their duties towards their benefactors in Tehran. Here is how Hassan Nasrallah, leader of the Lebanese branch of Hezballah, paid tribute to Khamenehi: "Many think that by saying we are members of the party of the Supreme Guide, they are insulting us. Today, I declare once again something that is not new: I am a member of the party of the Supreme Guide, who is just, learned, sagacious, brave, honest and sincere. Let everyone know that we are the party of the Supreme Guide."[2]

Nevertheless, it is possible that Khamenehi is not as affected by this cult of personality as Khomeini had been. Khomeini genuinely believed that he was somehow "chosen" (*nazar-kardeh*) by the imams to save Islam. Khamenehi, on the other hand, knows that he is where he is by accident. Between 1979 and 1981, counterrevolutionaries assassinated half a dozen senior mullahs who, headed by Khomeini, provided the revolution with its leadership. Had they not died, any of them could have succeeded Khomeini as Supreme Guide. More importantly, Khomeini's designated heir as Supreme Guide, Ayatollah Hussein-Ali Montazeri, decided to break with the regime in 1986 because of his opposition to mass executions and the regime's repressive policies. Thus, when Khomeini died in 1989, he lacked a clearly identifiable successor.

In a deft political maneuver, Hashemi Rafsanjani, then speaker of the Islamic Majlis, leading the faction that had forced Montazeri out, succeeded in naming Khamenehi as Supreme Guide based on what later turned out to be a forged note from the late ayatollah. The scenario, written by Rafsanjani, was that Khamenehi would leave the presidency to become Supreme Guide, thus making sure that their faction controlled the key organ of the regime. In exchange, Khamenehi, once sworn in as Supreme Guide, would support Rafsanjani's bid to become president. The secret deal, which also involved Khomeini's son Ahmad, was based on a twenty-year friendship between Rafsanjani and Khamenehi. In the tandem, Rafsanjani was recognized as the "strongman," while Khamenehi, who looked more like a mullah than Rafsanjani ever could, was supposed to provide the necessary clerical cover. Khamenehi realized that he had moved to the highest position in the regime largely because he had happened to be in the right place, at the right time, and on the right side. He had been among some one hundred mullahs who had been objects of assassination attempts by counterrevolutionaries. Most had died; he had survived. In 1989, when Rafsanjani had the constitution amended to abolish the post of prime minister and increase the powers of the presidency, Khamenehi knew that his friend and ally regarded him as little more than a second fiddle. It was to take Khamenehi sixteen years to build his own power base within the regime, thus restoring the position of Supreme Guide as the true center of power in the Islamic Republic.

The fact that Rafsanjani devoted a good part of his considerable talents and energy to amassing a personal fortune, now regarded as the largest in Iran, helped Khamenehi. As he became richer, Rafsanjani, nicknamed Kusseh (the Shark) by Iranians, became politically more vulnerable. Iranians love to become rich themselves but hate the rich, especially if they made their money through questionable public contracts. That Khamenehi was not interested in amassing a personal fortune endeared him to the hardcore revolutionaries and won him grudging admiration within the population at large. As Supreme Guide, Khamenehi cultivated his image as a simple if not austere man, devoting his time to defending Islam and the revolution. People saw him sit on the floor rather than use expensive furniture, eat with his hands as poor Persians did until recently, and wear inexpensive clerical garb. Unlike most mullahs, who seemed addicted to taking young "temporary wives" on an almost annual basis, Khamenehi remained strictly monogamous. He seemed to be uninterested in the three things that fascinate the average Muslim in "developing countries": money, sex, and travel. As soon as he became Supreme Guide, Khamenehi decided he would not travel outside Iran, further enhancing his image as a modest man. At the same time, people would see leaders from all over the world coming to Tehran to "pay their respects to the Supreme Guide" as the official media claimed.

The media also showed Rafsanjani and Khatami, who succeeded him as president in 1997, embarking on costly foreign trips with the kind of pomp and ceremony they could not reconcile with revolutionary pretensions. In some anecdotes from his memoirs, published in April 2008, Khamenehi recalled his encounters with several revolutionary leaders, including Mozambique's President Samora Machel in the 1980s. Khamenehi says he was "shocked and horrified" to see Machel living in a grand Portuguese colonial palace complete with black servants dressed in scarlet velvet uniforms. The banquet that Machel had thrown in Khamenehi's honor proved so sumptuous that the visiting mullah lost his appetite. During another visit, this time to Harare in Zimbabwe, Khamenehi decided to skip Robert Mugabe's banquet of honor because the African despot was behaving like a monarch. Khamenehi preferred to stay in his hotel room, dine on a simple plate of cheese and grapes, and pray. (The Zimbabweans announced that Khamenehi had refused to attend the banquet because Mugabe had invited women, including his Ghanaian wife, who refused to wear the hijab.)

Khamenehi's insistence on advertising his simple lifestyle and his shunning of luxuries that many other mullahs crave is a theme of many jokes that circulate about him in Tehran and have earned him the sobriquet of "Ali Gedda" (Ali the Beggar). Having tried to make up for the lacunae in his theological studies by increasing the size of his turban and the length of his beard, the accidental Supreme Guide poses as a paragon of virtue in a sea of vice.

Some Iranians believe that Khamenehi's claimed virtues could ultimately prove deadlier than Rafsanjani's alleged vices. The real test is whether Khamenehi would be prepared to sacrifice the interests of the revolution to safeguard Iran's interests as a nation-state. Will he be able to see beyond the schizophrenia that has afflicted Iran under the bizarre system created by Khomeini? In his Jekyll-and-Hyde situation, whose side will he take? There are no ready answers to these questions. Khamenehi has made all the usual noises against Iran's pre-Islamic civilization, although far less viciously than Khomeini. Also, he never misses an opportunity to warn against the supposed dangers of Iranian patriotism. Nevertheless, patriotic themes occasionally sneak into his speeches, hinting at the possibility that he might baulk at the prospect of sacrificing Iran at the altar of Khomeini's lunatic ideology.

In 1980, days after Saddam Hussein's armies had invaded Iran, Khamenehi drove to the battlefront in the company of a ramshackle band of lightly armed men. On his way, he exhorted the population in villages and towns to take up arms, including "knives and batons," and move to the front to stop the invader. His theme was one of defending a homeland (*vatan*), not an ideology. On the front, he saw firsthand that Iranians from all backgrounds, faiths, and ethnic origins were ready to fight and die for their homeland, while Khomeini's sick ideology divided them against one another. Khamenehi's patriotic oratory in those days was in contrast with a notorious speech by Khomeini, a day after the invasion, in which he said he did not bother about "a handful of earth and a bit of water." As deputy secretary of defense in those crucial days, Khamenehi also played a role in forcing the release of army officers and air force pilots imprisoned by Khomeini because they had served under the shah. There is no doubt that Khamenehi's action played a part in helping organize Iranian resistance against the Saddamite invaders in the first phase of the war.

For the past five years, Khamenehi's health has been a subject of speculation, with his death announced by the rumor mill on more than one occasion. In the absence of official information regarding his health, however, it is difficult to be certain. Today, Khamenehi is still twenty years younger than Khomeini was at the time of his death, and based on the mullahs' average life expectancy, which is fifteen years higher than that of the average Iranian, he may well continue for two or more decades. His demise, however, could plunge the system into a crisis the outcome of which is unpredictable. There is no consensus candidate for succession, and rival factions appear poised for a power struggle that could tear the regime apart.

20

Six Centers of Power

Designed to reserve ultimate, in fact absolute, power for the Supreme Guide, the Khomeinist system has tried to prevent its concentration around any of the traditional organs of the state. To that end, it has created a number of revolutionary organs operating in parallel with the state. This has led to a system of checks and balances in which the Supreme Guide is acknowledged as the ultimate arbiter of debate and final decision-maker. Western officials, including President George W. Bush in the United States, have often castigated the various revolutionary organs of the regime by describing them as "unelected." In fact, all organs of the Islamic Republic, including the position of Supreme Guide, are elected directly or indirectly. The point is that elections in the Islamic Republic are carefully limited to the supporters of the regime.

Theoretically, the most important of the revolutionary organs after the Supreme Guide is the Assembly of Experts (Majlis Khobregan), a ninety-two-man body of theologians elected through universal adult suffrage for a period of eight years. Legally, the assembly has the power to elect and to remove the Supreme Guide if he falls short of his constitutional duties or is afflicted by an incurable illness or is otherwise incapacitated. In practice, however, it is hard to imagine circumstances under which the assembly might make such a move. The assembly was led by Ayatollah Ali-Akbar Meshkini, the Friday prayer leader of the "holy" city of Qom and one of Khomeini's most radical associates, until his death in 2007. Since then it has been chaired by Rafsanjani, who has tried to flex muscles by reminding everyone of the assembly's right to choose, and dismiss, the Supreme Guide. In its current composition, however, the assembly will almost certainly produce a comfortable majority for Khamenehi if and when the matter comes to a vote.

The second important revolutionary organ is the Council of the Guardians of the Constitution (Shuray e negahban qanun assassi Jumhuri Eslami Iran). A twelve-man organ, the council is tasked with examining laws passed by the elected parliament to make sure it conforms to the Islamic principles of the constitution. More importantly, perhaps, the council decides who is allowed to stand for any elected position within the system. It also has the authority to declare the election of any individual, or even an entire election, null and void. Of the twelve members, six are appointed by the Supreme Guide, while the parliament names the other six with his assent. Again, the council, although enjoying a constitutional position, and thus considered a state structure, is better classified as a revolutionary organ because of ideological considerations. Over the past three decades, the council has acted as a bastion of revolutionary puritanism rather than a bona fide constitutional court. Virtually all its members have been picked from among individuals claiming a revolutionary record rather than constitutional, or theological, qualifications. The council's principal spokesman and secretary is Ayatollah Ahmad Janati, who is regarded as one of the leading spokesmen of the radical faction supporting President Ahmadinejad.

Another pseudo-constitutional but in fact revolutionary organ is the Council for the Discernment of the Interests of the Established Order (Shuray e Tashkhis e Maslehat e Nezam). This was at first created by Khomeini as an ad hoc extra-constitutional body in 1988 to iron out disputes among the prime minister, the president, and the parliament. (The post of prime minister was abolished in 1989.) The council was given constitutional standing in 1991. It now has thirty-two members, appointed by the Supreme Guide. The president of the republic, the speaker of the parliament, and the president of the Supreme Judicial Council are ex officio members. Rafsanjani, who heads the council, has tried to turn it into a power base for himself. He has co-opted most of his former collaborators fired by Khatami or Ahmadinejad. Pro-Rafsanjani newspapers present the council as something of a super organ that could overrule not only the president and the parliament but also the Supreme Guide. In 2005, the council announced that it had assumed charge of establishing a twenty-year development plan for the country, implying that it now stood above all organs of government. After an initial strong showing, partly thanks to a skillful propaganda campaign, the council has nevertheless faded into the background since Ahmadinejad's election as president. Its chief usefulness at present is that it provides a channel for direct communication among the top figures of the state and the revolution on a monthly basis. However, at a time of crisis triggered by the power struggle within the ruling clique, the council could help tip the balance in favor of one or another faction.

Another organ of the revolution, the Supreme Judicial Council (Shuray e Ali Qaza'i) is the equivalent of a supreme court, and should normally be regarded as an organ of the state. In practice, however, it has acted as a revolutionary organ and has sought to promote the revolutionary tribunals as a parallel judicial system alongside civilian courts of law inherited from the *ancien régime*. Its president, Ayatollah Mahmoud Hashemi Shahroudi, an Iraqi-born Shiite militant, has repeatedly said that in any conflict between the law and the interests of the revolution, the latter should have priority. To underline its revolutionary credentials, the court has intervened in a wide range of matters, from cases of national security to those of corruption and embezzlement. Since Ahmadinejad's election, the court has adopted a critical posture towards the government. Hashemi Shahroudi has specifically targeted Ahmadinejad's economic policy on the grounds that it has led to a massive flight of capital from the country.

The Supreme Council of Cultural Revolution (Shuray e Aali Enqelaab Farhangi), another key organ of the revolution, was created by Khomeini in 1979 with the task of purging the Iranian universities of all Western influence. In the past three decades, the council has become a locus of organization for militant Khomeinist intellectuals and university personnel dedicated to the doctrine of the Supreme Guide. The council plays a major role in the internal debate of the revolutionary establishment both directly and through various student organizations that it uses as fronts. Before Ahmadinejad's election, the council had faded into the background. Its chairman, Ayatollah Muhammad-Ali Taskhiri, appointed by Khamenehi, had focused his energies on promoting "convergence" among Islamic sects. In 2006, however, Ahmadinejad declared a "second Islamic cultural revolution" to purge the nation's institutions of higher education of "Zionist and satanic influences." Between 2006 and 2008, an estimated one thousand lecturers, professors, faculty deans, and other academics were expelled or forced into early retirement. A number of academics were arrested on their return to Iran from conferences abroad. In December 2006, student anger exploded with an unprecedented show of defiance when President Ahmadinejad visited Tehran's Amir Kabir University. Pictures shot on cell phones showed angry students chanting against the president, calling him a fascist and murderer. They held portraits of Ahmadinejad upside down with cries of "Death to the dictator." Using the Supreme Council of Cultural Revolution, Ahmadinejad retaliated by having hundreds of students expelled on spurious grounds. At least forty student associations were dissolved and court cases were filed against some seven hundred student activists.

In a show of defiance, Ahmadinejad appointed Ayatollah Amid Zanjani as chancellor of Tehran University, the nation's largest institution of higher education, with over 120,000 students. This was the first time that a turbaned head was put in charge of an institution that had been created by Reza Shah Pahlavi in the 1930s as the advance guard of secularism in Iran. Incensed by the coming of a mullah to their university, students demonstrated against Zanjani and simulated strangling him with his own turban. The ayatollah retaliated by retiring forty-five professors he claimed were "too old to teach," although every one was younger than himself. The students and their allies in the faculty scored a victory when the council decided to replace Zanjani on the grounds that protecting him would disrupt normal life at the university.

The most important of the parallel organs created by the Khomeinists is the so-called Islamic Revolutionary Guard Corps (IRGC), a paramilitary outfit with its own ground, air, and naval forces. At the same time, the IRGC is the country's biggest holding company, controlling hundreds of businesses, notably Iran's rapidly growing armament industry. For a quarter of a century, the regime established by Khomeini has been labeled a "mullahrchy," a theocracy dominated by the Shiite clergy. Today, however, it is safe to say that the dominant force within the ruling establishment in Tehran is the IRGC. This was perhaps one reason why the Bush administration decided to brand the IRGC a "terrorist organization" in 2007. The problem, however, is that the IRGC is not a monolith, and to label all of it as "terrorist" may make it difficult to cut deals with parts of it when an opportunity arises.

Any analysis of the IRGC must take into account a number of facts. First, the IRGC is not a revolutionary army in the sense that the ALN (National Liberation Army) was in Algeria or the Vietcong in Vietnam. Those two were born *during* the so-called revolutionary wars in which they became key players. The IRGC was created *after* the Khomeinist revolution had succeeded. This fact is of crucial importance. Those who joined the IRGC came from all sorts of backgrounds. The majority were opportunists who wished to board the gravy train. By joining the IRGC, an individual would not only obtain revolutionary credentials, often on fictitious grounds, but also secure a well-paid job at a time that economic collapse made jobs scarce. Joining the IRGC enabled many who had cooperated with the *ancien régime* to rewrite their CVs and obtain a new "revolutionary virginity," so to speak. Membership also ensured access to rare goods and services, from color television sets to more decent housing. One popular Iranian satirist has a poem about a young man who joins the IRGC to get a color television set so that his parents can see in Technicolor the blood he sheds in the streets in defense of Khomeinism.

As the years went by, IRGC membership provided a fast track to social, political, and economic success. By 2005, more than half of Ahmadinejad's cabinet ministers were members of the IRGC, as was the president himself. After the general election of March 2008, IRGC members held nearly a third of the seats in the Islamic Consultative Assembly (Majlis), which made the IRGC the largest party in the ersatz parliament. Twenty of Iran's thirty provinces had governors from the IRGC. Under Ahmadinejad, IRGC members also started capturing key posts in the diplomatic service. In 2008, for the first time, the Islamic Republic's ambassadors in such important places as the United Nations in New York and embassies in a dozen Western capitals were members of the IRGC.

More importantly, perhaps, the IRGC acts as a business conglomerate with interests in many sectors of the economy. By some accounts, the IRGC is Iran's third corporation after the National Iranian Oil Company and the Imam Reza Foundation in Mash'had. In 2004, a Tehran University study estimated the annual turnover of IRGC businesses at $12 billion. The privatization package announced by Ahmadinejad in 2007 increased the IRGC's economic clout. Almost all the public sector companies marked for privatization, at a total value of $18 billion, ended up in the hands of the IRGC or its individual commanders and their front men.

The IRGC also controls the lucrative business of "exporting the revolution," estimated to be worth $1.2 billion a year. It finances branches of Hezballah in at least twenty countries, including some in Europe, and provides money, arms and training for radical groups with leftist backgrounds. In recent years, it has emerged as a major backer of the armed wing of the Palestinian Hamas and both Shiite and Sunni armed groups in Iraq, Afghanistan, and Pakistan. The Islamic Republic is believed to have invested some $20 billion in Lebanon since 1983. In most cases, the Lebanese branch of Hezballah is nominally in control. A closer examination, however, reveals that in most cases the Lebanese companies are fronts for Iranian concerns controlled by the IRGC. Hezballah's business empire, the source of much of its power in Lebanon, is like a house of cards that could collapse with an adverse breeze from Tehran.

The crown jewel of the IRGC's business empire is the Islamic Republic's nuclear program, which has cost the nation over $10 billion so far. It is quite possible that even senior officials, including the president of the Islamic Republic, were not always properly informed about the true ambitions of the clandestine nuclear project. In 2007, the project became the central issue in the confrontation between the Islamic Republic and the United Nations. For years, a former oil minister and IRGC officer, Ghulam-Reza Aqazadeh, has led the nuclear project, reporting to the Supreme Guide. It is part of a broader scheme of arms purchases and manufacture, accounting for almost 11 percent of the annual national budget.

At the end of the war with Iraq in 1988, the leadership in Tehran engaged in a major debate about possible future threats and ways of countering them. The debate produced what was labeled the "National Defense Doctrine," with the IRGC at its core. Under this doctrine, the Islamic Republic decided to base its defenses on three pillars: a massive land army, a large arsenal of missiles, and a nuclear surge capacity. The idea of a massive land army had originally come from Khomeini in the early stages of the war against Iraq. The ayatollah had seen how masses of Iranian teenagers had effectively committed suicide by using their bodies to stop Iraqi tanks. At the time, Iran's demography—with annual growth rates of more than 3 percent, the highest in the world—could be regarded as a weapon. Khomeini also assumed that his regime's strongest potential enemy, the United States, would not be able to sustain casualties on the scale that his Islamic Republic, using its ideology of martyrdom, was able to sell to the Iranian people.

Khomeini had dreamed of "an army of twenty million," providing a virtually endless supply of cannon fodder. To build such an army, he created the Mobilization of the Dispossessed (Baseej Mustadafeen) to handle national conscription under IRGC supervision. Every male Iranian age sixteen or over must perform a six-month national service through the Baseej, which could place him with the IRGC or the regular armed forces or in one of the paramilitary organizations created in recent years. Demographically, the nation could supply the Baseej with half a million recruits each year. Soon, however, it became clear that the national budget could not support such a large number of recruits. Thus, the Baseej has been issuing exemptions to almost half of those who qualify for national service. At the same time, the restoration of the family planning program, scrapped by Khomeini as a "Zionist-American plot against Islam," has halved the annual population growth rate. Today, the Baseej is a force of around 400,000 at any given time, providing the IRGC with its manpower needs.

While they had to scale down their dream army of twenty million, Tehran decision-makers exceeded their expectations with regard to turning the Islamic Republic into a "superpower in missiles." The signal for this project was given as early as October 1985 by Rafsanjani: "What I wish to say openly is that Iran is determined to become a major missile power. It is possible that we won't be able to rival the superpowers in this domain but we shall become the world's second missile power after them."[1] A few months later, Rafsanjani made a similar boast in front of an Iranian audience: "We have made such innovations in radar defense systems and hawk missiles that if the Americans learned about our success they would have a fit of jealousy."[2] The decision to go for missiles was dictated by necessity. When the mullahs seized power, Iran's air force was almost entirely U.S.-equipped. The severing of ties with the United States meant that the new regime in Tehran would no longer have access to American suppliers. Building a new air force from scratch, assuming that other manufacturers of military aviation were prepared to sell materiel to a revolutionary regime, was simply too costly for a nation facing economic meltdown and war. The cheap solution was to go for missiles, the "weapon of the poor."

As early as 1984, the IRGC, using American and British models, started manufacturing crude missiles with limited range for battlefield use. At the time, the only country prepared to help the Islamic Republic was North Korea, which soon emerged as Iran's principal partner in developing a missile program. Iranian money, North Korean technology, and Soviet and Chinese models produced the generation of missiles named Shahab (Meteor). By 2008, three generations had been designed, tested, manufactured, and deployed, with technical and scientific input from India, Pakistan, China, Russia, and Brazil, in addition to North Korea. Initially, the IRGC's objective had been to possess short-range missiles to use in theater. This objective was achieved in 1988, when the war with Iraq was about to end. The IRGC's next objective was to produce longer-range missiles capable of hitting most targets in the Middle East. By 1998, this objective had also been achieved. In 2008, the consensus among military experts was that the Islamic Republic was manufacturing a new generation of missiles, designated as Shahab-III and Shahab-IV, with ranges of 1,500 to 2,500 kilometers, and thus capable of reaching all targets in the Middle East and, if fired from Iranian bases in Syria or Lebanon, several members of the European Union as well. Tehran tested another of its short-range missiles, known as Zalzal (Earthquake), with deadly effect through the Lebanese branch of Hezballah against Israel in the summer of 2006.

Missiles and rockets play a central role in the IRGC doctrine of *hojum ezdehami*, which, translated literally, means "attacking by crowding." The idea is to attack an enemy position or asset, such as an aircraft carrier, with a large number of men armed with small but deadly weapons. An American aircraft carrier, for example, could be attacked suddenly by scores of small IRGC speedboats on a suicide mission, firing an endless barrage of missiles and rockets—like Gulliver at the hands of the Lilliputians. American land positions, say in Iraq, could be overrun by wave after wave of suicide attackers firing rocket-propelled grenades and an assortment of short-range missiles. In 2007, Ahmadinejad announced that the Islamic Republic had developed "the fastest underwater missile in the world," an apparent threat to U.S. warships in the strategic Strait of Hormuz.

But it was the second pillar of the defense doctrine that was meant to provide the Islamic Republic with ultimate insurance against the United States, the only power capable of posing a military threat to the Khomeinist regime. In its time, the USSR had secured a similar insurance against being attacked in its homeland by becoming a nuclear power in the 1950s. With that insurance in its pocket, as it were, the Soviet Union had embarked on a global "anti-imperialist" campaign that included fomenting revolts, fighting proxy wars, and projecting political power throughout the world. The Islamic Republic wants to be in the same position—immune to attack in its home base, and thus free to challenge the Great Satan all over the world. Thus, there could be little doubt that the ultimate aim of the Khomeinist nuclear program is the creation of an arsenal of weapons.

With a two-year interlude in 2003–2005, the Islamic Republic has been enriching uranium as a high priority, although it has no nuclear power station where this could be used as fuel. The only nuclear power station under construction in Iran, in the Bushehr peninsula on the Persian Gulf, was designed by Germans in the 1970s and is being built by a Russian company that constructed Chernobyl. The Bushehr plant is designed to use a specially graded and codified fuel that is produced only in Russia; it cannot use the uranium enriched by Iran. Russia has contracted to supply the fuel needed in Bushehr for ten years and has announced its readiness to provide the needed fuel for the entire lifespan of the plant, which is estimated at thirty-seven years. Thus, Tehran's insistence on maintaining its uranium enrichment program at the cost of UN sanctions and other diplomatic and economic pressures appears suspicious, to say the least. There is one more reason to suspect that the Islamic Republic is trying to become a nuclear power. It is building a heavy water plant at Arak, west of Tehran, supposedly producing fuel for a nuclear power station using plutonium. However, the Islamic Republic has no such plant, nor has it even planned to build one. What is produced in Arak, therefore, could only have a military use.

In any case, Iran, owning the world's second largest oil and natural gas reserves—enough to supply its needs and provide it with export margins for at least four more centuries—has no need of costly and potentially hazardous nuclear energy. Furthermore, a study by a group of Tehran University scientists in 1999 warned the government that building nuclear power plants in Iran, one of the world's most active earthquake zones, was "irresponsible." The Bushehr nuclear plant is designed to resist earthquakes of up to magnitude 7.3 on the Richter scale. The area where the plant is being built has already experienced earthquakes of magnitude 7 on at least three occasions since the 1920s.

If the plant is destroyed in an earthquake, the environmental effects could be catastrophic not only for Iran itself but also for its neighbors in the Persian Gulf. The whole population of Kuwait, Bahrain, Qatar, and the United Arab Emirates, along with more than 20 percent of the populations of Iraq, Saudi Arabia, and Oman, live within 180 kilometers of the dangerous peninsula. The Islamic Republic's dogged determination to pursue its illicit nuclear program in the face of such dangers could be understood only if it had a purely military purpose.

Nevertheless, it is possible that the program as it stands today is aimed only at securing what is known in technical jargon as "surge capacity"— the scientific, technical, and industrial instruments necessary for building the bomb without necessarily doing so immediately. Several countries, notably Germany and Japan, have that "surge capacity" without wishing to build nuclear warheads.

One other factor may explain Tehran's readiness to risk war on this issue. It is possible that the IRGC is determined to secure this third pillar of the defense doctrine around which it has built all its plans for rolling back American power and establishing the Islamic Republic as the "regional superpower" in the Middle East. President Khatami's decision to suspend the nuclear program in 2003 as a sign of goodwill towards the European Union provoked a bitter reaction from the IRGC, some of whose commanders implicitly threatened to kill "those responsible for this shame." Let us also recall that it was Khatami, and not Ahmadinejad as it is commonly assumed, who resumed the program in 2005, ostensibly to pacify the angered IRGC leadership. The nuclear issue showed that the IRGC, although it may be more of a franchise chain than a corporation controlled by a board of directors, is united when it comes to the fundamental issues of military strategy.

The IRGC is divided into five commands, each of which has a direct line to the Supreme Guide Khamenehi, who was himself one of the earliest members of the force in 1980. As deputy defense secretary and then president of the republic, Khamenehi played a key role in building up the IRGC and using it as a political base for himself. Later, he projected the IRGC as a force with a global mission: "Today, the IRGC has a determining effect on all international political balances and calculations," Khamenehi told an audience of IRGC officers in 1984. "If one day this corps ceases to exist in our society, the authority of our Islamic revolution shall collapse, and the calculations of global politics will be upset."[3]

To minimize the risk of coup d'état, IRGC's senior officers are not allowed to engage in "sustained communication" with one another on "sensitive subjects." Of the five commands in question, two could be regarded as "terrorist" according to the U.S. State Department's definition—which, needless to say, is rejected by the Islamic Republic. One, which includes the so-called Jerusalem (Quds) Corps, is in charge of exporting the revolution. Apart from Hezballah and Hamas, it runs a number of radical groups across the globe. It is currently devoting most of its energies to Iraq in preparation for an American withdrawal. The idea is to put the Islamic Republic and its clients in Iraq in a position to claim credit for having "expelled the American infidels." The second command that could be targeted deals with internal repression. It operates through several auxiliary forces, including the notorious Karbala brigades charged with crushing popular revolts in Tehran and other urban centers. Many Iranians see these as instruments of terror.

The IRGC's officer corps, including those in retirement, numbers around 55,000 and is as divided on domestic and foreign policy as the rest of the society. A few former IRGC commanders who did not share the Islamic Republic's goals have already defected to the United States. Hundreds of others have gone into quiet exile, mostly as businessmen in the United Arab Emirates, Malaysia, and Turkey. An unknown number were purged because they refused to kill anti-regime demonstrators in Iranian cities. Many prominent IRGC commanders may be regarded as businessmen first and military leaders second. Usually they have a brother or a cousin in Europe or Canada to look after their business interests and keep a channel open to small and big Satans in case the regime falls. A few IRGC commanders, including some at the top, do not seek a major military conflict with the United States that could wreck their business empires without offering victory on the battlefield.

There is no guarantee that, in case of a major war, all parts of the IRGC would show the same degree of commitment to the Islamic Republic. IRGC commanders may be prepared to kill unarmed Iranians or hire Lebanese, Palestinian, and Iraqi radicals to kill others. But it is not certain they would be prepared to die for Ahmadinejad's ambitions. In 2007, these concerns prompted Khamenehi to announce a Defense Planning Commission controlled by his office.

A blanket labeling of the IRGC, as opposed to targeting elements of it that do mischief against the Iranian people and others in the region and beyond, could prove counterproductive. It could unite a deeply fractious force by leaving it no door through which some of its members could walk out of the dangerous situation they have helped create. This is all the more so now that the IRGC, with ambitions similar to those of most armies in the "developing world," is trying to recreate itself as a political party. Its domestic critics already call it "the party of the barracks." Having captured the presidency, the IRGC, faction-ridden though it is, will continue seeking an even greater share of power at all levels.

Islamic history is full of instances of the caliph's praetorian guards getting wise to the possibility of jettisoning their master and ruling for themselves. One day, Khamenehi may realize that his alliance with the IRGC against his rivals might not have been such a brilliant idea.

21

Six Rival Centers of Power

The six centers of revolutionary power are paralleled with six other centers of state power in a system that continues to vacillate between them. Despite their new appellations, all the six centers of state power are holdovers from the *ancien régime*, often continuing the same bureaucratic culture tinged with a bit of nationalism but always moderated by a certain realism. While hardcore revolutionaries still regard these institutions with deep suspicion, those who run them feel that the revolution has run its course and must now take the backseat as far as strategic decisions are concerned.

The principal institution among the six rival centers of power is the presidency of the republic. The use of the term "president" has been the source of much confusion in recent years. In reality, the president has the same powers and responsibilities that prime ministers had in the former regime. Despite his title, he is not the head of state. The use of the term "president" to designate an official who heads a council of ministers is not peculiar to the Islamic Republic. It was also used in the Fourth Republic in France to designate the prime minister, and likewise in Spain today. In the Khomeinist system, the president nominates the members of the cabinet but cannot appoint them without the approval of the Supreme Guide and the Islamic Consultative Assembly. Although directly elected through universal adult suffrage, the president is not confirmed in his position unless he receives a written "letter of appointment" from the Supreme Guide. He could not stand for more than two consecutive four-year terms as president. Candidates must be of Iranian parentage and of the Shiite faith. The president also needs the approval of the Supreme Guide and the parliament to apply his policies.

All this does not mean that the president of the Islamic Republic is nothing but a puppet in the hands of the Supreme Guide, or irrelevant, as Senator John Kerry has claimed. To start with, the president has a say on every single major decision that commits the resources of the Iranian state. He controls the national budget, including the secret budget allocated to the office of the Supreme Guide. He is also head of a bureaucracy that, directly or indirectly, employs almost two million people. Through the Ministry of the Interior and the Ministry of Intelligence and Security, he also controls a vast network of police, gendarmerie, and secret services, whose members look to him for budgets, policies, and promotions. Because of the dominating role the public sector plays in the Iranian economy, the president also enjoys endless opportunities for distributing favors to secure political support. More importantly, perhaps, the president—unlike the Supreme Guide, who is appointed by a college of mullahs—enjoys the unique advantage of drawing his legitimacy from direct universal suffrage. A strong president could easily assert greater authority as someone who represents both the will of the people and the interests of the state. It would be hard for any Supreme Guide, let alone one as weak as Khamenehi, to veto a package of popular reforms presented by a strong president. The presidency is a bully pulpit that, if used effectively, could mobilize public support for policies that the revolutionary organs might regard as not radical enough or even as counterrevolutionary.

As the principal spokesman for the machinery of state, the president has often come into conflict with revolutionary organs. Regardless of who is president, this office is also influenced by the inherent moderation of the bureaucracy that, over centuries, has learned to pursue its goals through consensus rather than conflict. In that sense, all but one of the five presidents of the Islamic Republic before Ahmadinejad proved to be relative "moderates" in their different ways because they came to represent the interests not of the revolution but of the state.

The first five presidents of the Islamic Republic adopted different strategies vis-à-vis a revolution to which they owed their position in the first place. The first of them, Banisadr, tried to govern *against* the revolution, believing that Iran needed to close the revolutionary chapter and start building a new nation-state. Caught in a bitter power struggle with the mullahs and facing the Iraqi invasion, he did not last long enough to test his theories in practice. His successor, Rajai, had just a few weeks as president before being assassinated by counterrevolutionaries. In that brief spell, he showed that he saw the presidency as another "revolutionary bunker." Had he survived, he would have governed *for* the revolution. The third president, Khamenehi, the first of three mullahs who successively occupied the position, did not try to govern at all. During his eight-year reign, Khomeini took all the key decisions as Supreme Guide, while the day-to-day matters were handled by the prime minister, a post that still existed, and the speaker of the Islamic Consultative Assembly. Khamenehi's style as president did not reflect his lack of interest in politics or absence of political ambitions. It was based on the belief that in a system already bedeviled by factional feuds, open conflict between state and revolution could prove suicidal for both.

The fourth president, Rafsanjani, a businessman-cum-mullah, was intelligent enough to recognize the need to restore and, when possible, strengthen the machinery of state that had been damaged by the revolution. In his eight-year tenure, he tried to govern *alongside* the revolution. This allowed the Iranian state to regain part of its self-confidence and rebuild some of its institutions alongside similar revolutionary organs. For example, Rafsanjani did not abolish the Islamic tribunals and the revolutionary courts, but he did enable the civil courts of the *ancien régime* to resume work alongside them. This created an *à la carte* system of justice in which people could take their litigations either to revolutionary tribunals applying the Shariah, or to civil courts operating with laws derived from the Napoleonic Code. Rafsanjani did not stop the various revolutionary organs from generating vast wealth for the mullahs and their associates. In fact, he and his family benefited immensely from the system. But he did allow the public sector of the Iranian economy to make a comeback, restoring part of the economic role that the state had lost to the revolution. Ultimately, however, he failed because he was unprepared, or unable, to close the chapter of revolution and let the nation rebuild its state.

Rafsanjani's successor, Khatami, another mullah, decided to govern *away* from the revolution by pretending that it did not exist, while doing nothing that might provoke its assertion of existence. During his presidency, Khatami spent a good part of his time traveling abroad, visiting more than forty countries and attending a string of conferences in Europe, Asia, and the Americas. At home, he talked of reform, without ever introducing a single reform project. Abroad, he tried to put a smiling face on a regime whose highest officials had been indicted for terrorism by criminal courts in Europe and Latin America. When it came to choosing between the state and the revolution, however, he sided with the latter, especially in its brutal repression of dissent.

The election of Mahmoud Ahmadinejad as president in 2005 heralded an entirely new experiment with a position caught between state and revolution. His predecessors had tried to govern against, for, alongside, or away from the revolution. Ahmadinejad, whose campaign slogan was "We Can," has tried to fuse the two and govern *for* the revolution. We shall discuss his original approach in more detail later on.

It is through the Council of Ministers or the cabinet that the president, as head of the executive, exercises power. The council consists of up to twenty-five portfolios dealing with the different tasks of government under the direct supervision of the president. Because the state directly or indirectly controls almost 70 percent of the gross domestic product, the government, headed by the Council of Ministers, wields immense practical powers that are often neglected by observers bedazzled by the light and fire of the revolutionary organs. It is through the Council of Ministers that the powerful octopus of Persian bureaucracy exerts much of its influence in the decision-making process, at times quietly overruling even the Supreme Guide himself. The council also controls the Central Bank and thus the fixing of interest rates and the volume of money in circulation, thus playing a key role in shaping the regime's overall economic policies.

Legally, the Council of Ministers is answerable to the Islamic Consultative Assembly (Majlis Shuray e Islami). This is a 290-seat unicameral parliament directly elected by universal adult suffrage once every four years. The Majlis has often been identified as a hotbed of radicalism. In reality, however, only the second Majlis, where leftist Islamists held a majority, sided more with the camp of the revolution than with that of the state. The Majlis is dominated by a conservative majority that is less revolutionary, in Western terms, than Ahmadinejad. In 1997, the speaker of the Majlis, Ayatollah Ali-Akbar Nateq-Nuri, stood as a presidential candidate and was defeated by Khatami. The outside world saw Nateq-Nuri as a radical "revolutionary" and Khatami as a reformist "moderate." Khatami won because he was the unknown "outsider," not because Nateq-Nuri was a radical revolutionary. In terms of both economic and foreign policies, in fact, Nateq-Nuri was more conservative than Khatami, who models himself on Western leftist figures.

The Majlis is the legislative power that must approve all government bills before they become law with the approval of the Council of Constitutional Guardians and the assent of the Supreme Guide. It also has the right to propose legislation, and often does, much to the chagrin of the ministers. The Majlis can remove ministers it regards as incompetent or worse. Because its members are in direct contact with their constituencies, the Majlis, regardless of the peculiar circumstances under which it is elected, often acts as a barometer of public opinion. The general election of 2008, spread over March and April, produced a two-thirds majority for radical candidates from the IRGC, giving rise to fears that the Majlis may abandon its traditional role as a defender of Iran as a state and join the institutions of the revolution. Nevertheless, the Majlis is unlikely to do this. The new IRGC majority is divided into three factions, at least two of which appear to want the revolutionary phrase of Iran's history to be closed as soon as possible, albeit with the IRGC in power. In May 2008, only one faction loyal to Ahmadinejad, and accounting for about 40 percent of the seats, appeared determined to redefine the role of the Majlis in the context of the president's plans for "global and permanent revolution."

Just as almost every revolutionary organ has a state double, the IRGC is doubled by the Armed Forces of the Islamic Republic of Iran (Niruhay e Mossllah e Jumhuri Islami Iran). These consist of the regular army, the gendarmerie, the urban police, the border police, the forest guard, the industrial guard, and the oil industry protection guard. The organ as a whole accounts for 600,000 men, including civilian ancillary personnel. The armed forces are under the command of the Supreme Guide. Nevertheless, their esprit de corps, traditions, and objective interests keep them closer to the state rather than the revolution. Themes of Iranian nationalism, such as the purification of the Persian language, are emphasized by the armed forces in opposition to the revolution's efforts to bring Iran closer to the Arab and Islamic worlds. The backbone of the armed forces consists of men from middle-class backgrounds with relatively high levels of education and technical expertise compared with the IRGC. Many traditions established during the years of Iran's close association with the West, especially the United States, have survived in the armed forces, notably some knowledge of the English language in contrast with the IRGC, where Arabic and Russian are favored.

For the past three decades, the regular army has played the "grand dumb one," as the French say, careful not to become involved in anything remotely political. There were two reasons for this. First, the army knew that in 1979 and 1980 it came close to total destruction by Khomeini. In fact, had it not been for the Iraqi invasion, the ayatollah who had executed thousands of officers and NCOs, often without trial, would not have allowed the army to remain in existence in any form. Even after the Iraqi invasion, many revolutionary mullahs continued to campaign for the destruction of what they saw as "the Shah's army." Thus, any dabbling in politics by the army would have given its enemies the excuse they needed for a new wave of purges and massacres. The second reason for the army's quietist posture was a well-established tradition under which the Iranian military did not intervene in politics. In 1978–79, that tradition had prevented them from staging a coup, dismissing the shah and crushing the revolt led by the mullahs. Since then some Iranians have continued to look to the army, as a national institution and not an instrument of revolutionary repression, to emerge as the leader of Iran's renaissance as a nation-state. But if Iran is to have a Bonaparte, he is more likely to come from the IRGC than from an apolitical army.

As a rentier state, the Islamic Republic depends heavily on oil revenue. At the center of the industry that produces those revenues stands the National Iranian Oil Company (NIOC) (Sherkat e Melli Naft e Iran), created by Mossadeq in 1951 after he wrested control of Iran's principal wealth from the British. Although under the nominal control of the minister for petroleum, with a seat in the cabinet, the NIOC and its offshoots—which number at least a hundred companies, notably in the petrochemical industry—must be regarded as a powerful autonomous organ of the state. In 2008, the oil industry accounted for some 40 percent of the Iranian GDP and provided 65 percent of the government's income and some 90 percent of the nation's export earnings. The NIOC's voice is thus a powerful one within the decision-making process. That influence is augmented by the fact that the NIOC spends billions of dollars inside and outside the country each year, purchasing services and equipment. The NIOC and its affiliates have lobbied for a moderate foreign policy for years. Their key argument is that, as a result of decades of underinvestment, Iran's energy industry is heading for a crisis. In 2008, Iran's maximum oil-producing capacity was estimated at 3.8 million barrels a day, compared with almost 8 million in 1978. Many oilfields, old and tired, were in need of rejuvenation through gas injection and a process known as secondary recovery. Iran itself, however, lacks the technology and the massive investments needed. Most of NIOC's oil and gas exploration projects have remained on hold, with no prospect of finding the estimated $150 billion they would need in investments over the next two decades.

The 180,000 employees of the NIOC and its affiliates are aware of their strategic power and often use it to further their particular interests and to support policies they favor. In the 1990s, they succeeded in overcoming opposition from the revolutionary organs and signed a landmark

$1 billion contract with Amoco, a medium-sized U.S. oil company. However, the Clinton administration canceled the contract, which was then awarded to the state-owned French company Total. The Iranian oil industry has been a key target of sanctions imposed by the United States, including measures to punish any company that invests more than $25 million a year in Iran's energy sector.

The NIOC and its affiliates act as a pool of management skills for the state as a whole, providing competent personnel for other departments of the government at various levels. The NIOC was the first major institution to expel the mullahs who acted as "revolutionary guides" at all levels of its management. It was also the NIOC that initiated the famous debate between "experts" and "believers" in the late 1980s that led to the reinstating of many officials and technicians who had been purged by the revolution. In the past few years, the NIOC and its affiliates have emerged as major instruments in furthering the regime's foreign policy in a number of regions. In Latin America, Africa, and South Asia, the NIOC is at the center of attempts by the Islamic Republic to project its power and influence as a state. Holding the world's second largest oil and natural gas reserves, Iran is likely to remain a major player in the global energy market for the foreseeable future. And that means a continued role for the NIOC and its affiliates as key organs of the Iranian state.

Even before he seized power, Khomeini had vowed to destroy the mechanism for secular justice developed by the Pahlavi Shahs between 1925 and 1979. Copied from the "infidel model," the mechanism was used to transform Iran from a society ruled by Islamic Shariah into one governed by a corpus of laws adopted from Roman traditions. The key organ in that mechanism was the Ministry of Justice (Vezarat e Dadgostari), which Khomeini wanted to abolish but could not. The ministry still offers a system of justice largely patterned on that of western Europe. This is in contrast with Islamic tribunals that operate as organs of revolutionary justice under ambiguous constitutional arrangements with the blessings of the High Council of the Judiciary. The Ministry of Justice recognizes Western-style lawyers and procedures for both civilian and criminal cases, something that is in direct violation of Islamic legal principles. The ministry employs women as assistant judges and advocates, again in defiance of the Islamic Shariah.

The existence of two parallel organs of justice creates an *à la carte* situation that, in turn, could lead to conflicts between the state and the revolution. Decisions taken by Islamic tribunals are often overruled on appeal by ordinary courts, and vice versa. This could be of crucial importance in business and regarding property rights. This is one reason why many legal experts believe that the Islamic Republic does not have any clear set of laws dealing with property ownership. An Islamic tribunal could seize an individual's property at any time, on the grounds that the owner is "waging war on Allah." Then, an ordinary court could annul the decision. However, a revolutionary tribunal could reverse that decision, too. The Ministry of Justice is supported by a powerful lobby consisting of people who at one time or other graduated in Western-style law and worked as lawyers, judges, jurists, and notaries public, before and after the revolution.

22

Power Points in a No-Man's Land

Over the last three decades, there have been countless occasions on which the interests of Iran as a nation-state have clashed with those of Iran as a vehicle for the Islamic Revolution. In most cases, though by no means all, the interests of the revolution have prevailed. Nevertheless, the rival interests are given ample opportunity to compete for support within the regime. Several institutions are used as venues for that competition. The most important of these is the Supreme Council for National Security (Shuray Aali Amniyat Melli). Chaired by the president of the republic, who also appoints its secretary general, the council includes the speaker of the Islamic Majlis, the president of the Supreme Judicial Council, key ministers, and the commanders of both the IRGC and the armed forces.

Created during the Iran-Iraq war to supervise and coordinate policy, the Supreme Council for National Security has become a permanent organ of the state enshrined in the constitution. Nevertheless, it vacillates between the state and the revolution, now siding with one and now with the other. In 2003, for example, the council decided that it was in "Iran's national interest" to suspend the uranium enrichment program so as to deny the United States a pretext for pre-emptive attack. At the time, the Islamic Republic leaders had been unnerved by the speedy victory that the U.S.-led coalition had achieved in Iraq while there was much talk of "Iran next" in Washington. In 2005, however, the same council, now certain that there would be no U.S. attack, decided to resume uranium enrichment because it "served the highest interests of our Islamic Revolution."

Critics of the council argue that its hybrid nature undermines its principal mission, which is to ensure the security of the nation. For example, on a number of occasions, the council has endorsed the brutal repression of citizens' protest against government policies, something that does not serve the interests of Iran as a nation. The council has also approved support for radical terrorist groups in a number of countries on the grounds that they share Khomeini's revolutionary ideals. Such support, however, could undermine Iran's national security by exposing it to retaliation by countries affected by Iranian-sponsored terrorism. Since Ahmadinejad's election as president, the council has clearly tilted towards the revolution. Its dismissal of Ali Ardeshir Larijani as secretary general in 2007 was a signal that Ahmadinejad wanted the council to endorse his radical foreign policy regardless of its effects on Iran's longer-term interests.

In the no-man's land between state and revolution, we also find a number of business concerns that play major roles in both economic and political domains. The most important of these is the Foundation for the Dispossessed and Self-Sacrificers (Bonyad Mostazafan va Janbazan). This is a trust that existed under the name of the Pahlavi Foundation before the revolution, under the shah's control. Since 1979, the *bonyad* has seized the assets of a further 17,000 small and medium-size companies. Its annual turnover is estimated at around $12 billion, making it the nation's third largest business concern. The foundation owns banks and insurance companies, shipping and airlines, hotels, armament factories, cash-crop farms, feature-film companies, advertising agencies, and hundreds of smaller businesses throughout the country. Its head is named by the Supreme Guide, who must also approve all nominations to the board of directors. The foundation is used to distribute favors among the supporters of the regime, and thus tends to side with the revolutionary camp whenever it comes into conflict with the state. Nevertheless, the foundation knows how far it can go in its relations with the state, which is needed for legal protection as well as lucrative contracts. For example, the foundation does good business in supplying the armed forces with some of their needs.

The Foundation for the Dispossessed is not alone in its role as a means of "democratizing" corruption and distributing favors in the Islamic Republic. In 1979–80, the Khomeinist regime seized the assets of over 1.2 million Iranians. These included 750,000 housing units and over 50,000 businesses. Under the revolutionary regime, these assets have been distributed among a number of "foundations." The latest register available in 2005 showed the existence of 113 such foundations, each of which was headed by an influential mullah. These are all based on the same model as the *bonyad.* They never publish their accounts, pay no taxes to the state, and ignore most laws, especially as far as terms of employment are concerned. One of the key grievances of independent trade unionists concerns the fact that the foundations do not respect even the so-called Islamic Labor Code in force. The best known of these foundations are the Martyrs' Foundation (Bonyad e Shahid) and the Fifth of June Foundation (Bonyad 15 Khordad).

The Supreme Guide appoints almost all the heads of these foundations. Virtually all the foundations seek their legitimacy in real or imaginary revolutionary pedigrees, fearing that normalization—that is to say a restoration of state authority at the expense of the revolution—could undermine their position and threaten their interests. At the same time, they depend on the state for part or sometimes the whole of their income. They also need the state for privileges, such as reserved places at universities for children of revolutionary families introduced by the foundations. One example of the contradictory behavior of the foundations is the decision by the Fifth of June Foundation to continue announcing a prize for the murder of the British novelist Salman Rushdie even after President Khatami had declared that the dispute had been settled. In some Muslim countries, the financing of radical groups is done through the foundations often in defiance of the Iranian government. In 2000, for example, while Iran as a state was trying to improve ties with Saudi Arabia, various foundations continued to finance groups dedicated to causing trouble in the kingdom. There are periodic calls from advocates of normalization for the state to assume direct control of the foundations.

So far, however, the balancing act has continued with both sides seeking to use the foundations for their own purposes.

The foundations often act in the style of the Italian Mafia. The method is to contact businessmen and ask for "voluntary donations" to support charitable projects in favor of "families of martyrs" or in aid of Islamic causes abroad, especially in Palestine. This is always backed by the implicit threat that refusal to make a "voluntary donation" could lead to "complications with our martyrdom-seeking youth," social ostracism of the guilty businesses, or boycott of their goods and services. In some cases, businessmen who have refused to pay have been accused of being Baha'is, a charge that amounts to a death sentence, and have had their businesses ransacked and burned. Even foreign companies doing business with Iran are subjected to this kind of pressure. French businessmen claim that up to 5 percent of all contracts they conclude in the Islamic Republic go to secret accounts held by the *bonyads.* No one knows what actually happens to the money. It is certain, however, that at least part of it is distributed among the five thousand or so mullahs who provide the backbone of the regime. These mullahs have their unofficial bodyguards and maintain their own networks of favor distribution, and thus need a steady flow of cash.

The most powerful of the foundations operating as a state within the state is the Sacred Precinct of Imam Reza (Astan e Qods e Razavi). This is, in effect, a major holding company that handles assets bequeathed to the shrine of Imam Reza, the eighth imam of shiism, in Mash'had, capital of the northeastern province of Khorassan. The *astan* existed before the revolution, with the shah as its nominal head. Its assets are estimated at around $50 billion, with an annual turnover of some $15 billion, making it the nation's second largest business entity after the NIOC. The *astan* owns vast tracts of land, a massive real estate portfolio, factories, hotels, gold, turquoise and lapis lazuli mines, farmlands, orchards, and its own bank. It also owns an airline, several intercity coach companies, and a share in the natural gas fields of Sarakhs on the border with Turkmenistan. It holds a virtual monopoly on the production and sale of saffron, of which Iran is the world's number-one exporter. The *astan* also runs a university and provides scholarships for thousands of students each year. The wealth of the *astan* increases every year because many believers leave a part or the whole of their inheritance to it in their testaments.

Ruling over the *astan* is Ayatollah Abbas Va'ez Tabassi, a man who, according to his critics, behaves as an almost independent potentate, disregarding instructions from Tehran. The ayatollah has his unofficial "embassies" in a number of capitals, including some in the European Union, and concludes his separate trade agreements with foreign governments and companies. During the presidential campaign of May 1997, Ayatollah Tabassi publicly barred Muhammad Khatami from visiting his fiefdom in Mash'had. The wealth of the *astan* is used to distribute favor among supporters of the revolution, especially in Khorassan, which was initially cool or hostile to Khomeinism. At the same time, however, the *astan* must take the interests of the state into account because of its need for legal protection, import-export licenses, and business permits. The *astan* has organized its own security force and at times pursues its own policies in such neighboring countries as Afghanistan and the Central Asian republics.

Another power point in the no-man's land between state and revolution is the so-called Holy Struggle for Construction (Jihad Sazandegi). The genesis of this organ predates the revolution. The shah created three corps in which high school and university graduates could spend all or part of their compulsory national service of eighteen months instead of going into the army. In practice, the three corps—respectively dealing with literacy, health, and reconstruction—absorbed the extra manpower that the regular army could not accommodate in those years of high demographic growth. Later, a fourth corps, the Universal Legion of the Servants of Mankind, was added with the specific task of implementing aid projects in developing countries, especially in Africa.

Initially, Khomeini ordered the four corps to be disbanded as relics of the Pahlavi regime. By 1980, however, he was forced to backtrack because of pressure from lobby groups that had emerged around the four corps over the years. What he did, however, was to merge all the four corps into a single one directly responsible to himself. Since then, the Jihad Sazandegi has been represented within the cabinet by a minister of its own. Nevertheless, it could be regarded as a hybrid organ because it has become home to many revolutionary cadres who use it as a means of mobilizing young people and keeping contact with the rural population. The Jihad needs the state for its budget and general legal support, but looks to the revolution for inspiration and guidance. Involved in thousands of projects at home and abroad, it has countless lucrative contracts to offer as a major business concern. But its principal role is to further the goals of the revolution through indoctrination linked with small public projects, especially in the rural areas.

The process of decision-making in the Islamic Republic also involves a number of other bodies that are hard to classify either as revolution-based, state-controlled, or hybrid. These bodies pursue particular interests, and could side with either the state or the revolution in accordance with their own agenda. Many of them overlap with the organs described above and some exist as their appendages. Using Western terminology, one could describe them as lobbies pursuing precise goals. They make a contribution to decision-making by mobilizing support for or against this or that policy within the revolutionary microcosm and, whenever possible, in society at large. Some even act as political parties in all but name, fielding candidates at elections and competing for positions of power within the public sector. The revolutionary microcosm finds part of its cohesion in family relations among its members. The who's who of the Khomeinist elites reveals an astonishing degree of kinship based on blood or marriage among its members. For example, former president Khatami is married to a sister-in-law of Ahmad, Khomeini's son. Khatami's brother, Muhammad-Reza, is married to a granddaughter of Khomeini. Business ties further strengthen the elites' family relations. In some cases, a majority of board members of a company might find themselves together again as members of the executive committee of a government organ or a political group.

Until Ahmadinejad's election as president, the most influential of the lobby groups was the so-called Society of Combatant Clergy (Jameh e Rouhaniyat Mobarez). Initially created as a club for Khomeinist mullahs in Tehran in 1979, it was for long headed by Ayatollah Muhammad-Reza Mahdavi-Kani, a former prime minister and *éminence grise* in the ruling establishment. The society later opened branches in the provinces and tried to organize itself as a political party. This effort ran into opposition from Khomeini, who was determined not to allow Western-style political parties to emerge in Iran. The society has forged close ties with the traditional bazaars and religious circles in Tehran and major provincial cities. Its candidates have been defeated in all presidential elections since 1997, but it still has a strong presence in the Assembly of Experts.

Its chief rival is the Society of Combative Clergymen (Jameh e Rouhanyoun e Mobarez), a splinter group from the original organization, hence the almost identical name. This one brings together left-wing mullahs who were eliminated from the cabinet and the parliament by Rafsanjani in 1994. The "clergymen" made a bit of a comeback by supporting Khatami, who won the presidency in 1997. Former parliament speaker Ayatollah Mehdi Karrubi, Ayatollah Assadallah Bayat, and former interior minister Ayatollah Ali-Akbar Mohtashami-Pour are key figures in this group, which is largely confined to Tehran and a few other major cities. They control a number of small foundations and publish several newspapers and magazines in Tehran and the major provincial centers.

Another group on the left of the Khomeinist establishment is the Holy Warriors of the Islamic Revolution (Mujahedin e Enqelaab Eslami). This is a small but influential organization bringing together technocrats, former officials, businessmen, and university teachers, often with a leftist background. Many members came from various proto-Marxist groups that were active before the revolution and converted to Khomeinism after the mullahs seized power. The group's leader is Behzad Nabavi, a former deputy prime minister and industry minister. The group's political "godfather" is former prime minister

Mir-Hussein Mussavi Khamenehi, who has emerged as a symbolic leader for the Khomeinist left.

Theoretically at least, the Scientific Center of Qom (Howzeh e Elmieh e Qom) should be a bastion of Khomeinism. But it is not. (The "scientific" in the name refers to theology rather than modern sciences.) The center groups together several thousand teachers of theology and their students and thus wields considerable influence within the Shiite clergy in Iran. It has had an uneasy relationship with the revolutionary establishment, benefiting from its favors, but at the same time implicitly opposing the principle of *walayat e faqih*, or rule by the theologian. The best-known members of this group are Ayatollahs Nasser Makarem Shirazi and Muhammad Fazel Lenkorani, who died in 2007. The latter was a teacher of Khamenehi, and thus enjoyed considerable influence within the establishment.

Another grouping of mullahs is known as the Association of Friday Prayer Leaders (Jamiat e A'emeh Namaz Jamaat). This groups together an estimated eight thousand mullahs who lead Friday prayer ceremonies at mosques in all localities in Iran with a population of ten thousand or more. Most of them have been appointed by the Supreme Guide and receive monthly stipends from his office. Some, however, owe their position to local notoriety and thus speak more independently on issues. The group meets several times a year, and plays a role in launching new ideas and starting debate on issues, often with more than a hint from the office of the Supreme Guide.

The Tehran Chamber of Commerce and Industry (Otaq e Bazargani va Sanay e Tehran) could also be regarded as a lobby group. This is the most powerful organization of businessmen and private industrialists in Iran with influence beyond the capital. It has a mass following through a range of charity organizations it has financed for decades. The powerful *bazaaris* who backed Khomeini against the shah have now rallied within the chamber to exert influence on the government. Their principal leaders are the former commerce ministers Habiballah Askar-Owladi and Hadi Khamoushi. In the presidential election of 1997, the chamber backed Nateq-Nuri, the losing candidate, against Khatami. In 2005 it supported Rafsanjani, who also lost, against Ahmadinejad. Nevertheless, at least a third of the members of the Majlis (parliament) depend on the chamber for campaign finance and other forms of support.

The Khomeinist regime won power by seizing control of the streets through violence and terror. Therefore, it is always concerned about losing the streets to its many opponents. To prevent that, the regime has created a number of groups that recruit, train, and deploy street fighters. The most important of these is the Victorious Companions of the Party of God (Ansar e Hezballah). A semi-clandestine organization, this branch of Hezballah is believed to be financed by the office of the Supreme Guide. Its members are recruited from among the professional "tough guys" of south Tehran's rough neighborhoods and used as shock troops against opposition on the streets. Hezballah also has the task of organizing the "spontaneous" demonstrations that the establishment needs every now and then. The Iranian branch of Hezballah is the hardcore of an international movement with branches in seventeen other Muslim countries, notably Turkey, Lebanon and Saudi Arabia. The best-known spokesman for Hezballah is Ayatollah Ahmad Janati Kermani, a close advisor of the Supreme Guide. Hezballah's shock brigades are led by Reza Allah-Karam, who wears a military-style uniform and calls himself "General." In the 1997 presidential election, Allah-Karam backed Nateq-Nuri and announced he would never allow Khatami to serve a full term as president. Allah-Karam's shock brigades are used for raiding the offices of newspapers regarded as "deviant" and homes of individuals critical of the regime. Estimates put the number of Hezballah's full-timers at around 50,000, all of them on a special payroll provided by the office of the Supreme Guide. However, the group also employs over 250,000 part-time "strugglers" when larger numbers are needed to confront an opposition demonstration.

Leaders of the various branches of Hezballah around the world gather in Tehran every February, along with representatives of other radical Islamic movements, to compare notes, pay tribute to Khomeini's memory, and coordinate strategy in various countries.

If Hezballah is in charge of crushing political dissent in the streets, the task of curbing social and cultural "deviations" is assigned to another organ of repression known as the Committee to Propagate the Good and Prevent the Evil (Komiteh Amr be Maarouf va Nahy az Munkar). This is a strictly religious version of Hezballah and is used to impose rules regarding dress, and the ban on alcoholic beverages and other "objects of evil" such as chessboards, playing cards, Western CDs, video and audio cassettes. The enforcement arm of the organization is called the Blood of Allah (Thar Allah) and consists of men and women driving separately in special vehicles, looking for "un-Islamic" behavior. Thar Allah units often take position in shopping centers, close to cinemas and theaters, in streets near university campuses, in hotel lobbies, and other places where "un-Islamic" acts may be committed. The purely female branch is known as the Sisters of Zaynab (Khaharan Zaynab), mostly volunteers who give the organization a few hours a week. Many women, especially in Tehran, regard the ferocious-looking "sisters" with terror.

Born in an atmosphere of conspiracy and intrigue, the Khomeinist movement, like fascist movements elsewhere, always depended on a number of clandestine organizations to shield it against the outside world. Even today, almost thirty years in power, the Khomeinist movement relies on secret societies to recruit supporters, collect information, and isolate the "outsiders." The most important of these secret organizations is the Society of the Pledge (Jamiyat e Hojatieh), a religious group that made its first appearance in the 1950s with a massive and at times violent campaign against the Baha'i community. In 1950, the Hojatieh persuaded Shamseddin Jazayeri, minister of education in the cabinet of Prime Minister Haj Ali Razmara, to purge Baha'is and other "deviants," such as followers of the secularist intellectual Ahmad Kasravi, from government schools. Within months, over four thousand teachers were purged. The society then allied itself with conservative monarchists against the centrist government of Prime Minister Muhammad Mossadeq and its Communist supporters. After Mossadeq's dismissal by the shah in 1953, Hojatieh reaped the rewards of its cooperation with monarchists in the form of a green light from the government for another nationwide campaign against the Baha'is. The principal Baha'i religious center, known as Hazirat al-Quds (the Holy Precinct) in Tehran, was razed to the ground while thousands of Baha'is were thrown out of the civil service. From the mid-1950s until his death in 1997, Hojatieh's best-known figure and possibly leader was Ayatollah Mahmoud Halabi, a cleric of Syrian origin who had studied in the Iranian "holy" city of Qom and acquired Iranian nationality. The main theme of his message was that the Hidden Imam was preparing his return and that Shiites should also prepare to receive him by purging unbelievers and deviants from their midst.

There is evidence that Hojatieh had some ties with the SAVAK, the secret police under the monarchy; but who used whom remains unclear. It is possible that Hojatieh used SAVAK to secure a free hand for its own activities and to benefit from secret funds funneled by the government. During the 1978–79 revolutionary turmoil, Hojatieh played a marginal part, mostly to counter Communists and other atheists within the anti-shah coalition. It is certain that Halabi opposed Khomeini's doctrine of *walayat e faqih,* or rule by a theologian. According to Halabi, all rule belonged to the Hidden Imam and, in his absence, to the Shiite community as a whole. While Khomeini sought a fusion of the mosque and the state, Halabi believed in their strict separation.

In the 1983, Khomeini formally disbanded the Hojatieh, seeing it as a threat to his ideological hold over the regime. The Hojatieh, which had never officially announced its existence, took the unusual step of publicly announcing its own dissolution. Nevertheless, many key figures of the establishment are known to be members of the Hojatieh, which operates as a series of secret societies pretty much like Russian matryushka dolls. Under its different appellations, including the Society of Mahdaviat, Hojatieh continues to wield financial influence through the countless business concerns it wholly owns or controls. In the duel between the state and the revolution, Hojatieh has generally supported the state because it believes that the clergy should not become directly involved in government. In 2002 and 2003, the government ordered a crackdown against Hojatieh, after accusing it of trying to seize power through infiltration and permeation of key organs of the state. The minister of the interior, Abdolvahed Mussavi-Lari, even claimed that Hojatieh represented "a clear and present danger for national security." In the end, however, no action was taken, largely because it was never clear who the Hojatieh members were.

The Hojatieh sponsor some parliamentary candidates, control scores of mosques throughout the country, and maintain close ties with rural areas through a network of religious front organizations supposedly designed to celebrate the birthday of the Hidden Imam and other religious occasions. Ahmadinejad and his religious mentor Ayatollah Mesbah-Yazdi are believed to be members of the Jamkaran branch of Hojatieh, along with Ayatollah Janati, the powerful secretary general of the Council of the Guardians of the Constitution. Another key figure rumored to be a member is Ghulam-Reza Aqazadeh, the man who heads Iran's controversial nuclear program. The most reliable studies of Hojatieh and offshoots put the number of members and sympathizers at several hundred thousand.

* * *

Far from being a monolithic system, the Islamic Republic allows an unusual measure of freedom of debate within the perimeters of its fascist ideology. Lacking a single overall political organization, such as the party in the former Communist states, the Islamic Republic has developed a system of decision-making unique in the so-called developing world.

Apart from the bodies described above, many other smaller interest groups contribute to the debate, and thus to decision-making, at least on specific issues. These include the associations representing such large immigrant groups as the Iraqi refugees (estimated to number about a million), and Lebanese Shiite militants (believed to number around 25,000) who have settled in Iran, often marrying Iranians and securing positions at the middle levels of the revolutionary establishment. Many influential mullahs recruit their personal bodyguards from among Iraqi and Lebanese Shiite militants who are believed to be more dedicated to Khomeini's universal Islamic revolution.

A number of press organizations, notably the two giants *Kayhan* ("Universe") and *Ettelaat* ("Information"), also play important roles in guiding the debate and thus affecting the process of decision-making within the establishment. Because no single organ is capable of imposing a blanket censorship of the press, some newspapers have emerged as genuine voices of at least some sections of society, thus giving the established order an additional safety valve. While *Kayhan* is known as the standard-bearer of the hardcore Khomeinists, *Ettelaat* has cultivated its image as a moderate voice for the machinery of state, taking some distance from the revolution.

Iran is a lively and dynamic society where change is a slow but constant factor. Despite appearances, Iranian society today is more open than two decades ago, with the balance of power shifting in favor of civil society. There are as yet few organs through which civil society can directly take part in the debate and decision-making process. But there is no doubt that it exerts some influence through many of the existing organs of the regime.

The constitution provides for the formation of political parties and trade unions, although this provision has not been put into effect, largely because Khomeini and to some extent Khamenehi have been suspicious of what they regard as models imported from the West. Nevertheless, it is possible to say that Iran is moving towards a reorganization of its political life through the creation of political parties. In a sense, major political currents are already to be found within the establishment and could in time be transformed into political parties. Once this happens, the parties would have to seek support beyond the confines of the establishment and within civil society.

Leaving aside the "Islamic" terminology used by almost everyone within the present establishment, the undercurrents of Iranian society could be described as conservative, liberal, social-democrat, and fascist. With Ahmadinejad's election, the fascist tendency is in the driver's seat, supported by the Supreme Guide, and is trying to absorb the state into the revolution and lead the Islamic Republic towards conflict and war with the outside world. Nevertheless, the central theme of Iranian politics concerns the role that the state ought to play in the economy and society as a whole. The revolutionary terminology and the theological shorthand in use could be described as the trees that hide the forest.

Trying to understand Iranian politics and the process of decision-making in religious terms would be missing the point. The central issue of Iranian politics, like politics everywhere, is the acquisition of power and its use for specific purposes. The revolutionary establishment has developed its own vested interests, which defend the status quo and fear change. The machinery of the state, however, is trying to reimpose its supremacy, including in the ideological field, where it emphasizes Iranian nationalism as opposed to Khomeinist pan-Islamism. Many powerful interest groups in Iran see their interest in a re-emergence of the state as the dominant factor in Iranian politics. That would mean the state's final absorption of the revolution, and the start of the long-promised but so far elusive Iranian Thermidor. Unless this happens, Iranian decision-making is likely to remain erratic, contradictory, and confusing in some areas.

One man who is determined to prevent this from happening is Ahmadinejad, the first of the six Islamic Republic presidents who wishes to put the state at the service of the revolution, not the other way round.

23

The "Nail" of the Imam

In April 2007, just before he announced that Iran had gate-crashed the "nuclear club," President Mahmoud Ahmadinejad disappeared for several hours. He was in Natanz, the nerve center of Iran's nuclear project, where Iranian scientists are producing the enriched uranium needed for atomic warheads. The ceremony was delayed because the president was having a *khalvat* (tête-à-tête) with the Hidden Imam, the twelfth and last of the Imams of Shiism, who went into his Grand Occultation in the year 941. According to Shiite lore, the Imam, although in hiding, remains the true Sovereign of the World and Master of Time.

In every generation, the Imam chooses thirty-six men (and no women, for obvious reasons) as the *owtad* or "nails" whose presence, hammered into mankind's existence by the "Hidden Hand," prevents the universe from "falling off" into eternal chaos. No one knows how the "nails" are chosen. One theory is that the Hidden Imam appears to the elect in their dreams and informs them of the awesome blessing bestowed upon them. Although the "nails" are not known to common mortals and do not know one another, at times it is possible to identify one of them by his deeds.

It is on this basis that some of Ahamdinejad's more passionate admirers claim that he is one of the "nails," a claim he does not discourage. For example, he has maintained that in September 2006, as he addressed the United Nations General Assembly in New York, the Hidden Imam was present in the audience and "drenched the place in a sweet light." In 2005, it was after another *khalvat* with the Hidden Imam that Ahmadinejad announced his intention to stand for president. And after the first round of voting, in which he had come in second, it was again the Hidden Imam who informed him that he would win in the second round. Ahmadinejad claims that the Imam has elevated him to the presidency of the Islamic Republic for a single task: provoking a "clash of civilizations" in which the Muslim world, led by Iran, takes on the infidels, led by the United States, and defeats them in a slow contest that, in military jargon, sounds like low-intensity asymmetrical war.

In Ahmadinejad's analysis, the burgeoning Islamic "superpower" has decisive advantages over the infidels. Islam has five times as many young males of fighting age as the "decadent West," which is the realm of aging populations. Hundreds of millions of Muslim *ghazis* (holy raiders) are keen to become martyrs, while the infidel youth fear death and would not fight. Islam also has four-fifths of the world's oil reserves, thus controlling the lifeblood of the infidels. To all this must be added the fact that the United States, the sole infidel power still capable of fighting, is hated by other infidel nations and even by a substantial segment of its own population. According to this analysis, echoed in Ahmadinejad's discourse and spelled out in commentaries by his strategic guru Hassan Abbasi, President George W. Bush is an aberration, an exception to a rule under which all American presidents since John F. Kennedy, when faced with a serious setback abroad, have "run away." From the start, therefore, Ahmadinejad's strategy was to "wait Bush out." And that, by "divine coincidence," also covers the time Iran needs to develop a nuclear arsenal, thus matching the only advantage that the infidels still enjoy.

Moments after Ahmadinejad announced the "nuclear miracle" in 2007, the head of the Iranian nuclear project, Ghulam-Reza Aqazadeh, unveiled plans for manufacturing 54,000 centrifuges, which are needed to enrich enough uranium for hundreds of nuclear warheads. "We are going into mass production," he boasted. The Iranian game plan was simple: dancing the diplomatic dance for another two years until Bush became a "lame duck" unable to persuade his people to take military action against the Khomeinist regime.

While "waiting Bush out," the Islamic Republic did all it could to consolidate its gains in the region. Iran is now the strongest presence in both Afghanistan and Iraq, after the United States. It has turned Syria and Lebanon into part of its glacis, which means that for the first time since Khosrow Parviz, the Persian King of Kings in the seventh century, Iran is militarily present on the Mediterranean coast. The Islamic navy is building a base in the Syrian port of Latakiya to keep an eye on the U.S. Sixth Fleet and, when the time comes, to project power on the doorsteps of Europe. The IRGC already controls the Beirut airport and, through Hamas and Hezballah, controls firepower on the Mediterranean. In a massive political jamboree in Tehran in February 2007, the Islamic Republic also assumed control of the so-called "Jerusalem Cause," which includes "wiping Israel off the map" on behalf of the Muslim world. The Ahmadinejad government has also reactivated Iran's network of Shiite radical organizations in Bahrain, Kuwait, Saudi Arabia, Pakistan, and Yemen, while resuming contact with Sunni fundamentalist groups in Turkey, Egypt, Algeria, and Morocco.

From early boyhood, Shiites are told to cultivate two contradictory qualities. The first is *entezar*, the capacity to wait for the return of the Hidden Imam in patience. The second is *taajil*, actions needed to hasten the Mahdi's return. Thus "waiting Bush out" was not a difficult game for Ahmadinejad to play. The task of *entezar* is tackled in cycles of seven years, which means Iran has ample time to build a nuclear arsenal. And that would remove the only advantage that the infidels have. The infidels do not have the stomach for a long conventional war in which they could sustain high casualties. Thus, they may feel forced to "nuke" the Islamic Republic. This advantage would be lost if the Islamic Republic became a nuclear power. In one of his lectures, Abbasi claimed that the United States would never have been able to defeat and conquer Japan without using nuclear weapons. The reason was that the United States could not have sustained the human losses that the Japanese were prepared to inflict. Once the infidel power loses its nuclear advantage, it could be worn down in a long low-intensity war, at the end of which surrender to Islam would appear the least bad of all options. And that would be a signal for the Hidden Imam to reappear.

At the same time, not to forget the task of hastening the Mahdi's second coming, Ahmadinejad will pursue his provocations. For the past three years, he has presided over the biggest show of military force Tehran has ever seen. In 2006, the Islamic Republic fire-tested what it presented as "the fastest underwater antisubmarine missile ever." This was followed by the unveiling of a "flying assault ship" as part of a massive military exercise held in the Persian Gulf; it was described as a "present to Prophet Muhammad" on his 1424th birthday. The exercise was designed to show that Iran could close the Persian Gulf and stop the flow of half the world's crude oil. Enjoying his moment of triumph, Ahmadinejad was as candid as ever: "To those who are angry with us, we have one thing to say: be as angry as you like until you die of anger!"

According to Abbasi, "The Americans are impatient and, at the first sight of a setback, they run away. We, however, know how to be patient. After all, we have been weaving carpets for thousands of years." Ahmadinejad did not invent the claim that the Islamic Republic is the government of the Hidden Imam and must, therefore, rule the world. The claim was the organizing principle of the Khomeinist system from the start. Addressing IRGC commanders in 1981, Khomeini said: "The Imam of the Time, the Awaited Mahdi, may my soul be sacrificed to Him, is personally your Commander. He looks after you personally, and the reports of your activities are sent to him on a daily basis."[1]

Apart from his thirty-six "nails," the Hidden Imam needs 313 "pure Shiites," the same number as Muhammad's companions in his most decisive battle, to conquer the world. Christians will instantly rally to the Mahdi because he has enlisted Jesus Christ as his special assistant. The Mahdi rides a white steed while Jesus follows on a brown one. At the same time, everyone knows that the Mahdi's mother was a Roman princess, thus passing on to him a dynastic claim to rule the West as well. One sign that the world was beginning to take notice of the Hidden Imam came last spring when the cyclone that struck Myanmar (Burma) was named Nargiss, after the Hidden Imam's mother.

For centuries Shiite life has vacillated between fear and hope: fear that the Imam will not return in one's lifetime, and hope that he might. The overwhelming majority of Shiites could be described as *entezaaris*, that is to say those who know how to wait until the Imam decides to return in his own good time. Some Shiites have even used the term *entezaari* or its variants such as Montazeri as family names. The theory of *entezaar* leads to political quietism. Since the believer is not aware of the Imam's intentions, he had better refrain from actions that might not accord with them. In practical politics, this means doing the minimum, or avoiding involvement altogether if possible. Ahmadinejad, however, is a political activist, not the typical *entezaari*. He and his theological guide, Mesbah-Yazdi, are *taajilis*, people who believe that they could and should hasten the Imam's return through their own action.

According to Shiite tradition, the Imam will return when "seven wonders" (*al-aja'eb al-sabaah*) appear. First comes a massive storm of locusts that destroys all cultivation. This is followed by an invasion of snakes and serpents that appear all over the place as if pouring from the skies. Next comes a huge fire that burns several cities. An unprecedented famine follows, triggering a pandemic of many hitherto unknown diseases. Finally, Shiite girls suddenly lose their virginity for no clear reason. Ahmadinejad sees the "seven wonders" as metaphors for actual contemporary events. In speech after speech he passes the coded message about the imminence of the Imam's return to audiences that see the growing hardship of life and constant talk of martyrdom and war as confirmations of the president's messianic vision.

In a sense, Ahmadinejad is a creature of the shah's regime, a kind of Frankenstein's monster that ends up threatening to kill its creator. He was born in 1956 in the village of Aradan, a suburb of Garmsar, itself a dusty hamlet in Semnan, one of Iran's poorest provinces on the edge of the Kavir Lut, a lunar desert the size of Germany. Originally, the family was known by the name Sabrian. A year after Mahmoud's birth, an earthquake struck their village and razed most of its mud-brick houses. The Ahmadinejads had to leave, and after months of peregrination they ended up in Tehran, where Ahmadinejad senior started work as an apprentice ironsmith. In the capital, Mahmoud and his siblings became the first in the history of their family to go to school, along with millions of other Iranians who had come of age at a time that the country was able to offer all of its children primary education for the first time.

By the time Ahmadinejad had completed his primary education, Iran was on the threshold of what was to become its economic and social golden age. Thanks to a series of reforms backed by rising oil revenues, the booming economy was generating enough growth to finance a massive expansion of public services. These included free education for all, from primary school to university. Between 1968, when Ahmadinejad graduated from secondary school, and 1978, when the mullahs launched their revolt, the average annual income per capita in Iran more than doubled, lifting millions of people out of poverty and creating a new middle class. The Ahmadinejads prospered beyond their wildest dreams. Mahmoud's father, now a skilled worker earning good wages, was able to move the family to Narmak, a new neighborhood built by French town planners east of Tehran with easy access to the center of the capital on one side and the nearby ski slopes on the other. All the children of the family were able to receive secondary and university education while also discovering such middle-class privileges as annual holidays and foreign travel.

As the Khomeinist revolt started in 1978, Ahmadinejad was where none of his ancestors would have dreamed of being: in an undergraduate course at the University of Science and Technology in Tehran, where he was to obtain his Ph.D. in transportation engineering after the revolution. He had every reason to be happy, but he was not. In fact, he claims that he felt "a deep sense of sadness" as he observed what he calls "the process of de-Islamicization" under the shah. Although his family were not religious, Ahmadinejad claims that they, too, were concerned about what they feared was an "irrevocable Westernization" of the country. According to Muhammad-Ali Sayyed-Nezhad, a friend of Ahmadinejad in his youth, the future "nail of the Imam" was specially shocked to see girls wearing hot-pants and mini-skirts in the streets of Tehran and on the campus of the university. "It was as if we were in Paris, not Tehran, the capital of a Muslim country," Sayyed-Nezhad recalls. "We wondered what was going to happen. Was this catastrophe a sign that the Mahdi was about to return?"[2] It was as if the prophecy about Shiite girls suddenly losing their virginity were being fulfilled. Ten years earlier, students in Paris had revolted partly to demand greater sexual freedom. In the late 1970s, many Iranian students, like Ahmadinejad, were in revolt because they thought there was too much sexual freedom.

Attending special indoctrination sessions at madrassas and mosques, the young Ahmadinejad was easily convinced that the only path to salvation was a return to Islam and "active waiting" for the return of the Hidden Imam. Some of his entourage claim that Ahmadinejad was in his teens when the Hidden Imam approached him with the startling news that he was to be one of the "nails." It is quite possible, though hard to prove, that the madrassas and mosques Ahmadinejad attended in his leisure time were run by mullahs working for SAVAK, the shah's secret service. At the time, SAVAK was trying to play the Islamic card against the left, especially among teenagers and students. That this might have been the case is indicated by the militant anti-left positions of Ahmadinejad within the Khomeinist student movement. At any rate, Ahmadinejad's generation was the first to be economically comfortable enough to indulge in political activities against the regime. Unlike his father, who had worked since the age of five, Ahmadinejad did not need a job to pay for his keep. The government paid his school fees plus a generous stipend, providing him with ample time and resources to devote himself to the overthrow of the regime.

At university, Ahmadinejad joined the radical Islamist and anti-Marxist group led by Hussein Esrafilian, a young lecturer close to Hojatieh, and became an editor of their monthly, *Jigh va Daad* ("Hue and Cry"), in opposition to the monthly *Ahangar* ("Ironmonger"), the organ of Communist students. When the shah's regime fell, Ahmadinejad was elected as a representative of his university in an audience granted by Khomeini to leaders of over a hundred student organizations. After the audience, he was elected as one of the five members of the Council for the Consolidation of the Students' Unity, known by its Persian acronym, Tahkim.[3] It was in this capacity that Ahmadinejad, in October 1979, more than seven months after the victory of the revolution, found himself in a defining moment of his early political career. At one of its weekly meetings, the council discussed reports that the U.S. embassy in Tehran was receiving and shipping a large quantity of diplomatic boxes through the Mehrabad Airport in Tehran. One of the council members claimed that this pointed to a possible plot by the United States to seize control of the revolution with the help of the Bazargan government, five of whose ministers were either U.S. citizens or holders of American "green cards." The two radical leftist members of the council suggested the occupation of the U.S. embassy compound for two or three days to probe "suspicious activities" there and attract public attention to whatever plot was being hatched. The suggestion led to a heated debate in which Ahmadinejad led the opposition to the leftist plan.

"Aren't we also facing provocations by Marxist groups and interventions by the Soviets in our domestic affairs?" Ahmadinejad asked. "If we are to react, why should we pick America [alone]? Why shouldn't we confront the Soviets as well? Because of the treacherous deeds of the leftists, the Soviets should be our priority. Who says the threat from America is greater than that [from] the Soviets?"[4]

From the various accounts of the meeting, it is not clear what actually happened. It seems that three of the five members voted for a raid on the U.S. embassy, leaving Ahmadinejad isolated. When the raid took place and won Khomeini's approval, Ahmadinejad feared that his revolutionary career might end. Like hundreds of thousands of young men and women, Ahmadinejad had joined the revolution in its penultimate phase as it stood on the threshold of victory. The revolutionary period itself, spanning just a few months, had not been long enough to allow newcomers to build up their CVs as soldiers of the revolution. The shah had quickly left the country, allowing the revolution to succeed with unexpected·ease. There had been no big struggle between two camps, no civil war, and few occasions for self-styled revolutionaries to create romantic autobiographies. As Mehdi Bazargan noted, the Khomeinists had pushed a door that was already ajar. The shah, his suitcase packed and his aircraft's engines running, had appeared on television to say: You want a revolution? OK, go ahead and have it!

Poor souls like Ahmadinejad had had no opportunity to show bravery and self-sacrifice against a regime that didn't want to kill them. The shah had not thrown them in prison, even for a single day, or sent them into exile or denied them the chance to attend university. Nor had his police beaten them up or tortured them, let alone killed them in the streets. Their sole hope for securing a revolutionary biography was to do something radical *afterwards*, claiming that they were defending the victorious revolution against its enemies. In a sense, even today Ahmadinejad is still trying to write the revolutionary autobiography that the shah didn't let him have before the revolution.

The raid on the U.S. embassy provided a golden opportunity for *post-factum* revolutionaries to secure the coveted CV. Middle-class boys and girls who had lived privileged lives were suddenly able to grow beards, wear battle fatigues, tote Uzi machine guns, and claim that they were "humbling the arch-imperialist" power. In complete safety themselves, protected by IRGC units posted outside the embassy, these spoiled middle-class brats had an opportunity to compose revolutionary CVs by torturing and humiliating their American captives, often in front of television cameras. With those CVs in hand, many of them rose to the highest positions in government. They became ministers, ambassadors, members of parliament, governors of provinces, and chief executives of public sector companies. The U.S. embassy, or "Nest of Spies" as the hostage-takers dubbed it, became a high-speed elevator for social mobility.

Ahmadinejad had missed that elevator and had to sweat for years to secure a place on it. He had believed SAVAK's subtle message that the Soviet Union, huge and right next door, was a bigger threat to Iran than the United States could ever be. Khomeini, however, thought differently: Communism would never appeal to Iranians, while American-style democracy and "pursuit of happiness" would. Ahmadinejad had to wait before he had another opportunity to write his revolutionary biography. Ten months after the seizure of the U.S. embassy, Saddam Hussein invaded Iran. Ahmadinejad jumped on the opportunity to become one of the first volunteers to accompany the defense minister, Mostafa Chamran, to the battlefront. Ahmadinejad had the last laugh. While his leftist fellow students were still bogged down at the embassy and bullying the American hostages, he could wear the Baseej battle fatigues and do his bit of a "Che" with Chamran if not with "Che" Guevara.

For the first five years of the war, Ahmadinejad was involved mostly in logistics and ancillary activities and saw no combat. In 1986, he joined the IRGC's Ramadan brigade, which specialized in raids deep inside Iraq. According to some accounts, on at least one occasion Ahmadinejad accompanied a mixed force of IRGC and Iraqi Kurdish fighters in a raid on the Iraqi town of Kirkuk's oilfields. That was the start of his connection with Iraqi Kurds and his interest in the Kurdish issue in general. In 1987, he was appointed commander of an engineering unit in an IRGC division, a position he held for a year, after which he joined the IRGC's intelligence unit. Technically, he never became a member of the IRGC's officer corps, always being seconded to the force through Baseej. It was in this capacity that in 1989, once the war with Iraq had ended, he accompanied a delegation sent by Rafsanjani to Vienna to negotiate with the exiled leaders of the opposition Democratic Party of Iranian Kurdistan (PDK). On the last day of the negotiations, a Khomeinist hit squad raided the hotel room where the two teams had gathered, and machine-gunned the four Kurdish leaders, including their president, Abdul-Rahman Qassemlou. Ahmadinejad, who probably had not been told that the mission was a trap for the Kurdish leaders, was slightly wounded but managed to escape aboard an Iran Air jet before the Austrian police could arrest him along with three other Khomeinist negotiators. From then on, as a reserve officer of the IRGC, Ahmadinejad knew that he had a strong political base. Ideologically, his home was Hojatieh; politically, it was the Baseej and the IRGC.

Back to civilian life after the war, Ahmadinejad served in a number of posts in various provinces and in 1994 was appointed governor of the newly created province of Ardebil in the northwest. By all accounts, he did well in Ardebil, at least well enough for his fellow governors to name him "Outstanding Governor of the Year" in 1995 and 1996. Using his provincial base, Ahmadinejad helped create a network of young radical revolutionaries who labeled themselves "Builders of the Islamic Iran" (Abadgaran Iran Islami).

With help from that network, he was able to get himself elected mayor of Tehran in 2003. Now under the national limelight, he started building his persona. He presented himself as the son of a poor blacksmith from a poor district of the capital, who had known hunger and deprivation. He attacked the "new rich" and accused "bigwigs," whom he never named, of "plundering the nation in the name of Islam." Tehranis who had never warmed up to the Khomeinist regime began to see Ahmadinejad as something of an opposition leader. The fact that he seldom mentioned either Khomeini or Khamenehi, preferring to refer directly to the Hidden Imam, created the impression of an outsider angry about the regime's corruption, brutality, and inefficiency. Ahmadinejad was everything that most other grandees of the regime were not. He refused to get a salary as mayor, preferring to depend on his income as a part-time lecturer at his alma mater; he drove his own car, a battered old Peugeot; and he continued to live in his modest house rather than the mayor's official residence. The man who manufactured Ahmadinejad's image as an Islamic Robin Hood was one Mojtaba Hashemi Samareh, a friend from his student days. It was also Samareh who encouraged Ahmadinejad to think of standing for the presidency. In 2005, most Iranians felt betrayed by the ruling elite, symbolized by Khatami and his promises of reform. Also, they were fed up with mullahs. In the subsequent presidential campaign, a woman approached Hashemi Rafsanjani, the candidate of the establishment, and knocked his turban off with the cry "No More Mullahs!"

24

We Can!

Ahmadinejad entered the presidential race with the slogan "We Can!" This was designed as a rejection of the outgoing President Khatami's claim that his administration had been unable to fulfill its promise of reform because of gridlock in the system. At first, few people gave Ahmadinejad any chance of registering on the electoral radar. Unlike the mullahs and the hostage-holders of the U.S. embassy, who had won notoriety thanks to the media, Ahmadinejad was a total unknown outside Tehran and Ardebil, where he had served as governor. Also, he had no money to spend on lavish advertising campaigns as did Rafsanjani, Iran's richest man, and the other main candidates, including the former police chief Muhammad-Baqer Qalibaf and the mullah Mehdi Karrubi, the well-funded candidate of Khatami's faction. However, Ahmadinejad had three advantages over his rivals.

First, he immediately came across as sincere. Revolutionary slogans mouthed by people like Rafsanjani, Karrubi, and Qalibaf sounded false. Here were wealthy men living in palatial mansions and spending vast sums on advertising, and yet talking about "the poor, the dispossessed." Their expensive clothing and bulletproof limousines told a different story. In contrast, Ahmadinejad traveled by bus, had no bodyguards, spent no money on posters, gave no free meals to would-be voters who attended his meetings, and lambasted "the lying rich, the corrupt moneybags, the leeches bloated by our blood." His signature item of clothing was a blouson of the type that were on sale in Tehran's poor districts for the equivalent of three dollars. The overly made-up and bejeweled ladies supporting Rafsanjani mocked Ahmadinejad by calling him *amaleh*, a derogatory word for construction workers. But he welcomed the sobriquet and made it a campaign theme: "We are the *amaleh* of the Imam and the people!" he would shout, bringing wild cheers.

Ahmadinejad's second advantage was that he could run as an opposition candidate because, in the minds of most Iranians, he was not identified with the regime. Iranians knew Rafsanjani too well to trust him again. They could not trust Karrubi, who appeared as a down-market version of Khatami minus the smile. Qalibaf was disliked because, as chief of police, he had crushed demonstrations by students and workers, and earned the title of "the Butcher of Tehran." Worse still, he had as his chief of staff for the campaign a certain Mohsen Khamenehi, son of the Supreme Guide and a notorious influence peddler. Ali Larijani, head of the state-owned radio and television and the candidate of the radical wing of he IRGC, also suffered because people knew him too well. For over a decade, he had given them a radio and TV network that offered nothing but lies, propaganda, and low-quality entertainment. If the voters wanted "none of the above," their choice had to be Ahmadinejad.

Finally, Ahmadinejad benefited from the fact that Khamenehi and the high command of the IRGC were determined that the next president not be turbaned. Khamenehi was concerned about growing popular anger against the mullahs who occupied all key positions, and he hoped that replacing a turban with a hat, even a military cap, might ease tensions. The IRGC commanders believed that after twenty-four years with the mullahs at the top, it was their turn to occupy the presidency.

Ahmadinejad, Larijani, and Qalibaf were all candidates of the IRGC, the last one as the favorite. Khamenehi and the IRGC commanders assumed that no one would win in the first round of voting and that the second round would be between a mullah and a "hat-wearer" (*mukalla*). Until the last moment, they believed that Karrubi would be the mullah and Qalibaf the *mukalla*. The results of the first round provided a big surprise, however: the second round was to be fought between Rafsanjani and Ahmadinejad, with Qalibaf coming in a poor fourth. Everyone knew that Khamenehi would never allow Rafsanjani to return as president and regain the position of strongman he had lost eight years earlier.

Khamenehi and Rafsanjani had been friends for thirty years before becoming rivals, the surest recipe for unquenchable hatred. Qalibaf had made a fool of himself by dropping hints that he would become a benevolent despot like Reza Khan, the founder of the Pahlavi dynasty, and rescue the nation from economic meltdown, social breakdown, and war. To Khamenehi, this portrayed a man too big for his boots. The Supreme Guide and the IRGC top brass had no choice but to help Ahmadinejad crush Rafsanjani, which he did in the second round by winning almost 63 percent of the votes.

Many wondered how a candidate who was unknown six weeks earlier could collect seventeen million votes without any advertising campaign. In Khomeinist Iran, however, voters form only part of a more complex mix that produces the results. If necessary, ballot boxes could be filled or emptied, and even the dead could be made to vote in thousands. Announcement of the results was postponed three times until the Supreme Guide and the IRGC top brass had agreed on who should win and by how much. Karrubi, embittered by his poor showing, quipped: The evening of voting day, I went to bed convinced that I had won. The following morning, I woke up a loser!

Despite all that, Ahmadinejad is the first president of the Islamic Republic who does not feel himself indebted to individuals or circles within the regime. He just happened to be the right man at the right time, the second choice of rival factions who realized that their first choice could not be imposed. This is why Ahmadinejad seldom mentions either Khomeini or Khamenehi. He goes directly to the Hidden Imam, making it more difficult for his rivals to attack him. Building his populist image further, he is the first president of the Islamic Republic to go on periodic tours to all provinces, holding the meetings of his cabinet in provincial centers rather than Tehran. In these tours, he also distributes a great deal of money, something he can do thanks to spiraling oil prices. In his first year as president, Ahmadinejad has had more oil money to play with than all of Iran's previous rulers combined since the first oil well was inaugurated in Masjed Suleiman in 1908.

Ahmadinejad's critics within the establishment have a dilemma. They seek supporting Khomeinist terms but speak a technocratic language that sounds odd in a revolutionary context. They accuse Ahmadinejad of provoking hyperinflation by just splashing money around. Ahmadinejad, however, says he is trying to help the poor on behalf of the Hidden Imam. "Economics is nothing when it comes to the science of *ladduni* [i.e. secret knowledge of the imams]," he says. What is "socially just" could never be wrong even if it is economically inadvisable. In other words, his devil-may-care economic policy is justified because he is trying to serve Allah.

To many in the West, especially in the European Union, Ahmadinejad's election was the worst news possible. They had deluded themselves into believing that Khatami's presidency was a golden age of liberty, brutally ended by Ahmadinejad. In 2005 it was fashionable to knock "neocons" and conservatives in general, so the Western glitterati presented Ahmadinejad as both an unhinged adventurer and a champion of the "conservative" faction in Tehran.

Ahmadinejad is neither. He is a radical revolutionary acting in accordance with the character of the Khomeinist ideology, a messianic movement whose ambition is to reshape the world after its fashion. On every one of the controversial issues that have provoked Western glitterati ire against Ahmadinejad, his rivals in Tehran, including Rafsanjani and Khatami, have always held identical views. On the nuclear issue, the program was revived under Rafsanjani just weeks after Khomeini's death in 1989. Iran's clandestine relations with A.Q. Khan, the Pakistani scientist who sold Tehran nuclear knowhow and equipment, started under Khatami. It was under Khatami that the budget allocated to the nuclear project was increased fivefold. In 2005, it was Khatami who ended a two-year suspension of Iran's uranium enrichment program. Neither Khatami nor Rafsanjani has ever accepted the Holocaust as a historical fact. Nor has either of them acknowledged the right of Israel to exist. Throughout Rafsanjani's presidency, the Islamic Republic waged a proxy war against Israel through the Lebanese Hezballah. Under Khatami, the

Islamic Republic emerged as the principal source of funding for radical Palestinian groups and, in 2002, was caught red-handed smuggling arms to Yasser Arafat's Al Fatah group in the *Karin A* cargo ship. In 2003, King Abdullah II of Jordan revealed that Tehran had set up seventeen secret cells on Jordanian territory for "terrorist operations." The Rafsanjani-Khatami duo often spoke of a "dialogue of civilizations" but allowed no dialogue inside Iran itself. Under Khatami, the Islamic Republic occupied the second position on the list of nations for the number of executions, just behind the People's Republic of China, with a population twenty times that of Iran. More newspapers and magazines were closed under Khatami than during Ahmadinejad's presidency—at least up to the spring of 2008.

Ahmadinejad rejects the "dialogue of civilizations" because he believes that there is no civilization outside Islam. Instead, he speaks of a "clash of civilizations" both inside Iran and in the world at large. He does not want a seat at any international panel; his dream is to abolish the capitalist system that has produced the world as we know it. He does not want Iran to become a member of the World Trade Organization, which he has described as "a club of global thieves." Nor is he tempted by the offer of preferential trade relations with the European Union, which he sees as "a family of fat parasites living off other nations."

Ahmadinejad's major sin is his refusal to practice *kitman,* an old tradition under which lying for a cause that one believes to be good is not only permitted but obligatory. He is saying aloud what Rafsanjani and Khatami have always thought in silence. He has already purged the Ministry of Foreign Affairs of so-called reformist diplomats, seized control of the two ministries that deal with security, and sponsored a major reshuffle of the top brass both in the IRGC and the regular armed forces. Over four thousand people have lost top jobs in government and/ or the public sector of the economy controlled by the state—jobs that have gone to Ahmadinejad's friends and allies. Ahmadinejad has also ordered the Ministry of the Interior and the Ministry of Islamic Guidance to crack down on all forms of "heathen" influences, from CDs and DVDs to colorful *pashminas* for women. One of his first moves was to pass the law on the Islamic National Dress Code and unleash the "moral squads" against transgressors. Over the past three years, the Islamic Moral Brigades have been clashing with groups of young Iranians on the streets of Tehran and other major cities over "immodest dress." Television footage of young men and women engaged in scuffles with "moral squads" may lead some in the outside world to assume that the opposition to the Khomeinist regime is mostly urban and middle class, and solely concerned with greater social freedoms. That, however, is only part of the story. While social issues continue to poison life in Iran, it is economic issues that spell the most trouble for Ahmadinejad's presidency.

A review of Ahmadinejad's first term as president provides two contrasting pictures. He has won much admiration at home, some of it grudging, by claiming that he has managed to stand up to the United States without incurring major costs. Each time he thumbs his nose at the Great Satan, his revolutionary base feels flattered. More broadly, beyond his base, he is admired for his attempt at fighting corruption, though his tough talk has seldom translated into concrete action. Ahmadinejad has also strengthened his links with the military, especially the IRGC. In his three national budgets so far, expenditure on defense has risen by a whopping 21 percent, the biggest increase in the history of the Islamic Republic. The president is clearly convinced that a war is coming and the Islamic Republic had better be as prepared for it as possible. A new multibillion-dollar accord with Russia would supply the Islamic Republic with a range of modern weapons, including a generation of long-range surface-to-air missiles capable of hitting high-flying U.S. bombers. Arms deals have also been signed with China and North Korea, giving the IRGC the sense that the military is receiving the priority they felt they had lost under Khatami.

While consolidating his base in the IRGC and among groups of seasonal workers and ruined peasants who have poured into cities—groups that sociologists describe as the lumpen—Ahmadinejad has provoked the emergence of a new internal opposition to the regime. In 2006, tens of thousands of angry workers, forming an illegal umbrella organization, flexed their muscles against Ahmadinejad on International Labor Day (May 1) in Tehran and a dozen provincial capitals. Marching through the capital's streets, the workers carried a coffin draped in black with the legend "Workers' Rights" inscribed on it. They shouted "No to slave labor! Yes to freedom and dignity!" Ahmadinejad had centered his 2005 presidential campaign on a promise to "bring the oil money to every family's dinner table." After the election, his position was boosted by a dramatic rise in oil prices, providing him with more than $100 million a day in state revenues. And, yet, all official statistics show that, with inflation running around 20 percent and unemployment jumping to more than 30 percent, the average Iranian is worse off than three years ago. Under Khatami, the Islamic Republic scored average annual economic growth rates of around 4 percent. In a nation that needs to create a million new jobs to cope with its demography, that kind of growth was not enough to point to any Eldorado anytime soon. But it was enough to prevent the economy from sinking. Under Ahmadinejad, however, the growth rate has dropped to around 3 percent—despite rising oil revenues.

Because it controls the oil revenue, which comes in U.S. dollars, the Khomeinist regime has a vested interest in a weak national currency. (It could get more rials for the same amount of dollars in the domestic market.) Ahmadinejad has tried to exploit that opportunity by printing an unprecedented quantity of rials. Economists in Tehran speak of "the torrent of worthless rials" that Ahmadinejad has used to finance his extravagant promises to eradicate poverty. The result has been massive flights of capital, mostly into banks in Dubai, Malaysia, and Austria. Ayatollah Shahroudi, the Islamic chief justice, claims that as much as $300 billion may have left the country since Ahmadinejad was sworn in as president. Other estimates put the figure at three times that. According to Abbas Abdi, a Tehran researcher and loyal critic of the regime, Iran is experiencing its worst economic crisis since the late 1970s. The effects are seen in the slumping of real estate prices for the first time since 1997, even in Tehran's prime districts. Printing money and spending on a no-tomorrow basis are not the only reasons for the crisis. Ahmadinejad's entire economic philosophy seems to be designed to do more harm than good.

The president's favorite catchword is *khodkafa'i*, or "self-sufficiency." To the horror of most Iranians, especially the millions connected with the bazaars, who regard trade as the noblest of pursuits, Ahmadinejad insists that the only way Iran can preserve its "Islamic purity" is to reduce foreign commerce. "Whatever we can produce, we should do ourselves," he likes to say, "even if what we produce is not as good, and more costly." His rationale goes something like this: The global economic system is a "Jewish-Crusader conspiracy" to keep Muslim nations in a position of weakness and dependency. Thus, Muslims would do better relying on their own resources even if it means lower living standards. One of President Ahmadinejad's first moves was to freeze a six-year-old policy designed to help the Islamic Republic become a member of the World Trade Organization. In Ahmadinejad's book, the WTO is just another "Jewish-Crusader" invention to make the inferior position of Muslim economies a permanent feature of international life.

It was with reference to *khodkafa'i* that Ahmadinejad decided to harden the regime's position on the nuclear issue, even if that meant United Nations sanctions and even war. The president claims that the seven countries currently capable of producing nuclear fuel plan to set up a global cartel and control the world market for enriched uranium, once mankind, having exhausted fossil fuels, is forced to depend on nuclear energy. On such a day, the Islamic Republic will find itself at the mercy of the infidels, unless, of course, it learns how to produce its own nuclear fuel.

Convinced that Islam is destined for war against the infidels—led by the United States—Ahmadinejad is determined to preserve what he regards as the Islamic Republic's "independence." One of his favorite themes is the claim that good Muslims, forced to choose between freedom and independence, would prefer the latter.

Khodkafa'i has had catastrophic results in many sectors of Iran's economy. Unable to reduce, let alone stop, imports of mass consumer goods controlled by powerful mullahs and Revolutionary Guard commanders, including almost half the nation's food, Ahmadinejad has tightened import rules for a range of raw materials and spare parts needed by factories. The policy has all but killed the once buoyant textile industry, destroying tens of thousands of jobs. It has also affected hundreds of small and medium-size businesses that, in some cases, have been unable to pay their employees for months.

Ahmadinejad has also used *khodkafa'i* as an excuse to freeze a number of business deals aimed at preventing the collapse of Iran's aging and semi-derelict oil and gas fields. He has vetoed foreign participation in building oil refineries, forcing the Islamic Republic to import more than 40 percent of the refined petroleum products consumed in Iran. The prospect of a prolonged duel with the United Nations and a possible military clash with the United States has also hurt the Iranian economy under Ahmadinejad.

One result of the president's policy is the series of strikes that have continued in Tehran and at least twenty other major cities since last autumn. In 2005, one major strike by transport workers in Tehran brought the capital city of fifteen million inhabitants to a standstill for several days. At any given time, tens of thousands of workers are on strike in industries as diverse as gas refining, paper and newsprint, automobile manufacture, sugar cane plantations, and copper mining.

Ahmadinejad, however, is determined to impose what looks like a North Korean model on the Iranian economy. He has already dissolved the Syndicate of Iranian Employers as a capitalist cabal, and replaced it with a government-appointed body. He is also pushing a new labor code through the Islamic Majlis to replace the existing one written with the help of the International Labor Organization in the 1960s and amended in 1991. The proposed text abolishes most of the rights won by workers throughout the world thanks to decades of social struggle and political reform. Ahmadinejad believes that Western-style trade unions and employers' associations have no place in a proper Islamic society, since the division of people into employees and employers is a "Jewish-Crusader" invention. In Islam, employers and employees are part of the *ummah* (community of the faithful), bound by divine laws that can't be questioned. They ought to operate through the institution they both share, the Islamic state, which can keep the "community of the faithful" free of class struggle—a typical affliction of infidel societies. Ahmadinejad insists that an individual's life is a "borrowed gift" meant to be spent only on preparing the return of the Mahdi, and thus all talk of fixing working hours and annual holidays is a sign of impiety. According to the new labor code, presented to the Majlis at the end of 2007, terms of employment are to be fixed by the employer and the employee through an agreement between "two Muslim brothers." The code would outlaw the formation of unions, abolish the minimum wage, and allow employers to fire any worker they wished instantly and without compensation.

When confronted with bad economic news or news of growing social unrest, Ahmadinejad has always been philosophical: We are preparing for a transformation of man's existence, something never before experienced in history; the Imam is coming back and Islam is to rule the world! Should we allow petty issues of this life to divert our attention from the glory that awaits us? This kind of discourse resonates with the radical Khomeinist base and elements benefiting from the rentier state. Even some in the senior ranks of leadership are seduced by this upbeat message of hope, especially because it comes after eight years of generally pessimistic signals from Khatami. To outsiders, the idea that Iran is now at the vanguard of a universal revolution may look like a sure sign of hubris. To Khomeinist insiders, however, it is the fulfillment of the late ayatollah's promise. "The Islamic Republic of Iran is the heart of the Muslim nation and the center of the worldwide awakening of Islam," Khamenehi said in May 2008. "This is why the bullying power and oppressors are afraid of increasing attention by Muslims everywhere to this Iranian model. All the political, economic, security, and propaganda attacks of the Imperialists against the Islamic Republic is to prevent Muslims from adopting the model of our Islamic Republic."[1]

Ahmadinejad is a typical "hastener" of the Imam's return. He sees the signs of "return" everywhere and all but openly claims regular sightings of the Mahdi. A generation ago, most Iranians would have regarded anyone holding such views as deranged. It was considered arrogant, if not impious, to try to force the Imam's hand. Today, however, one finds "hasteners" everywhere in Iran. According to the official media there are hundreds of sightings of the Hidden Imam each year and all over the country. And, as might have been expected, there are men, and one woman, who claim to be the Returning Imam, much to Ahmadinejad's chagrin. The female Hidden Imam is a certain Ruqiyah Begum, a seventy-seven-year-old seamstress from Kerman who in 2006 claimed that she was inhabited by the Mahdi. Ahmadinejad has also tried to connect Now-Ruz, Iran's national and non-Islamic New Year, to the idea of the Hidden Imam. He started his New Year message on March 21, 2008, with a special prayer of the "hasteners," imploring the Mahdi to hurry up to lead his followers on a campaign for establishing justice throughout the world.

25

A Case of National Schizophrenia

What to do about Iran? As we have seen, the question has haunted successive administrations in Washington for three decades. The real question, however, is the one asked by most Iranians themselves: what to do about the Islamic Republic in Iran?

As we have shown, since the establishment of the Khomeinist regime in Tehran, there are two Irans. There is Iran as a nation-state with a long history going back three millennia, and a culture of beauty and diversity. As a builder of civilizations, this Iran, despite the numerous ups and downs of its history, has demonstrated a rare degree of resilience. Dozens of nations in the Middle East, the first birthplace of nations and cradle of civilizations, have disappeared. Sumer, Akkad, Babylon, Anshan, Elam, Phoenicia, Carthage—all are gone, leaving behind only names. Iran, however, is still around. Ernest Renan described this Iran as an eternal stream that may disappear underground for a while, but always resurfaces with greater energy.

Then there is the other Iran, the transient one, which is perceived by many as a threat to regional stability and, indeed, world peace. This Iran is the vehicle for Khomeinism, a fascist movement based on a perverted interpretation of Shiism, itself a minority version of Islam. Like all other fascist states, this second Iran is a destroyer of civilization, starting with Iran's own heritage, and a practitioner of terror and violence both at home and abroad. It has killed Iranians by the tens of thousands, and caused the deaths of hundreds of thousands outside Iran. It has driven more than five million Iranians into exile and has turned a further four million into displaced persons inside the country. Khomeinism has provoked what the World Bank calls "the biggest brain drain in history." It has tried to de-Iranize Iran, thus seeking to achieve what Arab, Mongol and Turkic invaders failed to do over almost fifteen centuries. It has sponsored and organized terrorist operations in more than two dozen countries on all continents. Iran today is a nation hijacked by a mad ideology and its adepts, who claim they have discovered the ultimate version of Truth and regard it as their duty to impose that Truth on all of mankind. The problem that humanity faces today is not with Iran as a nation-state and a country; it is with Iran as a vehicle for Khomeinism, Iran as the Islamic Republic, Iran as a cause rather than a country. This makes the task of making policy in Iran difficult. A hijacked aircraft laden with explosives and with hundreds of innocent people on board is a clear and present danger. But the problem is not with the aircraft or the passengers; it is with the hijackers. The question, therefore, is how to neutralize the hijackers without harming the passengers and the aircraft.

This is not the first time that Iran has been hijacked and transformed from a country into a cause. For almost a century under direct Arab rule, Iran was used as source of manpower for Islamic expansion. In the region of Isfahan alone, over sixty thousand young men were press-ganged into the armies of the caliph and sent to North Africa to take part in wars of conquest there and in southern Europe. None of them returned. Islamic wars of conquest remained a drain on the population of Khorassan for two more centuries. Nor is Iran the first nation to be hijacked and transformed into a vehicle for the pursuit of a diabolical cause. In more recent times, this is what happened to Russia under the Bolsheviks, to Italians under the Fascists, and to Germans under the Nazis. The problem that the world had was not with Russia, Italy, or Germany as countries but with sick ideologies of which Khomeinism is one of the latest bastards.

As a nation-state, Iran could be a rival or even an adversary of other nation-states. It could even go to war against them. But it would never pose an existential threat to them. Nation-states, even when they make war, always end up accepting some rules of coexistence. This cannot be the case with causes. Khomeinism is not seeking territory, border changes, greater markets, access to natural resources, or even influence and prestige—things that any normal nation-state might seek. Khomeinism wants to seize control of other people's lives, at individual and national levels, and remold them into future soldiers of the returning Hidden Imam. In normal political parlance, Khomeinism does not want anything in particular; it wants everything.

Khomeinism is like the beasts in the Chekhov story in which a man riding a troika in the snows of Siberia is pursued by a pack of wolves. To stop the wolves, the man continues to throw food at them. He ends up killing the dogs that pull his troika one by one, feeding them to the wolves. Only then does he realize that what the wolves wanted all along was to devour *him*. Many Iranians have had a similar experience under Khomeinism. In the Persian alphabet, the three vowels *a, o,* and *i* are labeled *horouf elleh,* which means "sick letters." This is because they can be interchangeable, according to dialects. Thus, the word *Irani,* meaning "Iranian," could become *Irooni* in its "infirm" form. The word *Irani* means "noble, upright, brave." The word *Irooni,* on the other hand, means "devious, opportunist, cowardly." As the Iranian nationalist writer Zabih Behrouz explained, *Irani* and *Irooni* could coexist as the two sides of the same coin, but would never become one. *Irani* resists injustice and tyranny, and is prepared to suffer prison, go into exile, or even die, but would not submit to anti-Iranian rule. If none of these options is available to him, he could remain on the sidelines, retreat into his Sufi fraternity, and wait until the time comes for action. *Irooni,* on the other hand, tries to accommodate himself to the established order. The rulers want him to grow a beard, so he grows one, using his face as an advertising space for the dominant ideology. The rulers demand that he pray five times a day; he underlines his devotion by praying twice as many times. *Irooni* wears the hijab in Iran but discards it abroad. He or she flatters the rulers with the most flowery of lexicons, but curses them behind their backs in the vilest language possible. In the end, the effect that *Irooni* has on the despot could be as deadly, if not deadlier, than that of his *Irani* counterpart. *Irooni* is known as *pesteh khandan* (smiling pistachio) because he always looks pleased when he is in the presence of his oppressors. What the oppressors do not know is that the "smiling pistachios" are keeping their poisoned daggers well hidden behind their backs.

Like his *Irani* counterpart, *Irooni* knows how to wait. It is not for nothing that the theme of waiting is so important in Iranian culture, both religious and secular. In pre-Islamic Iran, the waiting was for King of Kings Kaykhosrow, who had disappeared in the snows of Mount Damavand at the peak of his power and glory. In Islamic Iran, the waiting is for the Hidden Imam. Khomeinism, like other totalitarian ideologies, forces ordinary people into either becoming heroes and risking their lives or operating as plotters in the dark. The Khomeinist despot will never know what "his people" really think until the pillars of his rule begin to crumble.

The first step towards effective policymaking on Iran is to understand the duality of the Iranian reality today: how to restrain and ultimately neutralize Mr. Hyde without killing Dr. Jekyll or turning him into an enemy? The starting point should be the choice of vocabulary. When we oppose the export of terror we must make it clear that it is the Islamic Republic, and not Iran, that is doing the exporting. President Clinton's first secretary of state, Warren Christopher, called Iran a terrorist nation. He would have been correct had he said that the Islamic Republic was a terrorist regime. His successor, Madeleine Albright, called Iran a rogue nation; again, a rogue regime would have been the apt expression. President George W. Bush recognized the subtle, but vital, distinction by constantly saying that he and the people of the United States had no problem with Iran as a nation. Bush underlined the theme by sending special messages to the people of Iran on the occasion of Now-Ruz, the Iranian New Year, which coincides with the spring equinox.

Lobbyists for the mullahs, and incurable anti-Americans who share the Khomeinist hatred of the United States, make a point of using Iran to mask the ugly face of the fascist regime. One typical example was an op-ed written by the former Islamic Republic ambassador to the United Nations for the *New York Times*. He described himself as "Iran's ambassador" and made sure that the term "Islamic Republic" was never mentioned. He made no reference to Ahmadinejad, as if he did not exist. He wanted the *Times'* readers to gain the impression that there was no such thing as an Islamic Republic; there was only Iran, a soft and reassuring concept. The American linguist Noam Chomsky and the French neofascist Jean-Marie Le Pen, two defenders of the Khomeinist regime in the West, never refer to the Islamic Republic. They talk of Iran, a heroic Third World nation standing up to "American imperialism." The word "Iran" generally evokes pleasant images: beautiful carpets, Persian miniatures, aristocratic cats, golden caviar, the roses of Isfahan, and persimmons, peaches, and pistachios. Those with a wider general knowledge would think of the poets Rumi, Omar Khayyam, and Hafez, and of Cyrus the Great, the first major defender of human rights in history. Others may think of the splendors of Persepolis and Susa, and the glories of ancient and/or Safavid Iran. The term "Islamic Republic," on the other hand, recalls hostage-taking, terrorist operations, crowds chanting "Death to America," and mullahs stoning women to death. Today, the two images come together. In policymaking, however, it is important to distinguish the two in order to discern potential friend from actual foe.

Fellow travelers and useful idiots often tried to soften the image of the Stalinist regime by referring to the USSR as "Russia." For Russia, too, struck sympathetic chords, at least outside countries that had suffered from its imperial expansion. Russia was the Bolshoi Ballet and *Swan Lake*, Pushkin and Tolstoy, borsht and blini, and, of course, Tchaikovsky and Borodin.

President Clinton—genuinely though mistakenly sympathetic towards the Khomeinist regime—looked on the map and recognized Iran as a large country in a vital geostrategic location. He also noticed that Iranians, according to numerous polls and other studies, had a favorable opinion of Americans. Thus, he offered a "grand bargain," which included the acknowledgement by the United States of Iran's position as the principal regional power, something that President Nixon had also done in the 1970s. Clinton did not understand that he was dealing not with Iran but with the Islamic Republic. He didn't realize that while it was possible to deal with Iran, dealing with the Islamic Republic was an impossibility. The "grand bargain" was not to be, however. Scheduled to be unveiled during the millennium summit at the United Nations in New York with an "accidental" encounter and handshake between Clinton and Khatami, it was scrapped at the last minute by the Islamic Republic's Supreme Guide, Ali Khamenehi, who had decided there was no point in striking a bargain with a U.S. president on the point of leaving office. Clinton was left pacing the corridors of the UN, waiting in vain for his "accidental" meeting.

Initially, the administration of President George W. Bush was inclined to ignore the Islamic Republic—a "tar-baby" that if touched would bring only grief. But the attacks of 9/11, followed by the U.S. campaign to liberate Afghanistan and Iraq, inevitably moved the Islamic Republic closer to the center of White House attention. By an accident of history, the mullahs actually shared Bush's objectives in Afghanistan and Iraq, since both the Taliban and the Baath movement were sworn enemies of the Islamic Republic. For a few months, Tehran and Washington conducted bilateral talks and even cooperated on the ground in Afghanistan. Soon, however, it became clear that they held diametrically opposed visions of the future of the Middle East.

Bush had concluded that the terrorist attacks on the United States had flowed out of six decades of American support for a Middle East status quo dominated by reactionary and often despotic regimes. To ensure its own safety, America now had to help democratize the region. The Islamic Republic, by contrast, saw the elimination of its two principal regional enemies as a "gift from Allah" and an opportunity to advance its own, contrary vision of the Middle East as the emergent core of a radical Islamist superpower under Khomeinist leadership. Still, throughout its first term, the Bush administration did its best to skirt the Iran issue, despite occasional rhetorical outbursts like the president's linkage of the Islamic Republic with Iraq and North Korea in an "axis of evil." When asked about the administration's Iran policy, officials would respond that there was a policy, only it was not on paper. By the start of the second term, the Bush administration had identified the Islamic Republic as a principal obstacle to the president's policy of democratization. By now, indeed, Tehran had become actively engaged in undermining the U.S. position in both Afghanistan and Iraq, while creating radical Shiite networks to exert pressure on such American allies as Saudi Arabia, Kuwait, and Bahrain. Nor was that all: the Islamic Republic was gaining influence over radical Palestinian groups, including Islamic Jihad and Hamas, by supplying them with funds and weapons. Khomeinism was recognized as a transnational movement whose interests did not always coincide with those of Iran as a nation-state.

Then came the ominous revelations of a secret Iranian program to produce enriched uranium as a first step towards manufacturing nuclear warheads. To this, the initial and by now well-practiced Western response was to blink. At the urging of the European Union, the International Atomic Energy Agency pointedly refrained from penalizing the Islamic Republic for violating the terms of the Nuclear Non-Proliferation Treaty (of which Iran under the shah had been an early signatory). Instead, the EU, working through Britain, France, and Germany, offered the Islamic Republic a series of economic and political "incentives" in exchange for stopping what it should not have started in the first place. After months of diplomatic wrangling, Tehran agreed to suspend its uranium processing and enrichment activities—without, however, agreeing to a method of effective verification. The program was resumed in 2005, indicating that the Islamic Republic does not consider itself bound by any agreements reached with infidels.

In May 2006, the United States joined the EU initiative in an expanded framework of talks that also included Russia and China. Condoleezza Rice even opened the possibility of direct talks with Tehran, with hints at concessions to the Islamic Republic. But Tehran declined to play. To the contrary, Mahmoud Ahmadinejad, then recently elected president, announced that the Islamic Republic was relaunching its uranium enrichment program on an even larger scale. Describing the West's demands as a species of "nuclear apartheid," Ahmadinejad vowed that

Iran would now work to achieve "mastery of the full cycle of nuclear science and technology." By September 2006, he had ignored three deadlines for changing his mind. As we have shown, Ahmadinejad considers a "clash of civilizations" to be both inevitable and welcome. Of course, he is ready to talk—so long as the Islamic Republic is not required to make *any* concessions. In a speech in Zanjan in the summer of 2006, Ahmadinejad assured his listeners that the United States would never be permitted to create "an American Middle East." "The new Middle East," he promised, "will be Islamic."

Why does the Islamic Republic behave as it does? The answer is that, as the spearhead of a revolutionary cause, it can do no other. The Islamic Republic is unlike any of the other regimes in its environment, or indeed anywhere in the world. Either it will become like them—i.e., a nation-state—or it will force them to become like it. As a normal nation-state, Iran would have few major problems with its neighbors or with others. As the embodiment of the Islamic Revolution, it is genetically programmed to clash not only with those of its neighbors who do not wish to emulate its political system but also with other powers that all too reasonably regard Khomeinism as a threat to regional stability and world peace. For as long as the Islamic Republic continues to behave as a revolutionary cause, it will be impossible for others, including the United States, to consider it a partner, let alone a friend or ally. This does not exclude talks, or even periods of relative détente, as happened with the USSR during the Cold War. But just as the Soviet Union remained an enemy of the free world right up to the end, so the Islamic Republic will remain an enemy until Iran once more becomes a nation-state.

Hopes that the Khomeinist regime might somehow transform into a friend and ally of the democracies are based on an old illusion. There were those who also hoped the USSR could be reformed. Mikhail Gorbachev devoted his considerable energies to the cause of reform only to realize that a leopard cannot shed its spots. Having talked of glasnost and perestroika, in 1988 he ended up using chemical weapons to quell riots in Tbilisi, the capital of Georgia, and ordered a full-scale invasion of Baku, capital of Azerbaijan, to crush another popular uprising. Gorbachev had to use such extreme measures because the USSR lacked the normal mechanisms for conflict resolution. In its political DNA, it was programmed to use violence. It had no choice but to behave in accordance with its nature. There had been other attempts at reforming unreformable regimes in Hungary with Nagy, in Poland with Gomulka, and in Czechoslovakia under Dubcek during the so-called Prague Spring. For a time, some Western self-deceivers even believed that the Ceausescu regime in Romania could be reformed. It was in that spirit that President François Mitterrand of France tried to save Ceausescu's regime until the very last phase of its existence. The Khomeinist regime, too, is unreformable, if only because it lacks the mechanisms needed for meaningful transformation.

26

Pre-emptive War or Pre-emptive Surrender?

How, then, should one deal with Iran in its current phase? There are several options. The most obvious is to do nothing. Among the attractions of this option is that, at least theoretically, it would deny the Islamic Republic the chance to cast itself as the grand defender of Islam against the depredations of the infidel camp, led by the United States. It would also allow internal tensions in Iran to come to the fore, helping speed the transition from cause to state. But the risk in the do-nothing option is clear. Interpreting it as yet another sign of weakness on the part of its adversaries, the Islamic Republic may hasten its program to "export the revolution" around the Middle East and, more importantly, develop a credible arsenal of nuclear weapons. The result would be an even bigger challenge to the regional balance of power and to the world.

An alternative to the do-nothing option is the one favored, today as yesterday, by the apostles of dialogue: namely, to reach an accommodation with the Islamic Republic on *its* terms, in the hope that this will somehow, in time, help to modify its behavior. Some Europeans clearly back this option. What matters, they say, is to engage the Islamic Republic as a partner in some kind of international arrangement that, over an unspecified period, will end up imposing restraints on its overall behavior. The risk here is equally obvious. Having won an initial concession from the infidels, the Khomeinist leadership could instantly and reflexively demand more. The Khomeinist revolution, after all, dreams of conquering the world in the name of Islam, just as Hitler aimed to do in the name of the Aryan master race and the USSR in the name of Communism. Indeed, Khatami's idea of a "Yalta-like" accord with President Clinton was itself inspired by the mullahs' claim to be the legitimate successors to the USSR as the global challengers to "American imperialism."

Those who pursue the elusive goal of behavioral change assume that a regime like that of the Khomeinists is a character actor that can easily switch from one role to another, one day playing a fiendish foe and the next reappearing as a faithful friend. In other words, this actor could play both the wolf and the grandmother. Within a democracy such as the United States, rival theories about how to deal with Iran may be aired and compared, and a change of administration can lead to a change of official behavior. But in totalitarian systems like the Islamic Republic, no such exchange of ideas is possible even within the narrow confines of the ruling elite. The United States is the foe that must ultimately be defeated and destroyed. Paradoxically, a policy aimed solely at behavioral change could encourage the Khomeinist regime to adopt an even more aggressive stance. Once assured that its hold on power in Iran is not in danger, the regime would try to pursue its strategic goal of total domination with even greater zeal. Foreign policy, of course, is a continuation and reflection of domestic policy. A regime that oppresses and terrorizes its own people, in fact is at war against them, cannot offer peace and understanding to other nations. Change of behavior on the foreign policy front comes only after behavioral change on the domestic scene. In 2008, however, the Khomeinist regime was behaving even more hysterically at home than ever. The hardening of its foreign policy positions reflected its harsher domestic policies, at least in part. A Persian proverb says: "Threaten him with death so that he accepts a fever!" This reflects the political psychology of the Khomeinist regime: it changes its behavior only when it feels its very existence is in danger.

A regime that boasts a messianic mission cannot change its behavior on any of the major issues of foreign policy; and even if it did, this could be nothing but a tactical repositioning. Like other fascist and totalitarian regimes, the Khomeinist one behaves as it does because, like Goethe's Mephistopheles, it cannot do otherwise. The scorpion does not sting because it wishes to behave badly; it stings because it is genetically programmed to do so. Machiavelli advised his prince never to wound an enemy and let him live. The wise prince, he said, would either turn the wounded enemy into a friend, or kill him. That advice, however, applies to mere enemies, not implacable foes bent on the total destruction of an adversary. Under the Khomeinist regime, Iran can never again be a friend and is certain to remain an implacable foe. This has been repeatedly illustrated by Ahmadinejad and Khamenehi, both of whom appear to have concluded that they have pushed the United States onto the defensive and all they need do now is push further until they accomplish its total defeat and perhaps even its destruction.

In June 2008, Ahmadinejad told a summit of the Food and Agricultural Organization of the United Nations that the United States was largely responsible for hunger and famine in the world. Nevertheless, he announced the "good news" that the Great Satan would disappear soon. "Today, the time for the fall of the satanic power of the United States has come and the countdown to the annihilation of the emperor of power and wealth has started. . . . I tell you that with the unity and awareness of all the Islamic countries all the satanic powers will soon be destroyed." He also announced Israel's destruction: "I must announce that the Zionist regime [Israel], with a sixty-year record of genocide, plunder, invasion and betrayal, is about to die and will soon be erased from the geographical scene." It was clear that Ahmadinejad saw his policy of "waiting Bush out" as vindicated. The Bush presidency was drawing to a close and the only U.S. leader who had shown readiness to use force against its enemies since the 1960s had not taken action against the Islamic Republic. Was this not in itself a sign that the Hidden Imam was behind the Islamic Republic and about to return? "With the appearance of the promised savior . . . and his companions such as Jesus Christ, tyranny will soon be eradicated in the world," Ahmadinejad said, implying that this return would mean the annihilation of the United States.[1] To make sure that no one believed he was just addressing the gallery, Ahmadinejad repeated his analysis in several meetings with other leaders attending the summit in Rome. "The U.S. domination is on the decline. Iran and Japan as two civilized and influential nations should get ready for a world minus the U.S.," he told the Japanese prime minister, Yasuo Fukuda, and called for cooperation between the two countries. "Enemies do not wish Iran and Japan to find their historical and true status. The time has come for both countries to draw up the horizon for their long-term cooperation."

In 2004 the Spanish prime minister, Jose Maria Aznar, revealed that Khamenehi had told him in a meeting in Tehran that the Islamic Republic was waiting for the return of the Hidden Imam and the expected destruction of Israel and the United States. Spanish leftists booed Aznar as a "warmonger" trying to incite Western powers against a Third World nation "standing up to Imperialism." There were even suggestions that Aznar should apologize to the Islamic Republic. Ahmadinejad blocked such possibilities for obfuscation by stating his regime's deep-held position with clarity. Thus, policies aimed at behavioral change through "engagement" and "constructive dialogue" with the Khomeinist brand of fascism are doomed to failure.

There remains another option: regime change. The very mention of this term drives some people up the wall, inspiring images of an American invasion, a native insurgency, suicide bombers, and worse. In other words, regime change has a bad name these days. Nevertheless, even the most ardent opponents of regime change cannot deny that in some cases it *could be* an option. What is wrong with wanting to change an obnoxious regime that is oppressing its people and threatening others? Was it not regime change that ultimately ended the Cold War, removing the threat of a global thermonuclear war between the free world and the Soviet bloc? And how many millions of people across the globe fought to change the apartheid regime in South Africa? This does not mean that regime change is always easy or even practical. What it means is that we should have the moral courage to stand for regime change when and if we sincerely believe that a regime deserves to be changed. In any case, military intervention and pre-emptive war are not the only means of achieving regime change. Between pre-emptive war and pre-emptive surrender— as the men of Munich practiced in their time and their heirs preach today—lie a range of options that anyone seriously interested in fighting evil regimes should consider.

What matters is to be intellectually clear about the issue at hand. This requires a consensus on a definition of the Khomeinist regime. Is it one of those adolescent-like regimes that, intoxicated with hubris, make a bit of mischief to get noticed? Something like this has happened in many countries on different occasions. Juan Perón's dictatorship did give Argentina a teenage rage for a while. Castro's Cuba has been a nuisance for its neighbors for half a century. Today, Hugo Chavez is behaving like an adolescent in heat. Muammar Kaddhafi has presided over another angry teenager regime for four decades. The Burmese military junta, offering a cocktail of bad Buddhism and misunderstood Marxism, has ruined the lives of its people and produced millions of refugees across the region. But none of these regimes represents an existential threat to its neighbors and others. This is because none has had messianic pretensions or seen itself as the vanguard of global conquest in the name of religion.

There are some Western politicians, like the former German foreign minister Joschka Fischer and the new American president Barack Obama, who believe, or claim, that Khomeinism could not be a threat because it lacks the resources. Still others, such as Senator John Kerry, argue that Ahmadinejad may not even mean what he says. Some self-styled American scholars have devoted time to arguing that Ahmadinejad's utterances are mistranslations or misstatements. Another view, held by President Bush among others, is that the United States will not be safe as long as Iran, a key country in a region of vital importance to the world economy and to international stability, remains the embodiment of the Khomeinist cause. If this last diagnosis is correct, the United States cannot allow the Khomeinist movement, itself a version of global Islamism, to achieve further political or diplomatic gains at the expense of the Western democracies.

Consider the consequences: The most immediate result would be to strengthen the mullahs and demoralize all those inside Iran who have a different vision of their country's future and an active desire to bring it about. In 1937 and 1938, many professional army officers in Germany, realizing that Hitler was leading their nation to disaster, had begun to discuss possible ways of getting rid of him. But the Munich "peace" accords, negotiated by the British prime minister Neville Chamberlain, handed Hitler a diplomatic triumph and with it a degree of international legitimacy that, from then on, any would-be putschists could hardly ignore. In the Middle East, this story has been repeated many times. The United States helped the Egyptian dictator Gamal Abdel Nasser transform the Suez fiasco into a political triumph, thereby encouraging an even bigger, and for Egypt more disastrous, war in 1967. The 1991 ceasefire that allowed Saddam Hussein to remain in power in Baghdad after the expulsion of his army from occupied Kuwait was interpreted by him as a signal of American weakness, and emboldened him to eliminate his domestic opponents and begin preparations for a bigger war against the infidels. After the first al-Qaeda attack on New York's World Trade Center in 1993, President Clinton dispatched a string of envoys to Afghanistan to strike a bargain with Mullah Muhammad Omar and the Taliban. Clinton's envoy at the United Nations, Bill Richardson, endured particular humiliation when he was kept waiting for two days for a meeting with the mullah only to be told that the "Emir" would not receive him. This was seen as "a sign of weakness in the Crusader-Zionists," to quote the Taliban foreign minister, and it immensely enhanced the prestige of al-Qaeda and Osama bin Laden. In addition, it discouraged the anti-Taliban forces, many of whom concluded that there was no point in fighting a foe backed by the world's only superpower.

That is the effect that reaching an accommodation with the Khomeinist regime will have on Iran's own democrats and reformers. And it will have the same weakening effect on the growing democratic movement elsewhere in the Middle East. Some signs of this are already visible. For example, the fragile consensus belatedly formed around the idea of a two-state solution for Israel and the Palestinians is under pressure from a new "one-state" formula propagated by the "defiance front" led by Iran and including Syria, Hezballah, Hamas, Islamic Jihad, Libya, and Sudan. In Lebanon, Hezballah and its allies have been encouraged by Tehran to pursue a systematic armed bullying of the democratically elected government of Prime Minister Fouad Siniora. In Syria, the pro-reform camp has been defeated, and the Baathist regime, a vicious menace in its own right, has entered into an unprecedented dependence on Tehran. In May 2008, Tehran and Damascus signed a new defense treaty, consolidating the Islamic Republic's position in Syria. Even major powers like Russia, China, France, and Germany calibrate their relations with the Islamic Republic with reference to how they suspect Washington will, or will not, act.

By contrast, in opting for regime change, the United States would send a strong signal to the democratic movement inside Iran, as well as throughout the Middle East, that the Bush Doctrine remains intact and that the Khomeinist movement is doomed. Such a policy would also encourage Iran's neighbors, and other powers concerned about aggressive Khomeinism, to resist the political and diplomatic démarches of the Islamic Republic without fear of being caught out by a surprise deal between Tehran and Washington. European, Russian, and Chinese officials tell us that while they know that the Islamic Republic is a danger to everyone, they also take two points into consideration. The first is that if the Islamic Republic really runs out of control and embarks on some major mischief, the United States and/or Israel will deal with it. Thus others need do nothing but wait and watch and, when possible, profit from doing business with the Khomeinist regime. The second consideration is that any attempt at undermining the Khomeinist regime might be suddenly disrupted by a deal between Tehran and Washington. A U.S. commitment to regime change in Tehran would send a clear signal that no such surprises would be possible. It would also convince others that doing business with the Khomeinists might not be all that profitable after all.

In the United States itself, a policy of regime change vis-à-vis the Islamic Republic would have the immense advantage of moral and political clarity. If backed by the requisite political will, it could open the way for a truly bipartisan approach to dealing with a regime now identified as the United States' most determined and potentially dangerous adversary in the region. For it is hard to imagine a democratic and pro-Western Middle East being built without Iran, the largest piece in any emerging jigsaw puzzle. Nor could U.S. victories in Afghanistan and Iraq be consolidated without change in Iran, or meaningful progress be made towards resolution of the Israel-Palestinian conflict as long as the Khomeinist regime is determined to pursue its "wipe-Israel-off-the-map" strategy. Abroad, a U.S. policy of regime change would give heart to all those who are rightly worried by the alliance that Ahmadinejad is trying to build with thugs and lunatics like North Korea's Kim Jong-Il, Zimbabwe's Robert Mugabe, Venezuela's Hugo Chavez, and the Castro brothers in Cuba. Ahmadinejad has also talked of a Tehran-Moscow-Beijing axis to confront the United States. He has attended the summit of the Shanghai Group—composed of Russia, China, Kazakhstan, Tajikistan, and Kyrgyzstan—as a guest, and applied for full membership. More importantly, today, Tehran is the ideological capital of international terrorism, with more than sixty groups from all continents gathering there each February for a global terror-fest. A triumphant Ahmadinejad, armed with nuclear weapons, would only boost the international terrorist movement, thus further undermining the security of the United States and its allies. This alone is a powerful argument for regime change.

Some might object: even granting the virtue of the idea, how realistic is regime change in Iran? Can it happen? The short answer is yes. Without underestimating the power still held by the mullahs over the Iranian people, let alone their ability to wreak havoc in places near and far, a number of factors suggest that, like other revolutionary regimes before them, their condition is more fragile than may at first appear.

The Islamic Republic is one of those cause-stricken regimes that cannot stop unless they are stopped. Ahmadinejad himself has described it as "a train without brakes"; it has to surge ahead until it hits something hard in its path. The Fascist and Nazi regimes of Italy and Germany came to an end when they hit something hard in their way. The same happened to the militarist regime in Japan. Nasser's regime in Egypt came to a close when it, too, hit something hard in 1967. In a sense, even the collapse of the USSR was in part due to its military defeat in Afghanistan combined with unprecedented firmness on the part of Moscow's American adversaries.

Khomeini was not the first mullah to seize control of a community and use its resources for war and oppression in the name of a messianic mission. In the nineteenth century, the Akhund of Swat, in the tribal mountains of what is now Pakistan, fought the British and the local emirs for a generation. Mullah Hassan, labeled the "Mad Mullah," in the Horn of Africa and the self-styled "Mahdi" in Sudan featured in similar versions of "jihad against the infidel." In every case, their enemies, including the British, tried all variations possible on appeasement, and failed. To the illusion-stricken mullahs, any suggestion of negotiations and compromise sounded like an admission of guilt and weakness by the infidels. We have seen the latest illustration of this in Afghanistan, where the Taliban under Mullah Muhammad Omar proved unable to make the slightest concession even to save their regime. The Taliban foreign minister Mullah Ahmad Wakil Mutuwakkil described Osama bin Laden as "a chicken bone stuck in our throats," but he was categorical that his regime could not agree to extradite bin Laden even for an Islamic trial by judges in his native Saudi Arabia. Remembering Bill Richardson's "begging posture" at Kandahar, Mullah Mutuwakkil was convinced that the United States would have "no stomach for a war."[2]

In 1979, at the start of the Khomeinist regime, the ayatollah feared hostile action on the part of the United States. That fear was one reason he was prompted to wear a reassuring mask by appointing the pro-American Mehdi Bazargan as prime minister. The ayatollah dispatched Bazargan for a meeting with Brzezinski to reassure the Carter administration. But then came the raid on the U.S. embassy, and Washington reacted with attempts at appeasement. This only encouraged the more radical elements in the Khomeinist ruling clique, and within months almost all moderate elements were purged.

When Reagan became president, the perception of the United States in Tehran changed. Reagan not only toughened the diplomatic discourse against the Khomeinist regime but also took military action against it in 1987. The combined effect was a retreat of the radicals. The ayatollah immediately stopped disrupting Arab oil shipping in the Persian Gulf, agreed to a UN resolution to end the war with Iraq, and expelled the radical elements, then led by Prime Minister Mussavi Khamenehi, by abolishing his post altogether. American toughness helped the rise of the more moderate elements led by Rafsanjani.

Under the first President Bush, who briefly attempted appeasement, the tide turned against the moderates in Tehran as the radicals, assured that the United States would not act against the regime, made a spectacular comeback and won control of the Islamic Majlis under Ayatollah Ali-Akbar Nateq-Nuri. Then came the Berlin trials that charged the Supreme Guide, the president, and two key ministers of the Islamic Republic with complicity in the murder of four Iranian Kurdish dissident leaders in Germany. Once again, the regime had bumped into something hard. It retreated by putting forward the smiling face of Muhammad Khatami as president.

President Clinton's attempts at appeasement also produced the opposite results as the Khomeinist establishment concluded that it could pursue its ambitions without encountering resistance. The regime speeded up its nuclear program in the face of international opposition.

Then came the liberation of Afghanistan and Iraq, and the Khomeinists feared that they may be the next target. To placate the United States, they briefly cooperated in stabilizing post-Taliban Afghanistan and also suspended uranium enrichment. Soon, however, they concluded that the United States divided against itself was in no position to take any meaningful action against them. The nuclear program was resumed with greater vigor and the regime went on the offensive throughout the region. The combined outcome of Clinton's appeasement and Bush's inability to develop any policy on Iran was the victory of the most radical faction of the regime under Ahmadinejad.

Even now, another signal of appeasement from the United States under a new administration is sure to translate into a further radicalization of the Khomeinist regime. Is someone more radical than Ahmadinejad possible? The answer is yes. The Khomeinist system is programmed to retreat when it meets something hard, but to surge ahead when it encounters no barriers in its way. Thus, even if one seeks mere behavioral change, that is to say tactical concessions, from a regime that remains a strategic foe, only a policy perceived to be aimed at regime change could produce the right impression on the Khomeinists.

27

Conditions for Regime Change

For regime change to happen, a number of conditions must obtain. First among these is the loss of regime legitimacy. The Islamic Republic owed its initial legitimacy to the revolution of 1979. Since then, successive Khomeinist administrations have systematically dismantled the vast, multiform coalition that made the revolution possible. The Khomeinists have massacred their former leftist allies, driven their nationalist partners into exile, and purged even many Islamists from positions of power, leaving their own base fractured and attenuated.

The regime's early legitimacy also derived from referendums and elections held regularly since 1979. In the past two decades, however, each new election has been more "arranged" than the last, while the authoritarian habit of approving candidates in advance has become a routine part of the exercise. Many Iranians saw the presidential election of 2005, in which Ahmadinejad was declared a surprise winner, as the last straw: credited with just 12 percent of the electorate's vote in the first round, he ended up being named the winner in the second round with an incredible 60 percent of the vote. In the parliamentary election of March 2008, voter turnout fell to 47 percent, the lowest since 1979. More significantly, perhaps, the turnout in Tehran and other major cities was below 30 percent. A triple alliance of hard-line Khomeinists won almost two-thirds of the seats in the Islamic Majlis with just 13 percent of those eligible to vote.

Still another source of the regime's legitimacy was its message of "social justice" and its promise to improve the lives of the poor. This, too, has been subverted by reality. Today, more than 40 percent of Iran's seventy million people live below the poverty line, compared with 27 percent before the Khomeinists seized power. In 1977, Iran's GDP per capita was the same as Spain's. Today, Spain's GDP is four times higher than Iran's. As the gap between rich and poor has widened to an unprecedented degree, the corruption of the ruling mullahs and their ostentatious way of life have made a mockery of slogans like "Islamic solidarity."

A report prepared by the Welfare Organization (Sazman Behzisiti) in the Ministry of Public Health, leaked in March 2008 and widely published on the Internet, offers a devastating portrayal of life in the Islamic Republic.[1] It shows that as far as life expectancy is concerned, Iran, which was in the 45th place among members of the United Nations before the revolution, has dropped to the 133rd place, and the average Iranian's life is six years shorter than in 1977. The report also speaks of "suicides reaching epidemic scale." In 2007, there were more than 42,000 officially recorded suicides, compared with 1,612 in 1977. Before the revolution, divorce was rare in Iran and unknown in some rural areas. Now, over 30 percent of all marriages end up in divorce, according to the report. The main reasons for this "epidemic of divorce" are unemployment, poverty, drug addiction and depression. The number of drug addicts is estimated at around 4.5 million, a tenfold increase over the pre-revolutionary era. A marginal phenomenon confined to big cities before the revolution, prostitution has developed into a growing industry. Tehran alone is reported to have almost half a million full-time or part-time ladies of leisure, in a total population of twelve million. In some cases, the true extent of prostitution is masked because some of it is presented as temporary marriage or *mut'ah*, which is regarded by the mullahs as praiseworthy. The ministry's report warns that depression is becoming "a national disease." It estimates that between 10 and 12 percent of the population, almost 15 million people, suffer from chronic depression. As reasons for this, the report cites "poverty, sociopolitical violence, domestic violence, unemployment, divorce, drug addiction, the feeling of lack of freedom, social disappointment, prostitution, inflation, discrimination, violation of the rights of citizenship." The report notes: "In the past, too, our society faced similar problems. However, depression has spread much more widely in recent years. The age of depression has dropped from 27 years to 17."

In an implicit criticism of what it labels "a policy of denial," the report recalls that "it took years before Iranian government leaders and officials stopped denying the existence of social ills. It was not so long ago that we were told that there was no AIDS in Iran and no prostitution, and no suicides."[2] By sending a clear message that they support regime change, the United States and other major democracies will further undermine the Khomeinist regime's claim of legitimacy.

Khomeinism had also sought legitimacy by claiming it would empower the poorest sections of society. Three decades after the revolution, however, it has created a new nomenklatura enjoying power and privilege unknown to its counterpart under the shah. This new class of rulers consists of mullahs and their siblings, the military, and the *bazaaris* allied to them. The shah's critics claimed that a club of "a thousand families" ruled the country. Today, critics of the regime speak about a club of just "a hundred families." The initial phase of the revolution that had allowed thousands of people from modest social backgrounds to achieve a degree of social mobility ended in the late 1980s; since then, only regime insiders have been allowed to ride the social elevator.

A second condition for regime change is the presence of a major split within the ruling establishment itself. The list of former Khomeinists who have distanced themselves from today's regime reads like a who's who of the original revolutionary elite. It includes former "student" leaders who raided the U.S. embassy in 1979, former commanders of the Islamic Revolutionary Guard Corps, and dozens of former cabinet ministers and members of the Islamic Majlis. Most have adopted a passive stance vis-à-vis the regime, but a surprising number have clearly switched sides, becoming active dissidents and thereby risking imprisonment, exile, or even death. Any decline in the regime's international stature could deepen this split within the establishment, helping to isolate the most hard-line Khomeinists.

Here, one might apply what could be labeled the "Yeltsin test," after the first president of post-Communist Russia. At some point in the late 1980s, Boris Yeltsin, who had been a top Communist apparatchik and Politburo member, realized that the Soviet system could not be reformed. After the so-called August coup against Gorbachev, Yeltsin decided it was time to come out of the closet, so to speak, and publicly announce what he had believed in private for some time: that the only way forward was regime change. In a historic address to the Russian nation, Yeltsin described the Bolshevik Revolution as a catastrophe and invited his people to build a free society.

Applying the Yeltsin test to Khomeinist leaders is not easy, if only because most dare not speak their mind for fear of assassination. Nevertheless, it is clear that many figures within the establishment have concluded, at least in private, that only regime change could save Iran from its present crisis and greater catastrophes. Among those who might pass the Yeltsin test and who are still in Iran are Grand Ayatollah Hussein-Ali Montazeri; Ayatollah Abdallah Nuri, a former interior minister; Ayatollah Mohsen Kadivar, a former parliamentarian; Hashem Aghjari, a former IRGC member; and Emadeddin Baqi, a prominent ex-Khomeinist writer and preacher. There are others who have understood the lesson of Yeltsin but lack the courage, or perhaps the wisdom, to come into the open.

Still others have succumbed to despair about a revolution for which they gave so much only to observe with horror the tragedy it has created for Iran. Some have withdrawn from public life, or even gone into exile. A few have destroyed their lives with drugs and alcohol. Cafes in Paris's Left Bank are still full of aging, sometimes derelict Iranian revolutionaries including former high officials of the Khomeinist regime, trying to drown their chagrin in cheap wine and nostalgia. Their endless talk hovers around "what we dreamed of, and what we created." Some are in touch with internal dissidents and still hope to save the revolution, not knowing that the revolution's worst enemy is itself.

The principal theme of internal dissidents is the need for the secularization of the political system, chiefly by abolishing the concept of *walayat e faqih* or rule by a single theologian. According to President Khatami, speaking in 2005, "Those who preach secularization seek the destruction of our Islamic system. Whatever we do, we must make sure that religion remains paramount in all aspects of life." That speech marked a break between Khatami and small but influential circles of intellectuals who, while remaining within the regime, advocate some measure of secularization in the hope of leading the Khomeinist system out of impasse. To be sure, secularization in the current Iranian context does not mean anything like the "separation of church and state" in the West or the Kemalist enterprise in Turkey. In the Iranian context secularization has a more limited meaning and more modest ambitions.

Iranian secularization appeared in its earliest version in the last years of the nineteenth century and grew to play a role in the Constitutional Revolution of 1906. In what may look like an intellectual sleight of hand, Iranian secularists proposed that political power be looked at from two angles. The first concerned the origin of power. They had no difficulty admitting that power was of divine origin, which bestowed on it a certain dignity that, they hoped, would protect it against abuse by ambitious individuals and groups in pursuit of selfish goals. The second angle concerned the exercise of power, in other words its practical reality. Here, Iranian secularists emphasized the human rather than the divine aspect. While power in itself was *noble* because divine, its exercise by humans could involve *ignoble* deeds.

Early secularists such as Mirza Malkam Khan, Jamaleddin Assad-Abadi (also known as al-Afghani), and Hassan Taqi-Zadeh took care to present their theses in Islamic terms so as to reassure both the mullahs and the illiterate masses. Most students of Iranian history agree that they succeeded at least in part. The structures of the Iranian state in time were secularized and remain so today. This means that, with a few notable exceptions, Iran *as a state* operates in accordance with its own *political* interests and not in the interests of Islam or its Shiite version. The early secularists, however, paid virtually no attention to the secularization of the collective consciousness, what political scientists call "subjective profanation." For years, some of the intellectuals within the Khomeinist establishment have been warning that the real threat to the system is not the secularization of structures, which may already be irreversible, but the secularization of the consciousness.

Every state has two functions, primary and secondary. Primary functions consist of upholding a system of law and order and ensuring society's internal peace and external security. Even in states whose raison d'être is religion, like Pakistan and Israel, these primary functions are secularized in practice. The state is a *cold monster;* it does not care who is pious and who is not as long as all obey the law, keep the peace, and pay their taxes. The secondary functions of the state pertain to religion, art, literature, and culture in general. Some Khomeinist reformers, notably Abdul-Karim Sorush, warn that while the ruling mullahs focus on preventing the secularization of the primary functions, a cause that is already lost, Iran is experiencing secularization in the secondary functions. Sorush proposes a united front with the ruling mullahs to combat this "secondary secularization."

One finds numerous mullahs in key government positions. But when it comes to religion, literature, art, and culture, Iran is almost entirely secularized. There are no *religious* philosophers, poets, writers, filmmakers, architects, or painters in Iran today—a sharp contrast with a generation ago. Even when it comes to Islamic, and specifically Shiite, theology, the only innovative work being done is by Western-educated scholars. Creators may be believers as individuals, but the work they produce is *secular* and *Western.* Sorush himself is an example. As an individual he may be a believer, but his work is *entirely* secular. A disciple of Karl Popper, the British philosopher, he draws heavily on Foucault, Habermas, Kuhn, Gouldner, and Russel, among others. As a philosopher he has *absolutely no* Islamic ancestry. Sorush warns that the very reading of Shiism is becoming increasingly secularized.

Here is the paradox, according to Sorush: the more the Iranian state becomes "Islamicized" at the level of government policy and personnel, the *less* Islamic it becomes at the level of existence. Under the shah, a secularist-nationalist ideology controlled the apparatus of the state, meaning its primary functions, but could not make serious inroads into the secondary functions, where religion remained strong. Since the mullahs seized power in 1979, the situation has been reversed. A series of recent surveys conducted by the government reveal the astonishing fact that fewer people go to the mosques in Iran today than they did before the Khomeinist takeover. In March 2008, President Ahmadinejad lamented the fact that no one was building new mosques in Tehran and other major cities, and announced the allocation of $17 million from government funds to build mosques in the capital. Genuine Islamic themes have all but disappeared from Persian literature and art, as well as the now immensely popular theater and cinema.

Sorush is trying to persuade the mullahs to accept a *tactical* retreat to avoid a *strategic* one. He wants the mullahs to admit that religion can no longer act as the sole organizer of all aspects of human society and its conscience. The quest for power cannot be equated with the quest for truth. This does not mean that Iranians have lost their thirst for a metaphysical explanation of existence. Their quest for transcendence continues, but in the form of a patchwork of personal convictions, beliefs, even fantasies, often in direct opposition to the state-sponsored ideology. Sorush argues that because religion *cannot kill* rationality it had better aim at *making it humble.* The result would be salutary for both: Religion would not enter a losing game, while rationality would not self-destruct through arrogance. The idea is that unless we allow the public space to become secularized we risk secularization in the private space. People will act as believers in public but as pagans in private. "Reformation is needed to anticipate and prevent secularization," Sorush asserts. He also takes care to reassure the mullahs. "I have no quarrel with the clergy," he says. "They have treated me kindly."

The problem with Sorush's position is that it assumes that the issue of power could be settled in purely theoretical terms. He thinks that the mullahs will listen to his reasoned arguments and say: Yeah, you're right!

Let's go back to the seminaries and focus on theology! Sorush's project is even less serious now that radicals like Ahmadinejad are publicly calling for a yet greater Islamicization of Iran. Sorush says Iran, by trying to become too Islamic, risks losing its Islamic identity. Ahmadinejad and the mullahs who support him claim that Iran, after twenty-eight years of Khomeinist rule, is not Islamic enough. Sorush wants to give religion a sacred space of its own. The Khomeinist radicals oppose any space not covered exclusively by their version of the faith.

The ideological and political split within the establishment is too deep to be bridged through tactical concessions by the regime. If persuaded that the major democracies, led by the United States, will not eventually make a deal with the regime and help it out of its diplomatic, economic, and political problems, those who support the gradual secularization of the system will be all the more determined to resist the Talibanization of Iran. The emergence of an organized and vocal opposition within the Khomeinist camp itself will, in turn, strengthen the position of those who support a direct regime change.

A third condition for regime change is that its coercive forces have become increasingly reluctant to defend it against the people. Since 2002, the regular army, the Islamic Revolutionary Guard Corps, and the professional police have refused to crush workers' strikes, student demonstrations, and other manifestations of protest against the regime. In many instances, the mullahs have been forced to deploy other, often unofficial, means, including the Ansar Hezballah (Supporters of the Party of God) and the Baseej Mustadafeen (Mobilization of the Dispossessed). In 2006, Ahmadinejad was forced to postpone or cancel several of his planned provincial visits because the regime's coercive forces were deemed unwilling to ensure his protection. The five hundred or so powerful mullahs who provide the backbone of the regime have their own private armies, consisting of between a dozen and three hundred often heavily armed bodyguards. But even these do not always prove reliable. In May 2008, the armed guards preferred to stand back and watch as a group of Baluch rebels murdered a prominent mullah on the Kerman-Zahedan highway in the southeast. Some IRGC commanders are known to be unhappy with the regime's further radicalization, which threatens their business interests. In 2005, Abdolvahad Mussavi-Lari, the interior minister and a mullah, warned in a leaked report that the regime's coercive forces were not willing to crush protest marches in the industrial cities of Alborz and Arak during a wave of strikes. In its early days, the IRGC may have been prepared to kill unarmed opponents in the name of Khomeini. Today, however, Khomeini's successors, who lack his charisma and prestige, might not find the IRGC so keen in massacring Iranians.

Even when it comes to fighting a foreign aggressor, it is not at all certain that the IRGC today would show the same degree of commitment that it did in the 1980s when fighting the armies of Saddam Hussein. In 2007 and 2008, several senior commanders of the IRGC, in public addresses, dropped hints that the force lacked the means to confront a major adversary, i.e. the United States. However, it was not clear whether this show of reluctance was a ploy to secure more resources from the state or indicated doubts about the wisdom of the regime's adventurist foreign policy.

A fourth condition for regime change is the emergence of alternative sources of moral authority in society. Even in religious matters, more and more Iranians look for guidance to non-official or even anti-official mullahs, including the clergy in Iraq. Admittedly, this is partly due to the fact that the present Supreme Guide, Ali Khamenehi, is a mid-ranking mullah who would never be accepted by senior Shiite clergy as a first among equals. Nevertheless, even the more senior ayatollahs promoted by the regime lack the moral authority that their predecessors exercised before the revolution, when most Iranians saw the clergy as a counterweight to an authoritarian regime. Today, the clergy is perceived as the backbone of an even more oppressive government. Many of the more pious Shiites are angry at the Khomeinist regime for having politicized religion, thus exposing it to criticism if not derision.

One sign that Iranians seek religious authority outside the Khomeinist republic is the immense popularity of Grand Ayatollah Ali-Muhammad

Husseini Sistani, the primus inter pares of the Shiite clergy, who has lived in Najaf, Iraq, since the 1950s. Until the liberation of Iraq by a U.S.-led coalition in 2003, Sistani was under house arrest and denied contact with the outside world. Saddam Hussein's regime was especially anxious that Sistani should have no communications with Iran. Since 2003, however, Sistani has resumed contact with the clergy in Iran. In the spring of 2008 he was reported to have appointed more than four hundred special representatives in all Iranian provinces with the task of collecting donations, distributing his fatwas and ministering to the needs of the faithful. In addition, thousands of theology students from all over the world, including Iran itself, have transferred to Najaf to attend Sistani's classes, thus challenging some three decades of dominance by the Iranian "holy" city of Qom. According to the best sources on the current status of the Shiite clerics, in 2008 Sistani was top of the list of grand ayatollahs for the number of his "emulators" and the extent of charities under his supervision.

In a famous duel through fatwas in 2004, Sistani and the five government-sponsored ayatollahs of Qom, led by Ayatollah Nasser Makarem-Shirazi, offered conflicting views on whether or not Islam should forbid smoking. Answering a question sent to both by a group of Tehran University students, the two ayatollahs demonstrated fundamentally different approaches. Makarem-Shirazi ruled that smoking should be banned by the government, and smokers and those who procure and sell tobacco should be punished. Sistani responded by saying that the issue was not a theological one, and that it had better be debated by scientific experts. In any case, he stated, believers who were grownup and of sound mind should take care of their own lives as best they can and in ways of their choice. In other words, Sistani was offering a Shiism of discussion, and of personal responsibility and choice, as opposed to the Khomeinist version based on dogmatism and terror. The fact that believers now have a chance to obtain an alternative fatwa from Najaf makes it harder for Khomeinist mullahs to impose their despotic view. In some cases, Najaf fatwas have saved the lives of women accused of adultery and sentenced to be stoned to death by Khomeinist mullahs. The Khomeinist regime no longer enjoys the religious cover it had two decades ago. Most Iranians now see it as another Third World–style despotic regime backed by security services and the military, along with hired thugs and vile apologists paid with oil money.

As for nonreligious matters, there was a time when the regime enjoyed the support of the overwhelming majority of Iran's "creators of culture." Today, not a single prominent Iranian poet, writer, filmmaker, composer, or artist endorses the Khomeinists; most have become dissidents whose work is either censored or banned. Opposition intellectuals, clerics, trade-union leaders, feminists, and students are emerging as new sources of moral authority. A number of individuals and social groups are also emerging as alternative sources of secular morality in Iran. Regular army officers, who had been discredited as a corps because they effectively surrendered to street mobs in 1979, have regained much of their lost moral authority. Their record of bravery in the war against Saddam Hussein and the fact that they have not become instruments of oppression for the Khomeinist regime have provided them with a capital of goodwill that their counterparts in the IRGC could not dream of.

As a group, the intellectuals are also making a comeback after more than two decades in disgrace as punishment for their collaboration with Khomeini. Despite recent purges ordered by Ahmadinejad, there are still hundreds of academics who enjoy the kind of prestige and moral authority that no Khomeinist official can claim. Most of Iran's poets had welcomed the revolution, often without a proper understanding of what was happening. Most, however, turned against the revolutionary regime within months of its inception. The annual Tehran Book Fair is a good barometer of the cultural mood in the country. Every year, government departments participate with hundreds of books about Islam, Khomeini, hatred of Jews and Americans, and other supposedly revolutionary themes. These, however, never succeed in finding an audience. The Iranian people have moved on. What they crave are books sold under the counter and in the teeth of the official censor. Noam Chomsky's books, instantly translated and published by the Ministry of Islamic Guidance and Culture, no longer sell. Instead, the latest Gabriel Garcia Márquez, banned by the same ministry, sells tens of thousands. When the Brazilian novelist Paulo Coehlo visited Iran in 2002, he was greeted like a pop star in Tehran and Shiraz. In response to the warmth of his reception, he set up a prize to help translate Persian authors into at least one Western language. The regime made it clear to him that the scheme would not be allowed unless it included a prize for a text on Islam. The problem is that, aside from official propaganda that no one could disguise as literature or scholarship, Iranians no longer produce texts on Islam.

Avowedly antireligious Persian poets of the past—notably Omar Khayyam, Obeid Zakani, and Iraj Mirza—have found a new popularity that no one would have expected before the revolution. Even when it comes to contemporary poets and writers, those identified as opponents of the regime find the biggest audiences. A collection of poems by Nader Naderpour, who died in exile in California, has gone into several editions since 2000, produced and sold clandestinely. Essays by Saidi Sirjani, a scholar who died after months of torture by the regime, have become part of the must-read list of many Iranians. The same is true of books by Abdul-Hussein Zarrinkub, narrating the sufferings of the Iranian people under Arab-Islamic rule some fourteen centuries ago. Banned by the regime, they are published and widely distributed in what everyone now recognizes is an alternative Iranian space. The poems of Saeed Soltanpour, a young poet who was abducted from his wedding and put in front of a firing squad, have been set to music and, despite regime efforts, have become part of the Iranian collective memory. The poetess Simin Behbahani, who initially supported the revolution, has turned against it, thus finding a new audience. The former Tehran University chancellor Mahmoud Maleki, the Kurdish poet Jalal Qavami, and the Nobel Peace laureate Shirin Ebadi could also be regarded as part of the emerging alternative source of moral authority in Iranian society. Books and audiotapes of seminars by anti-Islam writers and scholars such as Shojaeddin Shafa, Ahmad Ahrar, Cyrus Amuzegar, Dariush Homayoun, Majid Roshangar, Elahe Boqrat, Kurosh Aryamanesh, Bahram Moshiri, Ali Mir-Fetros, Homer

Abrahamian, Firuz Fouladvand, Assad Homayoun, and Esmail Nuri-Ala have found growing audiences both in samizdat form and through the Internet. And it would be no exaggeration to say that the antireligion satirist Hadi Khorsandi and the antifascist modernist Esmail Khoei are currently Iran's most popular poets.

Thanks to the Internet and satellite radio and television, Iranians have access to a wide range of views. Some exile figures have found audiences inside Iran through these new means of communication. Radio and TV talk shows by Hussein Mohri, Hussein Hejazi, Pari Abasalti, Homa Sarshar, Nader Sadiqi, and Ali-Reza Maybodi now have larger audiences than some of the political programs offered by the regime's official media. Attempts by the regime to build a wall around Iran have failed. An estimated twenty million Iranians now have access to the Internet. Most also receive satellite radio and television. As far as the number of bloggers is concerned, Iranians are in second place in the world, after the Americans.

28

Repression and Resistance

Finally, regime change becomes possible when at least the outline of a political alternative becomes visible. Like nature, society abhors a vacuum. In the case of Iran, that vacuum cannot be filled by the dozen or so groups in exile, although each could have a role in shaping a broad national alternative. What is still needed is an internal political opposition that can act as the nucleus of a future government. The ingredients of such a nucleus exist already. However, such a nucleus cannot be created so long as the fear persists that the United States and its allies might reach an accommodation with the regime and leave Iranian dissidents in the lurch. And that fear has roots in reality. In the years 1999–2000, President Khatami succeeded in splitting the opposition by boasting of the terms of his forthcoming "grand bargain" with President Clinton. His message was ingeniously twofold: the deal would help solve the nation's economic problems and open the way for less repressive measures in social life and culture, but it would include a stipulation that America would never help opponents of the Khomeinist regime.

Although, as we have seen, the "grand bargain" came to naught, the message and its implications have not been forgotten. Many in the West believe that because opposition to the Khomeinist regime does not offer a single easily recognizable figurehead it cannot be taken seriously. The American dictum "You cannot beat anybody with nobody" tells it all. Totalitarian regimes, however, do not allow opponents to produce such figures. An opposition leader who begins to look menacing is imprisoned, forced into exile, or murdered. During Khatami's presidency, the nationalist leader Dariush Foruhar, once a cabinet minister under Khomeini, began to look menacing to the regime. In 2001, the regime decided that it was time to stop him. A hit squad was sent to his home in Tehran to murder him and his wife by chopping off their heads, a message to all that under the mullahs no one would be safe. Scores of other men and women who appeared to be emerging as opposition leaders at the local or national level have been eliminated by Khomeinist hit squads in various parts of the country. The regime has also used murder as a weapon against its opponents abroad. As soon as someone looked like a potential leader, a murder squad was sent to eliminate him. This is why the Iranian opposition, rather than promoting a single "somebody" who would beat the regime, has produced a number of leading figures at different levels and in different fields. Since the mid-1990s, the most active opposition to the regime has come from urban workers, women, students, teachers, and ethnic minorities. Each of these groups has produced leaders of their own—individuals who enjoy audiences beyond their social stratum.

Leading the opposition to Khomeinism since the late 1990s are Iran's urban workers, who had once supported the revolution. Symbolising this new and growing movement is a man some Western commentators have called "the Iranian Lech Walesa," after the Polish trade unionist who helped bring down the Communist empire. The mullahs ruling Iran, however, regard him as "a dangerous enemy of Islam." The man himself—Mansoor Osanloo, a fifty-year-old leader of one of the many illegal trade unions that have sprung up in Iran in the last few years— shies away from both sobriquets. "We do not have a political agenda," he says. "All we are asking is for Iranian workers to be treated as free human beings, not as slaves."[1]

Osanloo first made his name in 2004 when, along with fourteen fellow workers, he created the Syndicate of Workers of the Tehran United Bus Company. Within weeks, most employees of the company—which is owned by the Tehran municipality and controlled by the Interior Ministry—had joined the new union. That left the so-called Islamic Workers' Council, a regime-sponsored organ imposed in many industries as an ersatz union, exposed and isolated. Workers across the country soon emulated the Tehran example. On May Day, more than four hundred free trade unions, boasting a membership of millions, raised their banners in the capital. Osanloo and his colleagues were among the founders of the Workers' Organizations and Activists Coordinating Council (WOACC), which is emerging as the principal voice of wage earners—especially in the public sector, which accounts for more than 70 percent of Iran's economy. The emergence of independent unions has meant the demise of "Islamic councils" in many workplaces and the virtual death of the so-called Workers' House set up by the mullahs to control labor. The free unions have chased away hundreds of mullahs who headed the Islamic councils, often enjoying high salaries and perks.

Osanloo was first jailed in 2005, after his union launched an original form of labor action: Tehran bus workers announced free rides for all comers. When the authorities sent in armed security men, the workers went on strike—bringing Tehran, a city of twelve million inhabitants, to a virtual halt. The regime then tried terror and intimidation. A group of three hundred members of the Iranian branch of Hezballah, armed with clubs and knives, attacked Osanloo and his colleagues and beat up their families, including small children. Osanloo suffered knife wounds, including a deep cut in his tongue, inflicted by a Hezballah member who had vowed to "silence the enemy of Islam." A partial return to work was soon interrupted when bus drivers refused to implement a new rule under which women passengers were confined to back seats—which in practice meant that more than 80 percent of the seats in Tehran's double-decker buses were reserved for men.

Anxious to prevent a prolonged strike, the authorities released Osanloo eight months later, only to rearrest him, again without charge.

In February 2007, he was presented at a one-day trial held *in camera.* "They had a file against me running to 1,300 dense pages," Osanloo said later. "I wonder how the judge could go through all that in a single day." Released from prison in March on a bail of $325,000 (a huge fortune in the Islamic Republic), Osanloo was allowed to travel to London and Brussels to address the annual conferences of the International Transport Workers Federation and the International Trade Unions Conference.

Having spent almost a year in Tehran's dreaded Evin Prison—known as the "Islamic Alcatraz"—on two occasions, Osanloo knew that he risked being rearrested and jailed on his return to Tehran. But if the authorities hoped that allowing him to visit abroad might tempt him to stay in exile, they were disappointed. He had no intention of throwing in the towel.

"We are at the start of a long struggle," he said in an interview in Brussels. "We are fighting for what is a basic human right: the right of workers to organize themselves in free and independent trade unions and negotiate conditions under which they accept employment."[2] The current administration in the Islamic Republic considers such talk "dangerous for the faith and the state."

The avalanche loosed by the Tehran transport workers in 2004 has continued with hundreds of strikes, sit-ins, and other industrial actions throughout Iran. Over the past three years an estimated 2.2 million workers have gone on strike for varying lengths of time in a range of industries, from textile factories in the Caspian region to sugar plantations in the southwest province of Khuzestan. The strike by sugar plantation workers lasted over a year and was eventually quelled in a military operation launched by the Baseej (the revolutionary militia) and strikebreakers hired by the regime. "Iranian workers are discovering their power," Osanloo said in Brussels and London. "The authorities would be wise to acknowledge that power and address the legitimate grievances of workers. At present, however, there is no sign that this is the case." Osanloo was abducted in a Tehran street in July 2007; the regime denied any knowledge of the incident. It took the authorities more than a month to admit that the trade union hero was under arrest, facing charges of "treason against Islam." In a message smuggled out of his prison in April 2008, Osanloo called on Iranian workers to march during Labor Day on May 1 and appealed to "working people everywhere to oppose efforts to crush the independent trade union movement in Iran." As usual, the regime responded with repression. The crackdown in 2007 had not produced the desired results. According to the Workers' Organizations and Activists Coordinating Council (WOACC), over six hundred labor leaders were arrested or "made to disappear" in a crackdown against independent trade unions during April. A further 4,500 workers have been dismissed, often without pay, on vague charges of "fomenting unrest" in a number of state-owned building projects. The largest number of arrests were made during the May Day marches organized by independent trade unions in defiance of the state-sponsored ceremonies.

The May Day marchers carried portraits of Osanloo and another leading trade unionist, Mahmoud Salehi, leader of the Union of Bakery Workers in Sanandaj, the capital of Iranian Kurdistan. Salehi was picked up on April 9, 2007, when security men raided his home, beat up his family, and carried him to an unknown destination. He has never been formally charged, while rumors about his alleged misdeeds are spread through the state-controlled media. According to these patently absurd rumors, Salehi is a member of the Kurdish Communist Party (Komalah), is seeking to detach the province from Iran, and at the same time is working with the United States to bring "Jewish-Crusader democracy" to Iran. Branding Salehi a Communist, while Osanloo is known as a center-right democrat, is clearly designed to create a split in the workers' movement. As part of the crackdown under Ahmadinejad, the regime has closed four weeklies that reflected the view of the workers and shut down the Iran Labor News Agency, an independent service covering the free trade union movement. In April 2008, they also arrested a number of WOACC militants, including six members of the executive board of the Tehran bus drivers' syndicate.

Despite the repressive measures, the labor movement seems to be picking up momentum. A group of WOACC leaders has written to the director general of the International Labor Organization, Juan Somavia, calling for an international committee of enquiry to investigate the repression of the Iranian workers' movement. The good news is that Western trade unionists are beginning to pay attention to the struggle of their fellow workers in Iran. Several European trade unions have already called for Salehi, Osanloo, and other Iranian trade unionists to be released. In 2008, the AFL-CIO began to take an interest in the Iranian labor movement by hiring a researcher to monitor the situation. Even the Western media, often silent on crimes committed by the regime during this three-decade-long "Persian Night," have started to pay attention to the new popular resistance movement in Iran. The Western left, however, has remained indifferent or hostile. To American leftists, opposing the Khomeinist regime, described by Chomsky as "mass based," is tantamount to collaboration with U.S. "imperialism." The regime echoes this view by branding trade unionists as "an American fifth column" and, in the words of the mullah Dorri Najaf-Abadi, the prosecutor general of the Islamic Republic, "the most dangerous enemies of our Islamic system."

Repression, however, has not succeeded in crushing the Iranian workers' movement. In 2007 and 2008, free trade unionists organized fifty-one major strikes and over a hundred demonstrations in various parts of the country. They showed their muscle on International Labor Day in both 2007 and 2008, when tens of thousands of workers marched in Tehran and eighteen provincial capitals. The regime retaliated by arresting scores of trade unionists and expelling many others. According to Rajab-Ali Shahsavari, leader of the Union of Contractual Workers, 25,795 unionists were arrested in the first four months of 2007 alone. He estimated that over one thousand workers were losing their jobs each day, as the regime intensified its crackdown. Worse still, the number of suspicious deaths among workers has risen to an all-time high. According to the deputy labor minister Ibrahim Nazari-Jalali, 1,047 workers have died in "work-related accidents" in 2007. Labor sources, however, point out that none of the accidents was investigated, and in at least thirteen cases the workers who died may have been killed by goons hired by the regime. Repression and lack of jobs have forced many Iranian workers to flee the country, mainly headed for Persian Gulf states in search of work and a minimum of freedom. Often these would-be immigrants face death or imprisonment. In 2008, Kuwait alone was arresting an average of one thousand Iranian illegal immigrants each month. Not all those who flee the Khomeinist tyranny are manual workers. According to the International Monetary Fund, more than 150,000 highly educated members of the Iranian middle class flee the country each year, creating "the biggest recorded brain drain in history."

Fighting the regime alongside industrial workers are Iran's estimated 600,000 teachers, who have also set up a number of independent trade unions and chased away mullahs appointed by the regime to "guide" them. The teachers first flexed their muscles in 2006 when they succeeded in shutting thousands of schools across the nation in a strike over pay and conditions. By 2007, however, the movement had assumed distinctly political features. In meeting after meeting, protesting teachers called for an end to "mass brainwashing of our children in the name of Islam" and insisted that textbooks be written by professionals rather than government propagandists. They also condemned the government for forcing schoolchildren to interrupt their classes to attend revolutionary rallies and other manifestations of support for the regime. In June 2006, nine independent teachers' unions brought together over 100,000 people for a march on the building that houses the Islamic parliament. The regime, having deployed a large force of police and Khomeinist thugs armed with knives and clubs, decided not to try interrupting the demonstrations. This was the first major sign that Khomeinism, a master of street politics, could be challenged even on its preferred terrain. Women teachers have also campaigned for permission for schoolgirls not to wear the mandatory hijab inside the school building. Although less advanced than the workers' movement on its way to ultimate politicization, the teachers' movement has been assuming a greater political coloring since 2006.

Women's organizations and feminist activists are also in the vanguard of the fight against Khomeinism. In a traditional society where male domination is regarded as the natural order of things, many brave women have achieved almost cult status as fighters for freedom and equality. Pari Ardalan, Zohreh Shoja'ee, Shahla Sherkat, and Mehrangiz Kar are just a few examples. Even some Khomeinist women such as former Islamic parliamentarians Jamileh Kadivar and Elaheh Koulai, disillusioned with the regime, have tried to atone for political sins by joining the women's struggle for equality. For almost thirty years the regime has waged a persistent campaign against women activists. Women's magazines such as *Zanan* ("Women") and *Khanevadeh* ("Family") have been forced to close, while hundreds of women activists have been sentenced to prison terms of between a few months and fifteen years for alleged anti-state activities. The regime has also tried, and failed, to prevent the celebration of International Women's Day on March 8. Instead it has proposed its own Women's Day on December 16, which is supposed to mark the birthday of Fatima, Muhammad's only daughter. However, the move has drawn opposition even from some mullahs who claim that Islamic events cannot be fixed once and for all according to the Iranian and Gregorian solar calendars. Islam's calendar is lunar, which means that Fatima's birthday could not be fixed on December 16.

In 2007, several women's organizations launched a campaign to collect one million signatures for a petition calling for an end to inequality. In a statement on March 7, 2006, the Organization for Women's Liberation, one of the many groups fighting Khomeinism, had made it clear that Iranian women would not be satisfied with cosmetic changes. They were demanding major reforms that, if implemented, could undermine the ideological foundations of the Khomeinist system. The statement reads in part:

> The movement for women's liberation is, at the present time, the flagship of No to Inequality, No to Discrimination, No to Sexual Apartheid, No to the Veil, and is the flagship of defense of Women's Rights against Cultural Relativism, defense of Secularism and struggle against Political Islam. With its clear platform of action this movement is being organized and led. The progressive movement for women's liberation has, through its activities and influence in many protests, succeeded in pushing back and defeating the Islamic regime's attacks against women. The presence of a radical women's movement is an undeniable reality in Iran.

The statement adds:

> The measure of society's freedom is the freedom of women. To achieve freedom we must overthrow the medieval Islamic rule. So long as this regime is ruling, women and society will not be free. The struggle for women's freedom is part of the general struggle for freedom, equality, and welfare.

That the regime is incapable of delivering even on its promises of limited reform is illustrated by the case of the Lapidation Act, concerning stoning to death. In 2002, President Khatami, bowing to pressure from women's organizations, declared a moratorium on this barbarous practice. The more radical Khomeinist mullahs, however, reacted by issuing even more fatwas sentencing women accused of sexual intercourse outside marriage to death by stoning in public. Between 2003 and 2005, the number of such cases more than doubled as thirty-two women were stoned to death. The self-styled reformist president rubbed his hands together in mock despair. He could do nothing against fatwas that overruled the authority even of a self-styled Islamic state. The precedent was Khomeini's fatwa for the murder of Salman Rushdie. If that fatwa could not be revoked, no fatwa could. This situation could lead to total lawlessness in which any mullah could decide to sentence anyone to death on any charge.

While workers and women are engaged in a deep and long struggle against the fascist regime, the most visible opposition to Khomeinism has come from university students. In July 1999, thousands of Tehran University students revolted against the regime with cries of "Down with the Dictator" and "Freedom of Thought, always, always!" The movement quickly spread to the provinces and within a week had mobilized more than a million students. A photo of Ahmad Batebi, one of the leaders of the movement in Tehran, wearing a bloodstained T-shirt and holding a poster calling for freedom, made the rounds all over the world, prompting comments that Iran was on the verge of a "second revolution." As the movement gathered momentum, other opposition groups watched and waited for the right moment to join.

They waited too long. The regime, badly shaken at first and divided between those who urged immediate repression and those who counseled accommodation, pulled itself together and reacted with terror and bloody repression. Thousands of hired thugs from Hezballah were brought in to occupy the Tehran University campus, while special units of the Baseej, led by General Qalibaf, beat and arrested the protestors. Four students died and hundreds more were injured. Over three thousand others were arrested. In September, an Islamic kangaroo court sentenced six student leaders to death, among them Batebi and Manuchehr Mohammadi. The crackdown came after Khatami, who had initially hesitated, realized that the movement was targeting the very heart of the regime. The students were openly calling for a secular system based on a separation of mosque and state. They were calling on the mullahs to return to their mosques and seminaries, allowing the people to form a democratic government representing the nation's rich diversity. Khatami joined the crackdown after he was told that further hesitation could lead to direct intervention by the IRGC and possibly his own arrest. The uprising and the repression that followed killed all hopes of "change from within," known as *estehaleh* in Persian, and thus effectively ended Khatami's presidency. As one student leader, Akbar Mohammadi, was to observe a few months later, the regime had shown that it was incapable of reform. "We started the movement with the conviction that we were supporting efforts for reforming the system without changing it," he said. "When the movement was crushed and we were in prison, we realized that the only way that Iran could see real change was overthrowing the regime."[3]

Although calm was restored on the campus, the events of the summer of 1999 marked a major defeat for the regime, as it lost its image as the expression of a revolution and acquired a new one as an arbitrary power sustained by repression. Since 1999, Iran has witnessed countless student demonstrations and protests. In hundreds of resolutions passed during mass gatherings, students have challenged virtually every aspect of the Khomeinist ideology and the regime's domestic and foreign policies. One typical resolution passed repeatedly states that the people of Iran do not desire the destruction of Israel and do seek close and friendly relations with the United States. Every year in July, students mark the anniversary of the 1999 events. On October 8, 2007, students in Tehran greeted Ahmadinejad with cries of "Down with the Dictator" and "Forget about Palestine! Think about Us," forcing him to run away briefly with the help of his bodyguards. On March 8, 2008, students marched in some twenty cities across the nation calling for an end to "gender apartheid." This was in reaction to a decision by Ahmadinejad to put men and women students in separate classrooms. Under this scheme, the teacher will be physically present only in the male students' classroom, while female students in another room will follow the lecture on closed-circuit television. Female students who have questions will write them and fax them to the teacher from their separate classroom. Even Khomeini had not dared impose such a system of apartheid on Iranian universities. Khamenehi and Ahmadinejad, however, are persuaded that strict separation of the sexes is a precondition for the return of the Hidden Imam.

The student movement remains a potentially major threat to the regime. Despite the massive purges conducted under Ahmadinejad, accompanied by the entry of thousands of handpicked Khomeinist young men and women exempted from the rigorous entrance examinations because of their loyalty to the regime, the student community remains overwhelmingly hostile to the system. Ahmadinejad's purge of academic personnel has led to the expulsion of hundreds of antifascist lecturers, professors, and deans; yet it is safe to say that a majority of the teaching staff of universities sympathize with the broad aims of the student movement. While it enjoys immense support among young Iranians as a whole, the student movement on its own cannot bring about regime change. One reason is that the students, while united in rejecting Khomeinism, are divided when it comes to a successor. Here we find the entire spectrum of Iranian political opinion, from monarchist and nationalist to social-democratic, socialist, communist, even anarchist.

By all accounts, the generation born and raised after the revolution is the most indifferent, not to say hostile, to the Khomeinist discourse. Young Iranians—in contact with the outside world thanks to satellite TV, the Internet, and travels to Persian Gulf emirates—clearly wish to be part of what they regard as a world of many promises.[4] The popularity of some pre-revolutionary pop stars such as Gugush and Dariush, and the growing audience for Western-style popular music from beat to rap, show that Iranian youth are creating their own space of freedom beyond state control. This is also reflected in the way young Iranians dress. Things are harder for girls because they are forced to wear the hijab and the accursed *manto* in all seasons, yet they still manage to dress in ways that manifest their dislike of the regime. A colorful headscarf worn loosely to let a wild strand of hair fall into view and tight trousers in bright tones to attenuate the somberness of the *manto* do the trick, much to the chagrin of the fascist morality police. Sports occasions, especially soccer matches, also provide young Iranians with an opportunity to display their hatred of fascism while celebrating their favorite sport. Each time there is a major soccer match, the regime is compelled to deploy paramilitary units to prevent the crowds from translating their love of sport into a show of hatred for Khomeinism. In a report prepared for the interior minister, Mullah Mostafa Pour-Mohammadi, in October 2007, a group of Tehran social researchers warned that "growing segments of our youth are disconnected with the ideals of our revolution and the teachings of Islam." The report also showed that less than 5 percent of young people watched religious and/or political programs on the state-owned television networks.

Opposition to the regime and its Islamic-fascist ideology also comes from thousands of nongovernmental organizations active in all walks of life. Offering medical, educational, and cultural services to the community, these NGOs not only fill gaps left by the state but also provide an alternative space in which Iranians can meet and work together away from the hysterical atmosphere of government organs. These NGOs honor the writers and poets banned by the state, and look after those parts of the national cultural heritage neglected by the Khomeinists because of their pre-Islamic origin. Some NGOs also help the families of political prisoners and other victims of repression, whose numbers run into the millions. Families of political prisoners and the "disappeared"— dissidents abducted by the regime and never heard of again—are often in the vanguard of demonstrations against Khomeinism and for freedom and democracy.

Although at war against the Iranian people as a whole, Khomeinism is even more hostile to Iran's religious and ethnic minorities. We have already mentioned the hatred that Khomeinism has always manifested against Jews, Baha'is, and Sunni Muslims because these faiths offer spaces in which their adepts can build a moral and even physical alternative to the public space controlled by the Khomeinists. A totalitarian regime cannot tolerate the existence of any space where it does not enjoy full control. In recent years, the regime has developed a hostile attitude towards Christians and Zoroastrians as well, communities that had hitherto enjoyed slightly better treatment than Jews, Baha'is, and Sunnis. The reason is that a growing number of Iranians, especially the young, are converting to Zoroastrianism or Christianity. The authorities claim that this surge in conversions is due to the activities of evangelical missions dispatched by American Christian churches, and some Zoroastrian organizations in India, Europe, and the United States, to tempt young Iranians with promises of easy immigration and good jobs abroad. However, there is little doubt that many young Iranians, repulsed by the image of Islam as presented by the fascists, are shopping around for a faith with which they might feel more comfortable. In 2002, the Ministry of Intelligence and Security ordered all Christian churches to close their doors outside specially approved masses, and make sure that those who attended the mass were "Christians of long-standing well-known to their community."[5] The ministry also arranged for special agents to be present at all church ceremonies. Instantly recognizable by their look and attitude, these agents sit in the back pews and are referred to as "the cockroaches of the end." Their task is to make sure that no criticism of the regime is aired in church and, above all, that no Muslim apostates are admitted.

The regime's fear of a mass conversion of young people to Christianity was first aired under Khatami, who ordered the drafting of a law to deal with change of religion or apostasy. Before the revolution, there was no mechanism for preventing individuals or even whole groups from switching to another religion. The Khatami administration tried to fill the gap with a draft law completed in 2005. At the time, lawyers from the Ministry of Foreign Affairs warned that a law on apostasy would run counter to Iran's commitments under the Universal Declaration of Human Rights and other international obligations. The presentation of the text was delayed until after the presidential election that produced Ahmadinejad's victory. Nevertheless, a crackdown was started without any legal basis and hundreds of Muslim converts to Christianity had their homes raided and then were imprisoned on charges relating to espionage. Many Christian converts were held for weeks and were physically and psychologically mistreated. Astronomical bails were required for their release.

Forbidden to spread their faith and even to attend church, these converts created a new institution known as *Kelisa-Khaneh* or "house church," turning their homes into places of worship and religious study. According to Carl Moeller, president of Open Doors USA, a charity that supports converts in the Middle East, Iranian authorities "are recognizing that there's a mushrooming house church movement going on in Iran. . . . This indigenous house church movement doubles in size every six months. So the rate of growth is actually stunning."[6] Calling Iranians to Christianity is facilitated by the fact that in Persian literature, Jesus Christ is easily the most popular figure associated with religion.

In January 2008, Ahmadinejad vowed to "root out this new Christianity" in Iran. Soon he presented a draft law to the Islamic Majlis based on the text prepared by Khatami, but adding tougher punishments for apostates. The new text describes the act of abandoning Islam, whether for the purpose of converting to another religion or simply living with no religion at all, as "a crime against the security of the Islamic state." Those found guilty of apostasy would become "Corrupters on Earth" (*Mufsed fil*

Ardh) and thus punishable by the Islamic *hadd* (limit), which means capital punishment. By June 2008, the text had not yet been enacted into law, and there was a chance that it would not be, as the new Majlis elected in March was not bound to adopt the legislative program set by Ahmadinejad for the previous parliament. If adopted, the text under its Article 112 could expose anyone, whether of Iranian origin or not, who abandons Islam anywhere in the world to death fatwas issued from Tehran. Anyone born even with a single Muslim parent, grandparent or ancestor is automatically considered as Muslim and forbidden to change his or her faith. The proposed law also creates a new crime under the title "Insulting the Prophet" (*Sibb al-Nabi*), which would also be punishable by death. This law would officially sentence Rushdie to death once again, along with the Danish cartoonists of Prophet Muhammad. The new draft is especially dangerous for Baha'is of Iranian origin because all of them have had Muslim grandparents or ancestors.

In June 2008, over thirty Iranians, including a pregnant woman, were in prison on charges of apostasy, according to human rights groups. Of special concern to the Khomeinists is the fact that conversion to Christianity and Zoroastrianism does not appear to be a middle-class, urban phenomenon. The four hundred or so individuals arrested on such a charge and then released came from all over the country, including small towns and villages.

29

The Ethnic Time Bomb

In September 2005, a group of armed Kurdish rebels attacked an outpost of the Islamic Revolutionary Guard Corps (IRGC) in the Mount Qandil area, close to the border with Iraq. Although the operation did not cause serious casualties, it was significant because it marked an end to almost twenty years of calm in the three Iranian provinces where the Kurdish minority live. Something else was new in this operation: the group that carried it out did not belong to any of the traditional Kurdish parties active in Iran since 1940. It was a new group, designating itself as the Party of Free Life in Kurdistan, soon to be known under its Persian acronym, Pejak.

Tehran was surprised by the attack, if only because it thought it had the upper hand in the Kurdish area. Since 2004 it had bombed and raided a number of Kurdish villages in Iraq, ostensibly to destroy bases created there by two Iranian Kurdish opposition groups, the Communist Party of Kurdistan (Komaleh) and the Democratic Party of Kurdistan (PDK), with support from the newly liberated Kurds of Iraq. Tehran had hoped that its Kurdish arm, known as the Kurdistan Hezballah, operating in Iraq, would make sure that no Kurdish group dared attack the Islamic Republic. Pejak, however, was a new group set up by Iranian Kurds mostly living in exile in Germany and France. After the liberation of Iraq in 2003, they went to Iraqi Kurdistan and recruited a number of fighters from among disillusioned Komaleh and PDK members. Pejak also had strong links with the Kurdistan Workers' Party (PKK), a Communist outfit operating in Turkey since the 1970s.

Between 2004 and 2008, Pejak rebels carried out more than fifty operations against Iranian positions, killing dozens of IRGC men and wounding many more. In retaliation, the IRGC has raided Kurdish villages in Iraq, killing hundreds and capturing dozens of suspected militants. In March 2008, Pejak launched its most daring operations by entering the small Iranian Kurdish town of Mahkok and holding it for a few hours, and by raiding an IRGC position in Marivan, a much bigger town. These operations, although militarily insignificant, shattered the region's calm and revived talks of armed struggle amongst Kurds.

As an ethnic minority, the Kurds, most of whom are Sunni Muslims or heretical Shiites and Zoroastrians, felt doubly oppressed in the Islamic Republic. With Ahmadinejad's coming to power, they have been subjected to even more repressive measures. The only publications appearing in the Kurdish language were closed in 2006, and the only theater company offering plays in Kurdish dissolved. Worse still, the fascist regime has carried out a massive purge of the civil service, the teachers' corps, and the independent trade union movement, supposedly to weed out "Kurdish separatists." In June 2008, over a thousand Kurds were held as political prisoners by the regime, often on trumped-up charges of anti-state activity. This made the Kurds the ethnic minority with the largest number of political prisoners in the Islamic Republic. Between 2004 and 2008, more than fifty Kurdish activists were sentenced to death and executed, among them trade unionists, journalists, and schoolteachers. Some parts of the province of Kurdistan and the neighboring province of West Azerbaijan, where Kurds account for at least half the population, were turned into no-go areas in 2007, indicating the regime's loss of legitimacy and control. Ahmadinejad's iron-fist policy has created new risks of a long and costly war of the kind that Turkey has suffered in its Kurdish areas for three decades.

The fascist regime has also provoked ethnic unrest among Iran's Arab minority in the oil-rich province of Khuzestan. During the 1990s, both Rafsanjani and Khatami tried to dilute the Arab presence in sensitive areas close to the border with Iraq by bringing in settlers from other parts of Iran, especially the central province of Yazd. According to some estimates, over the past eighteen years more than 800,000

Arabs have been displaced from their ancestral villages, their places being taken by non-Arab settlers. Many of the displaced Arabs had left their homes after Saddam Hussein's invasion of Iran in 1980 and spent the eight years of war in temporary camps all over the country. At the end of the war and much to their surprise and anger, they were told that they could not go back to their villages and had to settle in other parts of the country. While the Kurds share ethnic and linguistic roots with other Iranians, the Arabs of Iran are a distinct people with their own ethnic and linguistic heritage. What binds them to Iran is the shared Shiite faith, the broad Iranian culture, and a common history going back three millennia. Iranian Arabs demonstrated their attachment to Iran as homeland by fighting the Saddamite invaders and sustaining more casualties than any other component of the nation. Yet the fascist regime has rewarded them with displacement, and cultural and political repression.

Not surprisingly, Iranian Arabs have reacted with massive demonstrations in more than a dozen cities, including the provincial capital of Ahvaz and the oil city of Abadan. Dozens of Arabs have been killed in clashes with the Baseej and other repressive forces of the regime. Between 2005 and March 2008, more than one hundred Iranian Arabs were executed or murdered by Khomeinist death squads, among them trade unionists, writers, musicians, and tribal figures. In March 2008, more than four hundred Iranian Arabs were still in prison or listed among the "disappeared." Tension was high in many parts of the province, especially in the border areas with Iraq, such as Dasht Mishan, Susangerd and Hoveyzeh. Several Arab tribes—including the Bani-Amer, the Bani-Turuf, and the Bani-Kaab—were reportedly buying arms to create self-defense units against the regime. The liberation of Iraq and the advent of a democratically elected government dominated by the Shiite majority had inspired immense hopes for the spread of democracy to Iran, thus giving Iranian Arabs the same rights that new Iraq had granted to its Kurdish minority. However, the opposite has happened. As free Iraq has built itself up in the teeth of opposition from Sunni extremists and sabotage by Tehran-backed groups, Iranian Arabs have been subjected to even greater repression.

In 2008, the Iranian Arab political movement was divided into three distinct trends. The most militant, still representing a small but active minority, operated under the label of Ahvaz Liberation Front. This is a secessionist group that dreams of a separate Arab state covering almost half the province of Khuzestan and most of its oil reserves. Using violence and terror, this group has been responsible for a number of bomb attacks in the province since 2005. Another trend is represented by a number of groups fighting for human rights and democratization. These are generally peaceful movements trying to operate within the limits of the Islamic Republic's constitution. They include the remnants of the Khuzestan Welfare Party (Hizb Saadat Khuzestan) of the 1940s, which promoted the idea of a federal Iran in which ethnic Arabs would enjoy a large measure of autonomy in areas where they formed a majority of the population. The third trend consists of groups dedicated to the overthrow of the Khomeinist regime but not willing to use arms against it. However, the fascist regime's increasingly repressive posture in the province risked weakening the position of the moderates, forcing more and more ethnic Arabs into the arms of the outright secessionists.

The regime is also facing ethnic unrest at the other end of the country, among the Baluch in the southeastern province of Sistan and Baluchistan. There, too, large chunks of Iranian territory have become no-go areas, with armed clashes between rebels and the IRGC an almost weekly occurrence. In 2008, Tehran accused Pakistan of encouraging and partly financing the most radical of the armed groups, named Jund-Allah (Army of Allah) and led by Abdul-Malik Riggi, a thirty-year-old former student, apparently in retaliation for the Islamic Republic's support for Pakistani Baluchi rebels since 1993. In parts of what is called the "Wild East" of the country, government officials and mullahs are forced to travel by helicopter or under heavy armed escort to avoid ambush by rebels. In some areas such as Pishin, Magas, and Jakeguvar, the Khomeinist regime has all but disappeared, leaving behind a no-man's land close to the borders with Pakistan and Afghanistan.

Like their Iranian siblings in Kurdistan and Khuzestan, the Baluch, though almost unanimous against the Khomeinist regime, are divided into several trends. The most militant consists of radical Sunni fundamentalists close to Salafist groups in the Arab world. Inspired by the Taliban in Afghanistan, these groups are even more reactionary than the Khomeinists. For example, they are so obsessed with the issue of hijab that they have forced everyone, male and female, to wear full-length burqahs in public from the age of six. In the enclave of Pishin, for example, a visitor gets the impression of a land of ghosts covered from head to toe with two holes left for the eyes. Although more than 80 percent of the Baluch are Sunni Muslims, these extremists have not been able to secure a large following. Financed by wealthy Salafi groups in Arab countries in the Persian Gulf, these groups are nevertheless able to buy some support among the poorest Baluch.

The second trend is represented by Jund-Allah and a number of tribal armed groups, fighting to overthrow the Khomeinist regime and replace it with a federal Iranian state in which ethnic minorities enjoy autonomous rights envisaged for them in the 1906 Constitution. They protest against the regime's efforts to convert the Baluch to Shiism through propaganda, force, and bribery. By 2008, however, none of these groups had succeeded in developing a political platform that could appeal to the broader strata of society, especially in urban areas.

Finally, there is a third trend consisting of outright secessionists such as the Baluch Liberation Front, led by elements from the Lashari (Shahbakhshi) tribe. At least some of these groups are partly financed by drug barons in Afghanistan and Pakistan. Their scheme is to create a Greater Baluchistan composed of all Baluch-majority parts of Afghanistan, Pakistan, and Iran. Such a state could then become a safe haven for drug barons who now control almost half of all heroin supplies in the world. Linked to the drug barons are organized smuggling gangs that sell billions of dollars of contraband goods in Iran, Pakistan, Afghanistan and Central Asia each year. Worse still, large chunks of the vast semi-desert area shared by Iran, Pakistan, and Afghanistan risk becoming safe havens for terrorists. The Khomeinist regime's repressive policies and its systematic violation of the basic human rights of the Baluch favor the darkest elements among them.

The fourth ethnic minority moving rapidly towards open rebellion against the regime is the Turkmen, who inhabit a vast arc of land from the Caspian Sea in the west to the northernmost corner of Iran's border with Afghanistan in the east. Like the Kurds and the Baluch, the Turkmen are mostly Sunni Muslims and distinguished from other Iranians by ethnic background and language. In the 1920s, Turkmen rose in revolt and declared a Soviet Republic with support from Moscow. Reza Khan, the general who became shah in 1925, destroyed their short-lived republic. Over two hundred Turkmen chiefs were hanged and hundreds of families transported far from Turkmen territories. However, from the 1930s until the seizure of power by the mullahs in 1979, the Turkmen did relatively well as their region was transformed into a major agricultural center producing cash crops, including almost 90 percent of Iran's cotton, much of it destined for export. In 1945, encouraged by Stalin, some Turkmen again rose in rebellion, this time under the red flag, but failed to make much of an impression as the overwhelming majority of Turkmen had no wish to live under Communism. The third revolt came in 1979 with the declaration of an autonomous Turkmen Republic, created by the People's Fedayeen Guerrilla Organization (PFGO), a Marxist-Maoist outfit dedicated to a Communist revolution. The adventure ended when the IRGC arrived to crush the rebels, most of whom were not Turkmen.

Since 2005, growing repression combined with widespread poverty has once again driven the Turkmen to revolt. The immediate cause of the latest wave of revolts that started in January 2008 is the IRGC's monopolization of fishing in the caviar-rich Caspian Sea, thus depriving thousands of Turkmen fishermen of their sole source of income. The trigger for the revolt came on January 4, when an IRGC gunboat shot and killed a twenty-year-old Turkmen fisherman in the coastal waters of

the Caspian. The authorities claimed that the fisherman, one Hissmaud-
din Khadivar, had been part of an illegal fishing expedition whose thirty
or so members were later arrested, and that his death was an accident.
As news of the incident spread, bands of angry Turkmen, some armed
with daggers and sticks, attacked government offices and set vehicles on
fire. One group attacked a police station; another tried to lay siege to the
local IRGC barracks near the fishing port of Bandar-Turkmen. The riots
continued for two days, ending after reinforcements flew in from other
cities. Over the two days, more than three hundred people were arrested
and taken away to unknown destinations. A spokesman for the Turkmen
Human Rights Group said that dozens were injured. How many might
have died was unclear, because the Guard took some of the injured with
them, ostensibly for hospitalization in other towns. In March 2008 it was
established that eleven people, including four children, had died in the
clashes. As antigovernment demonstrations rocked a number of other
cities, including Gonbad Kavous and Quchan, where Turkmen are a
majority, a state of emergency was imposed by the IRGC. The Turkmen
anger was so strong and widespread as to oblige the government in Ash-
gabat, capital of neighboring Turkmenistan, to stop its flow of natural
gas to Iran, provoking a diplomatic tussle with Tehran.

Khadivar is not the first Turkmen fisherman to be killed in an incident
involving the IRGC's naval units in the Caspian. Since Tehran banned
unauthorized fishing in the inland sea in 1996, dozens of men in search
of caviar-rich sturgeon have died in clashes with security forces. Why did
Khadivar's death trigger such anger? Some observers point to President
Ahmadinejad's economic policies, which have produced a 17 percent inflation rate and thrown thousands out of work. Unemployment among the
Turkmen is estimated at 40 percent, three times the official national rate.
Another grievance is the government's refusal to allow Turkmen even a
toehold in local administration. All top jobs in Golestan and in Turkmen
towns in other provinces are held by Shiites from other parts of Iran.
The government prefers to employ migrant workers from Afghanistan
and Baluchistan to work in the Turkmen area's vast state-owned cotton

fields. And besides making Caspian fishing a state monopoly, Tehran has also imposed central control on water distribution from the River Atrak, reserving the bulk of it for state-owned farms and estates, owned by rich mullahs and Guard commanders, where few Turkmen work. Turkmen farmers, mostly smallholders, are left with little or no water. Turkmen claim that they have the lowest life expectancy in Iran.

They also complain of a massive government campaign to convert them to Shiism. While no permit is issued for building Sunni mosques, the number of Shiite places of prayer and mourning has multiplied in Turkmen towns and villages. Shiite mullahs from Qom conduct periodic conversion "raids" into Turkmen towns and villages, using the promise of jobs and perks as inducements. Turkmen say that they are denied fair access to higher education. Those who manage to apply for university places are often turned away because they fail religious tests based on Shiism; and their inadequate mastery of Persian reduces their chances further.

Turkmen form a majority in Golestan province; they are also present in North Khorassan (along the border with the former Soviet Republic of Turkmenistan) and the Caspian province of Mazandaran. They say Tehran has gerrymandered them across four provinces to curtail their political influence by denying them the number of seats they might otherwise have won in the Islamic Majlis.

Tehran authorities blame the Turkmen revolt on "counterrevolutionaries," allegedly supported by the United States. In fact, the revolt highlights the failure of a narrowly based ideological regime to understand the pluralist nature of Iranian society and the legitimate aspirations of its diverse component parts for dignity, equal opportunity, and a fair share in decision-making.

Another area of Iran in a state of civil unrest—though not full revolt as is the case in Kurdistan, Sistan and Baluchistan, and Golestan provinces—is Talesh county, on the southwestern tip of the Caspian Sea. The Taleshis are of pure Iranian stock and speak one of the oldest Iranic languages. What distinguishes them from a majority of their fellow Iranians is their Sunni Muslim faith. Many Taleshis regard the fascist regime's aggressive Shiism as a permanent threat to their identity, as Tehran pours in massive resources of money and manpower to convert the Sunnis to the Khomeinist version of Shiism. The Taleshis also resent the regime's persistent refusal to declare their region a full province, thus making it eligible for greater financial aid from the central government. Tehran has elevated the neighboring town of Ardebil into a full province but refuses the same favor to Talesh. The reason is that the mullahs do not wish to create yet another province with a Sunni majority.

Over the coming years, the ethnic time bomb may prove the most serious threat to Iran's existence as a unified nation-state. Several neighboring countries believe that the only way to neutralize what they perceive as an Iranian threat is to push Iran towards Yugoslav-style disintegration. That is unlikely to happen, however. Unlike Yugoslavia, which was a recently created and totally artificial state, Iran is an ancient nation with deep cultural and historic roots binding its many peoples together. Even when backed by a superpower such as the USSR in the 1940s, secessionism failed to divide Iran into a number of mini states. This is why Iranian patriots should not use the fear of secessionism as an excuse for not even discussing the very real discrimination directed at ethnic, linguistic, and religious minorities. The fascist regime's policy of systematic repression is likely to lead the country into endless low-intensity war against rebels using ethnic and religious grievances as a pretext. The failure of both pre-liberation Iraq and Turkey to "solve" the Kurdish problem by force must be a lesson for Tehran decision-makers as they face what looks like a series of ethnic revolts in the four corners of the country.

While the fascist regime faces increasing opposition from workers, teachers, women, students, and ethnic and religious minorities inside the country, it is also challenged by a diverse and robust opposition in exile that covers virtually the entire spectrum of political ideologies. The presence of millions of Iranians of several generations abroad gives this opposition a space in which to develop and grow. The traditional view of exiles, of course, is that of a bunch of romantic idealists fighting ideological battles in the cafes of Paris and the lobby of the British Museum in London. Everyone remembers the quip by the Swiss pension manager who observed that Mr. Bronstein (Trotsky) and his comrades would never be able to topple the tsar. In 1999, a senior official in Saddam Hussein's government offered a reporter a substantial bet that the Hakim family would never return to Iraq. The reporter did not take the bet, but the Hakims returned to Iraq in 2003 to become part of a new governing elite, while the senior Saddamite was in prison.

The two largest exile movements among Iranians are the monarchists and the Mujahedin Khalq, the People's Holy Warriors. While the monarchists acknowledge Reza Pahlavi, heir to the Iranian crown, as their overall leader, they are divided into more than a dozen rival groups; by contrast, the Mujahedin look like a hermetic sect.

The more radical supporters of Reza Pahlavi want a straight return to monarchy, with the heir as the future shah. Others, including Reza Pahlavi himself, offer a referendum on the future system of government, leaving the choice to the people. Although they enjoy a great capital of goodwill, partly inspired by nostalgia for what many Iranians see as their "golden age," the monarchists have not succeeded in developing a coherent political program or promoting an easily identifiable leadership. Nevertheless, the monarchists remain a force to reckon with in forming a broad patriotic coalition to oppose and eventually replace the fascist regime.

The Mujahedin Khalq, better known under their acronym of MKO, are an active element of the exile opposition but have failed to broaden their original support base. The reason is their sectarian attitude, their insistence that they have already written a new constitution for Iran and even elected its future president in the person of Mrs. Maryam Rajavi, the estranged wife of their supreme leader Massoud Rajavi. The latter has lived in Iraq for the past quarter century, first under Saddam Hussein's protection, and since 2003 thanks to a policy of benevolent neglect by the U.S.-led coalition. The U.S. forces in Iraq have disarmed the 3,500 Mujahedin who had been armed by Saddam Hussein for broader raids against the Islamic Republic and put them under virtual arrest in their camp northeast of Baghdad. Originally a Marxist-Islamist movement, the MKO has developed into a sect dedicated to the destruction of the Khomeinist regime and the handover of the country to the Rajavi couple. In 2008, however, there were signs that at least a section of the MKO leadership was pondering a less sectarian program and possible alliances with other opposition movements. Were that to happen, the MKO, although declared a terrorist organization by the State Department in Washington, could emerge as a significant part of a broad anti-Khomeinist coalition.

Outside the monarchists and the Mujahedin, Iranian opposition in exile also includes a wide range of leftist parties, from the Tudeh (Masses) to social-democrats modeled on Western European parties. What is encouraging is that almost all the exile opposition groups have committed themselves to a pluralist and democratic system of government. Even the hard left no longer calls for the establishment of a one-party state in the name of the "dictatorship of the proletariat." This collective commitment to democracy, even if not sincere in every case, restores the situation that existed in Iran between the 1880s and the 1920s. In that period, Iranian intellectuals came into contact with modern Western political ideas and began to fight for an end to absolutism in Iran.

The Bolshevik Revolution in Russia in 1917 divided the Iranian intellectual elite into left and right, just as it had divided the European socialist movements. This division proved fatal for Iran's hopes of democracy. Fearing that democratization could lead to Communist revolution and the annexation of Iran by the Soviet Union, the intellectuals of the right decided that their priority was preserving the nation's independence rather than extending individual and collective freedoms. That analysis led them into collaboration with the authoritarian regimes of the two Pahlavi monarchs, a collaboration they tried to justify by pointing to the achievements of both shahs in uniting and modernizing the country. The intellectuals of the left, on the other hand, imitated Lenin in rejecting even the possibility of slow but steady reform. Under Soviet influence they believed that Iran had to break with the "imperialist" camp before it could have any chance of meaningful change. Based on that analysis, the Iranian left supported Khomeini and his obscurantist associates in seizing power.

Although the right-left divide remains, it is no longer an unbridgeable gap. Left and right could, and do, compete for support, but are no longer prepared to form alliances with Islamist fascists or secular absolutists. The disappearance of the USSR has removed the prospect of Soviet domination through an Iranian "fifth column," something that haunted the Iranian right as a nightmare for three generations. At the same time, a majority of Iranian leftists have realized that had they sided with the shah rather than Khomeini in 1979, Iran might have avoided this long Persian Night.

Because Iranian exiles of both left and right have lived in Western democracies, they have learned much from the political systems of their host countries. They have not only seen *how* democracy works but, more importantly perhaps, *that* it works. They have witnessed changes of governments through free elections and learned that coups, armed uprisings, and revolutions are not the only methods of attaining power. Since Ahmadinejad's coming to power, a number of the Khomeinist regime's internal critics and loyal opponents have also gone into exile, or they spend part of the year in Europe and the United States. These include Ghulam-Hussein Karbaschi, former mayor of Tehran and still a popular figure; Ata-Allah Mohajerani, former minister for Islamic guidance and culture; and Ibrahim Yazdi, a former foreign minister. Their presence abroad provided an opportunity for internal and external opponents of Khomeinism to establish a dialogue that, although at times hostile and marred by mutual suspicions, could help a larger segment of the regime part ways with it when the moment comes.

30

A Heaving Volcano

If many of the preconditions for regime change are in place, is the time right? To this, too, the answer is yes. Again without underestimating the power of the mullahs, the truth is that Iran today, far from being the island of calm portrayed in some leading American newspapers, is more nearly like a heaving volcano, ready to explode. This does not mean that the regime is going to collapse anytime soon or that the current economic crisis is sounding its death toll. What it means is that the Khomeinist regime has become overthrowable, something that it was not in the first two decades of its existence. But even overthrowable regimes do not fall on their own; someone must overthrow them.

In the words of Muhammad-Mahdi Pour-Fatemi, a member of the Islamic Majlis, Iran today is passing through "the deepest crisis our nation has experienced in decades." Because of "policies that have produced nothing but grief for our nation," Pour-Fatemi has courageously said, "the Islamic Republic today is isolated." The fall in value of the Iranian currency—despite rising oil revenues—and the massive increase in the rate of unemployment over the past two years signal an economic crisis already heralded by double-digit inflation. In some cases, the government has been unable to pay its employees—including the protesting teachers—on time. In 2006 and 2007, it faced difficulty financing over half its projects, forcing hundreds of private contractors into bankruptcy. Meanwhile, fear of an international crisis over the nuclear issue, and the possibility of even more biting sanctions imposed by the United Nations and/or the United States, have put a damper on the economy's only buoyant sector: real estate. According to Ayatollah Shahroudi, the regime's chief justice, the flight of capital from the Islamic Republic, which started as a hemorrhage, has been transformed in the past two years into "a flood."

It is not only on the economic front or in his confrontations with labor unions and women's and student organizations that Ahmadinejad is coming under pressure. As noted above, his regime also faces growing ethnic unrest that has led to bloodshed in provinces with non-Persian majorities: the Kurds in the west, the Arabs in the south, and the Baluch in the southeast, among others. Over the past eighteen months, hundreds of people have been killed in clashes with the central security forces. Dozens of ethnic leaders have been executed, thousands have been put under arrest, and many more have been driven into exile in Iraq, Turkey, and Pakistan. So uncertain is the security situation in the affected areas that Ahmadinejad has been forced to cancel planned visits to eight of the nation's thirty provinces.

In an effort to terrorize the people, the regime has ordered a dramatic increase in the number of executions, mostly by hanging in public. In 2007 alone, over 400 people were executed, while at least 150 more, including five women, were scheduled to be hanged or stoned to death, according to Saeed Mortazavi, the chief Islamic prosecutor.

The current wave of executions is the biggest Iran has suffered since 1984, when thousands of opposition prisoners were shot on Khomeini's orders. Not all executions take place in public. In the provinces of Kurdistan and Khuzestan, where ethnic Kurdish and Arab minorities are demanding greater rights, several activists have been put to death in secret, their families informed only days after the event. The campaign of terror also includes targeted "disappearances" designed to neutralize trade union leaders, student activists, journalists, and even mullahs opposed to the regime. According to the latest tally, more than thirty people have "disappeared" since the start of the new Iranian year on March 21. To intimidate the population, in 2007 the authorities also carried out mass arrests on spurious grounds. According to General Ismail Muqaddam, commander of the Islamic Police, a total of 430,000 men and women have been arrested on charges related to drug use. A further 4,209 men and women, mostly between ages fifteen and thirty, were arrested for "hooliganism" in Tehran alone. The largest number of arrests, totaling almost a million men and women according to Muqaddam, were related to the enforcement of the new Islamic Dress Code, passed by the Islamic Majlis in May 2006. Most of those arrested, he says, spent a few hours, or at most a few days, in custody as a "warning." According to the deputy chief of police, General Hussein Zulfiqari, an additional 6,204 men and women were in prison on charges of "sexual proximity" without being married.

The wave of arrests has increased pressure on the nation's inadequate prison facilities. At a press conference in Tehran in 2007, the head of the National Prisons Service, Ali-Akbar Yassaqi, appealed for a moratorium on arrests. He said Iran's official prisons could not house more than 50,000 prisoners simultaneously, while the actual number of prisoners at any given time was above 150,000. Yassaqi also revealed that each year on average some 600,000 Iranians spend some time in one of the 130 official prisons. Since Ahmadinejad ordered the crackdown, work on converting forty-one official buildings to prisons has started, with contracts for thirty-three other prisons already signed. Nevertheless, with the annual prison population likely to top the million mark in 2008, Yassaqi believes that even this new capacity might prove insufficient. There are, however, an unknown number of unofficial prisons as well, often controlled by the IRGC or militias working for various prominent mullahs. In 2008, human rights activists in Iran published details of a new prison in Souleh, northwest of Tehran, staffed by militants from the Lebanese branch of Hezballah. According to the revelations, the Souleh prison is under the control of the Supreme Guide, Ali Khamenehi, and is used for holding the regime's most "dangerous" political foes.

The nationwide crackdown is accompanied by efforts to cut Iranians off from sources of information outside the Islamic Republic. More than four thousand Internet sites have been blocked, and more are added to the list each day. The Ministry of Islamic Orientation has established a new blacklist of authors and book titles twice as long as the one in effect a year ago. In 2007, some thirty newspapers and magazines as well as two news agencies were shut down and their offices raided. At least seventeen journalists were in prison, two already sentenced to death by hanging.

The regime is trying to mobilize its shrinking base by claiming that the Islamic Republic is under threat from internal and external foes. It was in that context that the four Iranian-American hostages held in Tehran were forced to make televised "confessions" about alleged plots to foment a "velvet revolution." In 2007, over forty people were arrested on charges of espionage, twenty in the southern city of Shiraz. Khomeinist paranoia reached a new peak when the authorities announced, through the Islamic Republic News Agency, the capture of four squirrels in the Western city of Kermanshah and claimed that the furry creatures had been fitted with "espionage devices" by the Americans in Iraq and smuggled into Iran.

Ahmadinejad likes to pretend that he has no worries except "infidel plots" related to the Islamic Republic's nuclear ambitions. The truth is that, faced with growing popular discontent, the Khomeinist clique is vulnerable and worried—extremely worried. The outside world would do well to monitor carefully and, whenever possible, support the Iranian people's fight against the fascist regime in Tehran. Iran today is not only about atomic bombs and Iranian-American hostages. It is also about a growing popular movement that may help bring the nation out of the dangerous impasse created by the mullahs.

Since his election Ahmadinejad has been desperate to provoke a mini conflict with the United States in order to divert attention from the gathering storm inside Iran. He is trying to position himself as the leader of the Non-Aligned Movement, in the hope of creating an alliance of all the anti-American and antidemocratic forces in the world, including those in the West itself. His strategy is premised on the assumption that the West has no stomach for a real fight, and that the worst that could happen to his regime is a few attacks on its nuclear sites—something that would have the advantage of shifting the focus from his domestic problems and bestowing on his regime a veneer of victimhood. Most of all, he is hoping that the next American president will revert to the confused policies pursued by previous U.S. administrations.

In his address to the UN General Assembly in September 2006, President Bush showed unmistakably that he understands the desire of the people of Iran for freedom and self-determination. If that is the vision, the best way to proceed towards implementing it is to remain guided always by the recognition that the Islamic Republic is evil because its nature is evil—and that, although its behavior may intermittently be influenced, ultimately the regime itself must be defeated and replaced. With a clear compass, the litmus test for any particular policy towards Iran will likewise be clear: does this activity, program, or initiative help or hinder regime change? Under this general guideline, any number of specific policies can be envisioned, some of them already in place. For instance, the adoption of a regime-change strategy does not preclude American participation in diplomatic initiatives focused on particular issues, such as the efforts to engage the Islamic Republic in the matter of its nuclear ambitions. But the crucial criterion is that *process* must not be allowed to become a substitute for *policy*. In the hope of winning concessions from the mullahs, the three EU partners in the talks—Germany, France, and the UK—have chosen to ignore the question of the sanctions already envisaged under the Nuclear Non-Proliferation Treaty for the regime's repeated violations of its provisions; the United States, by contrast, can and should press for their application.

Flexibility is also key. No one knows for sure how long it will take the Islamic Republic to develop or deploy a serious arsenal of nuclear weapons. Just as diplomacy need not be ruled out on this and other issues, the military option should also remain on the table. Just as tactics of containment and even of détente need not be ruled out when and if they seem clearly designed to hasten regime change, neither should tactics aimed at rollback.

Like a pair of angry cats contesting the same space, Iran and the United States have been frowning and making warlike gestures over who should set the agenda in the Middle East for a quarter of a century. At some point, the two cats must jump at one another. In a sense, as we have already shown the two have been at war since 1979 when Khomeinist militants raided the U.S. embassy in Tehran and took its diplomats hostage. The question, therefore, is not whether to go to war, but how to end a war that has been going on for three decades.

Since Ahmadinejad's election, the Islamic Republic has been preparing for another high point in its protracted war. Tehran has intensified the arming of Hezballah, renewed contacts with Shiite militants in Arab states, and increased its military budget by 21 percent. It also resumed uranium enrichment to put its controversial nuclear program into high gear, thus provoking a diplomatic tussle with the United States and its allies. In Afghanistan, Iran reactivated Gulbuddin Hekmatyar's Hizb Islami militia, shipped arms to the Is'haqzai Pushtun tribe, and helped Hazara Shiites raise an army of 12,000. Iran also opened its borders to fleeing Taliban and al-Qaeda militants. According to Arab intelligence sources, some thirty senior "Arab Afghans" are in Iran. To exert pressure on another U.S. ally, Iran has shipped arms to Baluchi rebels in Pakistan, including Marri tribesmen led by Nawab Khair-Baksh. Next, Tehran established contact with Palestinian radicals, notably Hamas, feting its leaders in Tehran and providing aid worth $500 million. Last year's capture of Iranian military advisors in Gaza shows that Tehran was also involved in training Palestinian fighters. In the summer of 2006, Tehran fought a proxy war against Washington in Lebanon, as Israel, the United States' regional ally, dueled with Hezballah, the Islamic Republic's cat's-paw in the Arab world. A month before the war, Tehran had signed a defense treaty with Syria, turning it into a client state. In April and May 2008, Tehran, again using Hezballah, organized a political coup against the pro-Western government of Prime Minister Fouad Siniora in Lebanon. The conflict ended with Hezballah gaining an effective veto on government decisions, while two UN resolutions demanding that the Shiite militia be disarmed were put on the back burner.

Since 2006, however, Iraq has become the principal battleground in the indirect war between the Khomeinist regime and the United States.

Tehran strategists assume that if the Americans run away, Iraq will be divided into three mini states: Kurdish, Sunni, and Shiite. Invoking the nineteenth-century Treaty of Erzerum, which gives Iran certain rights in Iraq's Shiite areas, Tehran hopes to play "big brother" to a future mini state in southern Iraq. The list of U.S. accusations against Tehran includes:

- Supplying Iraqi militants with roadside bombs, known as explosively formed projectiles (EFPs), which have killed at least 170 U.S. soldiers and maimed over 600 others.

- Supplying Iraqi insurgents, both Sunni and Shiite, with sniper rifles bought by Iran from Austria in 2002.

- Recruiting, training, and financing a number of Iraqi Shiite militias, notably the Mahdi Army, led by Moqtada Sadr.

- Setting up command-and-control networks to coordinate insurgent attacks on U.S. forces in Iraq. Seventy-eight members of Iran's Islamic Revolutionary Guard Corps and security services have been arrested in Iraq, including seven senior officers captured in raids in Erbil and Baghdad. Among them were Muhsin Shirazi and Muhammad-Jaafar Sahraroudi, who have been in charge of pro-Iran militant groups abroad since the 1980s.

- Offering safe haven to anti-U.S. militants, including Jamal Jaafar-Muhammad, a member of the Iraqi National Assembly who coordinated the smuggling of EFPs into Iraq. Moqtada Sadr is also in Iran along with Abu-Hamza, a leader of al-Qaeda, and Ramadan al-Shalah, leader of the Islamic Jihad Organization.

The Islamic Republic cannot allow the imposition of a Pax Americana in which Khomeinism could have no place. The United States, for its part, cannot allow its Khomeinist foes to dominate a region that contains half the world's oil and gas reserves. The conventional wisdom is that with the U.S. Army bogged down in Iraq and Afghanistan, Washington cannot wage full-scale war against the Islamic Republic. This ignores the fact that the U.S. Navy and Air Force remain fully free and ready for action. In any case, the choice is not limited to either invading Iran or surrendering to the mullahs. Between the two, a range of options is available.

Some are already being used. These include moves known in military jargon as "proximity pressure." In 2007, President Bush changed the rules of engagement in Iraq to allow U.S. forces to capture or kill Khomeinist infiltrators. The arrival of two naval battle groups in the Persian Gulf soon afterwards represented the biggest concentration of firepower there since 1990. These could take out the Islamic Revolutionary Guards positions close to or along the Persian Gulf, including key strategic assets like the bases in Dezful, Bushehr, Bandar Abbas, the Jask Peninsula, and Konarak. The Islamic Republic's nuclear installations in Klardasht, Arak, Tehran, Natanz, and Isfahan, along with the uranium mines of Bafq and Sarcheshmeh, could also be destroyed, postponing the emergence of the Khomeinist regime as a nuclear power by years. Other targets include the bases and headquarters of the so-called Quds (Jerusalem) Corps that Tehran uses for "exporting revolution." Located in western Iran, close to Iraq, these could be taken out with a combination of air attacks and ground commando raids.

Such moves by the United States would face the Khomeinist leadership with a tough choice: whether to retaliate, thus provoking a full-scale war. The Islamic Republic could retaliate by using its Lebanese and Palestinian clients for attacks against Israel. It could also organize terror operations in several Arab states and in Europe, while making life harder for NATO in Afghanistan. Escalation, however, would provide Washington with the excuse to hit the command-and-control structures of the Khomeinist regime, including in Tehran itself. The idea is to show the Khomeinists that asymmetric warfare is a game that two can play, and that they, too, could end up having a dose of their own medicine.

Every time it has met something hard in its way, the Khomeinist regime has stopped or even backtracked. This is why the worst way to deal with it is through flattery and appeasement. In dealing with this dangerous enemy of democracy, the United States and other modern democracies should have the courage of their convictions. Remaining committed to Iraq and Afghanistan, and to promoting peace and democratization in the greater Middle East, are the surest means of preparing the ground for a strategic political defeat of Khomeinism, which is as doomed to destruction as were Communism, fascism, and pan-Arabism in their times.

Above all, the United States should be resolutely on the side of the Iranian people, as President Bush has repeatedly stated, including messages delivered on the Iranian New Year.. Programmatically, two things are needed here: assuring Iranians in no uncertain terms that the United States will never endorse or grant legitimacy to the current despotic regime, and helping to expose the Islamic Republic's repressive policies, human rights violations, rampant corruption, and wanton subsidization of some of the worst terror groups on the face of the earth. More important and ultimately perhaps more effective is for the United States to use its immense bully pulpit to publicize the Iranian people's struggle for freedom.

Ahmadinejad's strategy is based on two assumptions, one about going, the other about coming. The one about going is built around the belief that the next U.S. administration will abandon America's traditional positions in the Middle East, not to mention the victories won in Afghanistan and Iraq. The assumption about coming feeds on the illusion of the Mahdi's return.[1] In the spring of 2008, however, there was no evidence that the Americans were going or that the Mahdi was coming. A more robust and coordinated American posture on the economic, diplomatic, political, and moral fronts would create forceful pressure on the current leadership and inspire new courage in its opponents.

There is no denying that the mechanics of regime change are a delicate and often highly chancy matter, and that the historical record offers examples of failure as well as success. But there is also no denying that the game is worth the candle. The people of Iran have been fighting this evil regime for almost three decades. Hundreds of thousands of people have died and millions more have suffered in the struggle against Khomeinist tyranny in Iran. Today, the world should hear the cry of help that is coming out of Iran. Accelerating the collapse and replacement of this aberrant tyranny, an enemy of the Iranian people and a curse to the world, will also strike a blow against anti-Western and antidemocratic forces all over the globe and safeguard the strategic interests of the democratic world in the Middle East. The Persian Night can come to an end; Iran can become free; and the world can be saved from terror and wars triggered by an obscurantist fascist movement with messianic pretentions. Since the fall of the Soviet Empire and the apartheid regime in South Africa, the main theme of contemporary international life has been freedom. So why not Iran, and why not now?

Notes

Chapter 1: The World's Number-One Power

1   General David Petraeus in an interview with BBC Radio 4, March 24, 2008. Cf. Testimony by General Petraeus and Ryan Crocker, U.S. Ambassador to Baghdad, at the U.S. Senate hearing on April 8, 2008.

2   The congress elected a nine-man "Coordination Council" for the proposed jihad. Among its members were Turabi; Osama bin Laden, later to emerge as the leader of al-Qaeda; Ayman al-Zawahiri, of the Egyptian Jama'ah al-Islamiyah (Islamic Society) and later bin Laden's second-in-command; the Algerian Abdallah Jaballah of an-Nahda (Awakening) party; and Ayatollah Mehdi Karrubi, at the time speaker of the Islamic Consultative Assembly (Majlis), Iran's ersatz parliament.

3   *Cet animal est trop mechant,* / *Quant on l'attacque, il se defend!*

4   After the murder of 241 Marines in their sleep in 1982, President Ronald Reagan withdrew the U.S. task force from Lebanon despite the fact that they had been sent under a United Nations Security Council mandate and at the invitation of the Lebanese government to protect the Palestinians. In 1999, President Bill Clinton's secretary of state, Madeleine Albright, apologized to the Islamic Republic in Iran for unspecified aspects of past U.S. policy. Clinton also dispatched a string of emissaries, including his UN ambassador, Bill Richardson, to Kandahar, capital of the Taliban in Afghanistan, to court Mullah Muhammad Omar, but without success. On one occasion, Richardson was kept waiting for two days to see the mullah to deliver Clinton's message, before being told that he had to return home without a meeting. The mullah could not sully himself by meeting an "infidel" emissary!

5   See Kenneth M. Pollack, *The Persian Puzzle: The Conflict Between Iran and America* (New York: Random House, 2004).

Chapter 2: The Haven of Jihad

1   Cf. Carl Schmidt, *The Leviathan in the State Theory of Thomas Hobbes: Meaning and Failure of a Political Symbol*, trans. George Schwab, Erna Hilfstein (Westport, Conn.: Greenwood Press, 1996).

2   Here is how "Supreme Guide" Ali Khamenehi described the "deeper meaning" of the slogan in a sermon to Islamic Revolutionary Guards in Tehran on March 14, 2005: "Death to America is something every Muslim must say before every sura of the Koran. It is like saying anathema to Satan. It is because we have to be constantly aware that Satan is there to attack you." Broadcast live by Islamic Republic of Iran Broadcasting (IRIB).

3   Ayatollah Ahmad Khatami, a member of the Council of the Custodians of the Constitution, a key organ of the Khomeinist regime, put it this way: "After [the death] of the Prophet, the Koran was discarded and Koranic laws were pushed aside. Our revolution revived it, and is making [the laws of the Koran] triumph in every corner of the earth." Friday sermon on the campus of Tehran University, February 29, 2008, broadcast live by Islamic Republic of Iran Broadcasting (IRIB).

Chapter 3: The Focus of the Universe

1   Iran has land and sea frontiers with the following states: Russia, Kazakhstan, Turkmenistan, Afghanistan, Pakistan, Oman, United Arab Emirates, Saudi Arabia, Qatar, Bahrain, Kuwait, Iraq, Turkey, Armenia, Azerbaijan, and Nakhichivan (autonomous enclave).

2   The neighbors are Russia and Pakistan. The other three are China, India, and Israel. One could also include the United States, which may be considered a neighboring power thanks to its massive and semi-permanent presence in the Persian Gulf.

3   Persian belongs to the Indo-European family of languages, which includes such ancient languages as Sanskrit and Greek, and modern ones like German and English.

4   These include Kurdish, Baluchi, Pushtun, Sart, Ossetian, Tati, and Taleshi.

5   Yammut and Kokalan, also spoken in neighboring Turkmenistan, parts of Uzbekistan, and northwestern Afghanistan.

6   Other non-Iranic languages spoken by smaller communities in various parts of Iran include Armenian, Assyrian, Chaldean, and Tatar.

7   Sheikh Abdul-Aziz bin Baz, in conversation with the author in Riyadh, Saudi Arabia, in November 1996.

8   Each of these faith communities is, in turn, divided into several rival sects. Some, like the Yazidis, are closer to Zoroastrianism than Islam, while others, like Ali-Allahis—who believe that Muhammad's son-in-law Ali was an avatar of Allah—clearly fall outside the broadest perimeter of Islamic belief.

9   The phrase is from the historian Muhammad Mohit-Tabatabai (died in Tehran in 1988), who echoed Hegel's assertion that history began with the creation of the Persian Empire under Cyrus the Great.

Chapter 4: The Triple Oxymoron

1   The second caliph, Omar bin Khattab, was murdered by an Iranian war prisoner, Firuz, known as Abu-Laulau (Father of Pearls). The third, Osman Ibn Affan, was hacked to death by a group allegedly linked to Ali, Muhammad's cousin and son-in-law. Ali, who became the fourth and last of the "Well-Guided Caliphs," died when one of his former aides, Abdul-Rahman Ibn Muljem, cracked his skull with a sword.

2   The late Ayatollah Ali-Akbar Meshkini, longtime speaker of the Assembly of Experts, a high organ of the Islamic Republic in Iran, claimed in a sermon in Qom, in 2003, that only Iran had a "truly Islamic system of government." Others, including the "self-styled Islamic Republics" and the Saudi Arabian kingdom, were making "sordid claims" when they called their systems Islamic. Khomeini himself referred to the Saudi system as "American Islam."

3   Described as such because they believe in twelve imams, the last of whom went into "prolonged occultation" in 941 A.D. The Zaydis believe in a chain of only four imams and the Ismailis recognize seven.

4   Of the six grand ayatollahs of the time, three—Grand Ayatollah Muhammad Kazem Shariatmadari, Grand Ayatollah Muhammad Khonsari, and Grand Ayatollah Hassan Tabatabai-Qomi—openly rejected the Khomeinist system as "un-Islamic." Two others, Grand Ayatollah Shahabeddin Mar'ashi-Najafi and Grand Ayatollah Muhammad Golpayegani, practiced *taqiyyah*, the Shiite tradition of dissimulation, to avoid taking a clear position on the issue. The sixth, Khomeini

himself, was alone in regarding his system as "Islamic."

5 Cf. Colin Turner, *Islam Without Allah? The Rise of Religious Externalism in Safavid Iran* (Surrey, UK: Curzon Press, 2000).

6 In Arabic: *La ilah il-Allah! Muhammad an rasul Allah!* The formula is known as *she-hadatayn* or "the two testimonies." Anyone who pronounces it with sincere belief is immediately recognized as a Muslim.

7 Jaafar Ibn Muhammad Ibn Alil Ibn Hussein, a grandson of the Prophet, was the sixth imam of Twelver Shiites and the chief theoretician of their creed. This is why Twelver Shiites are also known as Jaafaris. His followers gave him the title *Al-Sadiq* ("the Truthful One").

8 Yaqub Kolini Razi, *Usul Kafi* [Sufficient Fundamentals], pp. 104–12. The book is one of the basic texts of Twelver Shiism.

9 Khomeini, *Kashf al-Asrar* [Revelation of Secrets], p. 100.

10 The original text is made of the following verses, repeated a number of times:

> Allah is the Greatest,
> There is no God but Allah,
> Muhammad is the Prophet of Allah.
> Come to reconciliation,
> Come to success.

The Shiite text contains two more hemistitches: "Ali is the Vicar of Allah" and "Come to doing good deeds."

11 They were Maulavi Abdul Quddus, Maulavi Yussef Sohrabi, and Mulavi Muhammad Omar Sarbazi.

12 Interview with Hussein Haj-Faraj-Allah Dabbagh, better known under his *nom de guerre* Abdul-Karim Sorush, in 2004. Sorush first made his name as secretary general of the Council for Islamic Cultural Revolution set up by Khomeini in 1979 to purge the Iranian universities. The council closed all universities for two years and purged over 6,000 professors and lecturers. Hundreds more were sent to prison. It also excluded over 15,000 students accused of being liberals, monarchists, nationalists, or Marxists. A few years later, Sorush joined the loyal opposition to the regime and eventually decided to go into exile in Britain.

13 The survey was commissioned by the deputy prime minister, Nassir Assar, but

was never published. Assar's successor in the post, Alinaqi Kani, showed the author a copy of the report in 1978.

14 Tehrani, who was married to Khamenehi's sister, spent almost ten years in exile in Iraq. He returned to Iran in 1995 and spent two years in prison, during which he attempted suicide on at least two occasions. He died in 2002.

15 See Amir Taheri, *The Spirit of Allah: Khomeini and the Islamic Revolution* (London: Hutchinson, 1985).

16 Some of Ayatollah Kazemeini Boroujerdi's sermons before his imprisonment in 2008 can be found on YouTube.

17 Ayatolla Mahmoud Tabatabai-Qomi in an interview with the author in London, January 2002.

18 Halabi was born in Yazd, central Iran, in 1897, and died in Tehran in 1999.

19 Najafabadi calls on fellow Shiiites to tone down some of their most excessive beliefs as a step towards reconciliation with the majority of Muslims.

Chapter 5: Democracy as Enemy

1 *Webster's New World Dictionary.*

2 M. Moin, *Persian Dictionary*, vol. 1 (Tehran, 1971).

3 Ibid.

4 The slogan was: "Independence, Freedom, Islamic Rule" (in Persian: *Esteqlal, Azadi, Hokumat Islami*).

5 The text was translated by Hassan Ibrahim Habibi, a French-educated Islamist who, supposedly "heartbroken" by the failure of the revolution, decided to withdraw from public life in 1997, having served as first assistant to the president of the Islamic Republic for almost two decades.

6 Montazeri in a meeting with the editorial board of the monthly *Nameh* ("The Letter") in his house in Qom. Quoted on the Peiknet website, April 16, 2008.

7 In 1981, Khomeini used that power to dismiss Abol-Hassan Banisadr. who had been elected the first president of the Islamic Republic the previous year. The dismissal came in the form of a nine-word decree dictated by Khomeini and scribbled by his son Ahmad on a piece of paper torn from a notepad in a hospital where the

ayatollah was undergoing medical tests. Banisadr had to flee to exile in France, disguised as a hijab-covered woman, aboard a jetliner hijacked by his future son-in-law Massoud Rajavi.

8   Ayatollah Muhammad Beheshti, quoted in M. Biazar Shirazi, *Yadha va Yadegarha* [Memoirs and Memories] (Tehran, 1988), p. 143.

9   The seven animals who go to paradise are: Buraq, the horse with a woman's face that Muhammad rode during his nocturnal visits to God (Shiites add Dhul-Jinah, Imam Hussein's steed during the Battle of Karbala in 680); Hout, the whale in whose belly the Prophet Yunes (Jonas) hid; Ezar, the donkey that Jesus rode to Jerusalem; Hoopoe, the bird that carried messages from Solomon to Belqees, Queen of Sheba; Naqeh, the young camel of the Prophet Saleh, which saved his life in the desert; Qitmir, the dog of the People of the Cave that watched over the Seven Sleepers for 309 years; Dik, the rooster that was the first animal to convert to Islam and became the muezzin of the animals, calling them to prayer every dawn; and, finally, Hureirah, the kitten that Muhammad loved to play with.

10   The categories are: *wajeb* (obligatory), *mostahab* (recommended), *halal* (permitted), *makruh* (permitted but best avoided), and *haram* (forbidden).

11   Mehdi Bazargan, *Enqelab-e Iran dar Dow Harekat* [Iran's Revolution in Two Moves] (Tehran, 1984), p. 87.

12   Ayatollah Ruhollah Khomeini, *Walayat Faqih* [Custodianship of the Theologian], pp. 58–62.

13   Ibid., p. 504.

Chapter 6: Iran and Anti-Iran

1   Paul Balta in interview with the author in Paris, 1986. There is also an account of this in the memoirs of the BBC reporter John Simpson, who witnessed the scene, and the Iranian journalist Mansur Taraji, who translated for Balta. Cf: Amir Taheri, *The Spirit of Allah: Khomeini and the Islamic Revolution* (London: Hutchinson, 1985).

2   He also suggested that the Persian name of the Caspian Sea, which is the Sea of Mazandaran, after an Iranian province on its littoral, be changed to please Russia and other neighbors. He unleashed a tsunami of protests, indicating that Iranians remained attached to their Iranian-ness.

3 The Iranian New Year starts precisely on the spring equinox. It is celebrated for thirteen days with rites that predate Islam. In Iranian mythology it marks the coronation of Jamshid, the first king of the mythical Pishdadi dynasty. A truly national and secular occasion, it brings together Iranians from all creeds and ethnic backgrounds. Now-Ruz is also the New Year for Afghans, Tajiks, Kurds, and many other ethnic groups in Central Asia, the Caucasus, Pakistan, and the Persian Gulf.

4 Quoted in Shojaeddin Shafa, *Jenayat va Mokafat* [Crime and Punishment], vol. 2 (Intercollegiate Press, USA, 1988), p. 1148.

5 Ibid., p. 1150.

6 The meeting took place at Khomeini's residence in Jamaran, north of Tehran, on February 10, 1983, launching the so-called Ten Days of Dawn ceremonies dedicated to his cult of personality.

7 Having numerous wives and concubines was regarded as one of the many signs of the special powers of the imams. For example, Hassan bin Ali, the second imam of Shiism, is reported to have had over two hundred wives and concubines.

8 During his revolutionary career, the ayatollah kept the fact that he had composed poetry a secret, possibly because he thought this would undermine his reputation as a ruthless ruler. Two volumes of his doggerel, however, have been published posthumously. The poems are syrupy and sentimental and ridden with grammatical errors and misspellings.

9 This is separate from *sahm e Imam* (the imam's share), which amounts to a flat 20 percent income tax, the proceeds of which go to an ayatollah of one's choice.

10 He was Nureddin Kianuri. Having collaborated with the mullahs, especially in hunting and destroying elements of the anti-Soviet left, the Tudeh in turn fell victim to Khomeinist repression from 1984 onwards. Hundreds of Tudeh cadres were executed or imprisoned without trial. Many more fled to Afghanistan, then ruled by fellow Communists.

11 Such as Abdul-Hussein (Slave of Imam Hussein) or even Kalb Ali (Dog of Imam Ali). Most Muslims regard such names as anti-Islamic because in Islam the believer is a slave only to Allah, best denoted in the name Abdallah.

12 They are Abol-Hassan Banisadr, the first president of the Islamic Republic; Muhammad-Ali Rajai, the second president; Ali Khamenehi, the third; and Muhammad Khatami, the fifth. Three of the six have been mullahs. Only the

fourth president, Rafsanjani, a mullah, does not claim to be a *sayyed*, although he used the *nom de guerre* Hashemi instead of his own family name, Bahremani, to claim some spiritual connection with the Prophet's clan.

13 Khomeini, meeting the family of Imam Musa Sadr, the Iranian leader of Lebanese Shiites, in Jamaran.

14 Khomeini, message to the Freedom Congress, Tehran, August 1980.

15 Khomeini at an audience with air force cadets in Jamaran, September 1980.

16 Khamenehi, address at the First Congress of Islamic Poets and Writers, Tehran, 26 Azar 1363 (December 17, 1984).

17 Ayatollah Khoiniha, interview with the daily *Kayhan*, Tehran, 13 Mordad 1361 (August 4, 1982).

18 *Two Centuries of Silence* (in Persian: *Do Qarn Sokut*) is the title of a book by Abdul-Hussein Zarrinkub, first published in 1960. After Khomeini seized power, the book became a bestseller, before being banned by the Islamic regime.

19 Persian has five letters more than the Arabic alphabet—letters that native Arabic speakers cannot easily pronounce. In exchange, Arabic has six letters that native Persian speakers cannot pronounce. Iranians also reformed the Arabic script by a process known as *A'ajamm* (literally: Persianization). This consists of adding dots to individual letters to distinguish them from one another. The technique made a proper reading of written Arabic, initially an oral language, possible for the first time, and helped stabilize the meaning of the Koran.

20 Persian in its current version is estimated to have a vocabulary twice as large as that of Arabic. The reason is that most Arabic words have been used in some Persian text at one point or another. It is possible to write Persian that is 85 percent Arabic. However, it is also possible to write a pure Persian with no Arabic words at all. The average Persian dictionary of over 100,000 words contains 12,500 Arabic words. Other languages from which Persian has borrowed include French (3,800 words), Turkish (1,500 words), Mongolian (700 words), Greek (500 words), and English (400 words).

21 The epic poem in 60,000 lines contains only 5 percent Arabic loan words.

22 The terrorist in question is Khalid Showqi al-Islambouli. The street named after him is where the Egyptian embassy is located in Tehran.

23 The exception is Sayyed Ali Hussein Khamenehi, the third president of the Islamic Republic and, since 1989, the Supreme Guide of the Khomeinist regime. He is fluent in spoken Arabic but unable to write in that language.

Chapter 7: Unwelcome Faith

1 Sura al-Towbah (Repentance), verse 29. Cf, Sura Baqarah (The Cow), verses 193 and 216, and Sura Muhammad, verse 4.

2 Abu Hanifa Ahmad ibn Dawood Dinwari, *Akhbar ut Tawal* [News of Old Times], p. 146.

3 Piruz married a Chinese princess, became a Chinese general, and led Chinese armies into conquests in Central Asia. However, he did not succeed in persuading the Chinese emperor to help him recover Iran, his own lost homeland.

4 The Islamic rule was revived in Iran under Khomeini. In 1979, the ayatollah ordered the execution of Habib Elqanian, a leader of the Iranian Jewish community. One of the charges brought against him was that he had built Iran's first high-rise block of offices in Tehran. The twenty-storey building was seen as an affront to Islam: a symbol of a Jew's attempt at "looking down on True Believers."

5 *Tarikh al-Tawarikh* [History of Histories], vol. 2 (Tehran, n.d.), p. 41. Also quoted in Javad Fazel, *Maasoum Chahrom* [The Fourth Infallible One] (Tehran, 1957), p. 88.

6 At an audience granted to students of theology in Qom. Reported by Mehr News Agency and quoted on the Peiknet website on April 2, 2008.

7 Sayyed Abol Hassan Bani-Sadr, interview with Iran Times, Washington, D.C., March 18, 1983.

Chapter 8: A Strange Beast

1 Also attending the conversation was the late Iranian diplomat and scholar Fereydoun Hoveyda, a lifelong friend of Rodinson's.

2 The *marja taqlid* or "source of imitation" is the mullah that the faithful choose to solve their religious problems. Traditionally, this is a voluntary matter, in which government does not intervene. Since 1979, however, the Khomeinist regime has tried to impose a handful of mullahs of its choice.

3 Literally "Claimant" and "Head," titles assumed by Arab dictators in modern times.

4 Ali Shariati in *Imam and Imamate* (Tehran, 1993), p. 592.

5 Khomeini in *Walayat Faqih* (Tehran, 2003), pp. 75–78.

6 One of the actors who played the role was Ali Mahzoon, a star of Iranian cinema in the 1950s. He revealed the deception in which he had played a part in a series of letters written to friends in 1984.

7 Tehran Radio broadcast, February 11, 1988. At the time, Khamenehi was president of the Islamic Republic.

8 Khamenehi in *Kayhan Havai*, 9 Ordibehesht 1366 (April 29, 1987), p. 8.

9 Hussein Tabatabai, *Ravabet Ejetemai dar Islam* [Social Relations in Islam] (Tehran, 2002), pp. 46–47.

10 Morteza Motahari, *Pyramoon Enqelab Eslami* [On Islamic Revolution] (Tehran, n.d.), pp. 103–4.

11 Tehran Radio broadcast, February 11, 1988.

12 Khomeini address on the anniversary of Prophet Muhammad's birth, 30 Azar 1363 (November 21, 1984).

13 At the University of California at Berkeley, for instance.

14 Mehdi Bazargan, *Enqelab-e Iran dar Dow Harekat* [Iran's Revolution in Two Moves] (Tehran, 1984), p. 84.

15 Daryush Shayegan, *Qu'est-ce qu'une revolution religieuse?* [What Is a Religious Revolution?] (Paris, 1985).

16 Bazargan, *Enqelab-e Iran dar Dow Harekat* (see n. 14).

17 Ibid.

Chapter 9: The Feeble Ones

1 Other reforms, approved in a popular referendum, included the distribution of land among landless peasants, a scheme for workers' participation in the capital of the companies that employed them, and the creation of a Literacy Corps in which young graduates would spend eighteen months teaching illiterate people

to read and write. The package was branded the "White Revolution," later to be renamed the "Revolution of the Shah and the People."

2   She was Mrs. Mehrangiz Manuchehrian, a senior judge who had also served as a member of the senate for years.

3   She was Mrs. Farrokhru Parsa, a veteran educationalist and one of the longest-serving ministers of education in contemporary Iran. In 1980, she was put to death on Khomeini's order—to symbolize the death of the Shah's pro-woman reforms.

4   Since the Persian language does not use gender, the constitution is vague on the gender of those who could seek the high offices. It uses the term *rejal*, a loan word that means "men" in Arabic but could mean "persons" both male and female, in Persian. So far, however, the mullahs have used the original Arabic meaning to bar women from becoming candidates for the presidency.

5   Freshteh Hashemi, in the weekly magazine *Zan Ruz* [Today's Woman], Tehran, 29 Dey 1358 (January 19, 1980).

6   At the Seminar on Islam and Women, Tehran, 16 Farvardin 1362 (April 5, 1983).

7   Some of these policies were later modified as the new regime created all-female police and military units. To impose the dress code, for example, female militants in uniform would deal with recalcitrant women.

8   Zahra Rahnavardi, wife of Prime Minister Mir Hussein Mussavi, addressing a group of Arab women visiting Tehran, *Weekly Kayhan*, 18 Mordad 1362 (August 9, 1983).

9   *Jumhuri Islami* [Islamic Republic], November 20, 2004.

10   Christians have identified the forbidden fruit as an apple. In Islam, however, the identity of the forbidden fruit remains obscure. There were no apple trees in Arabia and Muhammad is unlikely to have seen one. Most Islamic scholars believe the forbidden fruit of the Koran was a kind of wheat or barley.

11   Khomeini, *Tahrir al-Wassilah* [Release of the Means], vol. 2, p. 290.

12   Ebtekar, now in her fifties, became known to American television audiences as "Mary," a nineteen-year-old firebrand who nightly threatened the U.S. diplomats held hostage in Tehran with execution. Having grown up in the United States, she was chosen by the terrorists as spokesperson to address the citizens of the "Great Satan" in their own language and accent.

Chapter 10: The Prophet and Women

1 The Barmakids, a crypto-Zoroastrian family of Persian aristocrats, served as viziers and other high officials for Abbasid caliphs in Baghdad until their destruction under Caliph Haroun al-Rashid in the eighth century.

2 Under Muhammad's law, adultery is proven only if four male or eight female witnesses testify under oath that they actually witnessed the act of penetration take place between the accused couple. Since it is unlikely that anyone would perform an adulterous sexual act in public, the charge cannot be, and in fact never has been, proven in accordance with the strict rules of evidence fixed by the Prophet.

Chapter 11: The Eternal Conspirator

1 The claim is found in many books by Sunni scholars. The most direct one is *Mokhtasar al-Tuhfat al-Ithna-Ashariyah* [A Short Guide to Twelver Shiism] by Mahmoud Shukri al-Alloosi, an Iraqi scholar of the last century.

2 Muhsin al-Mulk, *Ayat al-Bayyanat* [Clear Signs], p. 88. Khomeini quotes the passage in his *Kashf al-Asrar* [Revelation of Secrets].

3 Among the visitors were Khalil Maleki, leader of the Titoist Third Force (Niruy e Sevvom) Party; the Islamist novelist Jalal al-Ahmad; the socialist novelist Nasser Khodayar; the sociologist Ihsna Naraqi, who became an advisor to President Hashemi Rafsanjani; and Abol-Hassan Banisadr, who became the first president of the Islamic Republic after Khomeini's seizure of power in 1979.

4 In 1970, Bakhtiar was assassinated in Baghdad by a SAVAK hit squad sent from Tehran.

5 The Khomeinists like the forged tract. In 1984, the newspaper *Imam* ("Faith"), published by the Islamic Republic embassy in London, serialized excerpts. In 1985,, the Ministry of Islamic Guidance and Culture in Tehran published a new edition in several hundred thousand copies. The periodical *Islami* later serialized the *Protocols* under the title: "Odor of Blood and Jewish Conspiracies."

6 Jerusalem had been part of various Persian Empires for some six centuries and was known as Hokhtgang Dezh (Fortress of Prophets). In the sixth century B.C., Cyrus the Great ordered and financed the rebuilding of the destroyed Jewish temple there.

7 Quoted in Shojaeddin Shafa, *Jenayat va Mokafat* [Crime and Punishment], vol. 2, (Intercollegiate Press, USA, 1988), p. 433.

8 Reported by the state-owned Entekhab News Agency, 19 Ordibehesht 1387 (May 8, 2008).

9 As Ahmadinejad's comments raised a storm of indignation all over the world, including in Iran itself, some "useful idiots" who have always acted as apologists for the Khomeinist regime tried to claim that he had not meant what he said. The phrase he used in Persian was clear, however: *Bayad az safheh ruzegar mahv garadad.* ("Must disappear from the pages of time.") The full texts of Ahmadinejad's various calls for Israel to be destroyed are available on his website.

10 Islamic Republic News Agency (IRNA), November 22, 2005.

11 IRNA, November 16, 2006.

12 IRNA, October 28, 2005.

13 Details of Ramin's background from the official Aftab News, 15 Bahman 1384 (February 4, 2006).

14 The Persian phrase he used was *falsafeh vojudi*, which, translated literally, means "the philosophy of existence."

15 The full text is available on Ahmadinejad's website.

16 IRNA, October 22, 2005.

Chapter 12: Esther and the King

1 From Khalkhali's *Collected Writings* (Tehran, 1999). The ayatollah ignores the fact that Esther and Cyrus were not contemporaries.

2 Named after Muhammad Abdul-Wahhab, founder of a radical, puritanical version of Islam in the seventeenth century.

3 The shah put Abbas Aram, a seasoned diplomat and former foreign minister and ambassador to Beijing, in charge of the initial studies for the project. Aram visited twenty-three countries in the Indian Ocean region, only to report that there was little support for the idea.

4 A tribal entity in parts of Afghanistan and the imamate in parts of Yemen were also semi-independent, although not yet constituted as proper states.

5   Nasser Khosrow wrote:

> Look at today's scientists of faith,
> Their minds closed to reason,
> Their mouths open for bribes.

6   The Khomeinist regime regards the defeat of the United States as a priority, and is thus hopeful of using Russia and China as political and diplomatic allies in driving the Americans out of the Middle East.

7   A mere enemy is designated by the word *khasm,* or in some cases *mu'aridh* (literally: "opponent"). A "foe," the equivalent of *hostis* in Latin, is designated with the Arabic word *adou.* A *khasm* today could become a friend tomorrow, something that an *adou* can never be. The Persian word for "foe" is *doshman.*

8   Speaking to the author on condition of anonymity in March 2008.

9   Talib Shabib, in conversation with the author in New York, 1998. Shabib served as foreign minister in the first Baathist regime in Baghdad in 1963 and was briefly Iraq's ambassador to the United Nations under Saddam Hussein.

10 In the 1960s, the song was shelved because Nasser decided to rename the Persian Gulf as the Arabian Gulf. This ruined the rhymes of the song's refrain: *Min al-Mohit al-Atlasi, Il al-Khalij al-Faresi!* ("From the Atlantic Ocean to the Persian Gulf.")

Chapter 13: The Great Satan

1   Translated literally, the slogan would read thus: "America is on the slippery slope [leading] to collapse."

2   Audience at Khomeini's residence in Jamaran on 19 Aban 1358 (November 1979).

3   In *Eqtesad Towhidi* [Monotheistic Economics] (Tehran, n.d.), p. 113.

4   From Khomeini's letter to Mikhail Gorbachev, *Kayhan,* January 30, 1989. Also in *Los Angeles Times,* February 1, 1989.

5   In conversation with the author in New York, February 1982.

6   *New York Times,* January 28, 1979.

7   Peiknet website, February 9, 2007.

8   Abbas Ali Khalatbari, Iran's foreign minister from 1971 to 1978, explained the symbolic color scheme as "a rainbow of threats" that always loomed on the Iranian horizon. In 1978, the shah added a new color to the "rainbow": black, which he said was "the color of domestic religious reaction." Thus, he branded the Khomeinist revolution as "the coalition of red and black," red representing the Communists, their fellow travelers, and the habitual "useful idiots."

9   See Amir Taheri, *Nest of Spies: America's Journey to Disaster in Iran* (London: Hutchinson, 1988).

10 Editorial in *Besuy e Ayandeh* [To the Future], organ of the Tudeh Party, 26 Tir 1330 (July 18, 1951).

11 See Taheri, *Nest of Spies.*

Chapter 14: Five Days in August

1   These included such popular papers as *Mardom* (People), *Shahbaz* (Eagle), *Razm* (The Fight), *Zafar* (Victory), *Challengar* (Ironsmith), and *Besuy e Ayandeh* (Towards the Future).

2   Queen Soraya and Princess Ashraf, in conversations with the author in Paris in the 1980s.

3   The main pro-Mossadeq group, known as the National Front (Jebheh Melli), split into two factions, only one of which remained loyal to him right to the end. Among those who broke with Mossadeq was Hussein Makki, the front's most charismatic leader, and Abol-Hassan Haerizadeh, an elder statesman who published an open letter to the United Nations secretary general, Trygve Li, accusing Mossadeq of dictatorship. Other pro-Mossadeq parties that broke with him were Niruy-e-Sevvom (Third Force), led by Khalil Maleki; Hezb Zahmatkeshan (Laborers' Party), led by Mozaffar Baqai; Hezb Pan-Iranist, led by Mohsen Pezeshkpour; and a number of religious groups loyal to Grand Ayatollah Abol-Qassdem Kashani. Hezb Mardom Iran (Party of the People of Iran), led by Dariush Foruhar, also distanced itself from Mossadeq because of the prime minister's refusal to curb Tudeh activities. Foruhar, however, did not join active opposition to Mossadeq.

4   Some details of the events of those fateful days are drawn from Ghulam-Hussein Sadiqi, *Khaterat* [Memoirs] (Tehran, 1991).

5   In 1977, Roosevelt received a retainer from the shah's court to write a biography of

the monarch. But when the shah fell in 1979, he switched his project to his fantasy about his heroic mission to Tehran in 1953.

6   Donald N. Wilber, *Regime Change in Iran: Overthrow of Premier Mossadeq of Iran, November 1952–August 1953* (Abm Komers, 2000), p. 52.

7   Ibid., p. 86.

8   Ibid., p. 110.

9   Ibid., p. 51.

10   Ibid., pp. 53–54.

11   Fred Halliday, *Iran: Dictatorship and Development* (London: Penguin, 1979), pp. 25–26.

12   Among them were Ali Shayegan, who had been finance minister under Mossadeq, and Karim Sanjabi, who had served as education minister in the same cabinet.

13   In 1978, Dariush Foruhar, a senior Mossadeqist leader, wrote a letter to President Carter seeking U.S. help in forcing the shah to reform his regime. In a private conversation with the author, Foruhar claimed that the United States had always favored "the Mossadeq alternative" but had been misled by the British in siding with the shah in 1953.

14   The Iranian delegation was led by the deputy foreign minister, Jalal Abdoh.

15   The concept of "Finlandization" had some supporters among the shah's advisors, including Ahmad Mirfenderesky, who served as ambassador to Moscow in the 1970s and foreign minister in 1978.

16   In 1972, the shah allowed the establishment of seventeen American "listening posts" on Iranian territory along the borders with the USSR to monitor Soviet missile tests. This was done at the behest of Moscow and Washington in the context of the Strategic Arms Limitation Treaty (SALT). Iran's ambassador to the United Nations at the time, Fereydoun Hoveyda, who chaired the UN's Disarmament Committee, negotiated the tripartite deal.

17   Iran sent a contingent to Vietnam after the United States and North Vietnam had signed a truce to monitor the ceasefire. In 1968, the Iranian diplomat Fereydoun Hoveyda, using his French left-wing contacts, had helped organize the first contacts between Washington and Hanoi at the request of President Lyndon B. Johnson.

18 Close ties with Beijing enabled Tehran to play intermediary between China and the United States. The contacts led to secret visits to Beijing by President Richard Nixon's national security advisor, Henry Kissinger, and later to the historic visit by Nixon himself.

19 OPEC Fund was set up by the thirteen members of the Organization of Petroleum Exporting Countries, with initial donations from Iran and Saudi Arabia. Its first director was Muhammad Yeganeh, a former Iranian cabinet minister.

20 This analysis is based on a number of interviews the author had with the shah in the late 1970s.

21 Ibid.

Chapter 15: A Universal Ideology

1 Islamic Republic News Agency (IRNA), January 5, 2005.

2 IRNA, April 9, 2004.

3 Sermon, IRNA, June 1, 2007.

4 Major General Mohsen Rezai, secretary of Expediency Council. IRNA, June 8, 2006.

5 The defectors included one Davoud Muhammad, a former Nation of Islam member, wanted in the United States for the murder of Ali-Akbar Tabatabai, a pro-Shah Iranian diplomat in Washington in 1980, and Lynda Santiago, a black convert to Islam briefly married to Ayatollah Ehsan Bakhsh.

6 IRNA.

7 IRNA, May 18, 2007.

8 IRNA, November 1, 1999.

Chapter 16: Sunrise Power against Sunset Power

1 FBI director Louis Freeh, in conversation with the author, December 2000, Washington, D.C.

2 See Amir Taheri, "Who Should Apologize to Whom?" *Arab News*, March 6, 2005.

3 Ibid.

4   IRNA, January 22, 2001.

5   The mullahs provoked the incident after two Christian Georgian ladies who had been kidnapped and sold as concubines managed to flee the homes of their enforced "husbands" and sought refuge at the Russian embassy. The minister plenipotentiary, Griboidev, refused to surrender the refugees, and the mullahs declared "jihad" against the tsar.

Chapter 17: Crazy Eddie and Martyr Hussein

1   Friday prayer sermon at Tehran University campus, January 7, 1989.

2   Khomeini, *Kashf al-Asrar* [Revelation of Secrets], p. 292.

Chapter 18: West Stricken, Arab Stricken

1   Al-Ahmad was a charming man with a keen sense of humor. I first met him in 1960 in London, where I was a student. In later years, we met on and off, including at his home in north Tehran, mostly to discuss French literature, which he admired.

2   I made Fardid's acquaintance in 1973 when we appeared together in a series of televised debates. At the time, he was ferociously anticlerical, a position he subsequently concealed thanks to the Shiite practice of *taqiyyah* (dissimulation).

3   Khomeini, *Sahigfat al-Anwar*, p. 112.

4   The most popular Arab writer translated into Persian was Georgie Zaydan, a Lebanese Christian who wrote a series of fantasized accounts of Islamic history.

Chapter 19: State or Revolution

1   Hadi Khorsandi, one of Iran's most popular satirical poets, has published a series of imitation Khomeini speeches that capture the late ayatollah's style, or lack of it, to much comical effect.

2   Nasrallah in televised address in Beirut, May 26, 2008. Account published by *Asharq Alawsat*, May 27, 2008.

Chapter 20: Six Centers of Power

1 Rafsanjani, interview with Japanese TV, Tokyo, June 11, 1985.

2 Rafsanjani, prayer sermon, Tehran, October 20, 1985.

3 Khamenehi, prayer sermon, Tehran, October 7, 1984.

Chapter 23: The "Nail" of the Imam

1 Khomeini meeting IRGC commanders in Jamaran on 4 Esfand 1360 (March 1981).

2 Interview with the monthly *Shahrvand,* Tehran, April 2008.

3 Other members were Muhammad-Ali Sayyed-Nezhad, Muhammad Mirdamadi, Asghar Zadeh, and Muhammad Bitaraf.

4 Reported by Sayyed-Nezhad in interview published by Peiknet website, May 2008.

Chapter 24: We Can!

1 Khamenehi, speaking in Shiraz, May 8, 2008, Iranian Students' News Agency (ISNA).

Chapter 26: Pre-emptive War or Pre-emptive Surrender?

1 The Islamic Republic's official Mehr News Agency, report from Rome, June 3, 2008.

2 Interview with the author in Kabul, November 2001.

Chapter 27: Conditions for Regime Change

1 Published on the Fararow website, May 28, 1981. Also published by Iran Press News.

2 The denial policy continues, however, on at least one issue: homosexuality.

President Ahmadinejad maintains that there are no gays in Iran, although in the past two decades more than three hundred men have been hanged under Article 110 of the Penal Code of the Islamic Republic, which makes same-sex relations punishable by death.

Chapter 28: Repression and Resistance

1   Interview with the author in Brussels, June 2007.

2   Ibid.

3   *Nimrooz Weekly*, January 11, 2001.

4   Each year, half a million Iranians living on the coasts of the Persian Gulf are allowed to make visits of up to forty-eight hours to the United Arab Emirates to engage in border trade. This gives them an opportunity to have a look at the outside world.

5   In his splendid travelogue *A Persian Odyssey*, Ramin Yelda, an Iranian doctor living in Chicago, relates how surprised he was to find that the doors of the church where he had been baptized as a child in Kermanshah, western Iran, were closed to him. He had to find the priest and prove that he was not a Muslim seeking conversion in order to be allowed to enter a church that his family had attended for over a century.

6   Right Side News website, June 5, 2008.

Chapter 30: A Heaving Volcano

1   It is strange that some American "scholars" encourage this illusion. In an anti-American conference in Mash'had attended by Baseej soldiers on June 1, 2008, Abdul-Aziz Schedina, who was presented as "a leading American scholar and professor at the University of Virginia," endorsed Ahmadinejad's claim that the Hidden Imam was about to reappear. Reported by IRNA, June 2, 2008.

Index

389